THEORETICAL FOUNDATIONS OF QUANTUM COMPUTING

THEORETICAL FOUNDATIONS OF QUANTUM COMPUTING

DAOWEN QIU

ELSEVIER
MK
MORGAN KAUFMANN PUBLISHERS
AN IMPRINT OF ELSEVIER

Morgan Kaufmann is an imprint of Elsevier
50 Hampshire Street, 5th Floor, Cambridge, MA 02139, United States

ISBN: 978-0-443-27704-7

For information on all Morgan Kaufmann publications
visit our website at https://www.elsevier.com/books-and-journals

Publisher: Mara Conner
Acquisitions Editor: Stephen Merken
Editorial Project Manager: Naomi Robertson
Publishing Services Manager: Deepthi Unni
Production Project Manager: Surya Narayanan Jayachandran
Cover Designer: Greg Harris

Typeset by VTeX

Printed in Great Britain

Last digit is the print number:
9 8 7 6 5 4 3 2

Contents

Preface *ix*

1. Development history and potential applications of quantum computing **1**

1.1. Development history of quantum computing 1
1.2. Potential applications of quantum computing 6
1.3. Quantum hardware development 7
1.4. Summary 9
References 9

2. Fundamental concepts of quantum computing **11**

2.1. Quantum bit 11
2.2. Classical logic gates and circuits 14
2.3. Basic quantum gates and circuits 18
2.4. Summary 21
References 22

3. Fundamentals of linear algebra **23**

3.1. Linear independence and basis 23
3.2. Linear operators and matrices 23
3.3. Pauli matrices 24
3.4. Cauchy–Schwarz inequality 24
3.5. Eigenvalues and eigenvectors 25
3.6. Adjoint operators and Hermitian operators 26
3.7. Operator functions 26
3.8. Operator decomposition theorem 27
3.9. Quantum mechanics assumptions 32
3.10. Density operator 33
3.11. Partial trace 36
3.12. Superoperator 39
3.13. Summary 42
References 43

4. Basic protocols in quantum communication **45**

4.1. BB84 protocol 45
4.2. B92 protocol 49
4.3. E91 protocol 51
4.4. Superdense coding 52
4.5. Quantum teleportation 53
4.6. Summary 55
References 56

5. Quantum computing models **57**

5.1. One-way quantum finite automata 57
5.1.1. Measure-once 1QFA 57
5.1.2. Measure-many 1QFA 65
5.1.3. 1QFA together with classical states 71
5.1.4. Other important types of 1QFA 73
5.2. Two-way quantum finite automata 78
5.3. Two-way finite automata with quantum and classical states 83
5.4. Quantum pushdown automata 94
5.5. Quantum grammars 97
5.5.1. Context-free grammars and regular grammars 97
5.5.2. Quantum regular grammars 98
5.5.3. * Quantum context-free grammars 100
5.6. Quantum Turing machines 102
5.7. Quantum circuits 106
5.7.1. Quantum gates 106
5.7.2. Polynomial-time simulation of QTM 108
5.8. Summary 116
References 117

6. Quantum algorithms **119**

6.1. Basic relationships between probabilistic and quantum algorithms 119
6.2. Quantum query model 123
6.3. Query complexity and polynomial degree 124
6.4. Deutsch's algorithm 127
6.5. Deutsch–Jozsa algorithm 130
6.6. Simon's algorithm 133
6.7. Quantum Fourier transform 143
6.8. Quantum phase estimation 147
6.9. * Detailed probabilistic analyses of quantum phase estimation 152
6.10. Shor's factorization algorithm 159

6.11. Shor's discrete logarithm algorithm 165
6.12. Hidden subgroup algorithm 169
6.13. Grover's algorithm 176
6.14. Quantum amplitude amplification 179
6.15. Quantum amplitude estimation 183
6.16. * HHL algorithm 190
6.17. * Variational quantum eigensolver algorithm 196
6.18. * Quantum approximate optimization algorithm 201
6.19. Summary 203
References 204

7. Quantum computational complexity **207**

7.1. Revisiting quantum query model 210
7.2. Quantum state distinguishability 212
7.3. Lower bound for the search problem 214
7.4. Polynomial method 220
7.5. Adversary method 227
7.6. Summary 236
References 237

8. Quantum error correction **239**

8.1. Classical bit-flip error correction 239
8.2. Quantum bit-flip error correction 241
8.3. Quantum phase-flip error correction 243
8.4. Shor code 245
8.5. Linear code 249
8.6. CSS code 258
8.7. * Stabilizer code 262
8.8. * Binary quantum MDS code 265
8.9. Summary 275
References 275

Index *277*

Preface

This book is a textbook on the basic theory of quantum computing, aimed at computer science majors as well as undergraduates and graduate students in science and engineering. At the same time, it also has certain reference and guidance value for researchers engaged in quantum computing. This book introduces the most important basic knowledge and research content in quantum computing, and also appropriately mentions some recent advancement in related fields.

This book includes eight chapters, as follows.

Chapter 1 briefly introduces the development history, background, and current situation of the quantum computing, and points out the advantages and potential applications of quantum computing.

Chapter 2 describes some basic concepts related to quantum computing. By comparing basic quantum gates with classical logic gates, we can clearly understand the basic relationship between quantum computing and classical computing: classical computing is a special case of quantum computing.

Chapter 3 outlines the basic linear algebra and mathematical foundations related to quantum computing, including the concepts of linear operators, Pauli matrices, basic postulates of quantum mechanics, density operators, partial trace, and superoperators. In particular, this chapter systematically summarizes the relevant theorems related to operator decomposition.

Chapter 4 states the basic quantum information and communication protocols, mainly including discrete variable quantum key distribution protocols, such as BB84 protocol, B92 protocol, and E91 protocol, as well as quantum superdense coding and quantum teleportation protocols.

Chapter 5 describes the basic quantum computation models. Because finite automata are the basic and important computational models in classical computing theory, the content of this chapter includes quantum finite automata, quantum Turing machines, basic quantum circuits, and the effective simulation of quantum Turing machines by quantum circuits. These are the formal descriptions of quantum computers and the essential characterization of the computational power of quantum computers.

Chapter 6 is the core content of quantum algorithms. It starts with the first quantum algorithm—Deutsch's algorithm, followed by Deutsch–Jozsa algorithm and Simon's algorithm. Then it describes quantum phase estimation method, and from there, it elaborates on Shor's algorithm for large-number factorization. After that, it explores Grover's search algorithm and its basic principle of quantum amplitude amplification. Finally, it covers HHL algorithm for solving linear systems of equations, VQE algorithm, and QAOA algorithm. At the same time, this chapter also briefly introduces quantum algorithms for solving hidden subgroup problems.

Chapter 7 focuses on the basic knowledge of quantum computational complexity, mainly including the quantum query model, the basic concepts of quantum query complexity, and the polynomial method and adversary method for solving the lower bounds of quantum query complexity.

Finally, Chapter 8 is dedicated to the basic concepts and methods of quantum error correction, mainly including Shor codes, linear codes, CSS codes, stabilizer codes, and MDS codes, along with explanations of their error correction principles.

Note: Chapters marked with an $*$ are optional and can be considered advanced topics.

Daowen Qiu
Sun Yat-sen University

Instructor resources for this textbook may be accessed by visiting https://www.educate.elsevier.com/book/details/9780443277047

CHAPTER 1

Development history and potential applications of quantum computing⊛

Nowadays, quantum computing is one of the most important research areas in nonclassical computing, and is considered a promising research direction for future advancement since the era of Moore's law. It has attracted significant attention from countries worldwide.

Quantum computing has achieved substantial theoretical research results and has also gained extensive research progress in experimental aspects. This chapter briefly introduces the major achievements in the development of quantum computing and discusses the advantages as well as potential applications of quantum computing.

1.1 Development history of quantum computing

The concept of quantum computing was first proposed by Benioff [1] and Feynman [2] in the early 1980s. Feynman [2] believed that simulating quantum mechanical systems on classical computers were extremely difficult and suggested that a computer based on the principles of quantum mechanics might be able to overcome these difficulties.

Generally speaking, quantum computing is a new computing mode that utilizes quantum mechanical principles to manipulate quantum information units for calculation. It differs from existing classical computing modes. To better understand the concept of quantum computing, it is often compared to classical computing correspondingly. In classical computing, binary numbers are used for encoding, with the digits always being in a definite state—either 0 or 1. In contrast, quantum computing takes advantage of quantum superposition, enabling the parallel processing of superposed states. A quantum state can represent not only 0 or 1 but also a superposition of 0 and 1 simultaneously. Thus quantum computing utilizes the

⊛ This book has a companion website hosting complementary materials. Visit this URL to access it: https://www.elsevier.com/books-and-journals/book-companion/9780443277047.

Theoretical Foundations of Quantum Computing
https://doi.org/10.1016/B978-0-44-327704-7.00006-2

characteristics of superposition and entanglement in quantum mechanics, operating algorithms through a novel computing device. The features of quantum computing are higher computational speed, stronger information processing capability, broader application scope, and so on.

A computational model is considered reversible if and only if the input can be uniquely determined from the output. In reality, irreversible computations (such as the classical logic operations $\wedge$ and $\vee$) lead to the loss and erasure of bits, resulting in heat dissipation. In 1973, Bennett [3] proved that any Turing machine can be efficiently simulated by a reversible Turing machine. In 1985, Deutsch [4] designed a quantum Turing machine that can simulate any quantum machine [5] (in exponential time) and proposed the quantum Church–Turing thesis: Any algorithm can be efficiently simulated by a quantum Turing machine. In fact, reversible Turing machines can be thought of as special cases of quantum Turing machines (quantum Turing machines with the amplitudes of transfer functions being 0 or 1 are reversible Turing machines). Since the computational process of a quantum Turing machine satisfies unitarity, quantum computation is inherently reversible [3]. In 1989, Deutsch proposed the quantum circuit model. Subsequently, Yao [6] proved a significant result in 1993, that is, quantum circuits can efficiently simulate quantum Turing machines. Bernstein and Vazirani [5] further demonstrated that not only do universal quantum computers exist, but they can also simulate other quantum Turing machines in polynomial time. They clarified the fundamental relationships between quantum computation, probabilistic computation, and reversible computation.

Quantum algorithms are specific algorithms that run on quantum computers. When dealing with certain problems, quantum algorithms exhibit an exponential speedup advantage over classical algorithms (such as Shor's algorithm). They are likely to provide solutions to large-scale computational problems required in cryptography, weather forecasting, oil exploration, and drug design. Also, they may reveal complex physical mechanisms such as in high-temperature superconductivity and quantum Hall effect, which lay the foundation for advanced materials manufacturing and new energy development.

Deutsch [4] designed the first quantum query algorithm in 1985 to determine whether a Boolean function $f : \{0, 1\} \rightarrow \{0, 1\}$ is a balanced function or a constant function. Deutsch's algorithm only requires one query to accurately determine the result, while classical query algorithms require two queries. This shows the initial advantage of quantum computation. Deutsch and Jozsa [7] further extended Deutsch's algorithm in 1992. They generalized it to determine the properties of the function $f:\{0,1\}^n \rightarrow \{0,1\}$. This function is promised to be either a constant function (i.e., $f \equiv 1$ or 0) or a balanced function (a function which half of the values in the domain are 0, and the other half are 1). The quantum query algorithm (D-J algorithm) designed by Deutsch and Jozsa requires only one query to obtain the result, while the query number of the classical algorithm is $2^{n-1}+1$, further demonstrating the advantage of quantum computation. It is worth noting that in 1998, Cleve, Ekert, Macchiavello, and Mosca [8] further improved D-J algorithm.

A symmetric function on $\{0,1\}^n$ is a Boolean function whose value depends only on the Hamming weight of the input string. A partial function is a Boolean function whose domain is a subset $D \subseteq \{0,1\}^n$. In 2016, Qiu and Zheng [9] proved that any symmetric partial Boolean function f has the exact quantum 1-query complexity if and only if f can be computed by the D-J algorithm. The generalized D-J problem can be described as: Suppose the function $\mathrm{DJ}_n^k:\{0,1\}^n \longrightarrow \{0,1\}$, where n is even and $0 \leq k < \frac{n}{2}$, $\mathrm{DJ}_n^k = 1$ if $|x| = \frac{n}{2}$; $\mathrm{DJ}_n^k = 0$ if $0 \leq |x| \leq k$ or $n-k \leq |x| \leq n$. We can see that when $k=0$, DJ_n^0 is D-J problem; when $k=1$, Montanaro, Jozsa, and Mitchison [10] discussed its upper bound (but the lower bound is unknown). Qiu and Zheng [11] gave an optimal exact quantum query algorithm for computing the generalized D-J problem DJ_n^k (which also obtained the lower bound when $k=1$).

In 1994, Simon [12] proposed Simon's problem and presented a quantum algorithm to solve this problem, known as Simon's algorithm. Simon's problem can be described as follows: Given a Boolean function $f:\{0,1\}^n \rightarrow \{0,1\}^m$, where $n-1 \leq m$, and it satisfies the following conditions: there exists an $s \in \{0,1\}^n$ with $s \neq 0^n$ such that for any $x, y \in \{0,1\}^n$, $f(x)=f(y)$ if and only if $x \oplus y \in \{0^n, s\}$, where $x_1 \cdots x_n \oplus y_1 \cdots y_n = (x_1 \oplus y_1) \cdots (x_n \oplus y_n)$ and s is the target to be found.

Simon's algorithm is not exact, and its query complexity is $O(n)$ [12]. The lower bound for the quantum query complexity of Simon's problem was proven to be $\Omega(n)$ by Koiran, Nesme, and Portier [13]. de Wolf [14] proved that the classical probabilistic query complexity is $\Theta(\sqrt{2^n})$. This further demonstrates the advantage of quantum computing.

In 1997, Brassard and Höyer [15] proposed an exact quantum query algorithm to solve Simon's problem, with a query complexity of $O(n)$ (this algorithm further developed the amplitude amplification method used in Grover's algorithm). Subsequently, Mihara [16] simplified the algorithm's process, but the construction of Oracles was relatively complicated. Therefore in 2018 Cai and Qiu [17] utilized the idea of amplitude amplification to present a concise and clear exact quantum query algorithm for solving Simon's problem and the query complexity of the algorithm is also $O(n)$. Additionally, they provided a classical deterministic algorithm to solve Simon's problem with a query complexity of $O(\sqrt{2^n})$, which is the same as the classical probabilistic algorithm. Consequently, they obtained the optimal separation between the quantum and classical complexities of Simon's problem.

In particular, soon after Simon's algorithm was proposed, Shor [18], inspired by the D-J algorithm and Simon's algorithm designed a polynomial-time quantum algorithm for integer factorization in 1994, known as Shor's algorithm. It is well known that the best classical algorithms for integer factorization still have sub-exponential time complexity. Since integer factorization is the foundation of the security of RSA public-key cryptography, it has very important theoretical and practical implications. Since then, quantum computing has attracted much more attention and interest. In Shor's algorithm, quantum Fourier transform is implemented by a polynomial-time quantum circuit, which is a key technique for quantum phase estimation and become an important technique and basic tool in quantum algorithm design.

In 1995, Grover [19] proposed a quantum search algorithm for unstructured databases, known as Grover's algorithm. Its complexity is a square root faster than classical algorithms. More specifically, suppose a function $f: \{0,1\}^n \rightarrow \{0,1\}$ satisfies $f(x_0) = 1$ and $f(x) = 0$ when $x \neq x_0$. The goal is to find x_0. The query complexity of classical algorithms is $\Theta(2^n)$, while the query complexity of Grover's algorithm is $\Theta(\sqrt{2^n})$.

In Grover's algorithm, a new quantum algorithm design technique, amplitude amplification, was discovered. This technique was subsequently studied in depth by Brassard, Höyer [15], and many other researchers. It has now become another important tool and fundamental method in quantum algorithm design.

It is worth noting that in 2009, Harrow, Hassidim, and Lloyd [20] cleverly utilized quantum phase estimation to design a quantum algorithm for solving systems of linear equations. In some cases, its time complexity has an exponential advantage over classical algorithms.

Quantum finite automata (QFA [21,22]) is a simpler quantum computational model than quantum Turing machines. QFAs were first proposed by Moore and Crutchfield [21], and Kondacs and Watrous [22]. Moore and

Crutchfield proposed one-way QFAs, which only measure once during the computation process, and conducted some research on quantum grammars. The one-way QFA proposed by Kondacs and Watrous measures at each step of the computation process. In particular, they initiated important research on two-way QFA (2QFA). Because the tape heads of 2QFA perform quantum operation, which is difficult to be implemented in physics, Ambainis and Watrous proposed two-way QFA with classical and quantum states (2QCFA) in 2002, where the tape heads are classical. In particular, 2QCFA can recognize the non-regular language $L_{eq} = \{a^n b^n : n \in \mathbb{N}\}$ in polynomial time; and can recognize the palindrome language $L_{pal} = \{x \in \{a, b\} : x = x^R\}$ in exponential time, where x^R denotes the reverse of x. However, the relationship between 2QFA and 2QCFA is currently unclear, which is an interesting topic for further exploration.

Quantum complexity encompasses both quantum computational complexity and quantum communication complexity [23]. Bernstein and Vazirani first began the in-depth study of quantum computational complexity, proving the existence of universal quantum computers and their ability to simulate other quantum Turing machines in polynomial time. In the meantime, they demonstrated that quantum computers are at least as powerful as classical computers. There are generally two fundamental methods for determining lower bounds on quantum computational complexity: the polynomial method [24] and the adversary method [25].

Quantum computing represents a rapidly developing and important emerging technology. Countries around the world are paying close attention to quantum computing. Governments and industries are increasing their investment in quantum computing research and development. Both public and private institutions are investing significant resources.

In the report of the 20th National Congress of the Communist Party of China, President Xi Jinping emphasized the importance of "adhering to the frontiers of world science and technology, focusing on the main economic battlefields, meeting major national needs, promoting the health of the people, and accelerating the realization of high-level technological self-reliance and self-strength." As a major frontier of world science and technology, quantum computing is one of the most important races in the global competition for technological advancement, and it has significant research value. On October 16, 2020, the Political Bureau of the CPC Central Committee held its 24th collective study on the research and application prospects of quantum technology. In presiding over the study, President Xi Jinping emphasized the need to "fully recognize the importance and urgency of promoting the development of quantum technology, strengthening strategic planning and systematic layout for the development of quantum technology, grasping the overall trend, and making a good move." Therefore it is necessary and urgent to conduct in-depth research on quantum computing and attract more high-level talents to join the research. Based on the spirit of the 20th National Congress, this book introduces the basic theory of quantum computing, aiming to promote quantum computing research, inspiring more scholars to conduct original explorations, encouraging more people to learn about quantum computing and potentially achieving outstanding innovative results.

1.2 Potential applications of quantum computing

Quantum computing has demonstrated significant advantages in certain areas. For example, the representative quantum algorithms stated previously all show superiorities over classical computing, and these algorithms highlight the potential impact of quantum computing and provide basic methods of study.

Shor's algorithms require $O((\log N)^3)$ time and $O(\log N)$ space on a quantum computer to factor an integer N and to solve the discrete logarithm problem over $\mathbb{Z}_N^*$. As is known, Shor's algorithms have advantages of sub-exponential time and space complexity over existing classical algorithms. Therefore Shor's algorithms can be used to attack various cryptographic protocols, such as RSA and elliptic curve cryptography, potentially having a disruptive impact on security.

Quantum search algorithm proposed by Grover requires only $\Theta(\sqrt{N})$ time complexity to find a specific target in an unstructured database of size N, while classical algorithms require $\Theta(N)$ time complexity. This demonstrates the potential of quantum algorithms to significantly accelerate the search for specific information.

HHL algorithm offers a significant advantage over classical algorithms in terms of time complexity for solving linear systems of equations. Because it needs to solve a large amount of linear equations in fields such as big data, artificial intelligence, and deep learning, researchers begin to explore the integration of quantum computing with these fields. HHL algorithm, in particular, has been applied to quantum machine learning.

Beyond these, quantum computing has a broad range of applications across various industries as follows:

Biomedical Industry—Structural biology and protein structure simulation require a vast amount of computational resources, making drug development a complex and time-consuming process. Quantum computers can make trillions of molecular configurations in a short time and rapidly identify the most promising combinations, effectively reducing the cost and time of new drug development.

Weather Forecasting—Even with the most advanced instruments for analyzing temperature and pressure, it is challenging to keep up with the ever-changing atmospheric movements. As the forecast period lengthens, the accuracy of weather forecasts decreases. Additionally, weather forecasts often rely on calculations and analyses of historical data by meteorologists, resulting in potential errors. In order to make more accurate weather predictions, computational speed must keep pace with the speed of weather changes. In 2019, IBM introduced the Global High-Resolution Atmospheric Forecasting System (GRAF), using its supercomputer to perform more specific regional analyses. As quantum computers become maturer, it is expected that weather forecasting will also benefit from quantum computing.

Financial Services—Quantum computing may help eliminate data blind spots overlooked by financial analysts, preventing losses. In cases involving thousands of interconnected assets, quantum computing can be used to better identify attractive investment portfolios and more effectively detect financial fraud patterns. In 2021, Rigetti, a quantum computing startup and senior technical scientists from Commonwealth Bank of Australia collaborated on a study to optimize portfolio rebalancing by using quantum computing, to understand the potential applications of quantum computing in financial services.

Information Encryption—Quantum computers can be used to crack the encryption codes we use today to protect sensitive data and electronic communications. Conversely, quantum encryption technology can also be used to protect data from quantum hacking. In quantum communication, if an eavesdropper wants to copy the state of a particle, they must first measure the state of the particle. However, according to the no-cloning theorem of quantum mechanics, such a measurement will cause the quantum states to collapse, which can be detected by the communicating parties.

1.3 Quantum hardware development

Given the quantum computer's powerful computing capabilities and its potential applications in fields such as military defense, finance, information security, and disaster prediction, then many governments, universities, and companies in developed countries in the United States and Europe, as well as various organizations, have been actively involved in research and development. However, realizing a fault-tolerant universal quantum computer still requires significant theoretical and technological innovations. Nevertheless, specialized quantum computers that demonstrate quantum speedup are more likely to achieve practical applications sooner.

Currently, the physical systems, which can be used for experimental quantum computing research, mainly include superconductors, ion traps, photons, quantum dots, nitrogen-vacancy centers in diamond, cold atomic gases, and nuclear magnetic resonance, as well as topological quantum systems that are still under theoretical investigation. These systems each have their own advantages and also face critical challenges that need to be addressed.

Quantum computers can be broadly categorized into two types: universal quantum computers and special-purpose quantum computers. General-purpose quantum computers can be programmed by using quantum logic gates to execute any quantum algorithm within a certain error tolerance. Special-purpose quantum computers, on the other hand, are designed to run specific types of quantum circuits and perform pre-defined tasks. They generally cannot execute other quantum algorithms. Examples of special-purpose quantum computers include the Ising model quantum annealer developed by D-Wave Systems and China's "Jiuzhang" Boson sampling machine.

Since 2010, major research companies have made significant breakthroughs in hardware and software of quantum computing. In 2013, D-Wave Systems released a 512-qubit quantum computer. In 2016, IBM introduced a 6-qubit programmable quantum computer. In 2019, IBM launched the world's first standalone quantum computer, IBM Q System One; Google developed a 53-qubit quantum chip, "Sycamore." In 2020, China's "Jiuzhang" achieved a "Gaussian Boson Sampling" calculation with 76 photons. In 2021, China built a 62-qubit superconducting quantum computer, "Zuchongzhi"; IBM developed a 127-qubit superconducting quantum computer, "Eagle." In 2022, IBM launched a 433-qubit superconducting quantum computer, "Osprey." As a new computing paradigm, hardware research of quantum computing is rapidly advancing and is poised to revolutionize various fields.

Questions

1.1. Prove that DJ_N^0 is equivalent to *D-J* problem, where $N = 2^n$.

1.2. Suppose *D-J* problem does not require exact computation, but only an error less than $\frac{1}{2}$. How can you design such a probabilistic algorithm?

1.4 Summary

From the development history and potential applications of quantum computing, we can see that quantum computing, as a new computing paradigm, has unique superposition and entanglement properties that cannot be explained by classical physics. At the same time, we can see that quantum algorithms have an exponential speedup advantage over classical algorithms in solving certain specific problems, which provide solutions to many problems that require large-scale computation.

Currently, there are various physical systems that can be used for experimental research in quantum computing, and each system has its own advantages. The development of quantum computers is still in its infancy, and there is still a long way to go before the realization of universal quantum computers. Once universal quantum computers come into being, it will be a major milestone in human technological civilization.

References

[1] P. Benioff, Quantum mechanical Hamiltonian models of Turing machines, Journal of Statistical Physics 29 (3) (1982) 515–546.
[2] R.P. Feynman, Simulating physics with computers, International Journal of Theoretical Physics 21 (6/7) (1982) 467–488.
[3] C.H. Bennett, Logical reversibility of computation, IBM Journal of Research and Development 17 (6) (1973) 525–532.
[4] D. Deutsch, Quantum theory, the Church-Turing principle and the universal quantum computer, Proceedings of the Royal Society of London. Series A, Mathematical and Physical Sciences 400 (1818) (1985) 97–117.
[5] E. Bernstein, U. Vazirani, Quantum complexity theory, SIAM Journal on Computing 26 (5) (1997) 1411–1473.
[6] A.C.C. Yao, Quantum circuit complexity, in: Proceedings of 1993 IEEE 34th Annual Foundations of Computer Science, 1993, pp. 352–361.
[7] D. Deutsch, R. Jozsa, Rapid solution of problems by quantum computation, Proceedings of the Royal Society of London. Series A, Mathematical and Physical Sciences 439 (1907) (1992) 553–558.
[8] R. Cleve, A. Ekert, C. Macchiavello, et al., Quantum algorithms revisited, Proceedings of the Royal Society of London. Series A, Mathematical, Physical and Engineering Sciences 454 (1969) (1998) 339–354.
[9] D.W. Qiu, S.G. Zheng, Characterizations of symmetrically partial Boolean functions with exact quantum query complexity. 2016, arXiv:1603.06505.
[10] A. Montanaro, R. Jozsa, G. Mitchison, On exact quantum query complexity, Algorithmica 71 (4) (2015) 775–796.
[11] D.W. Qiu, S.G. Zheng, Generalized Deutsch-Jozsa problem and the optimal quantum algorithm, Physical Review A 97 (6) (2018) 062331.
[12] D.R. Simon, On the power of quantum computation, in: Proceedings of the 35th Annual Symposium on Foundations of Computer Science, 1994, pp. 116–123.
[13] P. Koiran, V. Nesme, N. Portier, A quantum lower bound for the query complexity of Simon's problem, in: International Colloquium on Automata, Languages, and Programming, 2005, pp. 1287–1298.

[14] H. Buhrman, R. de Wolf, Complexity measures and decision tree complexity: a survey, Theoretical Computer Science 288 (1) (2002) 21–43.
[15] G. Brassard, P. Höyer, An exact quantum polynomial-time algorithm for Simon's problem, in: Proceedings of the Fifth Israeli Symposium on Theory of Computing and Systems, 1997, pp. 12–23.
[16] T. Mihara, S.C. Sung, Deterministic polynomial-time quantum algorithms for Simon's problem, Computational Complexity 12 (3) (2003) 162–175.
[17] G.Y. Cai, D.W. Qiu, Optimal separation in exact query complexities for Simon's problem, Journal of Computer and System Sciences 97 (2018) 83–93.
[18] P.W. Shor, Algorithms for quantum computation: discrete logarithms and factoring, in: Proceedings 35th Annual Symposium on Foundations of Computer Science, 1994, pp. 124–134.
[19] L.K. Grover, A fast quantum mechanical algorithm for database search, in: Proceedings of the Twenty-Eighth Annual ACM Symposium on Theory of Computing, 1996, pp. 212–219.
[20] A.W. Harrow, A. Hassidim, S. Lloyd, Quantum algorithm for linear systems of equations, Physical Review Letters 103 (15) (2009) 150502.
[21] C. Moore, J.P. Crutchfield, Quantum automata and quantum grammars, Theoretical Computer Science 237 (1–2) (2000) 275–306.
[22] A. Kondacs, J. Watrous, On the power of quantum finite state automata, in: Proceedings of the 38th IEEE Conference on Foundations of Computer Science, 1997, pp. 66–75.
[23] P. Kaye, R. Laflamme, M. Mosca, An Introduction to Quantum Computing, Oxford, 2006.
[24] R. Beals, H. Buhrman, R. Cleve, et al., Quantum lower bounds by polynomials, Journal of the ACM 48 (4) (2001) 778–797.
[25] A. Ambainis, Quantum lower bounds by quantum arguments, Journal of Computer and System Sciences 64 (2002) 750–767.

CHAPTER 2

Fundamental concepts of quantum computing⊛

In this chapter, we introduce the mathematical notation, concepts, and their properties that are relevant to this book, with a particular focus on the fundamental concepts closely related to quantum computing, including qubits and basic quantum gates. Let $\mathbb{N}$, $\mathbb{Z}$, $\mathbb{Q}$, $\mathbb{R}$, and $\mathbb{C}$ denote the sets of natural numbers, integers, rational numbers, real numbers, and complex numbers, respectively.

2.1 Quantum bit

A qubit (quantum bit) can be represented by a two-dimensional unit column vector, $\begin{bmatrix} \alpha \\ \beta \end{bmatrix} \in \mathbb{C}^2$. $\begin{bmatrix} 1 \\ 0 \end{bmatrix}$ and $\begin{bmatrix} 0 \\ 1 \end{bmatrix}$ are two special quantum bits, called the computational basis states. A general single-qubit state $\begin{bmatrix} \alpha \\ \beta \end{bmatrix}$ can be represented as $|\psi\rangle$, meaning $|\psi\rangle = \begin{bmatrix} \alpha \\ \beta \end{bmatrix}$. Thus $|\psi\rangle = \alpha|0\rangle + \beta|1\rangle$, where $|\alpha|^2 + |\beta|^2 = 1$.

Since $|\alpha|^2 + |\beta|^2 = 1$, there exist real numbers θ, φ, and γ such that

$$\alpha = e^{i\gamma} \cos\left(\frac{\theta}{2}\right), \ \beta = e^{i(\gamma+\varphi)} \sin\left(\frac{\theta}{2}\right). \tag{2.1}$$

The proof of this conclusion is left as an exercise. It can be shown that $e^{i\gamma}$ has no effect on the observation, so it can be ignored. Therefore $|\psi\rangle$ can also be represented as

$$|\psi\rangle = \cos\left(\frac{\theta}{2}\right)|0\rangle + e^{i\varphi} \sin\left(\frac{\theta}{2}\right)|1\rangle, \tag{2.2}$$

where $\theta \in [0, \pi]$, $\varphi \in [0, 2\pi)$.

⊛ This book has a companion website hosting complementary materials. Visit this URL to access it: https://www.elsevier.com/books-and-journals/book-companion/9780443277047.

Theoretical Foundations of Quantum Computing
https://doi.org/10.1016/B978-0-44-327704-7.00007-4

It can be seen that any single-qubit state $|\psi\rangle$ corresponds to a point on the Bloch sphere, as shown in Fig. 2.1.

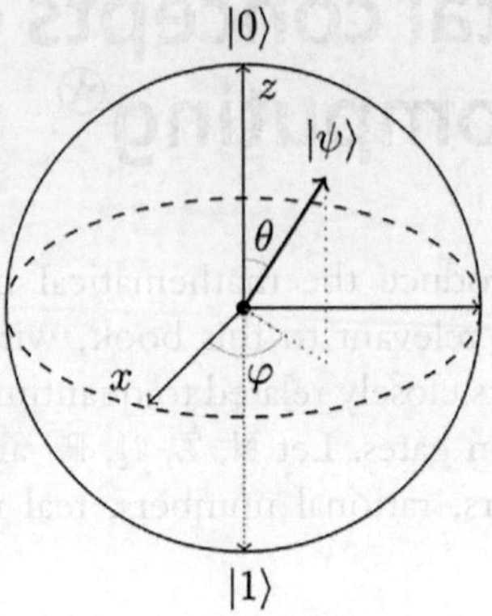

Figure 2.1 Bloch sphere.

We further consider the representation of double quantum bits. A two-qubit system has four basic states: 00, 01, 10, 11. The computational basis states of a two-qubit system are $|00\rangle$, $|01\rangle$, $|10\rangle$, $|11\rangle$, where $|ab\rangle = |a\rangle \otimes |b\rangle$, and $\otimes$ represents tensor product. The tensor product of any two matrices $A = \begin{bmatrix} a_{11} & \cdots & a_{1n} \\ \vdots & \ddots & \vdots \\ a_{m1} & \cdots & a_{mn} \end{bmatrix}$ and B is defined as

$$A \otimes B = \begin{bmatrix} a_{11}B & \cdots & a_{1n}B \\ \vdots & \ddots & \vdots \\ a_{m1}B & \cdots & a_{mn}B \end{bmatrix}. \tag{2.3}$$

Therefore any two-qubit state $|\psi\rangle$ can be represented as

$$|\psi\rangle = \sum_{i=0}^{1}\sum_{j=0}^{1} \alpha_{i,j}|ij\rangle, \tag{2.4}$$

where $\alpha_{i,j}$ are complex numbers and $\sum_{i=0}^{1}\sum_{j=0}^{1} |\alpha_{i,j}|^2 = 1$.

An important two-qubit entangled state is the Bell state (also known as the EPR pair),

$$\frac{|00\rangle + |11\rangle}{\sqrt{2}}. \tag{2.5}$$

Furthermore, n qubits can be represented as $|i_1 i_2 \cdots i_n\rangle$, where $i_j \in \{0, 1\}$ and $j = 1, 2, \cdots, n$. Therefore any n-qubit state $|\psi\rangle$ can be represented as

$$|\psi\rangle = \sum_{i_1, i_2, \cdots, i_n = 0}^{1} \alpha_{i_1, i_2, \cdots, i_n} |i_1 i_2 \cdots i_n\rangle, \tag{2.6}$$

where $\alpha_{i_1, i_2, \cdots, i_n}$ are complex numbers, and $\sum_{i_1, i_2, \cdots, i_n = 0}^{1} |\alpha_{i_1, i_2, \cdots, i_n}|^2 = 1$.

Similarly, $|i_1 i_2 \cdots i_n\rangle = |i_1\rangle \otimes |i_2\rangle \otimes \cdots \otimes |i_n\rangle$. Since the tensor product is associative, the order of tensor product operations does not affect the result.

$i_1 i_2 \cdots i_n$ corresponds to a binary number. If we represent it in decimal, then it belongs to $\{0, 1, \cdots, 2^n - 1\}$. If $i_1 i_2 \cdots i_n = k$, then we can write $|i_1 i_2 \cdots i_n\rangle = [\ \overbrace{0 \cdots 0}^{k}\ 1\ 0 \cdots 0\ ]^T$. Obviously, the dimension of the vector here is 2^n.

$\langle\psi|$ represents the conjugate transpose of $|\psi\rangle$, that is,

$$\langle\psi| = \sum_{i_1, i_2, \cdots, i_n = 0}^{1} \alpha^*_{i_1, i_2, \cdots, i_n} \langle i_1 i_2 \cdots i_n|, \tag{2.7}$$

where $\alpha^*_{i_1, i_2, \cdots, i_n}$ is the complex conjugate of $\alpha_{i_1, i_2, \cdots, i_n}$, $\langle i_1 i_2 \cdots i_n|$ is the conjugate transpose of $|i_1 i_2 \cdots i_n\rangle$ and is a row vector.

Suppose $|\psi^{(j)}\rangle = \sum_{i_1, i_2, \cdots, i_n = 0}^{1} \alpha^{(j)}_{i_1, i_2, \cdots, i_n} |i_1 i_2 \cdots i_n\rangle$, $j = 1, 2$. Then the inner product $\langle\psi^{(2)}|\psi^{(1)}\rangle$ is defined as

$$\sum_{i_1, i_2, \cdots, i_n = 0}^{1} \left(\alpha^{(2)}_{i_1, i_2, \cdots, i_n}\right)^* \alpha^{(1)}_{i_1, i_2 \cdots, i_n}, \tag{2.8}$$

which is the usual inner product $\left(|\psi^{(2)}\rangle, |\psi^{(1)}\rangle\right)$.

A non-empty set V with addition and scalar multiplication operations is called a vector space over the complex field $\mathbb{C}$, if it satisfies the following properties. Addition operation satisfies the following four rules:

(1) $\forall \alpha, \beta \in V$, $\alpha + \beta = \beta + \alpha$.

(2) $\forall \alpha, \beta, \gamma \in V$, $(\alpha + \beta) + \gamma = \alpha + (\beta + \gamma)$.

(3) $\exists 0 \in V$, $\forall \alpha \in V$, $0 + \alpha = \alpha$.

(4) $\forall \alpha \in V$, $\exists \beta \in V$, $\alpha + \beta = 0$.

Scalar multiplication satisfies the following two rules:

(5) $\forall \alpha \in V$, $1\alpha = \alpha$.

(6) $\forall k, l \in \mathbb{C}, \alpha \in V, k(l\alpha) = (kl)\alpha$.

Addition and scalar multiplication satisfy the following two rules:

(7) $\forall k, l \in \mathbb{C}, \alpha \in V, (k+l)\alpha = k\alpha + l\alpha$.

(8) $\forall k \in \mathbb{C}, \forall \alpha, \beta \in V, k(\alpha + \beta) = k\alpha + k\beta$.

For example, $\mathbb{C}^n = \left\{ \left[x_1, x_2, \cdots, x_n \right]^T \middle| x_i \in \mathbb{C}, i = 1, 2, \cdots, n \right\}$ is a vector space, where T denotes the transpose.

We define the inner product formally below. Let V be a vector space. A function $(\cdot,\cdot)$: $V \times V \rightarrow \mathbb{C}$ is called an inner product on V if it satisfies the following conditions:

(1) Conjugate linearity in the first argument: $|v_i\rangle, |w\rangle \in V, \alpha_i \in \mathbb{C}, i = 1, 2, \cdots, n$,

$$\left(\sum_{i=1}^{n} \alpha_i |v_i\rangle, |w\rangle \right) = \sum_{i=1}^{n} \alpha_i^* (|v_i\rangle, |w\rangle). \tag{2.9}$$

(2) Conjugate symmetry: $\forall |v\rangle, |w\rangle \in V$, $(|v\rangle, |w\rangle) = (|w\rangle, |v\rangle)^*$.

(3) Positive definiteness: The equality $(|v\rangle, |v\rangle) \geq 0$ holds if and only if $|v\rangle = 0$.

Define $\| |\varphi\rangle \| = \sqrt{\langle \varphi | \varphi \rangle}$. If for any real number $\epsilon > 0$, there exists a positive integer N, such that for any integers $n, m > N$, we have $\| |\varphi_n\rangle - |\varphi_m\rangle \| < \epsilon$. Then $\{|\varphi_i\rangle\}$ is called a Cauchy sequence.

A vector space equipped with an inner product is called an inner product space. If for any Cauchy sequence $\{|\varphi_i\rangle\}$ in the inner product space, there exists $|\varphi\rangle \in V$, such that $\{|\varphi_i\rangle\}$ converges to $|\varphi\rangle$, then V is called a complete inner product space, also known as a Hilbert space.

$|\psi^{(1)}\rangle\langle\psi^{(2)}|$ represents the tensor product, which is also the multiplication of two vectors, but its result is an $n \times n$ matrix. In fact, for any n-qubit state $|\varphi\rangle$, we have

$$\left(|\psi^{(1)}\rangle\langle\psi^{(2)}| \right) |\varphi\rangle = \left(\langle\psi^{(2)}|\varphi\rangle \right) |\psi^{(1)}\rangle. \tag{2.10}$$

2.2 Classical logic gates and circuits

Suppose a and b are the truth values of two propositions. Then

$$\text{NOT: } a \rightarrow \neg a = 1 - a, \tag{2.11}$$

$$\text{AND: } (a, b) \rightarrow a \wedge b = \min(a, b), \tag{2.12}$$

$$\text{OR: } (a, b) \rightarrow a \vee b = \max(a, b), \tag{2.13}$$

$$\text{XOR(exclusive OR): } (a, b) \rightarrow a \oplus b = (\neg a \wedge b) \vee (a \wedge \neg b). \tag{2.14}$$

Note: XOR is also called an XOR gate.

Let a and b be any truth values of two propositions. Then we have

$$a \vee b = \neg(\neg a \wedge \neg b), \tag{2.15}$$

$$a \oplus b = (a \wedge \neg b) \vee (\neg a \wedge b) \tag{2.16}$$

$$= \neg(\neg(a \wedge \neg b) \wedge \neg(\neg a \wedge b)). \tag{2.17}$$

We can see that $\neg$ and $\wedge$ can be used to represent other logical operations. Therefore $\{\neg, \wedge\}$ is called a complete set of Boolean operations. In fact, besides $\{\neg, \wedge\}$, the NAND gate is also a complete set. We denote NAND as $\uparrow$ and define that if a and b are two truth values, then

$$a \uparrow b = \neg(a \wedge b). \tag{2.18}$$

Since $\neg a = \neg(a \wedge a) = a \uparrow a$ and $a \wedge b = \neg(a \uparrow b)$, we know $\{\neg, \wedge\}$ can be represented by NAND and {NAND} is also complete.

Gate description:

NOT gate:

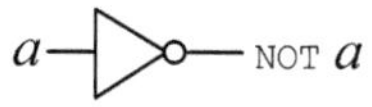

Figure 2.2 NOT gate.

AND gate:

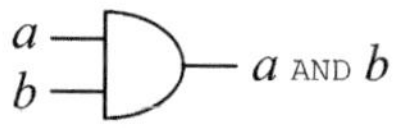

Figure 2.3 AND gate.

OR gate:

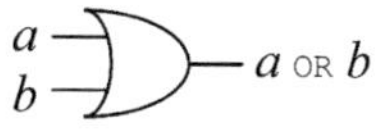

Figure 2.4 OR gate.

NAND gate:

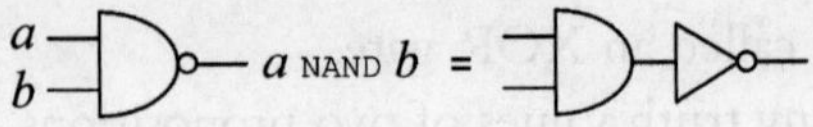

Figure 2.5 NAND gate.

Proposition 2.1. NAND *is a universal gate.*

Circuit representation of logic gates:

(1) Circuit diagram for $\neg(\neg a \wedge \neg b)$:

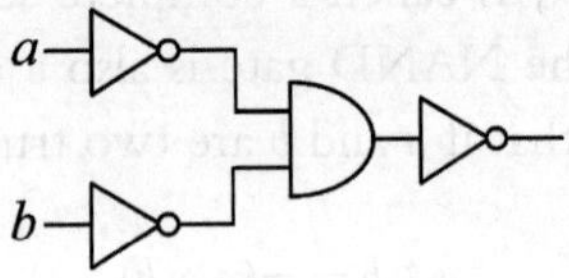

Figure 2.6 Circuit of $\neg(\neg a \wedge \neg b)$.

(2) Circuit diagram for $a \uparrow a$:

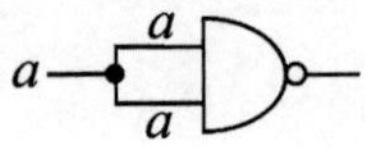

Figure 2.7 Circuit of $a \uparrow a$.

which represents a fan-out circuit.

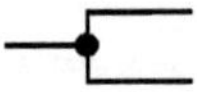

Figure 2.8 Fan-out circuit.

(3) Circuit diagram for $(a \uparrow b) \uparrow (a \uparrow b)$:

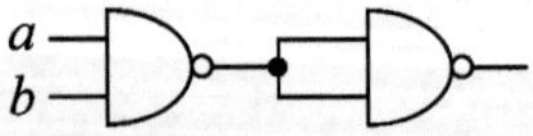

Figure 2.9 Circuit of $(a \uparrow b) \uparrow (a \uparrow b)$.

Circuit representation of reversible logic gates:

(4) Controlled NOT gate

$$(a, b) \xrightarrow{\text{CNOT}} (a, a \oplus b). \tag{2.19}$$

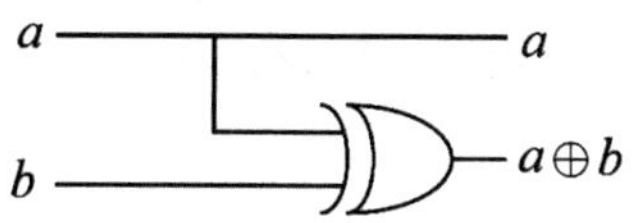

Figure 2.10 Circuit of controlled NOT gate.

which represents the circuit of XOR.

Figure 2.11 Circuit of XOR.

(5) Toffoli gate—also called CCNOT gate

$$(a, b, c) \xrightarrow{\text{CCNOT}} (a, b, (a \wedge b) \oplus c). \tag{2.20}$$

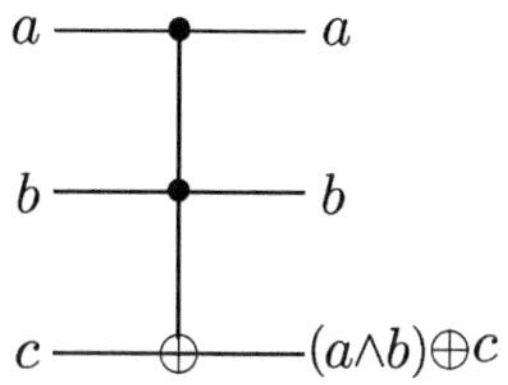

Figure 2.12 Circuit of Toffoli.

Note that $\mathrm{T}(a, b, 1) = (a, b, \neg(a \wedge b))$, so T gate can simulate NAND gate. In addition, because $\mathrm{T}(a, 1, 0) = (a, 1, a)$, T gate can also simulate fan-out.

$$(0, y, z) \xrightarrow{\text{CSWAP}} (0, y, z),(1, y, z) \to (1, z, y). \tag{2.21}$$

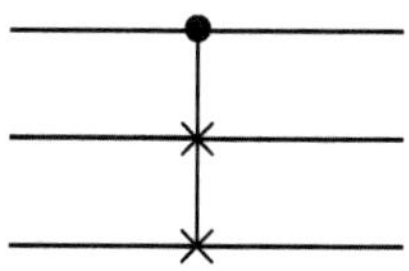

Figure 2.13 Circuit of Fredkin.

2.3 Basic quantum gates and circuits

Basic quantum gates:

(1) CNOT gate

$$|00\rangle \xrightarrow{\text{CNOT}} |00\rangle, |01\rangle \xrightarrow{\text{CNOT}} |01\rangle, \quad (2.22)$$

$$|10\rangle \xrightarrow{\text{CNOT}} |11\rangle, |11\rangle \xrightarrow{\text{CNOT}} |10\rangle. \quad (2.23)$$

CNOT can be represented in outer product form:

$$\text{CNOT} = |00\rangle\langle 00| + |01\rangle\langle 01| + |11\rangle\langle 10| + |10\rangle\langle 11|. \quad (2.24)$$

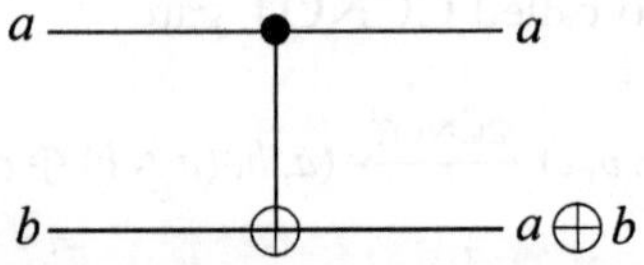

Figure 2.14 CNOT gate.

Since

$$\left(\frac{1}{\sqrt{2}}(|0\rangle + |1\rangle)|0\rangle\right) \xrightarrow{\text{CNOT}} \frac{1}{\sqrt{2}}(|00\rangle + |11\rangle), \quad (2.25)$$

the output is a Bell state (also an entangled state).

(2) I and Z gates

$$I = |0\rangle\langle 0| + |1\rangle\langle 1| = \begin{bmatrix} 1 & 0 \\ 0 & 1 \end{bmatrix}, \quad (2.26)$$

$$Z = |0\rangle\langle 0| - |1\rangle\langle 1| = \begin{bmatrix} 1 & 0 \\ 0 & -1 \end{bmatrix}. \quad (2.27)$$

(3) X and Y gates

$$X = |1\rangle\langle 0| + |0\rangle\langle 1| = \begin{bmatrix} 0 & 1 \\ 1 & 0 \end{bmatrix}, \quad (2.28)$$

$$Y = -i(|0\rangle\langle 1| - |1\rangle\langle 0|) = \begin{bmatrix} 0 & -i \\ i & 0 \end{bmatrix}. \quad (2.29)$$

(4) Hadamard gate

$$H = \frac{1}{\sqrt{2}}(|0\rangle + |1\rangle)\langle 0| + \frac{1}{\sqrt{2}}(|0\rangle - |1\rangle)\langle 1| = \frac{1}{\sqrt{2}}\begin{bmatrix} 1 & 1 \\ 1 & -1 \end{bmatrix}. \tag{2.30}$$

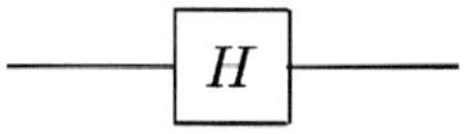

Figure 2.15 Hadamard gate.

No-cloning theorem is as follows:

Theorem 2.1. *There does not exist a quantum circuit U such that for any quantum state $|\psi\rangle$, $U|\psi\rangle|0\rangle = |\psi\rangle|\psi\rangle$.*

Proof. (Proof by contradiction) If there exists a unitary operator U satisfying the equation earlier, then we have

$$U|0\rangle|0\rangle = |0\rangle|0\rangle, \tag{2.31}$$

$$U|1\rangle|0\rangle = |1\rangle|1\rangle, \tag{2.32}$$

$$U\left(\frac{1}{\sqrt{2}}(|0\rangle + |1\rangle)|0\rangle\right) = \frac{1}{\sqrt{2}}(|0\rangle + |1\rangle)\frac{1}{\sqrt{2}}(|0\rangle + |1\rangle). \tag{2.33}$$

However,

$$U\left(\frac{1}{\sqrt{2}}(|0\rangle + |1\rangle)|0\rangle\right) \tag{2.34}$$

$$= U\left(\frac{1}{\sqrt{2}}(|00\rangle + |10\rangle)\right) \tag{2.35}$$

$$= \frac{1}{\sqrt{2}}(U|00\rangle + U|10\rangle) \tag{2.36}$$

$$= \frac{1}{\sqrt{2}}(|00\rangle + |11\rangle) \tag{2.37}$$

$$\neq \frac{1}{\sqrt{2}}(|0\rangle + |1\rangle)\frac{1}{\sqrt{2}}(|0\rangle + |1\rangle). \tag{2.38}$$

This is a contradiction. Therefore such a U does not exist, and the theorem has been proved. □

Simple quantum circuits:

(1)

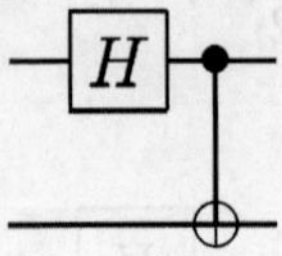

Figure 2.16 Circuit of CNOT $\cdot$ $(H \otimes I)$.

The matrix representation is CNOT $\cdot$ $(H \otimes I)$, where CNOT $= \begin{bmatrix} 1 & 0 & 0 & 0 \\ 0 & 1 & 0 & 0 \\ 0 & 0 & 0 & 1 \\ 0 & 0 & 1 & 0 \end{bmatrix}$. It can implement the following transformation:

$$|00\rangle \xrightarrow{\text{CNOT}\cdot(H\otimes I)} \frac{1}{\sqrt{2}}(|00\rangle + |11\rangle). \tag{2.39}$$

(2)

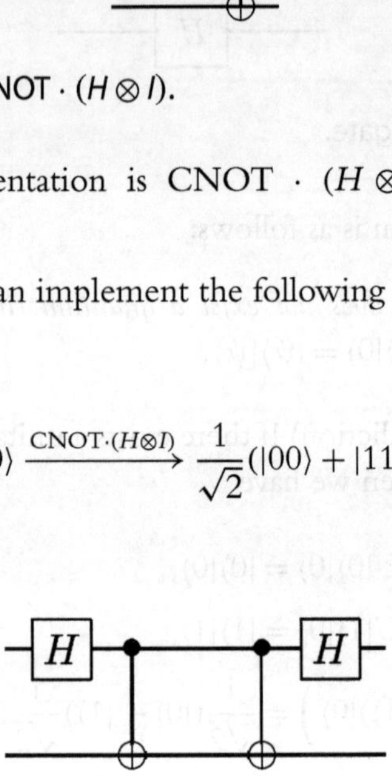

Figure 2.17 Circuit of $(H \otimes I)$ $\cdot$ CNOT $\cdot$ CNOT $\cdot$ $(H \otimes I)$.

The matrix representation is $(H \otimes I)$ $\cdot$ CNOT $\cdot$ CNOT $\cdot$ $(H \otimes I)$. It can implement the following transformation:

$$|00\rangle \xrightarrow{(H\otimes I)\cdot\text{CNOT}\cdot\text{CNOT}\cdot(H\otimes I)} |00\rangle. \tag{2.40}$$

Exercises

2.1. Prove that if $\alpha, \beta \in \mathbb{C}$, $|\alpha|^2 + |\beta|^2 = 1$, $|\psi\rangle = \alpha|0\rangle + \beta|1\rangle$, then there exist real numbers θ, φ, γ such that

$$\alpha = e^{i\gamma}\cos\left(\frac{\theta}{2}\right),\ \beta = e^{i(\gamma+\varphi)}\sin\left(\frac{\theta}{2}\right).$$

2.2. Prove that the tensor product operation is associative, that is, $(A \otimes B) \otimes C = A \otimes (B \otimes C)$.

2.3. Prove that if $i_1 i_2 \cdots i_n = k$, then $|i_1 i_2 \cdots i_n\rangle = [\,\overbrace{0 \cdots 0}^{k}\ 1\ 0 \cdots 0\,]^T$.

2.4. Use CNOT gate and Hadamard gate to generate the quantum states $\frac{|00\rangle - |11\rangle}{\sqrt{2}}$, $\frac{|01\rangle + |10\rangle}{\sqrt{2}}$, and $\frac{|01\rangle - |10\rangle}{\sqrt{2}}$.

2.5. Prove that $\left(|\psi^{(1)}\rangle\langle\psi^{(2)}|\right)|\psi\rangle = \left(\langle\psi^{(2)}|\psi\rangle\right)|\psi^{(1)}\rangle$.

2.6. What are the final states after the quantum states $|01\rangle$, $|10\rangle$, $|11\rangle$ passing through the following circuit?

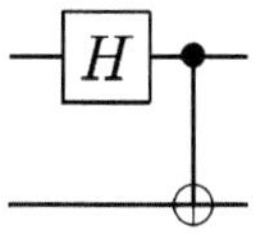

Figure 2.18 Circuit of CNOT $\cdot$ $(H \otimes I)$.

2.7. What are the final states after the four Bell states passing through the following circuit?

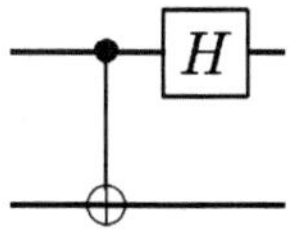

Figure 2.19 Circuit of $(H \otimes I)$ $\cdot$ CNOT.

Questions

2.8. Prove that if there exists a device that can perfectly distinguish two non-orthogonal quantum states $|\psi\rangle$ and $|\phi\rangle$, then the no-cloning principle is violated. Conversely, if there exists a device that can clone quantum states, then non-orthogonal quantum states can be perfectly distinguished.

2.9. Find the corresponding points on Bloch sphere for the eigenvectors of Pauli matrices.

2.4 Summary

In light of this chapter, we can learn about the mathematical symbols and concepts closely related to quantum computing, such as the column vector representation of qubits, the tensor product between matrices, the conjugate transpose of vectors and quantum states, the definition of inner product in vector spaces, and the outer product of vectors. Then we have reviewed the commonly used logic gates in classical computing, such as NOT gate, AND gate, OR gate, XOR gate, and NAND gate. We have also introduced the circuits of some commonly used logic gates. Finally, we have introduced some basic quantum gates, such as CNOT gate, X gate, Y gate, and Hadamard gate; also the no-cloning theorem and several simple quantum circuits have been described. These knowledge points are the foundation for further learning this book. In addition, more specific content can be found in [1,2].

References

[1] M.A. Nielsen, I.L. Chuang, Quantum Computation and Quantum Information: 10th Anniversary Edition, Cambridge University Press, 2010.

[2] P. Kaye, R. Laflamme, M. Mosca, An Introduction to Quantum Computing, Oxford, 2006.

CHAPTER 3

Fundamentals of linear algebra ⊛

In the previous chapters, we introduced Dirac notation and used it to describe quantum states, defining the tensor product, inner product, and outer product. These definitions are essentially the same as those taught in linear algebra, but Dirac notation makes many operations more concise and clear. In this chapter, we would like to provide further insight into linear algebra as it relates closely to quantum computing.

3.1 Linear independence and basis

Let $|v_1\rangle, \cdots, |v_n\rangle$ be n vectors in the vector space V. If $\forall \alpha_i \in \mathbb{C}$ and $\sum_{i=1}^{n} \alpha_i |v_i\rangle = 0$ implies $\alpha_i = 0$, $i = 1, 2, \cdots, n$, then $|v_1\rangle, \cdots, |v_n\rangle$ are said to be linearly independent.

If

$$\langle v_i | v_j \rangle = \begin{cases} 1, & i = j, \\ 0, & i \neq j, \end{cases} \tag{3.1}$$

then $\{|v_1\rangle, \cdots, |v_n\rangle\}$ is said to be a set of orthonormal vectors. Furthermore, if $\forall |v\rangle \in V$, there exist $\alpha_1, \cdots, \alpha_n \in \mathbb{C}$ such that $|v\rangle = \sum_{i=1}^{n} \alpha_i |v_i\rangle$, then $\{|v_1\rangle, \cdots, |v_n\rangle\}$ is said to be an orthonormal basis of V, and n is the dimension of V, denoted by $\dim(V)$.

3.2 Linear operators and matrices

Let V and W be any two vector spaces. Suppose A is a mapping from V to W and satisfies: $\forall |v_i\rangle \in V$, $\forall a_i \in \mathbb{C}$ $(i = 1, 2, \cdots, n)$, there is $A(\sum_{i=1}^{n} a_i |v_i\rangle) = \sum_{i=1}^{n} a_i A |v_i\rangle$, then A is said to be a linear operator from V to W.

The relationship between matrices and linear operators is discussed below. Let V and W be two vector spaces with $\dim(V) = n$ and $\dim(W) = m$, and let $A = [a_{ij}]_{m \times n}$ be an $m \times n$ matrix. Suppose $\{|v_1\rangle, \cdots, |v_n\rangle\}$ is an orthonormal basis of V, and $\{|w_1\rangle, \cdots, |w_m\rangle\}$ is an orthonormal basis of W.

⊛ This book has a companion website hosting complementary materials. Visit this URL to access it: https://www.elsevier.com/books-and-journals/book-companion/9780443277047.

Theoretical Foundations of Quantum Computing
https://doi.org/10.1016/B978-0-44-327704-7.00008-6

Then we define a mapping T_A from V to W: $\forall c_j \in \mathbb{C}$, $j = 1, 2, \cdots, n$, $T_A(\sum_{j=1}^{n} c_j|v_j\rangle) = \sum_{i=1}^{m}\sum_{j=1}^{n} a_{ij}c_j|w_i\rangle$. In fact, it can be proved that T_A is a linear operator from V to W.

On the other hand, let T be a linear operator from V to W. Suppose $\{|v_1\rangle, \cdots, |v_n\rangle\}$ and $\{|w_1\rangle, \cdots, |w_m\rangle\}$ are two orthonormal bases of V and W, respectively. If $T|v_j\rangle = \sum_{i=1}^{m} a_{ij}|w_i\rangle$, $j = 1, 2, \cdots, n$, then T corresponds to an $m \times n$ matrix $A = [a_{ij}]_{m\times n}$.

From these points, we have the following theorem.

Theorem 3.1. *Let V and W be n, m-dimensional vector spaces, respectively. Then there exists a one-to-one correspondence between the set of all $m \times n$ matrices and the set of all linear operators from V to W.*

In fact, quantum computation is studied on the complex Euclidean space $\mathbb{C}^n$, so we can think of the n-dimensional vector space as $\mathbb{C}^n$ usually.

3.3 Pauli matrices

The following four matrices are called Pauli matrices:

$$\sigma_0 = I = \begin{bmatrix} 1 & 0 \\ 0 & 1 \end{bmatrix}, \qquad \sigma_1 = \sigma_x = X = \begin{bmatrix} 0 & 1 \\ 1 & 0 \end{bmatrix},$$
$$\sigma_2 = \sigma_y = Y = \begin{bmatrix} 0 & -i \\ i & 0 \end{bmatrix}, \qquad \sigma_3 = \sigma_z = Z = \begin{bmatrix} 1 & 0 \\ 0 & -1 \end{bmatrix}. \tag{3.2}$$

Since $\{|0\rangle, |1\rangle\}$ is an orthonormal base of $\mathbb{C}^2$, the Pauli matrices are equivalent to the following four linear operators, respectively,

$$T_I = |0\rangle\langle 0| + |1\rangle\langle 1|, \tag{3.3}$$
$$T_X = |0\rangle\langle 1| + |1\rangle\langle 0|, \tag{3.4}$$
$$T_Y = -i(|0\rangle\langle 1| - |1\rangle\langle 0|), \tag{3.5}$$
$$T_Z = |0\rangle\langle 0| - |1\rangle\langle 1|. \tag{3.6}$$

3.4 Cauchy–Schwarz inequality

The following theorem describes the Cauchy–Schwarz inequality.

Theorem 3.2. *For any two vectors $|v\rangle$, $|w\rangle$ (unit vectors may not be required here) in a* Hilbert *space (say, H), then $|\langle v|w\rangle|^2 \le \langle v|v\rangle\langle w|w\rangle$, and the equality holds if and only if $|v\rangle$ and $|w\rangle$ are linearly dependent.*

Proof. Without loss of generalization, suppose $|v\rangle$ is a nonzero vector, otherwise it holds clearly. Denote $|i_0\rangle = \frac{|v\rangle}{\sqrt{\langle v|v\rangle}}$ and expand $|i_0\rangle$ into an orthonormal basis of H, denoted as $\{|j\rangle\}$. Then

$$|\langle v|w\rangle|^2 = \langle w|v\rangle\langle v|w\rangle \quad (3.7)$$

$$= \langle w|i_0\rangle\langle i_0|w\rangle\langle v|v\rangle \quad (3.8)$$

$$\leq \sum_j \langle w|j\rangle\langle j|w\rangle\langle v|v\rangle \quad (3.9)$$

$$= \langle w|\left(\sum_j |j\rangle\langle j|\right)|w\rangle\langle v|v\rangle \quad (3.10)$$

$$= \langle w|w\rangle\langle v|v\rangle. \quad (3.11)$$

$$\text{The equality holds} \Leftrightarrow \text{when } j \neq i_0,\ \langle w|j\rangle = 0 \quad (3.12)$$

$$\Leftrightarrow |w\rangle = \sum_j \alpha_j|j\rangle \text{ and when } j \neq i_0, \alpha_j = 0 \quad (3.13)$$

$$\Leftrightarrow |w\rangle = \alpha_{i_0}|i_0\rangle = \frac{\alpha_{i_0}|v\rangle}{\sqrt{\langle v|v\rangle}}. \quad (3.14)$$

□

3.5 Eigenvalues and eigenvectors

Let A be a linear operator on the vector space V and let $|v\rangle$ be a nonzero vector in V. If $A|v\rangle = \lambda|v\rangle$, where λ is complex number, then $|v\rangle$ is said to be the eigenvector of A and λ is the eigenvalue corresponding to $|v\rangle$. In fact, all the eigenvalues of the matrix A can be obtained by solving the eigenfunction $c(\lambda) = \det(A - \lambda I) = 0$, where $\det(A)$ denotes the determinant of the matrix A. We call the above equation $\det(A - \lambda I) = 0$ the characteristic equation with respect to A.

The eigenspace with regard to the eigenvalue λ is the set $\{|v\rangle \in V \mid A|v\rangle = \lambda|v\rangle\}$ (which is a subspace of V and is also called the eigenspace concerning λ). If $A = \sum_i \lambda_i|i\rangle\langle i|$, then it is called the diagonal representation of A, where $\{|i\rangle\}$ is an orthonormal basis of V, and λ_i is the eigenvalue with regard to $|i\rangle$. However, not all linear operators have diagonal representations. A linear operator A is said to be diagonalizable if there exists a diagonal representation of A.

3.6 Adjoint operators and Hermitian operators

Let A be a linear operator on Hilbert space V. If there exists a linear operator B on V such that $\forall|v\rangle, |w\rangle \in V$, we have $(|v\rangle, A|w\rangle) = (B|v\rangle, |w\rangle)$. Then B is called the adjoint operator (or Hermitian adjoint operator) of A, denoted by $A^\dagger$. In fact, if A is a matrix, then $A^\dagger$ is the conjugate transpose matrix of A.

Definition 3.1. If a linear operator (or matrix) A satisfies $A = A^\dagger$, then A is called self-adjoint or *Hermitian*.

Let W be a subspace of vector space V. Let $\{|1\rangle, \cdots, |k\rangle\}$ be an orthonormal basis of W, and let $\{|1\rangle, \cdots, |k\rangle, \cdots, |n\rangle\}$ be an orthonormal basis of V. Define the operator P as $P = \sum_{i=1}^{k} |i\rangle\langle i|$. Then P is called the projection operator from V onto W.

Definition 3.2. If a linear operator (or matrix) A satisfies $AA^\dagger = A^\dagger A$, then A is called a normal operator (matrix).

Definition 3.3. If a linear operator (or matrix) U satisfies $U^\dagger U = I$, then U is called a unitary operator (matrix).

Definition 3.4. If for any vector $|v\rangle$, a linear operator (or matrix) A satisfies $(|v\rangle, A|v\rangle) \geq 0$, then A is called a positive semi-definite operator (matrix).

3.7 Operator functions

Let A be a normal operator, and let $A = \sum_i \lambda_i |i\rangle\langle i|$. If f is a function, then the operator function is defined as

$$f(A) = \sum_i f(\lambda_i)|i\rangle\langle i|. \tag{3.15}$$

Let $A = [a_{ij}]_{n\times n}$ be an arbitrary n-order square matrix. The trace of A is defined as $\mathrm{Tr}(A) = \sum_{i=1}^{n} a_{ii}$. For any two matrices A and B, we have $\mathrm{Tr}(AB) = \mathrm{Tr}(BA)$; for any unitary matrix U, we have $\mathrm{Tr}(UAU^\dagger) = \mathrm{Tr}(A)$.

Let A be a linear operator. Define $\mathrm{Tr}(A)$ as the trace of the matrix corresponding to A in any orthonormal basis (the trace of A is invariant under different orthonormal bases). Equivalently, $\mathrm{Tr}(A) = \sum_i \langle i|A|i\rangle$, where $\{|i\rangle\}$ is an arbitrary orthonormal basis.

Let A be a linear operator and let $|\psi\rangle$ be any vector. Extend $\frac{|\psi\rangle}{\sqrt{\langle\psi|\psi\rangle}}$ to form an orthonormal basis, denoted as $\{|i\rangle\}$, then

$$\mathrm{Tr}(A|\psi\rangle\langle\psi|) = \sum_i \langle i|A|\psi\rangle\langle\psi|i\rangle \tag{3.16}$$

$$= \frac{\langle\psi|A|\psi\rangle\langle\psi|\psi\rangle}{\langle\psi|\psi\rangle} \tag{3.17}$$

$$= \langle\psi|A|\psi\rangle. \tag{3.18}$$

Theorem 3.3. *(Simultaneous diagonalization) Let A and B be two Hermitian operators. Then $AB = BA$ if and only if there exists an orthonormal basis $\{|i\rangle\}$ and real numbers a_i and b_i, such that $A = \sum_i a_i|i\rangle\langle i|$ and $B = \sum_i b_i|i\rangle\langle i|$.*

3.8 Operator decomposition theorem

Theorem 3.4. *(Spectral decomposition) Let V be a Hilbert space. Suppose A is a linear operator on V. Then $AA^\dagger = A^\dagger A \iff A = \sum_i \lambda_i|\varphi_i\rangle\langle\varphi_i|$, where λ_i are complex numbers, and $\{|\varphi_i\rangle\}$ is an orthonormal basis.*

Proof. The proof of "$\Leftarrow$" is obvious, so we only consider the proof of "$\Rightarrow$." We use mathematical induction on the dimension d of the image space of A.

If $d = 1$, it can be verified directly. Suppose it holds when $d \le k$. Then we prove that it holds when $d = k + 1$. Let λ be an eigenvalue of A, and let P be the projection operator onto the eigenspace of λ. Denote Q as the orthogonal complement of P (where Q is also a projection operator). Then $PAQ = QAP = 0$ and therefore $A = (P + Q)A(P + Q) = PAP + QAQ$.

It can be further verified that $PAP = \lambda P$ and QAQ is a normal operator. The former is obvious, so we prove the latter. Since $QA = QA(Q + P) = QAQ$, $QA^\dagger = QA^\dagger(Q + P) = QA^\dagger Q$, and the given condition $AA^\dagger = A^\dagger A$, we can get $QAQQA^\dagger Q = QA^\dagger QQAQ$. Due to the dimension of the image space of PAP being at least 1, we have the dimension of the image space of QAQ is at most k. By the inductive hypothesis, the theorem is proved. □

Theorem 3.5. *(Polar decomposition) Let A be a linear operator. Then there exist a unitary operator U and positive semi-definite operators J and K such that $A = UJ = KU$, where $J = \sqrt{A^\dagger A}$ and $K = \sqrt{AA^\dagger}$.*

Proof. In the light of the spectral decomposition theorem, let $J = \sqrt{A^\dagger A} = \sum_i \lambda_i |i\rangle\langle i|$ $(\lambda_i \geq 0)$. Denote $|\psi_i\rangle = A|i\rangle$. Then $\langle\psi_i|\psi_i\rangle = \langle i|A^\dagger A|i\rangle = \lambda_i^2$. Furthermore, denote $|e_i\rangle = \frac{|\psi_i\rangle}{\lambda_i}$ $(\lambda_i \neq 0)$, and extend $\{|e_i\rangle\}$ to form an orthonormal basis. As a result, define $U = \sum_i |e_i\rangle\langle i|$, and the theorem is proved. □

Theorem 3.6. *(Singular value decomposition) Let T be an arbitrary linear operator from V_1 to V_2. Then there exist two sets of orthonormal sets of vectors $\{|a_i\rangle\}$ and $\{|b_j\rangle\}$ and nonnegative real numbers λ_i such that $T = \sum_i \lambda_i |a_i\rangle\langle b_i|$.*

Proof. According to the polar decomposition theorem, let $T = UJ$ (U is a unitary operator and J is a positive semi-definite operator). By means of the spectral decomposition theorem, suppose $J = \sum_i \lambda_i |i\rangle\langle i|$, and then $T = U\sum_i \lambda_i |i\rangle\langle i| = \sum_i \lambda_i U|i\rangle\langle i|$. Define $|a_i\rangle = U|i\rangle$ and $|b_i\rangle = |i\rangle$, and thus the theorem is proved. □

The following proposition is clear.

Proposition 3.1. *Let $\mathcal{B} = \{|b_i\rangle \mid i \in B\}$ be an orthonormal basis of Hilbert space $\mathcal{H}$, where B is an index set. Then any linear operator T on $\mathcal{H}$ can be expressed as $T = \sum_{n,m\in B} T_{n,m} |b_n\rangle\langle b_m|$, where $T_{n,m} \in \mathbb{C}$.*

Now we present the Schmidt decomposition theorem.

Theorem 3.7. *(Schmidt decomposition) Let $|\psi\rangle$ be a pure state on two systems $\mathcal{A}$ and $\mathcal{B}$, and $\langle\psi|\psi\rangle = 1$, that is, $|\psi\rangle = \sum_{i,j} a_{ij}|i_\mathcal{A}\rangle|j_\mathcal{B}\rangle$, where $|i_\mathcal{A}\rangle$ and $|j_\mathcal{B}\rangle$ are orthonormal bases of $\mathcal{A}$ and $\mathcal{B}$, respectively. Then there exist $|\psi_{k,\mathcal{A}}\rangle$ and $|\psi_{k,\mathcal{B}}\rangle$ such that $|\psi\rangle = \sum_k \lambda_k |\psi_{k,\mathcal{A}}\rangle|\psi_{k,\mathcal{B}}\rangle$, where λ_k are nonnegative real numbers, and $\sum_k \lambda_k^2 = 1$.*

In order to prove the theorem, we need to do related preparations. For any $A, B \in L(V)$, define $(A, B) = \mathrm{Tr}(A^\dagger B)$. It can be proven that (A, B) is an inner product on $L(V)$. Furthermore, if d is the dimension of V, then the dimension of $L(V)$ is d^2.

Let $\{|\psi_i\rangle \mid i = 1, 2, \ldots, d\}$ be an orthonormal basis of V. Then $\{|\psi_i\rangle\langle\psi_j| \mid i, j = 1, 2, \cdots, d\}$ is an orthonormal basis of $L(V)$.

Let $\mathcal{A}$ and $\mathcal{B}$ be two Hilbert spaces. Let $\{|a_i\rangle \mid i = 1, 2, \cdots, d_a\}$ and $\{|b_j\rangle \mid j = 1, 2, \cdots, d_b\}$ be orthonormal bases of $\mathcal{A}$ and $\mathcal{B}$, respectively. $L(\mathcal{B}, \mathcal{A})$ is the Hilbert space of all linear operators from $\mathcal{B}$ to $\mathcal{A}$. Then $\{|a_i\rangle\langle b_j \mid$

$|i=1,2,\cdots,d_a, j=1,2,\cdots,d_b\}$ is an orthonormal basis of $L(\mathcal{B},\mathcal{A})$. Denote $E_{ij}=|a_i\rangle\langle b_j|$. The inner product in $L(\mathcal{B},\mathcal{A})$ is defined as $(A,B)=\mathrm{Tr}(A^\dagger B)$, where $A,B\in L(\mathcal{B},\mathcal{A})$.

Lemma 3.1. *There exists a one-to-one mapping between* $L(\mathcal{B},\mathcal{A})$ *and* $\mathcal{A}\otimes\mathcal{B}$.

Proof. Define $vec(E_{ij})=|a_i\rangle(|b_j\rangle)^*$ and $vec\left(\sum_{ij}\mu_{ij}E_{ij}\right)=\sum_{ij}\mu_{ij}|a_i\rangle(|b_j\rangle)^*$. Then for any $|\varphi\rangle\in\mathcal{A}$ and $|\psi\rangle\in\mathcal{B}$, we have $vec(|\varphi\rangle\langle\psi|)=|\varphi\rangle(|\psi\rangle)^*$. Therefore vec is a one-to-one mapping between $L(\mathcal{B},\mathcal{A})$ and $\mathcal{A}\otimes\mathcal{B}$. □

Now we are ready to prove the Schmidt decomposition theorem as follows.

Proof. Let $T_\psi\in L(\mathcal{B},\mathcal{A})$ such that $vec(T_\psi)=|\psi\rangle$. By the singular value decomposition, there exist two sets of orthonormal vectors on $\mathcal{A}$ and $\mathcal{B}$, $\{|a_i\rangle\}$ and $\{|b_j\rangle\}$, respectively, such that $T_\psi=\sum_i\lambda_i|a_i\rangle\langle b_i|$. Therefore $|\psi\rangle=vec(T_\psi)=\sum_i\lambda_i|a_i\rangle(|b_i\rangle)^*=\sum_i\lambda_i|a_i\rangle|c_i\rangle$. Let $|\psi_{k,\mathcal{A}}\rangle=|a_k\rangle$ and $|\psi_{k,\mathcal{B}}\rangle=|c_k\rangle$. Then the theorem is proved. □

Exercises

3.1. Let $\mathcal{V}$ and $\mathcal{W}$ be two Hilbert spaces, and let $\{|v_j\rangle\}$ and $\{|w_i\rangle\}$ be orthonormal bases for $\mathcal{V}$ and $\mathcal{W}$, respectively. Define $T_A:\sum_{j=1}^{n}c_j|v_j\rangle\to\sum_{j=1}^{n}c_j\sum_{i=1}^{m}a_{ij}|w_i\rangle$. Prove that T_A is a linear operator.

3.2. Prove the following four equations:
(1) $T_I=|0\rangle\langle0|+|1\rangle\langle1|$,
(2) $T_X=|0\rangle\langle1|+|1\rangle\langle0|$,
(3) $T_Y=-i(|0\rangle\langle1|-|1\rangle\langle0|)$,
(4) $T_Z=|0\rangle\langle0|-|1\rangle\langle1|$.

3.3. Provide the eigenvalues, eigenvectors, and diagonalization of the Pauli matrices.

3.4. Prove that the matrix $\begin{bmatrix}1&0\\1&1\end{bmatrix}$ is not diagonalizable.

3.5. Prove that for any two vectors $|w\rangle$ and $|v\rangle$, we have $(|w\rangle\langle v|)^\dagger=|v\rangle\langle w|$.

3.6. Prove that for any projection operator P, we have $P^2=P$.

3.7. Let A be a normal operator. Prove that A is a Hermitian operator if and only if the eigenvalues of A are real.

3.8. Prove that $H^{\otimes n} = \frac{1}{\sqrt{2^n}} \sum_{x,y \in \{0,1\}^n} (-1)^{x \cdot y} |x\rangle\langle y|$.

3.9. Find $\sqrt{\begin{bmatrix} 4 & 3 \\ 3 & 4 \end{bmatrix}}$ and $\ln \begin{bmatrix} 4 & 3 \\ 3 & 4 \end{bmatrix}$.

3.10. Prove that the Pauli matrices satisfy the relation:

$$\sigma_i \sigma_j + \sigma_j \sigma_i = \begin{cases} 0, & \text{if } i \neq j; \\ 2I, & \text{if } i = j, \end{cases} \tag{3.19}$$

where $i, j = 1, 2, 3$.

3.11. Let $\vec{v} \cdot \vec{\sigma} = \sum_{i=1}^{3} v_i \sigma_i$, where $\vec{v} = (v_1, v_2, v_3)$ is a unit real vector, $\sigma_1 = X$, $\sigma_2 = Y$, and $\sigma_3 = Z$. Prove that

$$\exp(i\theta \vec{v} \cdot \vec{\sigma}) = \cos(\theta) I + i \sin(\theta) \vec{v} \cdot \vec{\sigma}.$$

3.12. Prove that for any linear operators A and B, we have $\mathrm{Tr}(AB) = \mathrm{Tr}(BA)$.

3.13. Let A be a linear operator, and define $\mathrm{Tr}(A) = \sum_i \langle i|A|i\rangle$, where $\{|i\rangle\}$ is an orthonormal basis. Prove the validity of this definition, that is, for any other orthonormal basis $\{|j\rangle\}$, we have $\sum_j \langle j|A|j\rangle = \sum_i \langle i|A|i\rangle$.

3.14. Prove the following three items appearing in the proof of the spectral decomposition theorem:

(1) Verify that the theorem holds when $d = 1$;

(2) $PAQ = QAP = 0$;

(3) $PAP = \lambda P$.

3.15. Verify that for any $|\Phi\rangle \in \mathcal{A} \otimes \mathcal{B}$, there exists a unique $T \in L(\mathcal{B}, \mathcal{A})$ such that $vec(T) = |\Phi\rangle$.

3.16. Let $\mathcal{A}$ and $\mathcal{B}$ be two Hilbert spaces. Prove that for any $|\varphi\rangle \in \mathcal{A}$ and $|\psi\rangle \in \mathcal{B}$, we have $vec(|\varphi\rangle\langle\psi|) = |\varphi\rangle(|\psi\rangle)^*$.

3.17. Let V be a two-dimensional vector space with basis vectors $|0\rangle$ and $|1\rangle$. Let A be a linear operator from V to V such that $A|0\rangle = |1\rangle$ and $A|1\rangle = |0\rangle$. Write down the matrix representation of A when both the input and output bases are $|0\rangle$ and $|1\rangle$. Provide a different matrix representation of A when another set of basis vectors is used.

3.18. Define $((y_1, \cdots, y_n), (z_1, \cdots, z_n)) \equiv \sum_i y_i^* z_i$. Prove that this definition is an inner product on $\mathbb{C}^n$.

3.19. Prove that the first variable of any inner product $(\cdot, \cdot)$ has the property of conjugate linearity, that is,

$$\left(\sum_i \lambda_i |w_i\rangle, |v\rangle\right) = \sum_i \lambda_i^* (|w_i\rangle, |v\rangle).$$

3.20. Prove that the Gram–Schmidt algorithm generates an orthonormal basis for a vector space V.

3.21. In a two-dimensional Hilbert space, write down the operator representation related to the Pauli matrices in the standard orthonormal basis $|0\rangle$ and $|1\rangle$, and express each Pauli operator in the form of outer products.

3.22. Prove that for any linear operators A_i and complex numbers a_i, we have

$$\left(\sum_i a_i A_i\right)^\dagger = \sum_i a_i^* A_i^\dagger.$$

3.23. Let A be a linear operator. Prove that $(A^\dagger)^\dagger = A$.

3.24. Prove that the Pauli matrices are Hermitian and unitary.

3.25. Prove that eigenvectors corresponding to different eigenvalues of a Hermitian operator are orthogonal.

3.26. Prove that the eigenvalues of a projection operator are 0 or 1.

3.27. Prove that a positive operator is necessarily a Hermitian operator.

3.28. Prove that for any operator A, $A^\dagger A$ is a positive semi-definite operator.

3.29. Prove that the transpose, complex conjugate, and adjoint operations distribute over the tensor product, that is, $(A \otimes B)^* = A^* \otimes B^*$; $(A \otimes B)^T = A^T \otimes B^T$; $(A \otimes B)^\dagger = A^\dagger \otimes B^\dagger$. Here, A and B are matrices.

3.30. Provide the polar decomposition form of a Hermitian matrix.

3.31. Write the polar decomposition of the matrix $\begin{bmatrix} 1 & 0 \\ 1 & 1 \end{bmatrix}$ and prove it.

Questions

3.32. Suppose $A = \sum_i \lambda_i |i\rangle\langle i|$, f is a function, then $f(A) = \sum_i f(\lambda_i)|i\rangle\langle i|$. Question: Why is the definition of $f(A)$ reasonable?

3.9 Quantum mechanics assumptions

The fundamental assumptions of quantum mechanics are expressed in various ways, including four or five statements. In this book, we adopt four assumptions that are described mathematically by employing Hilbert space theory. Readers need to master and apply these assumptions proficiently.

Assumption 1. A physical system is characterized by a Hilbert space $\mathcal{H}$, and the states of the system are described by vectors in $\mathcal{H}$.

For example, $|\psi\rangle = \alpha|0\rangle + \beta|1\rangle$ is used to describe the states of a qubit system, where $|\alpha|^2 + |\beta|^2 = 1$ and $\alpha, \beta \in \mathbb{C}$.

Assumption 2. The state evolution of a closed quantum system is described by a unitary transformation, such that the transformation from any state $|\psi\rangle$ to state $|\psi'\rangle$ satisfies $|\psi'\rangle = U|\psi\rangle$, where U is a unitary operator.

For example, the Hadamard transform $H = \frac{1}{\sqrt{2}}\begin{bmatrix} 1 & 1 \\ 1 & -1 \end{bmatrix}$.

Assumption 3. Quantum measurement is described by a set of measurement operators $\{M_m\}$, which satisfy the completeness relation $\sum_m M_m^\dagger M_m = I$. These measurement operators act on the state of the system being measured, where m is the measurement outcome. If the quantum state before measurement is $|\psi\rangle$, then the probability of obtaining m is $p(m) = \langle\psi|M_m^\dagger M_m|\psi\rangle$, and the state of the system collapses to

$$\frac{M_m|\psi\rangle}{\sqrt{\langle\psi|M_m^\dagger M_m|\psi\rangle}}. \tag{3.20}$$

For example, if we take $M_0 = |0\rangle\langle 0|$ and $M_1 = |1\rangle\langle 1|$, then $\{M_0, M_1\}$ constitutes a set of measurement operators for a single qubit. If we take $|\psi\rangle = a|0\rangle + b|1\rangle$, then

$$p(0) = \langle\psi|M_0^\dagger M_0|\psi\rangle = |a|^2, \tag{3.21}$$

$$p(1) = \langle \psi | M_1^\dagger M_1 | \psi \rangle = |b|^2, \tag{3.22}$$

and after measurement, the states for these two cases are respectively as follows $\frac{a}{|a|}|0\rangle$ and $\frac{b}{|b|}|1\rangle$.

We discuss an application of measurement operators: the discrimination of quantum states.

Let $|\psi_1\rangle$ and $|\psi_2\rangle$ be two quantum states in the space and $\langle \psi_1 | \psi_2 \rangle \neq 0$. Then there does not exist a measurement $\{E_i \mid i = 1, 2\}$ such that

$$\langle \psi_i | E_j^\dagger E_j | \psi_i \rangle = \begin{cases} 0, & i \neq j, \\ 1, & i = j. \end{cases} \tag{3.23}$$

Proof. If such a measurement exists, then $E_2|\psi_1\rangle = 0$ and $E_1|\psi_2\rangle = 0$. Let $|\psi_2\rangle = \alpha|\psi_1\rangle + \beta|\psi\rangle$, where $\langle \psi_1 | \psi \rangle = 0$ and $|\beta| < 1$ (otherwise $\langle \psi_2 | \psi_1 \rangle = 0$). In this case, $E_2|\psi_2\rangle = \beta E_2|\psi\rangle$, and thus $1 = \langle \psi_2 | E_2^\dagger E_2 | \psi_2 \rangle = |\beta|^2 \langle \psi | E_2^\dagger E_2 | \psi \rangle \leq |\beta|^2 < 1$, a contradiction! Therefore such a measurement does not exist. □

Assumption 4. The state space of a composite system can be described by the tensor product of the state spaces of its subsystems. If $|\psi_i\rangle$ is the state of the ith system and there are n subsystems, then the state of the composite system is $|\psi_1\rangle \otimes |\psi_2\rangle \otimes \cdots \otimes |\psi_n\rangle$.

3.10 Density operator

In addition to using vectors (known as states), quantum systems can also be described by using density operators or density matrices (referred to as mixed states). Let a quantum system be in state $|\psi_i\rangle$ with probability p_i. Then $\{p_i, |\psi_i\rangle\}$ is called an ensemble of pure states, and the state of the system is defined by the density operator $\rho = \sum_i p_i |\psi_i\rangle\langle\psi_i|$.

ρ is also referred to as the density matrix. If the state evolution of a closed quantum system is described by a unitary operator U, then the evolution of the density matrix ρ is given by

$$\rho \xrightarrow{U} \sum_i p_i U|\psi_i\rangle\langle\psi_i|U^\dagger = U\rho U^\dagger. \tag{3.24}$$

If the initial state is $|\psi_i\rangle$, then the probability of measuring m is given by

$$p(m|i) = \langle \psi_i | M_m^\dagger M_m | \psi_i \rangle = \mathrm{Tr}(M_m^\dagger M_m |\psi_i\rangle\langle\psi_i|). \tag{3.25}$$

By the law of total probability, the probability of measuring m is given by

$$p(m) = \sum_i p_i p(m|i) \tag{3.26}$$

$$= \sum_i p_i \mathrm{Tr}(M_m^\dagger M_m |\psi_i\rangle\langle\psi_i|) \tag{3.27}$$

$$= \mathrm{Tr}(M_m^\dagger M_m \rho). \tag{3.28}$$

If the initial state is $|\psi_i\rangle$, then the state of measuring m is given by

$$|\psi_i^m\rangle = \frac{M_m|\psi_i\rangle}{\sqrt{\langle\psi_i|M_m^\dagger M_m|\psi_i\rangle}}. \tag{3.29}$$

Therefore the state of the system after obtaining the measurement result m is

$$\rho_m = \sum_i p(i|m)|\psi_i^m\rangle\langle\psi_i^m| \quad \left(p(i|m) = \frac{p(m,i)}{p(m)} = \frac{p_i p(m|i)}{p(m)}\right) \tag{3.30}$$

$$= \sum_i \frac{p_i p(m|i)}{p(m)} \frac{M_m|\psi_i\rangle\langle\psi_i|M_m^\dagger}{\langle\psi_i|M_m^\dagger M_m|\psi_i\rangle} \tag{3.31}$$

$$= \sum_i p_i \frac{M_m|\psi_i\rangle\langle\psi_i|M_m^\dagger}{p(m)} \tag{3.32}$$

$$= \frac{M_m \rho M_m^\dagger}{\mathrm{Tr}(M_m^\dagger M_m \rho)}. \tag{3.33}$$

The basic properties of density operators are given below.

Theorem 3.8. *ρ is a density operator if and only if:*

(1) $\mathrm{Tr}(\rho) = 1$;

(2) *ρ is a positive semi-definite operator.*

Proof. "⇒" If ρ is a density operator, then ρ can be expressed in the form $\rho = \sum_i p_i|\psi_i\rangle\langle\psi_i|$, where $\sum_i p_i = 1$ and $p_i \geq 0$. In this case, (1) and (2) are obviously satisfied.

"⇐" According to (2), we know that ρ has a spectral decomposition $\rho = \sum_i \lambda_i|i\rangle\langle i|$. In addition, by (1) we know that $1 = \mathrm{Tr}(\rho) = \sum_i \lambda_i$. As a result, $\{\lambda_i, |i\rangle\}$ forms an ensemble of pure states and therefore ρ is a density operator. □

State vectors can only be used to describe pure states. The description of mixed states requires the use of density operators. The four fundamental postulates of quantum mechanics can be redescribed by using the formalism of density operators.

Assumption 1. Any isolated physical system is characterized by a Hilbert space and the state of the system is described by a density operator. If the system is in state ρ_i with probability p_i, then the state of the system is given by the density operator

$$\rho = \sum_i p_i \rho_i. \tag{3.34}$$

Assumption 2. The state evolution of a closed quantum physical system is described by unitary operators. The state of the system is ρ at time t_1, and evolves to the state ρ' at time t_2 by the action of a unitary operator U, that is,

$$\rho' = U\rho U^\dagger. \tag{3.35}$$

Assumption 3. Quantum measurement consists of a set of measurement operators $\{M_m\}$, and satisfies $\sum\limits_m M_m^\dagger M_m = I$, where m refers to the measured result. If the current state of the system is ρ, then the probability of obtaining m after measurement is $p(m) = \mathrm{Tr}(M_m^\dagger M_m \rho)$ and the new state is

$$\frac{M_m \rho M_m^\dagger}{\mathrm{Tr}(M_m^\dagger M_m \rho)}. \tag{3.36}$$

Assumption 4. The state of a composite physical system is composed of the state tensors of each subsystem. If the states of system 1 to system n are $\rho_1, \rho_2, \ldots, \rho_n$, then the state of the composite system is $\rho_1 \otimes \rho_2 \otimes \cdots \otimes \rho_n$.

The density matrix (operator) has the following properties (proof can be found in the book of Nielsen and Chuang [1]).

Theorem 3.9. *If ρ is a density operator with representation $\rho = \sum\limits_i p_i |\psi_i\rangle\langle\psi_i| = \sum\limits_j q_j |\varphi_j\rangle\langle\varphi_j|$, where $\{p_i, |\psi_i\rangle\}$ and $\{q_j, |\varphi_j\rangle\}$ are the states of the ensemble, then $\sqrt{p_i}|\psi_i\rangle = \sum\limits_j u_{ij}\sqrt{q_j}|\varphi_j\rangle$, $i = 1, \ldots, m$, $j = 1, \ldots, n$, where $[u_{ij}]$ is a unitary matrix.*

Exercises

3.33. Let ρ be a density operator. Prove $\mathrm{Tr}(\rho^2) \leq 1$, and $\mathrm{Tr}(\rho^2) = 1$ if and only if ρ is a pure state.

3.34. (1) Prove the second-order density matrix of any mixed state ρ can be denoted as $\rho = \dfrac{I + \overrightarrow{r} \cdot \overrightarrow{\sigma}}{2}$, where $\overrightarrow{r}$ is a real three-dimensional vector and $\| \overrightarrow{r} \| \leq 1$, $\overrightarrow{\sigma} = (\sigma_x, \sigma_y, \sigma_z)$, vector $\overrightarrow{r}$ is referred to as the Bloch vector of ρ.

(2) Write the Bloch vector representation of $\rho = \frac{I}{2}$.

(3) Prove ρ is a pure state if and only if $\| \overrightarrow{r} \| = 1$.

(4) Prove the Bloch vector representation of pure state is the same as the representation in (1).

3.35. Prove:

(1) Hadamard gate H is unitary;

(2) $H^2 = I$;

(3) Find the eigenvalues and eigenvectors of H.

3.36. Prove:

(1) $|\psi\rangle = \dfrac{|00\rangle + |11\rangle}{\sqrt{2}}$ is an Entangled state;

(2) Bell states form an orthonormal basis.

3.11 Partial trace

Let a composite physical system AB be composed of two subsystems A and B, and let the Hilbert space $\mathcal{H}_A$ and $\mathcal{H}_B$ describe A and B, respectively. Therefore the system AB is described by $\mathcal{H}_A \otimes \mathcal{H}_B$. If $\rho^{AB} \in L(\mathcal{H}_A \otimes \mathcal{H}_B)$ is a density operator in AB, then one question is how to obtain the state information of each subsystem from ρ^{AB}? For this, it is necessary to introduce the definition of partial trace.

Let $\rho^{AB} = \sum_i \lambda_i |\psi_i\rangle_{AB}\, {}_{AB}\langle\psi_i|$, where $|\psi_i\rangle_{AB} \in \mathcal{H}_A \otimes \mathcal{H}_B$. According to Schmidt's decomposition theorem, it can be assumed that

$$|\psi_i\rangle_{AB} = \sum_j \mu_j^{(i)} |\psi_j^{(i)}\rangle_A |\psi_j^{(i)}\rangle_B, \tag{3.37}$$

where $\{|\psi_j^{(i)}\rangle_A\}$ and $\{|\psi_j^{(i)}\rangle_B\}$ are two sets of orthonormal vectors of $\mathcal{H}_A$ and $\mathcal{H}_B$, respectively.

Now,

$$|\psi_i\rangle_{AB}\, {}_{AB}\langle\psi_i| = \sum_{j,k} \mu_j^{(i)} (\mu_k^{(i)})^* |\psi_j^{(i)}\rangle_A |\psi_j^{(i)}\rangle_B\, {}_A\langle\psi_k^{(i)}|\, {}_B\langle\psi_k^{(i)}| \tag{3.38}$$

$$= \sum_{j,k} \mu_j^{(i)} (\mu_k^{(i)})^* |\psi_j^{(i)}\rangle_A\, {}_A\langle\psi_k^{(i)}| \otimes |\psi_j^{(i)}\rangle_B\, {}_B\langle\psi_k^{(i)}|. \tag{3.39}$$

Define

$$\mathrm{Tr}_A(|\psi_i\rangle_{AB}\ {}_{AB}\langle\psi_i|) \tag{3.40}$$

$$=\sum_{j,k}\mu_j^{(i)}(\mu_k^{(i)})^*|\psi_j^{(i)}\rangle_B\ {}_B\langle\psi_k^{(i)}|\cdot\mathrm{Tr}(|\psi_j^{(i)}\rangle_A\ {}_A\langle\psi_k^{(i)}|), \tag{3.41}$$

Similarly, define

$$\mathrm{Tr}_B(|\psi_i\rangle_{AB}\ {}_{AB}\langle\psi_i|) \tag{3.42}$$

$$=\sum_{j,k}\mu_j^{(i)}(\mu_k^{(i)})^*|\psi_j^{(i)}\rangle_A\ {}_A\langle\psi_k^{(i)}|\cdot\mathrm{Tr}(|\psi_j^{(i)}\rangle_B\ {}_B\langle\psi_k^{(i)}|). \tag{3.43}$$

Furthermore, define

$$\mathrm{Tr}_A(\rho^{AB})=\sum_i\lambda_i\mathrm{Tr}_A(|\psi_i\rangle_{AB AB}\langle\psi_i|) \tag{3.44}$$

and

$$\mathrm{Tr}_B(\rho^{AB})=\sum_i\lambda_i\mathrm{Tr}_B(|\psi_i\rangle_{AB AB}\langle\psi_i|). \tag{3.45}$$

Denote $\rho^A=\mathrm{Tr}_B(\rho^{AB})$, $\rho^B=\mathrm{Tr}_A(\rho^{AB})$.

In fact, ρ^A and ρ^B describe the state information of systems A and B in ρ^{AB}, respectively.

Of course, we can also define partial traces without requiring the application of Schmidt decomposition. Let $|\psi\rangle\in\mathcal{H}_A\otimes\mathcal{H}_B$. Suppose $|\psi\rangle=\sum_{i,j}\lambda_{i,j}|\psi_i\rangle_A|\psi_j\rangle_B$, where $\{|\psi_i\rangle_A\}$ and $\{|\psi_j\rangle_B\}$ are two orthonormal bases of $\mathcal{H}_A$ and $\mathcal{H}_B$, respectively. Then

$$|\psi\rangle\langle\psi|=\sum_{i,j}\lambda_{i,j}|\psi_i\rangle_A|\psi_j\rangle_B\sum_{k,l}\lambda_{k,l}^*{}_A\langle\psi_k|_B\langle\psi_l| \tag{3.46}$$

$$=\sum_{i,j,k,l}\lambda_{i,j}\lambda_{k,l}^*|\psi_i\rangle_{AA}\langle\psi_k|\otimes|\psi_j\rangle_{BB}\langle\psi_l|. \tag{3.47}$$

Define

$$\mathrm{Tr}_A(|\psi\rangle\langle\psi|)=\sum_{i,j,k,l}\lambda_{i,j}\lambda_{k,l}^*\mathrm{Tr}(|\psi_i\rangle_{AA}\langle\psi_k|)|\psi_j\rangle_{BB}\langle\psi_l|. \tag{3.48}$$

$\mathrm{Tr}_B(|\psi\rangle\langle\psi|)$ can be defined similarly.

Clearly, let $|\psi_A\rangle\langle\psi_A| \otimes |\psi_B\rangle\langle\psi_B| \in \mathcal{H}_A \otimes \mathcal{H}_B$. According to the definition mentioned previously, it can be inferred that

$$\mathrm{Tr}_A(|\psi_A\rangle\langle\psi_A| \otimes |\psi_B\rangle\langle\psi_B|) = \langle\psi_A|\psi_A\rangle|\psi_B\rangle\langle\psi_B|. \tag{3.49}$$

Tr_B can be defined similarly.

Actually, partial trace of a composite system composed of multiple systems $\mathcal{H}_{A_1} \otimes \mathcal{H}_{A_2} \otimes \cdots \otimes \mathcal{H}_{A_k}$ can be similarly defined. Let $\rho = |\psi_1\rangle\langle\psi_1| \otimes |\psi_2\rangle\langle\psi_2| \otimes \cdots \otimes |\psi_k\rangle\langle\psi_k| \in \mathcal{H}_{A_1} \otimes \mathcal{H}_{A_2} \otimes \cdots \otimes \mathcal{H}_{A_k}$, where $|\psi_i\rangle\langle\psi_i| \in \mathcal{H}_{A_i}$. Then we define

$$\begin{aligned}&\mathrm{Tr}_{A_i}(\rho)\\ =&\mathrm{Tr}(|\psi_i\rangle\langle\psi_i|)|\psi_1\rangle\langle\psi_1| \otimes \cdots \otimes |\psi_{i-1}\rangle\langle\psi_{i-1}| \otimes |\psi_{i+1}\rangle\langle\psi_{i+1}| \otimes \cdots \otimes |\psi_k\rangle\langle\psi_k|,\end{aligned} \tag{3.50}$$

where $i = 1, 2, \cdots, k$.

Example 3.1. Let

$$|\psi_{AB}\rangle = \frac{|00\rangle_{AB} + |11\rangle_{AB}}{\sqrt{2}}, \tag{3.51}$$

$$\rho^{AB} = |\psi\rangle_{ABAB}\langle\psi| \tag{3.52}$$

$$= \frac{|00\rangle_{ABAB}\langle 00| + |00\rangle_{ABAB}\langle 11| + |11\rangle_{ABAB}\langle 00| + |11\rangle_{ABAB}\langle 11|}{2}. \tag{3.53}$$

Then

$$\mathrm{Tr}_A(\rho^{AB}) = \frac{|0\rangle_{BB}\langle 0| + |1\rangle_{BB}\langle 1|}{2} \tag{3.54}$$

$$= \frac{I_B}{2}, \tag{3.55}$$

$$\mathrm{Tr}_B(\rho^{AB}) = \frac{I_A}{2}. \tag{3.56}$$

Exercises

3.37. Let $\rho \in \mathcal{H}_A \otimes \mathcal{H}_B$. Prove $\mathrm{Tr}_B((U \otimes I)\rho(U^\dagger \otimes I)) = U(\mathrm{Tr}_B\rho)U^\dagger$.

3.38. (1) Find a pure state $\rho^{AB} \in \mathcal{H}_{AB}$, such that $\rho^{AB} \neq \mathrm{Tr}_B(\rho^{AB}) \otimes \mathrm{Tr}_A(\rho^{AB})$.

(2) Prove that for any density operator ρ on a system A, there exists a pure state $|\psi\rangle$ on some large system $A \otimes B$ such that $\rho = \mathrm{Tr}_B|\psi\rangle\langle\psi|$ and $\dim(A) \geq \dim(B)$.

3.12 Superoperator

In a closed quantum system, a state $|\psi\rangle$ of the system evolves to $U|\psi\rangle$ under the application of unitary operator U. However, when the quantum system interacts with the outside environment, the state of the whole physical system would be described by a mixed state, which is mathematically represented by a density operator (or matrix) and denoted as ρ. At this time, the evolution of states needs to be acted upon by a more general quantum operation, which is actually an operator that maps from operator space to operator space, also called a superoperator. Actually, a special kind of superoperator is utilized here, which will be introduced in detail in this section.

Let V be a finite-dimensional Hilbert space, and let $L(V)$ be the set of all linear operators on V. In fact, $L(V)$ can also form a Hilbert space according to the following definition of inner product: $(A, B) = \mathrm{Tr}(A^\dagger B)$. The linear operators that map from $L(V)$ to $L(V)$ are called superoperators.

Let $\rho \in L(V)$ be a density operator. Suppose $A_i \in L(V)$, $i = 1, 2, \cdots, k$, and $\sum_{i=1}^{k} A_i^\dagger A_i = I$. Then we define

$$\mathcal{T}(\rho) = \sum_{i=1}^{k} A_i \rho A_i^\dagger, \tag{3.57}$$

where A_i is Kraus operator [2]. The above operator $\mathcal{T}$ is called *admissible quantum operation*, and Eq. (3.57) is called the representation of sum of operators. It is clear that $\mathcal{T}$ is a superoperator.

Definition 3.5. Let $\mathcal{T}$ be a superoperator that maps from $L(V)$ to $L(V)$. Then $\mathcal{T}$ is called a completely positive operator if it satisfies the following two conditions: (1) For any positive operator $A \in L(V)$, $\mathcal{T}(A)$ is a positive operator. (2) Let R be any finite-dimensional Hilbert space, and let $\mathcal{I}$ be an identity operator on $L(R)$. Then, for any $A \in L(R \otimes V)$, when A is a positive operator, $(\mathcal{I} \otimes \mathcal{T})(A)$ is also a positive operator.

In fact, the admissible quantum operation $\mathcal{T}$ defined by the previous equation (3.57) is a completely positive operator and trace-preserving. It is not difficult to prove that $\mathcal{T}$ is trace-preserving. Next, We will prove that $\mathcal{T}$ is completely positive.

First, we give the following lemma (the proof is provided as an exercise).

Lemma 3.2. *Let $A_i \in L(V)$. Then for any $A \in L(R \otimes V)$, $\sum_i (\mathcal{I} \otimes A_i)A(\mathcal{I} \otimes A_i^\dagger) = (\mathcal{I} \otimes \mathcal{T})(A)$, where $\mathcal{I}$ is the identity operator on L(R), and $\mathcal{T}$ is defined in equation* (3.57), in other words, for any $B \in L(V)$, $\mathcal{T}(B) = \sum_i A_i B A_i^\dagger$.

According to Lemma 3.2, we can directly prove that $\mathcal{T}$ is completely positive. For any positive operator $A \in L(R \otimes V)$ and any $|\psi\rangle \in R \otimes V$, we have

$$\langle\psi|(\mathcal{I} \otimes \mathcal{T})(A)|\psi\rangle = \langle\psi|\sum_i (\mathcal{I} \otimes A_i)A(\mathcal{I} \otimes A_i^\dagger)|\psi\rangle \tag{3.58}$$

$$= \sum_i \langle\psi|(\mathcal{I} \otimes A_i)A(\mathcal{I} \otimes A_i^\dagger)|\psi\rangle \geq 0. \tag{3.59}$$

Some examples are given as follows.

Example 3.2. Suppose that the quantum system V is expressed as $V \otimes E$ after interacting with the external environment E, both $\rho \in L(V)$ and $\rho_e \in L(E)$ are density operators, and U is a unitary operator applying to the whole system. Let superoperator $\mathcal{T}$ be defined as

$$\mathcal{T}(\rho) = \mathrm{Tr}_e[U(\rho \otimes \rho_e)U^\dagger]. \tag{3.60}$$

Let $\rho_e = \sum_i \lambda_i |\varphi_i\rangle\langle\varphi_i|$, where $\{|\varphi_i\rangle\}$ is an orthonormal basis of E, and let $\{|e_i\rangle\}$ be another orthonormal basis of E. Then we have

$$\mathcal{T}(\rho) = \sum_k (I_v \otimes \langle e_k|)U(\rho \otimes \rho_e)U^\dagger(I_v \otimes |e_k\rangle) \tag{3.61}$$

$$= \sum_k A_k \rho A_k^\dagger, \tag{3.62}$$

where $A_k = \sum_i \sqrt{\lambda_i}(I_v \otimes \langle e_k|)U(I_v \otimes |\varphi_i\rangle)$.

Furthermore, we have

$$\sum_k A_k^\dagger A_k \tag{3.63}$$

$$= \sum_k \Big(\sum_i \sqrt{\lambda_i}(I_v \otimes \langle\varphi_i|)U^\dagger(I_v \otimes |e_k\rangle)\Big)\Big(\sum_j \sqrt{\lambda_j}(I_v \otimes \langle e_k|)U(I_v \otimes |\varphi_j\rangle)\Big) \tag{3.64}$$

$$= \sum_k \sum_{i,j} \sqrt{\lambda_i}\sqrt{\lambda_j}(I_v \otimes \langle\varphi_i|)U^\dagger(I_v \otimes |e_k\rangle)(I_v \otimes \langle e_k|)U(I_v \otimes |\varphi_j\rangle) \tag{3.65}$$

$$= \sum_{i,j} \sqrt{\lambda_i}\sqrt{\lambda_j}(I_v \otimes \langle\varphi_i|)U^\dagger \cdot \sum_k (I_v \otimes |e_k\rangle)(I_v \otimes \langle e_k|)U(I_v \otimes |\varphi_j\rangle) \tag{3.66}$$

$$= \sum_{i,j} \sqrt{\lambda_i}\sqrt{\lambda_j}(I_v \otimes \langle\varphi_i|)U^+ \cdot (I_v \otimes I_e) \cdot U(I_v \otimes |\varphi_j\rangle) \tag{3.67}$$

$$= \sum_{i,j} \sqrt{\lambda_i}\sqrt{\lambda_j}(I_v \otimes \langle\varphi_i|)(I_v \otimes I_e)(I_v \otimes |\varphi_j\rangle) \tag{3.68}$$

$$= I_v, \tag{3.69}$$

where I_e and I_v are the identity operators on E and V, respectively.

According to the previous lemma, $\mathcal{T}$ is an admissible quantum operation and is also a completely positive operator with trace-preserving. □

In particular, when the state of the environment is a pure state $|\rho_0\rangle\langle\rho_0|$ interacting with the internal quantum system ρ,

$$\mathcal{T}(\rho) = \mathrm{Tr}_e(U(\rho \otimes |\rho_0\rangle\langle\rho_0|)U^\dagger). \tag{3.70}$$

At this time, $A_i = (I_v \otimes \langle e_k)U(I_v \otimes |e_0\rangle)$, where $\{|e_k\rangle\}$ is an orthonormal basis of the environmental system.

In the previous admissible quantum operation represented by the sum of operators, we require $\sum_i A_i^\dagger A_i = I$. In fact, if the operation does not involve measurement, quantum operations can also be expressed as the sum of operators, but $\sum_i A_i^\dagger A_i \leq I$.

Example 3.3. Suppose a physical system V interacts with an external environment E, and the density operators ρ and ρ_e represent the states of V and E, respectively. Assume U is a unitary operator acting on $\mathcal{H}_V \otimes \mathcal{H}_E$, and $\{P_i\}$ is a projection measurement on $\mathcal{H}_V \otimes \mathcal{H}_E$. Then the quantum operation is

$$\mathcal{T}_k(\rho) = \mathrm{Tr}_e(P_k U(\rho \otimes \rho_e)U^\dagger P_k). \tag{3.71}$$

Let $\rho_e = \sum_j \mu_j |\varphi_j\rangle\langle\varphi_j|$, $\mu_j \geq 0$ and $\sum_j \mu_j = 1$, and let $\{|e_i\rangle\}$ be an orthonormal basis on $\mathcal{H}_E$. Then

$$\mathcal{T}_k(\rho) = \sum_i (I_v \otimes \langle e_i|)P_k U(\rho \otimes \rho_e)U^\dagger P_k(I_v \otimes |e_i\rangle) \tag{3.72}$$

$$= \sum_{i,j} \mu_j (I_v \otimes \langle e_i|)P_k U(\rho \otimes |\varphi_j\rangle\langle\varphi_j|)U^\dagger P_k(I_v \otimes |e_i\rangle), \tag{3.73}$$

where I_v is the identity operator on $\mathcal{H}_V$.

Let $E_{i,j} = \sqrt{\mu_j}(I_v \otimes \langle e_i|)P_k U(I_v \otimes |\varphi_j\rangle)$. Then we can verify that the above $\mathcal{T}_k(\rho)$ is the representation of the sum of the following operators:

$$\mathcal{T}_k(\rho) = \sum_{i,j} E_{ij}\rho E_{ij}^{\dagger}. \tag{3.74}$$

Example 3.4. Consider a three-dimensional Hilbert space with orthonormal basis $\{|0\rangle, |1\rangle, |2\rangle\}$. Suppose $A_i = |i\rangle\langle i|$, $i = 0, 1, 2$, $|\psi\rangle = \sum_{i=0}^{2} \alpha_i |i\rangle$, $\rho = |\psi\rangle\langle\psi|$. Then $\mathcal{T}(\rho)$ is defined as follows:

$$\mathcal{T}(\rho) = \sum_{i=0}^{2} A_i \rho A_i^{\dagger} \tag{3.75}$$

$$= \sum_{i=0}^{2} |\alpha_i|^2 |i\rangle\langle i|. \tag{3.76}$$

Exercises

3.39. Let V be a finite-dimensional Hilbert space, and let $L(V)$ be the set of all linear operators on V. In fact, $L(V)$ can also form a Hilbert space according to the following definition of inner product: $(A, B) = \mathrm{Tr}(A^{\dagger}B)$.

Prove:

(1) $L(V)$ is a vector space.

(2) (A, B) is defined as the inner product.

(3) The dimension of $L(V)$ is $d(V)^2$, where $d(V)$ is the dimension of V.

3.40. Prove that the admissible quantum operations defined by function (3.57) are trace-preserving.

3.41. Prove Lemma 3.2 (Tips: Utilize Schmidt decomposition theorem).

3.42. Prove Eq. (3.74).

3.13 Summary

In contrast to classical physics, quantum mechanics offers a precise depiction of the microscopic world. Quantum mechanics is closely related to Hilbert space theory, so functional analysis is a mathematical foundation of it. To have a better understanding, the readers can refer to *Mathematical Foundations of Quantum Mechanics* by Von Neumann et al. In general, some basic knowledge of linear algebra and matrix analysis is enough for one to carry out research in quantum computing without learning quantum mechanics.

In this chapter, we first introduced some fundamental knowledge of linear algebra pertinent to quantum computing, including various operators and operator functions. Then we systematically introduced several crucial operators (matrices) decomposition theorems, and clarified the relationships among these results. After that, we used the state vector and density operator methods to give a description of the four basic assumptions in quantum mechanics (computing). It should be pointed out that state vectors can only be used to describe pure states, but density operators can describe pure states and mixed states. To characterize the properties of individual subsystems within composite physical systems, we introduced the concept and fundamental properties of partial trace. The evolution process from mixed states to mixed states is a mapping from density operators to density operators, which is a kind of superoperator, so we introduced the basic concepts and properties of superoperators in the last section.

References

[1] M.A. Nielsen, I.L. Chuang, Quantum Computation and Quantum Information: 10th Anniversary Edition, Cambridge University Press, 2010.

[2] P. Kaye, R. Laflamme, M. Mosca, An Introduction to Quantum Computing, Oxford, 2006.

CHAPTER 4

Basic protocols in quantum communication[⊛]

Quantum communication is a product of perfect combination of quantum mechanics and quantum information, including quantum key distribution (QKD) and quantum teleportation. According to the type of quantum resources used, existing QKD protocols can be divided into two major categories: discrete variable QKD and continuous variable QKD. The former encodes information on discrete variables in a finite-dimensional Hilbert space (such as photon polarization). Its main advantages include that its principles are very concise and it can transmit long distances. However, it requires perfect signal sources and high-performance detection devices, which can be costly. Typical discrete variable QKD protocols include BB84 protocol [1], B92 protocol [2], and E91 protocol [3]. Continuous Variable QKD encodes information on continuous variables in an infinite-dimensional Hilbert space (such as quadrature phase of light). Its main advantages are low cost and strong compatibility with traditional communication systems. However, its transmission distance is relatively short. The most famous continuous variable QKD protocol is GG02 protocol proposed by Grosshans and Grangier [4] in 2002. In the first three sections of this chapter, we mainly describe three basic protocols of discrete variable QKD. Then, in the fourth and fifth sections, we present the famous quantum superdense coding [5] and quantum teleportation protocols [6].

4.1 BB84 protocol

The first protocol in quantum cryptography is BB84 protocol, proposed by Bennett and Brassard [1] in 1984. This protocol is simple in principle and, therefore, easy to be implemented physically. Its unconditional security is guaranteed by the quantum no-cloning theorem and the fact that nonorthogonal states cannot be perfectly distinguished. Since then, QKD

⊛ This book has a companion website hosting complementary materials. Visit this URL to access it: https://www.elsevier.com/books-and-journals/book-companion/9780443277047.

Theoretical Foundations of Quantum Computing
https://doi.org/10.1016/B978-0-44-327704-7.00009-8

has attracted extensive theoretical as well as experimental research and has been developing in depth.

Suppose $Z = \{|0\rangle, |1\rangle\}$, $X = \{|+\rangle, |-\rangle\}$. The process of BB84 is as follows:

1: Alice prepares a sequence of random bits $a_1, a_2, \cdots, a_n$ composed by 0 and 1, and a sequence of basis choices $b_1, b_2, \cdots, b_n$, where $b_i \in \{Z, X\}$.

2: Alice encodes this random sequence into a sequence of qubits $|q_1\rangle, |q_2\rangle, \cdots, |q_n\rangle$. The encoding rules are: $|q_i\rangle$ is encoded as quantum state $|0\rangle$ if $a_i = 0$ and $b_i = Z$; $|q_i\rangle$ is encoded as quantum state $|+\rangle$ if $a_i = 0$ and $b_i = X$; $|q_i\rangle$ is encoded as quantum state $|1\rangle$ if $a_i = 1$ and $b_i = Z$; $|q_i\rangle$ is encoded as quantum state $|-\rangle$ if $a_i = 1$ and $b_i = X$.

3: Alice sends the sequence of qubits $|q_1\rangle, |q_2\rangle, \cdots, |q_n\rangle$ to Bob through a quantum channel.

4: For each received qubit $|q_i\rangle$, Bob randomly chooses either Z or X as basis to measure it.

5: Bob publicly announces the measurement bases he used for each qubit.

6: Alice tells Bob which of the measurement bases are the same and which are not.

7: Alice and Bob discard the qubits where they used different measurement bases and keep the qubits where they used the same measurement basis, thereby obtaining a raw key.

8: Alice and Bob use a portion of their raw key to compare. If the error rate is below a certain threshold R_0, they proceed to error correction and privacy amplification [7] for the remaining raw key and obtain a secure key. Otherwise, they abort the protocol.

The privacy amplification in the protocol can be defined as follows.

Let K_0 be the raw key shared between legitimate users Alice and Bob after information reconciliation. Suppose Eve estimates K_0 as K_e and $I(K_0 : K_e)$ is the mutual information between K_0 and K_e. Alice and Bob perform some operations on K_0, resulting in a new key K_0^*, and Eve estimates K_0^* as K_e^*. Now, $I(K_0^* : K_e^*) \approx 0$ means that Eve has almost no information about the final key. The process of reducing Eve's information about the final key is called privacy amplification.

Note that in steps 5 to 8 of the protocol, the information is transmitted via classical communication channels.

To better understand the key generation process, a simple example is provided as follows.

Example 4.1.

Random Bit Sequence	1	0	0	1	1	0	1	1	0
Alice Encoded Sequence	X	Z	Z	Z	Z	X	X	Z	X
Quantum State Sequence	$\|-\rangle$	$\|0\rangle$	$\|0\rangle$	$\|1\rangle$	$\|1\rangle$	$\|+\rangle$	$\|-\rangle$	$\|1\rangle$	$\|+\rangle$
Bob's Measurement Basis	X	X	Z	X	Z	X	X	Z	Z
Bob's Measurement Result	$\|-\rangle$	$\|-\rangle$	$\|0\rangle$	$\|+\rangle$	$\|1\rangle$	$\|+\rangle$	$\|-\rangle$	$\|1\rangle$	$\|0\rangle$
Bob Decoded Sequence	1	1	0	0	1	0	1	1	0
The Raw Key	1		0		1	0	1	1	

First, due to the quantum no-cloning theorem, the eavesdropper Eve cannot clone Alice's qubits. Second, since BB84 protocol uses nonorthogonal basis states $\{|0\rangle, |1\rangle\}$ and $\{|+\rangle, |-\rangle\}$, which cannot be perfectly distinguished, Eve cannot accurately measure each intercepted qubit. For example, when Eve performs the common intercept-retransmission attack, which will increase the error rate of the raw key, Alice and Bob can detect Eve's presence by analyzing the error rate. Unlike classical cryptography, whose security relies on the difficulty of solving some mathematical problems, the security of BB84 protocol stems from the fundamental principles of quantum mechanics and is independent of the eavesdropper's computational power.

BB84 protocol mentioned previously is based on the prepare-measure model. In order to conduct a quantitative security analysis, it can be transferred to an entanglement-based model equivalently. In 1999, Lo and Chau [8] proposed a protocol equivalent to BB84 based on the entanglement model, proving the unconditional security of BB84 protocol from the perspective of entanglement purification. The following theorem is a key point in the proof of unconditional security.

Theorem 4.1. Alice *prepares N pairs of* EPR *pairs:* $|\psi\rangle_N = \left(\frac{|00\rangle+|11\rangle}{\sqrt{2}}\right)^{\otimes N}$, *and shares them with* Bob *through a quantum channel. Suppose there is an eavesdropper* Eve *who can perform any attack on the quantum channel, and the density matrix* ρ_{AB} *is the shared state between* Alice *and* Bob. *If the fidelity between* ρ_{AB} *and* $|\psi\rangle_N$ *satisfies*

$$F(\rho_{AB}, |\psi\rangle_N) > 1 - 2^{-k}, \tag{4.1}$$

where k is a sufficiently large parameter, then the information obtained by Eve *about the final key is bounded by*

$$2^{-c} + O(2^{-2k}), \tag{4.2}$$

where $c = k - \log_2(2N + k + \frac{1}{\log_e 2})$.

The proof of Theorem 4.1 is mainly based on the following two lemmas.

Lemma 4.1. *(High fidelity implies low entropy) If the fidelity satisfies* $F(\rho_{AB}, |\psi\rangle_N) > 1 - \varepsilon$, *where* $0 < \varepsilon \ll 1$, *then the* von Neumann *entropy of* ρ_{AB} *satisfies*

$$S(\rho_{AB}) < -(1-\varepsilon)\log_2(1-\varepsilon) - \varepsilon \log_2(\frac{\varepsilon}{2^{2N}-1}). \tag{4.3}$$

We outline the basic idea of proving 4.1: If $F(\rho_{AB}, |\psi\rangle_N) = 1 - \varepsilon$, then in the N-Bell basis, the maximum eigenvalue of ρ_{AB} is greater than $1 - \varepsilon$. Suppose $\rho_{\max}$ is a diagonal density matrix, and its largest diagonal element is $1 - \varepsilon$ and the remaining $2^{2N} - 1$ elements are $\frac{\varepsilon}{2^{2N}-1}$, that is,

$$\rho_{\max} = \operatorname{diag}\{1-\varepsilon, \frac{\varepsilon}{2^{2N}-1}, \cdots, \frac{\varepsilon}{2^{2N}-1}\}. \tag{4.4}$$

Then the von Neumann entropy of ρ_{AB} is bounded by the entropy of $\rho_{\max}$.

Lemma 4.2. *(*Holevo *bound) Suppose the values of* Alice*'s classical event* X *are* $\{x_1, x_2, \cdots, x_n\}$, *where* x_i $(i = 1, \cdots, n)$ *has probability* p_i $(\sum_{i=1}^{n} p_i = 1)$, *and the corresponding quantum state is* ρ_i, *meaning that* Alice*'s encoded quantum state can be written as* $\rho = \sum_{i=1}^{n} p_i \rho_i$. *Then for any measurement* $\{M_y\} = \{M_0, M_1, \cdots, M_m\}$ *(with measurement outcome* Y*) performed by* Bob, *we have*

$$H(X : Y) \leq \chi(\rho) = S(\rho) - \sum_{i=1}^{n} \rho_i S(\rho_i), \tag{4.5}$$

where $\chi(\rho)$ *is called the* Holevo *bound.*

Thus the smaller ε is, the closer the quantum state ρ_{AB} after purification gets to $|\psi\rangle_N$. If a protocol can ensure that the fidelity of the shared quantum state between Alice and Bob is greater than $1 - \varepsilon$, then even if Eve can perform any attack (assuming the eavesdropper has infinite computational power), the amount of information she can obtain about the final key is bounded. Increasing the fidelity can be achieved through entanglement purification, which can be done by using quantum error correction.

Exercises

4.1. Given Alice's random bit sequence 0101001110, the encoding basis sequence is $ZXZZXXXZXZ$, and Bob's measurement sequence is $XXZXZXXZZX$. Find the shared raw key that Alice and Bob would obtain using BB84 protocol.

4.2. Assume Eve can intercept all the quantum states in the channel and measure them in the X basis. If the eavesdropper Eve implements a common intercept-retransmission attack, then what is the error rate of the raw key?

4.2 B92 protocol

B92 protocol was proposed by Bennett [2] in 1992. This protocol is similar to BB84 protocol, but it is a two-state protocol, using only two nonorthogonal quantum states (such as the quantum states $|0\rangle$ and $|+\rangle$) to complete key distribution. The protocol is as follows:

1: Alice prepares a random sequence $a_1, a_2, \cdots, a_n$, composed by 0 and 1.

2: Alice encodes the random sequence into a sequence of quantum states $|q_1\rangle, |q_2\rangle, \cdots, |q_n\rangle$. The encoding rules are as follows: if $a_i = 0$, then $|q_i\rangle$ is encoded as quantum state $|0\rangle$, and if $a_i = 1$, then $|q_i\rangle$ is encoded as quantum state $|+\rangle$.

3: Alice sends the qubit sequence $|q_1\rangle, |q_2\rangle, \cdots, |q_n\rangle$ to Bob via a quantum channel.

4: For each received qubit $|q_i\rangle$, Bob randomly chooses either Z or X basis to perform a measurement.

5: Bob announces to Alice via public channel. The measurement results can uniquely determine the qubit state (if the measurement results are $|1\rangle$ or $|-\rangle$, it can determine the initial quantum state to be $|+\rangle$ or $|0\rangle$, respectively), but the choice of measurement basis is kept secret.

6: Alice and Bob publicly discuss and keep only the qubits a_i, which can determine their quantum states $|q_i\rangle$, and discard the others. Thus this forms the raw key.

7: Via a classical channel, Alice and Bob use a portion of the raw key to analyze the error rate. If the error rate exceeds a certain threshold R_1, the protocol is terminated. Otherwise, they perform error correction and privacy amplification on the remaining raw key to obtain the final secret key.

Following is a simple example of B92 protocol to better understand the protocol.

Example 4.2.

Random Bit Sequence	0	0	1	1	0	1	0	0	1
Quantum State Sequence	$\|0\rangle$	$\|0\rangle$	$\|+\rangle$	$\|+\rangle$	$\|0\rangle$	$\|+\rangle$	$\|0\rangle$	$\|0\rangle$	$\|+\rangle$
Bob's Measurement Basis	Z	Z	X	Z	X	Z	Z	X	X
Bob's Measurement Result	$\|0\rangle$	$\|0\rangle$	$\|+\rangle$	$\|1\rangle$	$\|-\rangle$	$\|1\rangle$	$\|0\rangle$	$\|-\rangle$	$\|+\rangle$
Is it kept?	N	N	N	Y	Y	Y	N	Y	N
The Raw Key				1	0	1		0	

B92 protocol is theoretically unconditionally secure. Its security is guaranteed by the quantum no-cloning theorem and the fact that nonorthogonal states cannot be perfectly distinguished. The two quantum states used in B92 protocol are nonorthogonal, making it impossible for an eavesdropper to perfectly distinguish them without introducing disturbances in the system, which can be detected.

For rigorous proof of unconditional security, in 2003, Tamaki, Koashi, and Imoto [9] used the idea of entanglement purification to provide a security proof for B92 protocol over lossless channels. In 2004, Tamaki and others [10] extended this proof to noisy, lossy channels. The protocol is optimized in terms of the types of quantum states used, which is a two-state protocol, but its key generation efficiency is only half that of BB84 protocol, limiting its practical applications.

Exercises

4.3. Given Alice's random bit sequence 01010011 and the encoding rule: the binary numbers 0 and 1 are encoded as the quantum states $|0\rangle$ and $|+\rangle$, respectively. Bob's measurement basis sequence is *XXZXZXXZ*. Find the possible raw keys that Alice and Bob can share using B92 protocol.

4.4. Analyze and explain why the key generation efficiency of B92 protocol is only half that of BB84 protocol.

4.3 E91 protocol

In the previous two quantum communication protocols, the qubits used are single-qubit states. In 1991, Ekert [3], a young scholar at Oxford University, first used entangled pairs of qubits, EPR pairs, to design a quantum key distribution protocol. The security of the protocol is guaranteed by Bell's inequality. The protocol is as follows:

> 1: Alice and Bob share an EPR pair $|\psi^-\rangle = \frac{1}{\sqrt{2}}(|0_A 1_B\rangle - |1_A 0_B\rangle)$ where each party possesses one qubit of the pair.
>
> 2: Alice and Bob independently choose three unit vectors a_i and b_i in a three-dimension space. Let a_i and b_i be the measurement bases corresponding to base A_i and base B_i, where $i = 1, 2, 3$. Alice randomly chooses a measurement base from base A_i and measures her qubits using it. Similarly, Bob randomly chooses a measurement base from base B_i and measures his qubits using it.
>
> 3: Alice and Bob announce the bases they used for each measurement via classical channel. Then the measurement results are grouped into two categories. If their measurement basis are the same, then they keep the result into group one. Otherwise, the result is placed in the second group and the measurement result is publicly announced.
>
> 4: Using the measurement results from the second group, Alice and Bob can check the security of the system.
>
> 5: If the security check is passed, Bob inverts the bits of the measurement results from group one, which is the same raw key as Alice's.
>
> 6: Via the classical channel, Alice and Bob can use part of the raw key to analyze the error rate. If the error rate exceeds a certain threshold R_2, the protocol is terminated. Otherwise, perform error correction and privacy amplification on the remaining raw key to obtain the secret key.

Assume a_i and b_i are in XZ plane. Let the angle of a_i with respect to Z-axis be $\theta_i = \frac{\pi}{4}(i-1)$ and let its measurement basis be $A_i = \{|A_i\rangle_+, |A_i\rangle_-\}$. Let the angle of b_i with respect to Z-axis be $\theta_i' = \frac{\pi}{4}i$ and let its measurement basis be $B_i = \{|B_i\rangle_+, |B_i\rangle_-\}$, where $i = 1, 2, 3$. $P_{\pm\pm}(a_i, b_j)$ denotes the joint probability of eigenvalue ± 1 that Alice uses base A_i to measure and obtains the result $|A_i\rangle_\pm$, and the eigenvalue ± 1 that Bob uses base B_j to measure and obtains the result $|B_i\rangle_\pm$. For entangled states, there is a correlation coefficient denoted by the joint probability, defined as

$$E(a_i, b_j) = P_{++}(a_i, b_j) + P_{--}(a_i, b_j) - P_{+-}(a_i, b_j) - P_{-+}(a_i, b_j). \tag{4.6}$$

When both Alice and Bob choose the same measurement basis (such as A_2, B_1 or A_3, B_2), the correlation coefficient $E(a_i, b_j) = -1$. In this case, Alice and Bob's measurement results are anti-correlated. When the Bell inequality parameter $|C| = |E(a_1, b_1) - E(a_1, b_3) + E(a_3, b_1) + E(a_3, b_3)| = 2\sqrt{2}$, the system has not been disturbed by an eavesdropper, and it is secure. This is a key indicator of security for the protocol. If the correlation coefficient $|C| < 2\sqrt{2}$, it indicates that the channel has been disturbed.

In this protocol, because Alice and Bob share entangled Bell pairs, the qubits are in an indeterminate state during transmission. It is only after measurement that the qubits' states become definite. Therefore the eavesdropper cannot steal information during transmission. If the eavesdropper wants to obtain information about the key, she must copy the qubits in the channel and store them in some channel. Then she must wait for Alice and Bob to publicly announce their measurement results, and then choose the same measurement bases to measure the stored qubits. However, this is impossible due to the quantum no-cloning theorem and the current technological limitations of storing quantum states.

In lossy and noisy channels, the entanglement of the shared Bell pairs will decrease. E91 protocol can detect this disturbance and abort the key distribution process. In 1996, Deutsch and others [11] extended E91 protocol and first applied the concept of entanglement purification to prove its security in noisy channels.

Exercises

4.5. Verify the correlation coefficient $E(a_2, b_1) = E(a_3, b_2) = -1$ above.

4.4 Superdense coding

Quantum superdense coding protocol was proposed by Bennett and Wiesner [5] in 1992. It is a simple application of quantum entanglement in quantum communication. In this protocol, Alice and Bob share an EPR pair. Alice performs a quantum gate operation (like X gate) on her qubit and then sends it to Bob. Bob performs corresponding operations on both qubits and measures them to obtain two classical bits (like 01) that Alice intended to send. Thus Alice transmits two classical bits by sending only one qubit, achieving superdense coding.

The process of superdense coding is as follows:

> 1: Alice and Bob share an EPR pair $|\phi^+\rangle = \frac{1}{\sqrt{2}}(|00\rangle + |11\rangle)$, and Alice possesses the first qubit, Bob the second.
>
> 2: Alice, based on the two classical bits she wants to send, applies a specific quantum gate to her qubit. Then she sends her qubit to Bob.
>
> 3: Bob applies the circuit $(H \otimes I) \cdot \text{CNOT}$ to the two qubits and then measures them, and can obtain two classical bits that Alice intended to send.

In the second step, Alice wants to send two classical bits to Bob, which can be 00, 01, 10, or 11. Depending on the two bits Alice wants to send, she applies one of the gates described in Fig. 4.1 to her qubit:

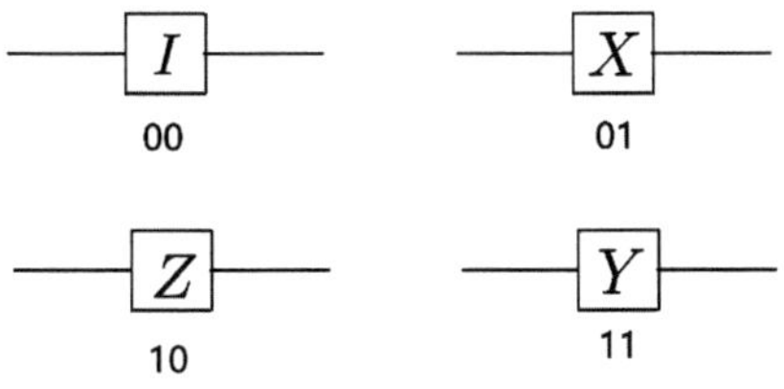

Figure 4.1 Gates used in superdense coding protocol.

Exercises

4.6. When the initial state is $|00\rangle$, what quantum gates can be used to prepare a Bell state $\frac{1}{\sqrt{2}}(|00\rangle + |11\rangle)$? Also, draw the quantum circuit for this operation.

4.7. If Alice and Bob share a quantum state $|\varphi\rangle = a|00\rangle + b|11\rangle$, where $|a|^2 + |b|^2 = 1$ and $|a| \neq |b|$, can they perform superdense coding? Why or why not?

4.5 Quantum teleportation

Quantum teleportation is another significant application of quantum entanglement. It was first proposed by Bennett and Brassard and others [6] in 1993. Quantum teleportation allows for the transmission of quantum states using classical communication.

Imagine Alice and Bob are separated by a distance, but they share an EPR pair. Additionally, Alice possesses another unknown quantum state

$|\psi\rangle$. In the quantum teleportation protocol, Alice can transmit the unknown quantum state $|\psi\rangle$ to Bob using classical communication.

The process can be described as follows:

1: Alice and Bob share a Bell state $|\phi^+\rangle = \frac{1}{\sqrt{2}}(|00\rangle + |11\rangle)$. Also, Alice has an unknown quantum state $|\psi\rangle = a|0\rangle + b|1\rangle$, where $|a|^2 + |b|^2 = 1$.

2: Alice applies a CNOT gate to her qubits. Then she applies a Hadamard gate.

3: Alice measures her two qubits by using measurement operators consisting of $\{|00\rangle\langle 00|, |01\rangle\langle 01|, |10\rangle\langle 10|, |11\rangle\langle 11|\}$, and sends the measurement result (via classical channel) to Bob.

4: Based on the result, Bob applies specific unitary operations to his qubit to reconstruct the original unknown state.

After the second step, the combined state of Alice and Bob's three qubits can be written as

$$\frac{1}{2}|00\rangle(a|0\rangle + b|1\rangle) + \frac{1}{2}|01\rangle(a|1\rangle + b|0\rangle)$$
$$+ \frac{1}{2}|10\rangle(a|0\rangle - b|1\rangle) + \frac{1}{2}|11\rangle(a|1\rangle - b|0\rangle).$$

In the fourth step, based on the received classical information, Bob performs the following specific unitary operations on his qubit.

If he receives 00, Bob directly obtains $|\psi\rangle = a|0\rangle + b|1\rangle$ without any operation.

If he receives 01, Bob applies X gate to his qubit.

If he receives 10, Bob applies Z gate to his qubit.

If he receives 11, Bob applies X gate followed by Z gate to his qubit.

The quantum teleportation process described previously can be realized by the quantum circuit illustrated in Fig. 4.2:

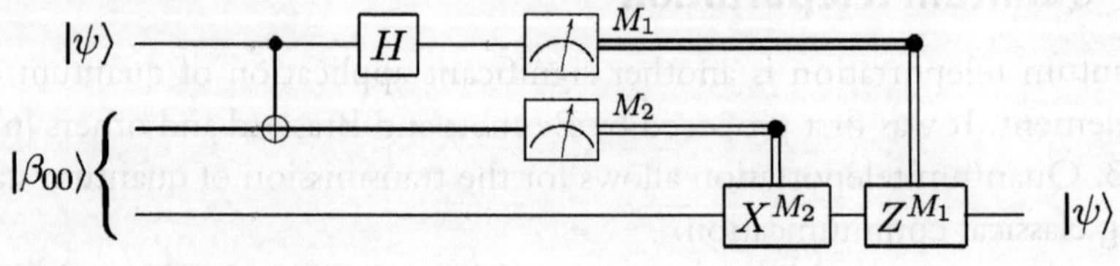

Figure 4.2 Quantum teleportation.

Exercises

4.8. If the initial entangled state is $\beta_{00} = \frac{1}{\sqrt{2}}(|01\rangle + |10\rangle)$, describe the quantum teleportation protocol.

4.9. Does this protocol imply that a quantum state can be cloned? Is there any superluminal communication involved?

4.6 Summary

In this chapter, we primarily introduced several fundamental quantum communication protocols, including three major discrete variable QKD protocols: BB84, B92, and E91, as well as the renowned quantum superdense coding and quantum teleportation protocols.

As quantum communication technology continues to be developed, the security analysis of quantum communication protocols has also attracted significant attention. Researchers have conducted detailed and in-depth studies on the security of quantum communication protocols from various perspectives. In 2001, Mayers [12] proved the unconditional security of symmetric quantum key distribution protocols (including BB84, B92, and E91) from the perspective of the amount of information an eavesdropper can obtain. Mayers demonstrated that regardless of the attack strategy employed by the eavesdropper, the average information they can acquire about the raw key is bounded.

While quantum communication is highly secure due to its unconditional security, practical implementation currently faces challenges such as the high cost of preparing and storing quantum states, and the susceptibility of quantum entanglement to environmental decoherence. How to achieve secure and reliable communication by using fewer quantum resources is a practical concern. In 2007, Boyer, Kenigsberg, and Mor [13] first proposed the concept of semi-quantum key distribution, where one party does not possess full quantum information processing capabilities. Building upon this foundation, in 2009, Zou and Qiu and others [14] presented a semi-quantum key distribution protocol using fewer than four quantum states. In 2015, Krawec [15] provided the first security proof for semi-quantum key distribution protocols under collective attacks and derived a lower bound on the key rate.

References

[1] C.H. Bennett, G. Brassard, Quantum cryptography: public key distribution and coin tossing, Theoretical Computer Science 560 (2014) 7–11.

[2] C.H. Bennett, Quantum cryptography using any two nonorthogonal states, Physical Review Letters 68 (21) (1992) 3121–3124.

[3] A.K. Ekert, Quantum cryptography based on Bell's theorem, Physical Review Letters 67 (6) (1991) 661–663.

[4] F. Grosshans, P. Grangier, Continuous variable quantum cryptography using coherent states, Physical Review Letters 88 (5) (2002) 057902.

[5] C.H. Bennett, S.J. Wiesner, Communication via one- and two-particle operators on Einstein-Podolsky-Rosen states, Physical Review Letters 69 (20) (1992) 2881–2884.

[6] C.H. Bennett, G. Brassard, C. Crépeau, et al., Teleporting an unknown quantum state via dual classical and Einstein-Podolsky-Rosen channels, Physical Review Letters 70 (13) (1993) 1895–1899.

[7] H. Guo, Z.Y. Li, X. Peng, Quantum Cryptography, National Defense Industry Press, 2016.

[8] H.K. Lo, H.F. Chau, Unconditional security of quantum key distribution over arbitrarily long distances, Science 283 (5410) (1999) 2050–2056.

[9] K. Tamaki, M. Koashi, N. Imoto, Unconditionally secure key distribution based on two nonorthogonal states, Physical Review Letters 90 (16) (2003) 167904.

[10] K. Tamaki, N. Lütkenhaus, Unconditional security of the Bennett 1992 quantum key-distribution protocol over a lossy and noisy channel, Physical Review A 69 (3) (2004) 032316.

[11] D. Deutsch, A. Ekert, R. Jozsa, et al., Quantum privacy amplification and the security of quantum cryptography over noisy channels, Physical Review Letters 77 (13) (1996) 2818–2821.

[12] D. Mayers, Unconditional security in quantum cryptography, Journal of the ACM 48 (3) (2001) 351–406.

[13] M. Boyer, D. Kenigsberg, T. Mor, Quantum key distribution with classical Bob, Physical Review Letters 99 (14) (2007) 140501.

[14] X.F. Zou, D.W. Qiu, L.Z. Li, et al., Semiquantum-key distribution using less than four quantum states, Physical Review A 79 (5) (2009) 052312.

[15] W.O. Krawec, Security proof of a semi-quantum key distribution protocol, in: 2015 IEEE International Symposium on Information Theory (ISIT), 2015, pp. 686–690.

CHAPTER 5

Quantum computing models⊛

Automata theory is a fundamental theory in computer science and has wide-ranging practical applications. Quantum automata are the most basic models of quantum computation. They have advantages over classical automata and are physically realizable to an extent. In this chapter, our goals are to introduce several fundamental quantum automata models, including Quantum Finite Automata (QFA), Quantum Pushdown Automata, Quantum Turing Machines (QTM), and Quantum Circuits.

First, we introduce the most basic and simple model: One-Way Quantum Finite Automata (1QFA).

5.1 One-way quantum finite automata

One-Way Quantum Finite Automata (1QFA) includes various types such as measure-once 1QFA, measure-many 1QFA, multi-letter 1QFA, 1QFA with control languages, and 1QFA with classical states. In the following sections, we introduce their definitions and ability to recognize languages.

5.1.1 Measure-once 1QFA

Measure-once 1QFA (abbreviated as MO-1QFA) is the simplest quantum automata. During its operation, it only performs a measurement after reading the last symbol of the input string. No measurements are made during the reading process.

Before we introduce quantum automata, let us recall probabilistic finite automata (PFA) and deterministic finite automata (DFA).

Definition 5.1. A PFA $\mathcal{M}$ over an alphabet Σ is a four-tuple

$$\mathcal{M} = (S, \pi, M(\sigma)_{\sigma\in\Sigma}, \eta),$$

where

- $S = \{s_1, s_2, \cdots, s_n\}$ is a finite set of states.

⊛ This book has a companion website hosting complementary materials. Visit this URL to access it: https://www.elsevier.com/books-and-journals/book-companion/9780443277047.

Theoretical Foundations of Quantum Computing
https://doi.org/10.1016/B978-0-44-327704-7.00010-4

- π is an n-dimensional row vector, representing the initial probability distribution over S.
- $\forall\sigma \in \Sigma$, $M(\sigma)$ is an $n \times n$ stochastic matrix (meaning each row is a transition probability vector), and $M(\sigma)(i,j)$ represents the probability of transitioning from state s_i to s_j after reading σ.
- $\eta = \left[\eta_1, \cdots, \eta_n\right]^T$ is an n-dimensional column vector with elements 0 or 1, where $\eta_i = 1$ indicates that s_i is an accepting state.

Remark 5.1. In the PFA defined previously, if all elements in $M(\sigma)$ are either 0 or 1, then $\mathcal{M}$ can be considered a DFA.

For any input string $x = x_1x_2 \cdots x_n \in \Sigma^*$, the probability that $\mathcal{M}$ accepts x is $\mathrm{P}_{\mathcal{M}}(x) = \pi M(x_1) \cdots M(x_n)\eta$.

Definition 5.2. A DFA is a five-tuple:

$$\mathcal{M} = (Q, \Sigma, \delta, q_0, F),$$

where

- Q is a finite set of states.
- Σ is a finite input alphabet.
- $\delta : Q \times \Sigma \to Q$ is the transition function.
- q_0 is the initial state.
- $F \subseteq Q$ is the set of final states.

For any input string $x = x_1x_2 \cdots x_n \in \Sigma^*$, if $\mathcal{M}$ can reach a final state by following the transition function, then we say $\mathcal{M}$ accepts x. Otherwise, $\mathcal{M}$ rejects x. The languages recognized by DFAs are regular languages.

Example 5.1. Fig. 5.1 shows a DFA that can recognize $\{a, b\}^*a$. (In the figure, q_0 is the initial state, and q_1 is the final state.)

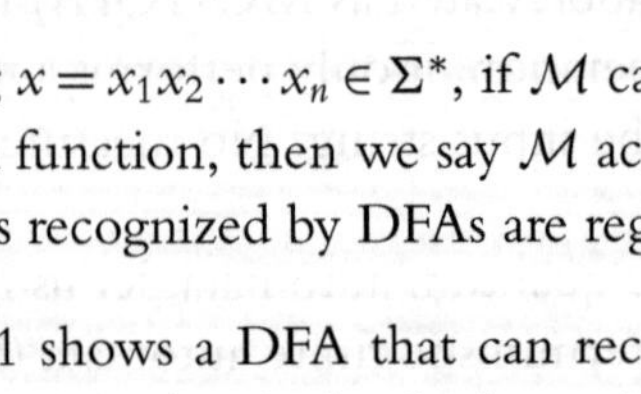

Figure 5.1 A DFA can recognize $\{a, b\}^*a$.

Unlike DFA, probabilistic finite automata and QFA accept input strings with a certain probability. We will introduce several definitions for language recognition. Suppose L is a language over a finite alphabet Σ, and $\mathcal{M}$ is an automaton with a finite input alphabet Σ. Then we denote the probability that $\mathcal{M}$ accepts the input string x as $\mathrm{P}_{\mathcal{M}}(x)$. There are several ways for $\mathcal{M}$ to recognize languages, and the simplest one is the exact recognition.

Definition 5.3. For $\forall x \in \Sigma^*$, $\mathrm{P}_{\mathcal{M}}(x) = 1$ if $x \in L$ and $\mathrm{P}_{\mathcal{M}}(x) = 0$ if $x \notin L$. Then we say that $\mathcal{M}$ exactly recognizes L.

We usually consider the situation of recognizing errors. Based on the different ways of error recognition, we roughly divide it into the following three definitions.

Definition 5.4. If $\exists \varepsilon > 0$ and $\lambda > 0$, $\forall x \in \Sigma^*$, $\mathrm{P}_{\mathcal{M}}(x) \geq \lambda + \varepsilon$ for $x \in L$, and $\mathrm{P}_{\mathcal{M}}(x) \leq \lambda - \varepsilon$ for $x \notin L$, then $\mathcal{M}$ recognizes L with bounded error, or $\mathcal{M}$ recognizes L with an isolated cut-point λ (and separation ε).

Definition 5.5. If $\forall x \in \Sigma^*$, $\mathrm{P}_{\mathcal{M}}(x) = 1$ for $x \in L$ and $\mathrm{P}_{\mathcal{M}}(x) \leq \epsilon$ for $x \notin L$, then $\mathcal{M}$ recognizes L with one-sided error ϵ.

Definition 5.6. If $\forall x \in \Sigma^*$, $\mathrm{P}_{\mathcal{M}}(x) > \lambda$ for $x \in L$ and $\mathrm{P}_{\mathcal{M}}(x) < \lambda$ for $x \notin L$, where $\lambda \in [0, 1)$, then $\mathcal{M}$ recognizes L with unbounded error.

Remark 5.2. In Definition 5.6, if "$<$" is changed to "$\leq$," then $\mathcal{M}$ recognizes L with a cut-point λ. Sometimes we consider probabilistic language recognition, that is, if $\forall x \in \Sigma^*$, $\mathrm{P}_{\mathcal{M}}(x) \geq p$ for $x \in L$ and $\mathrm{P}_{\mathcal{M}}(x) \leq 1 - p$ for $x \notin L$, where $p > \frac{1}{2}$, then $\mathcal{M}$ recognizes L with probability p.

The definition of MO-1QFA is as follows.

Definition 5.7. MO-1QFA $\mathcal{M}$ is a five-tuple: $\mathcal{M} = (Q, \Sigma, \delta, q_0, F)$, where

- $Q = \{q_0, q_1, \cdots, q_{n-1}\}$ is a finite set of states.
- Σ is a finite input alphabet.
- $\delta : Q \times \Sigma \times Q \rightarrow \mathbb{C}$ is a transition function satisfying: for any $q_1, q_2 \in Q$ and any $\sigma \in \Sigma$,

$$\sum_{p \in Q} \delta(q_1, \sigma, p)^* \delta(q_2, \sigma, p) = \begin{cases} 1, & q_1 = q_2, \\ 0, & q_1 \neq q_2, \end{cases} \tag{5.1}$$

where $\delta(q_1, \sigma, p)^*$ represents the conjugate complex number of $\delta(q_1, \sigma, p)$, $\delta(p, \sigma, q)$ ($|\delta(p, \sigma, q)|^2$) represents the amplitude (probability) of $\mathcal{M}$ that transfers from p to q after scanning σ.

- q_0 is the initial state.
- $F \subseteq Q$ is the set of accepting states.

The state space of $\mathcal{M}$ is a $|Q|$-dimensional Hilbert space $\mathcal{H}$, denoted as $\mathcal{H}_Q$. Arbitrary classical state $q_i \in Q$ is corresponding to a basic state $|q_i\rangle \in \mathcal{H}_Q$, where $|q_i\rangle$ is a column vector with the $(i+1)$-th element is 1 and the rest are 0. For example, $|q_0\rangle = (1, 0, \cdots, 0)^T$.

For any $\sigma \in \Sigma$, the transition function δ can be equivalently described by a unitary matrix $U(\sigma)$:

$$U(\sigma)(j, i) = \delta(q_i, \sigma, q_j). \tag{5.2}$$

The set of accepting states F is corresponding to a projector $P_{acc} = \sum_{q_i \in F} |q_i\rangle\langle q_i|$.

For any input strings $x = \sigma_1\sigma_2 \cdots \sigma_n \in \Sigma^*$, the computational process of $\mathcal{M}$ can be illustrated as follows: The initial state of $\mathcal{M}$ is $|q_0\rangle$, then the tape head scans the input symbols $\sigma_1, \sigma_2, \cdots, \sigma_n$. Once a symbol σ_i is scanned, a unitary matrix $U(\sigma_i)$ is applied to the current state. After the application of $U(\sigma_n)$, we apply a projective measurement $\{P_{acc}, I - P_{acc}\}$ on the state, and the accepting probability is

$$\mathrm{P}_{\mathcal{M}}(x) = ||P_{acc}U(\sigma_n)U(\sigma_{n-1}) \cdots U(\sigma_1)|q_0\rangle||^2. \tag{5.3}$$

Example 5.2. Let MO-1QFA $\mathcal{M} = (Q, \Sigma, \delta, q_0, F)$. Here, $Q = \{q_0, q_1\}$, $F = \{q_1\}$, $\Sigma = \{a\}$, q_0 is the initial state, the transition function δ is defined as $\delta(q_0, a, q_0) = \frac{1}{\sqrt{2}}$, $\delta(q_0, a, q_1) = \frac{1}{\sqrt{2}}$, $\delta(q_1, a, q_0) = \frac{1}{\sqrt{2}}$, $\delta(q_1, a, q_1) = -\frac{1}{\sqrt{2}}$. Then $U(a) = \begin{bmatrix} \frac{1}{\sqrt{2}} & \frac{1}{\sqrt{2}} \\ \frac{1}{\sqrt{2}} & -\frac{1}{\sqrt{2}} \end{bmatrix}$ and states q_0, q_1 are corresponding to the basic states $|q_0\rangle$, $|q_1\rangle$, respectively,

$$|q_0\rangle = \begin{bmatrix} 1 \\ 0 \end{bmatrix}, \ |q_1\rangle = \begin{bmatrix} 0 \\ 1 \end{bmatrix}. \tag{5.4}$$

The projective measurement $\{P_{acc}, I - P_{acc}\}$ is

$$P_{acc} = |q_1\rangle\langle q_1| = \begin{bmatrix} 0 & 0 \\ 0 & 1 \end{bmatrix}, \ I - P_{acc} = \begin{bmatrix} 1 & 0 \\ 0 & 0 \end{bmatrix}. \tag{5.5}$$

If aa is inputted, we can illustrate the computational process of $\mathcal{M}$ as follows: After $\mathcal{M}$ with the initial state $|q_0\rangle$ scanning first a, the quantum state of $\mathcal{M}$ will become $|\psi_1\rangle = U(a)|q_0\rangle = \frac{|q_0\rangle + |q_1\rangle}{\sqrt{2}}$. Next, $\mathcal{M}$ scans the second a, and changes the quantum state to $|\psi_2\rangle = U(a)|\psi_1\rangle = |q_0\rangle$. Finally, after applying projectors $\{P_{acc}, I - P_{acc}\}$ to the state $|\psi_2\rangle$, the accepting probability is obtained $\mathrm{P}_{\mathcal{M}}(aa) = ||P_{acc}|\psi_2\rangle||^2 = 0$.

Similar to the pumping lemma of DFA, we can also give a pumping lemma of MO-1QFA.

Theorem 5.1 (Pumping lemma of MO-1QFA [1]). *Let $\mathcal{M}$ be an MO-1QFA with the alphabet Σ. $\mathrm{P}_{\mathcal{M}}(x)$ is the probability of $\mathcal{M}$ accepting x. Then, for any $w \in \Sigma^*$ and any $\varepsilon > 0$, there exists a positive integer k such that $|\mathrm{P}_{\mathcal{M}}(uw^k v) - \mathrm{P}_{\mathcal{M}}(uv)| \leq \varepsilon$ for arbitrary $u, v \in \Sigma^*$.*

Proof. For the string $w = w_1 w_2 \cdots w_n$, suppose $U(w) = U(w_n)U(w_{n-1}) \cdots U(w_1)$. If V is the volume of an n-dimensional ball with radius ϵ', then there exists a $k \leq \frac{1}{V}$ such that the distance between $U^k(w)$ and the identity matrix is less than or equal to ϵ', where $U^k(w) = [U(w_n)U(w_{n-1}) \cdots U(w_1)]^k$ (the distance between matrix $U^k(w)$ and identity matrix I is defined as $||U^k(w) - I|| = \sup_{|||\psi\rangle||=1} ||(U^k(w) - I)|\psi\rangle||$). Therefore we can obtain $U^k(w) = I + \epsilon' J$, where J is a diagonal matrix and $\sum_{i=0}^{n} |J_{ii}|^2 \leq 1$. Consequently, we have

$$\begin{aligned}
\mathrm{P}_{\mathcal{M}}(uw^k v) &= ||P_{acc}U(v)U^k(w)U(u)|q_0\rangle||^2 && (5.6)\\
&= ||P_{acc}U(v)(I + \epsilon' J)U(u)|q_0\rangle||^2 && (5.7)\\
&= \mathrm{P}_{\mathcal{M}}(uv) + \epsilon' \langle q_0|U^\dagger(u)J^\dagger U^\dagger(v)P_{acc}^\dagger P_{acc}U(v)U(u)|q_0\rangle \\
&\quad + \epsilon' \langle q_0|U^\dagger(u)U^\dagger(v)P_{acc}^\dagger P_{acc}U(v)JU(u)|q_0\rangle \\
&\quad + \epsilon'^2 ||P_{acc}U(v)JU(u)|q_0\rangle||^2. && (5.8)
\end{aligned}$$

Since

$$\|P_{acc}U(v)JU(u)|q_0\rangle\| \leq 1, \tag{5.9}$$
$$\|P_{acc}U(v)U(u)|q_0\rangle\| \leq 1, \tag{5.10}$$

and

$$\begin{aligned}
&\langle q_0|U^\dagger(u)J^\dagger U^\dagger(v)P_{acc}^\dagger P_{acc}U(v)U(u)|q_0\rangle \\
&= (\langle q_0|U^\dagger(u)U^\dagger(v)P_{acc}^\dagger P_{acc}U(v)JU(u)|q_0\rangle)^*, && (5.11)
\end{aligned}$$

we have

$$\|\langle q_0|U^\dagger(u)J^\dagger U^\dagger(v)P_{acc}^\dagger P_{acc}U(v)U(u)|q_0\rangle\| \leq 1, \tag{5.12}$$

$$\|\langle q_0|U^\dagger(u)U^\dagger(v)P_{acc}^\dagger P_{acc}U(v)JU(u)|q_0\rangle\| \le 1. \tag{5.13}$$

If we denote

$$\begin{aligned} t = &\langle q_0|U^\dagger(u)J^\dagger U^\dagger(v)P_{acc}^\dagger P_{acc}U(v)U(u)|q_0\rangle \\ &+ \langle q_0|U^\dagger(u)U^\dagger(v)P_{acc}^\dagger P_{acc}U(v)JU(u)|q_0\rangle, \end{aligned} \tag{5.14}$$

then t is a real number such that $0 \le t \le 2$, and

$$\mathrm{P}_{\mathcal{M}}(uw^k v) = \mathrm{P}_{\mathcal{M}}(uv) + \epsilon' t + \epsilon'^2 ||P_{acc}U(v)JU(u)|q_0\rangle||^2. \tag{5.15}$$

Due to

$$\begin{aligned} &||P_{acc}U(v)JU(u)|q_0\rangle||^2 \\ =&||P_{acc}U(v)\sum_{i=1}^{n} J_{ii}|\psi_i\rangle\langle\psi_i|U(u)|q_0\rangle||^2 \\ \le&\sum_{i=0}^{n}|J_{ii}|^2 \\ \le&1, \end{aligned} \tag{5.16}$$

it follows that

$$\mathrm{P}_{\mathcal{M}}(uw^k v) - \mathrm{P}_{\mathcal{M}}(uv) \le 2\epsilon' + \epsilon'^2. \tag{5.17}$$

For any $\epsilon > 0$, $2\epsilon' + \epsilon'^2 \le \epsilon$ holds if we choose a suitable ϵ'. So, for any $w \in \Sigma^*$, and for any $\varepsilon > 0$, there exists a k such that

$$|\mathrm{P}_{\mathcal{M}}(uw^k v) - \mathrm{P}_{\mathcal{M}}(uv)| \le \varepsilon \tag{5.18}$$

for any $u, v \in \Sigma^*$. □

In practice, the languages accepted by MO-1QFA are closely related to *reversible finite automata* (RFA).

Definition 5.8. Given a DFA $\mathcal{M} = (Q, \Sigma, \delta, q_0, F)$, then $\mathcal{M}$ is called a RFA if for any $q \in Q$ and any $\sigma \in \Sigma$, there exists unique $p \in Q$ such that $\delta(p, \sigma) = q$. The languages recognized by RFA are termed as reversible languages.

Theorem 5.2. [2] *The class of languages recognized by* MO-1QFA *with bounded error is equivalent to the class of reversible languages.*

For example, from Fig. 5.1, it can be observed that the minimized DFA recognizing the regular language $\{a, b\}^*a$ is not a reversible finite automaton (RFA). Therefore $\{a, b\}^*a$ cannot be recognized by an MO-1QFA with bounded errors. To consider the case of unbounded error, we denote UMO as the class of languages recognized by MO-1QFA with unbounded error. Then UMO is a proper subclass of stochastic languages, which is the class of languages recognized by PFA with unbounded error [3].

Remark 5.3. Any finite language is not included in UMO, while finite languages can be recognized by PFA with unbounded error [4].

If the languages with cut-point are divided into strict and non-strict cases, we can define an automaton $\mathcal{M}$ recognizing languages $L_>$ and $L_\geq$ on Σ strictly and non-strictly with cut-point $\lambda \in (0, 1)$, respectively, that is, $L_> = \{x \in \Sigma^* | \mathrm{P}_\mathcal{M}(x) > \lambda\}$ and $L_\geq = \{x \in \Sigma^* | \mathrm{P}_\mathcal{M}(x) \geq \lambda\}$. For the decision problem of whether $L_>$ is empty, we have the following results.

Theorem 5.3. [5] *If $L_>$ is a language recognized by* MO-1QFA, *then it is undecidable that whether $L_>$ is empty. If $L_>$ is a language recognized by* PFA, *then it is decidable that whether $L_>$ is empty.*

Remark 5.4. "Decidable" can be simply understood as: It is possible to devise a mechanical method to decide the outcome in a limited period.

In classical automata theory, a significant problem is to decide whether two automata are equivalent.

Definition 5.9. Let $\mathrm{P}_{\mathcal{M}_1}(x)$ and $\mathrm{P}_{\mathcal{M}_2}(x)$ be the probabilities of two automata $\mathcal{M}_1$ and $\mathcal{M}_2$ accepting input string $x \in \Sigma^*$, respectively. If $\mathrm{P}_{\mathcal{M}_1}(x) = \mathrm{P}_{\mathcal{M}_2}(x)$ holds for any string x with length not exceeding k, then $\mathcal{M}_1$ and $\mathcal{M}_2$ are said to be k-equivalent: If $\mathrm{P}_{\mathcal{M}_1}(x) = \mathrm{P}_{\mathcal{M}_2}(x)$ for any x, then $\mathcal{M}_1$ and $\mathcal{M}_2$ are said to be equivalent.

The following methods and results are available for deciding whether different MO-1QFA are equivalent [3,6].

Theorem 5.4. *Two* MO-1QFA *$\mathscr{A}_1$ and $\mathscr{A}_2$ are equivalent if and only if they are $(n_1^2 + n_2^2 - 1)$-equivalent, where n_1 and n_2 are the number of states in $\mathscr{A}_1$ and $\mathscr{A}_2$, respectively. Furthermore, there exists a polynomial-time algorithm, which is related to n_1 and n_2, to decide whether $\mathscr{A}_1$ and $\mathscr{A}_2$ are equivalent.*

State minimization is also an important issue in classical automata theory [7]. An elegant method has been proposed to solve the state minimization problem of DFA [8]. In the case of PFA minimization, we usually focus on reducing the number of states and proving minimization [9]. For 1QFA, we also have methods to solve their minimization.

Theorem 5.5. [10] *The problem of state minimization for* MO-1QFA *is decidable within* EXSPACE.

Remark 5.5. Here, EXSPACE refers to problems that can be solved only by using exponential space on a deterministic Turing machine (which will be introduced later).

Although the class of languages that are recognized by MO-1QFA with bounded error is a proper subclass of regular languages, its state complexity offers substantial advantages over classical automata [11].

Theorem 5.6. *Suppose* $L_m = \{a^{km} | k \in \mathbb{N}\}$ *for any* $m > 0$. *If* $m = p_1^{\alpha_1} p_2^{\alpha_2} \cdots p_s^{\alpha_s}$, *then we have:*

(1) *A* DFA *(or* NFA*)* $\mathcal{M}$ *requires at least* m *states to recognize* L_m;

(2) *A two-way* DFA *(or* NFA*) or a one-way* PFA *requires at least* $p_1^{\alpha_1} + p_2^{\alpha_2} + \cdots + p_s^{\alpha_s}$ *states to recognize* L_m *with bounded error.*

Theorem 5.7. *For any* $m > 0$, L_m *can be recognized with bounded error by an* MO-1QFA $\mathcal{A}$ *with 2 quantum basis states.*

Proof. Suppose $\mathcal{A} = (Q, \Sigma, U(a), q_0, Q_{acc})$. Here, $Q = \{q_0, q_1\}$, $Q_{acc} = \{q_0\}$, $|q_0\rangle = |0\rangle$, $|q_1\rangle = |1\rangle$, $U_m(a) = \begin{bmatrix} \cos\frac{\pi}{m} & \sin\frac{\pi}{m} \\ -\sin\frac{\pi}{m} & \cos\frac{\pi}{m} \end{bmatrix}$. Then

$$U_m(a^k) = \begin{bmatrix} \cos\frac{\pi k}{m} & \sin\frac{\pi k}{m} \\ -\sin\frac{\pi k}{m} & \cos\frac{\pi k}{m} \end{bmatrix}, \tag{5.19}$$

and

$$\begin{aligned} \mathrm{P}_{\mathcal{A}}(a^k) &= ||P_{acc} U_m(a^k)|q_0\rangle||^2 && (5.20)\\ &= \cos^2\frac{\pi k}{m} && (5.21)\\ &= \begin{cases} 1, & k \mod m = 0, \\ \leq \cos^2\frac{\pi}{m}, & k \mod m \neq 0. \end{cases} && (5.22) \end{aligned}$$

Set $\lambda = \frac{1+\cos^2\frac{\pi}{m}}{2}$, $\epsilon = \frac{1-\cos^2\frac{\pi}{m}}{2}$. Then for any $a^k \in L$,

$$\mathrm{P}_{\mathcal{A}}(a^k) = 1 \geq \lambda + \epsilon; \tag{5.23}$$

for any $a^k \notin L$,

$$\mathrm{P}_{\mathcal{A}}(a^k) = \cos^2\frac{\pi k}{m} \leq \lambda - \epsilon. \tag{5.24}$$

□

5.1.2 Measure-many 1QFA

In a *measure-many 1QFA* (MM-1QFA), after scanning each symbol, the corresponding unitary operator will be applied, followed by a measurement. Then the new state obtained from the measurement is taken as the current state. The specific definition of an MM-1QFA is given as follows.

Definition 5.10. An MM-1QFA is a six-tuple $\mathcal{A} = (Q, \Sigma, \delta, q_0, Q_{acc}, Q_{rej})$, where

- Q is a finite set of states;
- Σ is a finite input alphabet;
- $\$ \notin \Sigma$ is end-mark (denote tape alphabet as $\Gamma = \Sigma \cup \{\$\}$);
- $\delta : Q \times \Gamma \times Q \rightarrow \mathbb{C}$ is a transition function satisfying Eq. (5.1);
- $q_0 \in Q$ is the initial state; Q can be divided into three subsets, that is, accepting states Q_{acc}, rejecting states Q_{rej}, and non-halting states Q_{non}.

The initial state q_0 of $\mathcal{A}$ can be represented by a unit vector $|q_0\rangle$ in a Hilbert space $\mathcal{H}_Q$. For any $\sigma \in \Gamma$, δ can be described by a $|Q| \times |Q|$ unitary matrix $U(\sigma)$, that is, $U(\sigma)(j, i) = \delta(q_i, \sigma, q_j)$; $\mathcal{H}_Q$ can be divided into three subsets, $E_{non} = \text{span}\{|q\rangle | q \in Q_{non}\}$, $E_{acc} = \text{span}\{|q\rangle | q \in Q_{acc}\}$ and $E_{rej} = \text{span}\{|q\rangle | q \in Q_{rej}\}$. Correspondingly, projectors P_{non}, P_{acc}, and P_{rej} that project states into these three subspaces constitute the projection measurement $M = \{P_{non}, P_{acc}, P_{rej}\}$ of $\mathcal{A}$.

Input $x = \sigma_1\sigma_2 \cdots \sigma_n$ to MM-1QFA $\mathcal{A}$, and the computation process of $\mathcal{A}$ whose input alphabet is $\sigma_1\sigma_2 \cdots \sigma_n\$$ can be illustrated as follows:

(1) Starting from $|q_0\rangle$, machine scans σ_1, and applies $U(\sigma_1)$ to $|q_0\rangle$. So, the state evolves to $|\psi_1\rangle = U(\sigma_1)|q_0\rangle$. Then we apply measurement $\{P_{non}, P_{acc}, P_{rej}\}$ to $|\psi_1\rangle$ and obtain the output $w \in \{\text{non, acc, rej}\}$ with probability $\mathrm{P}_1^w = ||P_w|\psi_1\rangle||^2$. The new state is $|\psi_1^w\rangle = \frac{P_w|\psi_1\rangle}{\sqrt{\mathrm{P}_1^w}}$.

(2) If the measurement output in (1) is "non", then the machine continues to scan the next symbol σ_2. After applying $U(\sigma_2)$ to $|\psi_1^{non}\rangle$, it will perform a measurement. The state evolution will be the same as described in (1).

(3) The process continues when the measurement result is "non". When the measurement result is "acc" or "rej", the computation stops and the input string $x = \sigma_1\sigma_2 \cdots \sigma_n$ is accordingly accepted or rejected.

It can be seen that $\mathcal{A}$ may stop running after scanning each symbol due to entering an accepting or rejecting state. Therefore when illustrating the operation process of $\mathcal{A}$, it is necessary to save the accepting and rejecting probabilities during the operation. For this purpose, we express the current state configuration of $\mathcal{A}$ as a three-tuple $(|\psi\rangle, p_{acc}, p_{rej})$. Here, $|\psi\rangle$ is the current unnormalized state, p_{acc} and p_{rej} are the cumulative accepting and rejecting probabilities, respectively. Obviously, the initial state configuration of $\mathcal{A}$ is $(|q_0\rangle, 0, 0)$. When the current configuration is $(|\psi\rangle, p_{acc}, p_{rej})$, after scanning a symbol σ, the process of changing to the next state configuration will be given by

$$(|\psi\rangle, p_{acc}, p_{rej}) \rightarrow (P_{non}|\psi'\rangle, p_{acc} + ||P_{acc}|\psi'\rangle||^2, p_{rej} + ||P_{rej}|\psi'\rangle||^2), \qquad (5.25)$$

where $|\psi'\rangle = U(\sigma)|\psi\rangle$.

In this way, we can define the probability of accepting, which can be represented as a function $f_{\mathcal{A}} : \Sigma^*\$ \rightarrow [0, 1]$ given by

$$f_{\mathcal{A}}(\sigma_1\sigma_2 \cdots \sigma_n\$) = \sum_{k=1}^{n+1} ||P_{acc}U(\sigma_k) \prod_{i=1}^{k-1} (P_{non}U(\sigma_i))|q_0\rangle||^2, \qquad (5.26)$$

where $\sigma_{n+1} = \$$ and $\prod_{i=1}^{n} A_i \triangleq A_n A_{n-1} \cdots A_1$.

Example 5.3. Let an MM-1QFA

$$\mathcal{A} = (Q, \Sigma, \{U(\sigma)\}_{\sigma\in\Sigma\cup\{\$\}}, q_0, Q_{acc}, Q_{rej}).$$

Here,

- $Q = \{q_0, q_1, q_{acc}, q_{rej}\}$;
- $Q_{acc} = \{q_{acc}\}$, $Q_{rej} = \{q_{rej}\}$;
- $\Sigma = \{a\}$;
- q_0 is the initial state;
- $\{U(\sigma)\}_{\sigma\in\Sigma\cup\{\$\}}$ can be represented as

$$U(a)|q_0\rangle = \frac{1}{2}|q_0\rangle + \frac{1}{\sqrt{2}}|q_1\rangle + \frac{1}{2}|q_{acc}\rangle,$$
$$U(a)|q_1\rangle = \frac{1}{2}|q_0\rangle - \frac{1}{\sqrt{2}}|q_1\rangle + \frac{1}{2}|q_{acc}\rangle,$$
$$U(\$)|q_0\rangle = |q_{acc}\rangle,$$
$$U(\$)|q_1\rangle = |q_{rej}\rangle.$$

In practice, we can define the mapping δ from the definition of U, such as $U(a)|q_0\rangle$: $\delta(q_0, a, q_0) = \frac{1}{2}$, $\delta(q_0, a, q_1) = \frac{1}{\sqrt{2}}$, $\delta(q_0, a, q_{acc}) = \frac{1}{2}$, $\delta(q_0, a, q_{rej}) = 0$. Additionally, undefined parts can be arbitrarily defined to maintain unitarity.

Consider the computational process of input $aa\$$:

(1) $|q_0\rangle$ is the initial state. After applying $U(a)$, we will obtain $\frac{1}{2}|q_0\rangle + \frac{1}{\sqrt{2}}|q_1\rangle + \frac{1}{2}|q_{acc}\rangle$. Then the machine performs a measurement. It will accept with the probability of $(\frac{1}{2})^2$ or it will obtain non-halting state with the probability of $\frac{1}{2}|q_0\rangle + \frac{1}{\sqrt{2}}|q_1\rangle$. After that, the machine continues to compute.

(2) After machine scanning second a the state $\frac{1}{2}|q_0\rangle + \frac{1}{\sqrt{2}}|q_1\rangle$ will evolve to $\frac{1}{2}(\frac{1}{2} + \frac{1}{\sqrt{2}})|q_0\rangle + \frac{1}{\sqrt{2}}(\frac{1}{2} - \frac{1}{\sqrt{2}})|q_1\rangle + \frac{1}{2}(\frac{1}{2} + \frac{1}{\sqrt{2}})|q_{acc}\rangle$. There are two possible results after measurement, that is, accepting and finishing the computation with the probability of $[\frac{1}{2}(\frac{1}{2} + \frac{1}{\sqrt{2}})]^2\ |q_{acc}\rangle$, or entering the non-halting state with the probability of $\frac{1}{2}(\frac{1}{2} + \frac{1}{\sqrt{2}})|q_0\rangle + \frac{1}{\sqrt{2}}(\frac{1}{2} - \frac{1}{\sqrt{2}})|q_1\rangle$. After that the machine continues to compute.

(3) The machine scans end-mark \$, and the state evolves to $\frac{1}{2}(\frac{1}{2} + \frac{1}{\sqrt{2}})|q_{acc}\rangle + \frac{1}{\sqrt{2}}(\frac{1}{2} - \frac{1}{\sqrt{2}})|q_{rej}\rangle$. Then a measurement is applied to the state, and we will obtain the accepting state $|q_{acc}\rangle$ with the probability of $[\frac{1}{2}(\frac{1}{2} + \frac{1}{\sqrt{2}})]^2$ or rejecting state $|q_{rej}\rangle$ with the probability of $[\frac{1}{\sqrt{2}}(\frac{1}{2} - \frac{1}{\sqrt{2}})]^2$.

Therefore the probability of accepting is

$$\left(\frac{1}{2}\right)^2 + \left[\frac{1}{2}\left(\frac{1}{2} + \frac{1}{\sqrt{2}}\right)\right]^2 + \left[\frac{1}{2}\left(\frac{1}{2} + \frac{1}{\sqrt{2}}\right)\right]^2 = \frac{5}{8} + \frac{1}{2\sqrt{2}}.$$

MM-1QFA recognizes a broader range of languages with bounded error compared to MO-1QFA (MM-1QFA can recognize a^*b^* [12]), while this class of languages is still a proper subclass of regular language [13]. The computing process of MM-1QFA is more complex than that of MO-1QFA, and the characterizations of language class recognized by MM-1QFA are still not clear.

Theorem 5.8. [12] *a^*b^* can be recognized by an* MM-1QFA *with a probability of $p \approx \frac{15}{22}$, where p is the root of function $p^3 + p = 1$. However, the probability that* MM-1QFA *recognizes a^*b^* is at most $\frac{7}{9}$.*

Theorem 5.9. [13] *The language recognized by any* MM-1QFA *with bounded error is a regular language, and the regular language $\{a, b\}^*a$ cannot be recognized by* MM-1QFA *with bounded error.*

There is a structure to characterize that MM-1QFA cannot recognize some regular languages with bounded error. The structure forbidden by MM-1QFA is shown in Fig. 5.2.

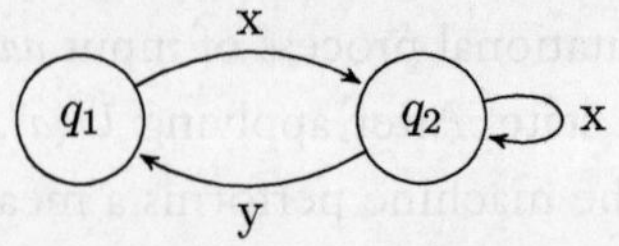

Figure 5.2 A structure forbidden by MM-1QFA.

Theorem 5.10. [3] *Let $\mathcal{M} = (S, \Sigma, \delta, q_0, F)$ be the minimized* DFA *that can recognize L. If there exist $q_1, q_2 \in S$ and $x, y \in \Sigma^*$ such that:*
(1) $q_1 \neq q_2$,
(2) $\delta^*(q_1, x) = q_2$,
(3) $\delta^*(q_2, x) = q_2$,
(4) $\delta^*(q_2, y) = q_1$,
then MM-1QFA *cannot recognize L with bounded error, where δ^* can be recursively defined as $\delta^*(s, \sigma) = \delta(s, \sigma)$ and $\delta^*(s, w\sigma) = \delta^*(\delta^*(s, w), \sigma)$ for any $s \in S$, $w \in \Sigma^*$, $\sigma \in \Sigma$.*

Remark 5.6. The class of languages recognized by MM-1QFA is closed under complementation, inverse homomorphisms, and word quotient operations, but it is not closed under homomorphism operations. Additionally, the closure under intersection and union operations remains an open problem [3].

The class of languages recognized by MM-1QFA with bounded error is also a proper subclass of regular languages, but it has advantages in the aspect of state complexity.

Theorem 5.11. [12] *Denote p as a prime number, and let language $L_p = \{a^i \mid i$ divisible by $p\}$. Then, for any $\epsilon > 0$, there exist an* MM-1QFA *and an* MO-1QFA *with basis states $\Theta(\log p)$ recognizing L_p with one-sided error ϵ. Moreover, a* PFA *is required to contain at least p states for recognizing L_p with bounded error.*

Certainly, for some languages, MM-1QFA may have a larger number of states than DFA. For example, any MM-1QFA recognizing $\{w1 \mid w \in \{0, 1\}^*, |w| \leq m\}$ will have an exponentially larger number of states than the corresponding minimized DFA [14].

For the fundamental problems of deciding whether two MM-1QFA are equivalent and the minimization of MM-1QFA, we have the following results.

Theorem 5.12. [6] *Any two* MM-1QFA *$\mathscr{A}_1$ and $\mathscr{A}_2$ are equivalent if and only if they are $(n_1^2 + n_2^2 - 1)$-equivalent, where n_1 and n_2 are the number of states in $\mathscr{A}_1$ and $\mathscr{A}_2$, respectively. Additionally, there exists a polynomial-time algorithm related to n_1 and n_2 to decide whether $\mathscr{A}_1$ and $\mathscr{A}_2$ are equivalent.*

Theorem 5.13. [15] *The problem of state minimization for* MM-1QFA *is* EXSPACE *decidable.*

Next, we will prove Theorem 5.9 by Proposition 5.1 and Proposition 5.2.

Suppose $\mathcal{V} = l_2(Q) \times \mathbb{R} \times \mathbb{R}$ is a Hilbert space and denote $\mathcal{B} = \{v \in \mathcal{V} \mid ||v|| \leq 1\}$. For any $(\psi, p_1, p_2) \in \mathcal{V}$, we define their norm as $||(\psi, p_1, p_2)|| = \dfrac{||\psi||_2 + |p_1| + |p_2|}{2}$ (denote $||\cdot||_2$ as the Euclidean norm).

Suppose $\text{span}\{|q\rangle \mid q \in Q_{acc}\}$, $\text{span}\{|q\rangle \mid q \in Q_{rej}\}$, and $\text{span}\{|q\rangle \mid q \in Q_{non}\}$ are the subspaces of $l_2(Q)$. Denote P_{acc}, P_{rej}, and P_{non} as the projective operators in these subspaces, respectively. $\{V_\sigma \mid \sigma \in \Gamma\}$ represents the unitary matrix derived from the transition function of MM-1QFA.

For any $\sigma \in \Gamma$, T_σ is given by

$$T_\sigma(\psi, p_{acc}, p_{rej}) = (P_{non} V_\sigma \psi, p_{acc} + ||P_{acc} V_\sigma \psi||_2^2, p_{rej} + ||P_{rej} V_\sigma \psi||_2^2), \quad (5.27)$$

and we define $T_x = T_{\sigma_n} T_{\sigma_{n-1}} \cdots T_{\sigma_1}$ for any $x = \sigma_1 \cdots \sigma_n \in \Gamma^*$.

If $(\psi, p_{acc}, p_{rej}) = T_{w\$}(|q_0\rangle, 0, 0)$, then MM-1QFA accepts w with the probability of p_{acc}.

Proposition 5.1. [13] *Arbitrary language L recognized by* MM-1QFA *with bounded error is regular language.*

Proof. Suppose there exist $\varepsilon > 0$ and $\lambda \in (0, 1)$, such that for any $x \in \Sigma^*$, if $x \in L$, then $P_{\mathcal{M}}(x) \geq \lambda + \varepsilon$; if $x \notin L$, then $P_{\mathcal{M}}(x) \leq \lambda - \varepsilon$.

The definition of "$\equiv_L$": for any $w, w' \in \Sigma^*$, $w \equiv_L w'$ if and only if $wy \in L \iff w'y \in L$ for any $y \in \Sigma^*$. It is clear that $\equiv_L$ is an equivalent relation on Σ^*. Classical automata theory [7] shows that Σ^* can be divided into a finite number of equivalence classes by $\equiv_L$ if and only if L is a regular language.

Let $W \subseteq \Sigma^*$ and assume the elements in W are not equivalent to each other on $\equiv_L$. In the following, we will prove that W is finite. For any w, $w' \in W$, w and w' are not equivalent on $\equiv_L$, so there exists $y \in \Sigma^*$ such that $wy \in L$ and $w'y \notin L$. Denote $v = T_w(|q\rangle, 0, 0)$, $v' = T_{w'}(|q\rangle, 0, 0)$, then $P_{\mathcal{M}}(w) \geq \lambda + \varepsilon$, $P_{\mathcal{M}}(w') \leq \lambda - \varepsilon$, and we have $||T_{y\$}v - T_{y\$}v'|| \geq 2\varepsilon$. There exists a $c > 0$ such that $||T_{y\$}v - T_{y\$}v'|| \leq c||v - v'||$ (the proof is left as an exercise). Then $c||v - v'|| \geq 2\varepsilon$, that is, $||v - v'|| \geq \frac{2\varepsilon}{c}$. Since it can be proved that the set $\{T_w(|q_0\rangle, 0, 0) \mid w \in W\}$ is finite ($\forall y \in \Sigma^*$), W is finite. □

Before proving that $\{a, b\}^*a$ cannot be recognized by MM-1QFA, we first present two lemmas.

Lemma 5.1. *Let U be an arbitrary unitary matrix. Then for any $\epsilon > 0$ and $N > 0$, there exists a positive integer $k > N$ such that $\|(U^k - I)x\| < \epsilon$ for any vector x with $\|x\| \leq 1$.*

Proof. This can be derived from the pumping lemma of MO-1QFA (Theorem 5.1). □

Lemma 5.2. [12] *Let U be an arbitrary $n \times n$ unitary matrix, denoting P as an arbitrary projective operator, and denote ψ as an arbitrary n-dimensional vector. Then ψ can be divided as $\psi = \phi_1 + \phi_2$, where $\langle \phi_1, \phi_2 \rangle = 0$. Hence, for any integer k, we have $(PU)^k \phi_1 = U^k \phi_1$ and $\lim_{m\to\infty} \|(PU)^m \phi_2\| = 0$.*

Now we can begin to prove that $\{a, b\}^* a$ cannot be recognized by MM-1QFA.

Proposition 5.2. *Let $L = \{a, b\}^* a$. Then L cannot be recognized by* MM-1QFA *with bounded error* [13].

Proof. Suppose L is the language recognized by an MM-1QFA $\mathcal{M}$. For any $x = \sigma_1 \sigma_2 \cdots \sigma_n \in \Gamma^*$, denote

$$\psi_x = (P_{non} V_{\sigma_n}) \cdots (P_{non} V_{\sigma_1}) |q_0\rangle. \tag{5.28}$$

Let $\mu = \inf\{||\psi_w|| \mid w \in \{a, b\}^*\}$. For any given $\xi > 0$, setting a suitable w with $||\psi_w|| < \mu + \xi$, we have $||\psi_{wa}|| \in [\mu, \mu + \xi)$.

According to Lemma 5.2, we know that $|\psi_{wa}\rangle$ can be divided as $\psi_{wa} = \phi_1 + \phi_2$, where $(P_{non} V_b)^k \phi_1 = V_b^k \phi_1$ and $\lim_{m\to\infty} \|(P_{non} V_b)^m \phi_2\| = 0$ for any positive integer k. Therefore for any N, the cumulative increase of the accepting and rejecting probabilities from the state ψ_{wa} to the state ψ_{wab^N} totally is at most

$$\|\phi_2 + \phi_1\|^2 - \|\phi_1\|^2 \leq (\mu + \xi)^2 - \mu^2 \tag{5.29}$$

$$= (2\mu + \xi)\xi. \tag{5.30}$$

According to $\langle \phi_1, \phi_2 \rangle = 0$, we have

$$\|\phi_2\|^2 \leq (\mu + \xi)^2 - \mu^2 \tag{5.31}$$

$$= (2\mu + \xi)\xi. \tag{5.32}$$

By combining with Lemma 5.1, there exists a positive integer k such that $\|(V_b^k - I)\phi_1\| < \xi$ and $\|(P_{non} V_b)^k \phi_2\| < \xi$. Therefore

$$\|\psi_{wab^k} - \psi_{wa}\| = \| V_b^k \phi_1 + (P_{non} V_b)^k \phi_2 - (\phi_1 + \phi_2)\| \tag{5.33}$$

$$\leq \|(V_b^k - I)\phi_1\| + \|\phi_2\| + \|(P_{non}V_b)^k\phi_2\| \tag{5.34}$$

$$\leq 2\xi + \sqrt{(2\mu + \xi)\xi}. \tag{5.35}$$

Since ξ can be arbitrarily small, $wa \in L$ and $wab^k \notin L$, $\mathcal{M}$ cannot recognize language L with bounded error. □

5.1.3 1QFA together with classical states

1QFA together with classical states (1QFAC) is a kind of hybrid model. In this model, we use classical states to determine the unitary operators that are applied on the quantum state after every time the tape head scanning an input symbol.

Let us illustrate the computational process of 1QFAC. First, the machine starts with its classical initial state as well as quantum initial state, and it scans the input string sequentially. Then, after scanning each input symbol, the current classical state as well as the current input symbol will determine a unitary operator that is applied to the current quantum state. Simultaneously the current classical state is updated based on the current input symbol. Once the last input symbol is scanned a measurement according to the final classical state is performed on the final quantum state, and consequently, we will obtain a measurement result.

For convenience the following notation is given: For any subset $B \subseteq Q$, $\mathcal{H}(B)$ represents the subspace of Hilbert space $\mathcal{H}(Q)$, and $\mathcal{H}(B) = \text{span}\{|q\rangle \mid q \in B\}$. I and O represent the identity operator and zero operator on $\mathcal{H}(Q)$, respectively. Here, we give the formal definition of 1QFAC as follows.

Definition 5.11. A 1QFAC $\mathcal{A}$ can be defined as a nine tuple: $\mathcal{A} = (S, Q, \Sigma, \Gamma, s_0, |\psi_0\rangle, \delta, \mathbb{U}, \mathcal{M})$. Here,

- Σ is a finite input alphabet;
- Γ is a finite output alphabet;
- S is a finite set of classical states;
- Q is a finite set of quantum states;
- $s_0 \in S$ is the initial classical state;
- $|\psi_0\rangle \in \mathcal{H}(Q)$ is the initial quantum state;
- $\delta : S \times \Sigma \to S$ is a classical transition function;
- $\mathbb{U} = \{U_{s\sigma}\}_{s\in S, \sigma\in\Sigma}$ is a set of unitary operators, where $U_{s\sigma}$ is the unitary operator in $\mathcal{H}(Q)$;
- $\mathcal{M} = \{\mathcal{M}_s\}_{s\in S}$, where $\mathcal{M}_s$, whose result is in Γ, is a projective measurement on $\mathcal{H}(Q)$. In this chapter, we only consider the case that

the measurement results only contain "accept" and "reject"), in other words, for any $s \in S$,

$$M_s = \{P_{s,\gamma}\}_{\gamma\in\Gamma}, \sum_{\gamma\in\Gamma} P_{s,\gamma} = I, \; P_{s,\gamma}P_{s,\gamma'} = \begin{cases} P_{s,\gamma}, & \gamma = \gamma', \\ 0, & \gamma \neq \gamma'. \end{cases} \tag{5.36}$$

If the machine locates in the classical state s_n and the quantum state $|\psi_n\rangle$ after scanning the whole input string, then the probability of resulting γ is $||P_{s_n,\gamma}|\psi_n\rangle||^2$.

We can depict the working process of a 1QFAC in Fig. 5.3.

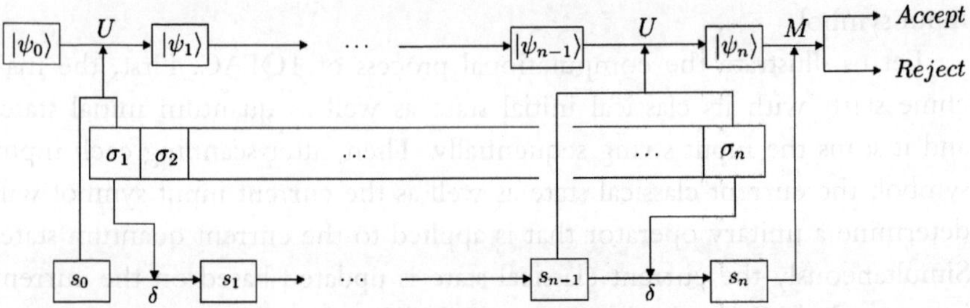

Figure 5.3 The working process of a 1QFAC.

Remark 5.7. If $\Gamma = \{a, r\}$, where a and r represent accepting and rejecting, respectively, then $M = \{\{P_{s,a}, P_{s,r}\} \mid s \in S\}$. Additionally, for any $s \in S$, we have $P_{s,a} + P_{s,r} = I$ and $P_{s,a}P_{s,r} = 0$. In this case, 1QFAC $\mathcal{A}$ is a recognizer of languages in Σ.

For any string $x \in \Sigma^*$, we define $\mu(x) = \delta^*(s_0, x)$.

After scanning symbol string $x = \sigma_1\sigma_2\cdots\sigma_m$ $(\sigma_i \in \Sigma)$, the classical state of 1QFAC $\mathcal{A}$ will transform to $\mu(x)$, and the quantum state will evolve to $U_{\mu(\sigma_1\cdots\sigma_{m-2}\sigma_{m-1})\sigma_m} U_{\mu(\sigma_1\cdots\sigma_{m-3}\sigma_{m-2})\sigma_{m-1}} \cdots U_{\mu(\sigma_1)\sigma_2} U_{s_0\sigma_1}|\psi_0\rangle$.

Let $v(x) = U_{\mu(\sigma_1\cdots\sigma_{m-2}\sigma_{m-1})\sigma_m} U_{\mu(\sigma_1\cdots\sigma_{m-3}\sigma_{m-2})\sigma_{m-1}} \cdots U_{\mu(\sigma_1)\sigma_2} U_{s_0\sigma_1}$. Then the probability that $\mathcal{A}$ accepts x is

$$\mathrm{P}_{\mathcal{A}}(x) = ||\mathrm{P}_{\mu(x),a} v(x)|\psi_0\rangle||^2. \tag{5.37}$$

1QFAC can exactly recognize all regular languages and the class of languages, which can be recognized by 1QFAC with bounded error, consists of all regular languages. The following two theorems show the advantages of state complexity in 1QFAC.

Theorem 5.14. *L is a regular language and the minimized* DFA *that can recognize L has m states. If there exists a* 1QFAC *that recognizes L with an isolated cut-point* λ *and a separation radius* ϵ*, then* $m \leq k(1+\frac{2}{\epsilon})^{2n}$.

Theorem 5.15. [16] *For any prime* $m \geq 2$*, the regular language* $L^{\circ}(m) = \{w0 \mid w \in \{0,1\}^*, |w0| = km, k = 1,2,3,\cdots\}$ *satisfies:*

(1) *Neither* MO-1QFA *or* MM-1QFA *can recognize* $L^{\circ}(m)$ *with bounded error;*

(2) *The number of states in the minimization* DFA *that can recognize* $L^{\circ}(m)$ *is* $m+1$*;*

(3) *For any* $\varepsilon > 0$*, there exists a* 1QFAC *with 2 classical states and* $O(\log m)$ *quantum states recognizing* $L^{\circ}(m)$ *with one-sided error* ε.

For any given finite regular language L, we can provide a precise lower bound on the number of classical states in 1QFAC that can recognize L [17]. It means that 1QFAC also has certain limitations. The state complexity concerning 1QFAC has been further studied deeply in [17].

Theorem 5.16. *For any given finite regular language L the number of classical states is not less than* $\max_{x\in L}|x| + 2$ *in arbitrary* 1QFAC *that recognizes L with isolated cut-point, and there exists a* 1QFAC *with* $\max_{x\in L}|x| + 2$ *classical states precisely recognizing L, where* $|x|$ *denotes the length of string x.*

We can also decide whether two 1QFAC $\mathcal{A}_1$ and $\mathcal{A}_2$ are equivalent.

Theorem 5.17. [16] *Any two* 1QFAC $\mathcal{A}_1$ *and* $\mathcal{A}_2$ *are equivalent if and only if they are* $[(k_1n_1)^2+(k_2n_2)^2-1]$*-equivalent. Additionally, there exists a polynomial-time algorithm whose time complexity is* $O([(k_1n_1)^2+(k_2n_2)^2]^4)$ *to decide whether two* 1QFAC $\mathcal{A}_1$ *and* $\mathcal{A}_2$ *are equivalent, where* k_i *and* n_i $(i=1,2)$ *are the number of classical basis states and quantum basis states of* $\mathcal{A}_i$*, respectively.*

5.1.4 Other important types of 1QFA

Besides the three types of 1QFA that we have already introduced, other types of 1QFA will be outlined in this subsection.

(I) 1QFA With Control Languages (CL-1QFA)

This model is similar to MM-1QFA, with a measurement being performed after each symbol is scanning. However, there are also some differences between CL-1QFA and MM-1QFA:

i. CL-1QFA can apply a more general measurement instead of projective measurement.

ii. The condition of accepting in CL-1QFA is different from that in the former model.

Definition 5.12. [18] Suppose Σ is a finite input alphabet. Denote $\$ \notin \Sigma$ as the end-mark, and let $\Gamma = \Sigma \cup \{\$\}$ be the tape alphabet. A CL-1QFA on Γ can be defined as a five-tuple $\mathcal{M} = (Q, |\psi_0\rangle, \{U(\sigma)\}_{\sigma\in\Gamma}, \mathcal{O}, L)$. Here,

- $Q = \{q_1, q_2, \cdots, q_n\}$ is the set of quantum basis states;
- $|\psi_0\rangle$ is a unit vector in Hilbert space $\mathbb{C}^n$, and it represents the initial state of $\mathcal{M}$;
- For any $\sigma \in \Gamma$, $U(\sigma)$ is an $n \times n$ unitary matrix;
- $\mathcal{O} = \{P(c_i) \mid i = 1, 2, \cdots, s\}$ is a projective measurement and output is in $C = \{c_1, \cdots, c_s\}$;
- $L \subseteq C^*$ is a regular language, and it is referred to control language.

For any input string $x = \sigma_1\sigma_2\cdots\sigma_n$, the symbols on the input tape are $\sigma_1\sigma_2\cdots\sigma_n\$$. First, starting from the state $|\psi_0\rangle$, $\mathcal{M}$ scans the first symbol σ_1. Then the machine performs the following operations:

(1) With the application of $U(\sigma_1)$, $\mathcal{M}$ will obtain the state $|\phi'\rangle = U(\sigma_1)|\psi_0\rangle$.

(2) Next, $\mathcal{M}$ applies a measurement $\mathcal{O}$ to $|\phi'\rangle$ and it will obtain c_k with the probability $\mathrm{P}_k = ||P(c_k)|\phi'\rangle||^2$. Then the state of $\mathcal{M}$ will collapse into $\frac{P(c_k)|\phi'\rangle}{\sqrt{\mathrm{P}_k}}$.

(3) After that, $\mathcal{M}$ will scan the next symbol and it will repeat previous process until scanning \$.

In the end, all the measurement results will form a sequence $\gamma_1\gamma_2\cdots\gamma_{n+1} \in C^*$ and the probability of generating this sequence is

$$\mathrm{P}(\gamma_1\gamma_2\cdots\gamma_{n+1}|\sigma_1\sigma_2\cdots\sigma_n\$) = \left\| \left(\prod_{i=1}^{n+1} \mathrm{P}(\gamma_i)U(\sigma_i) \right) |\psi_0\rangle \right\|^2, \tag{5.38}$$

where $\sigma_{n+1} = \$$, $\prod_{i=1}^{n+1} A_i = A_n \cdots A_1$.

Therefore the probability of $\mathcal{M}$ accepting x is

$$\mathrm{P}_{\mathcal{M}}(x) = \sum_{\gamma_1\cdots\gamma_{n+1}\in L} \mathrm{P}(\gamma_1\cdots\gamma_{n+1}|\sigma_1\cdots\sigma_n\$). \tag{5.39}$$

The class of languages that can be recognized by CL-1QFA with bounded error consists of all regular languages [19]. We have the following theorem regarding the equivalence decidability of CL-1QFA.

Theorem 5.18. [6] *For any two* CL-1QFA $\mathcal{A}_1$ *and* $\mathcal{A}_2$ *(with control languages* L_1 *and* L_2*, respectively) are equivalent if and only if they are* $(c_1n_1^2 + c_2n_2^2 - 1)$*-equivalent, where* c_1 *and* c_2 *are the minimized number of states in* DFA *that* *recognize* L_1 *and* L_2*, respectively. Additionally,* n_1*,* n_2 *are the number of quantum basis states in* $\mathcal{A}_1$ *and* $\mathcal{A}_2$*, respectively.*

(II) Multi-letter 1QFA

Multi-letter 1QFA are quantum versions of classical one-way multi-head finite automata [20]. To put them simply, a k-letter 1QFA has k tape heads that scan k symbols simultaneously. Its input of the state transition function is formed by k consecutive symbols (starting with k-1 space symbols followed by the first input symbol, tape heads will move to the next squares on the right in parallel until the rightmost symbol is scanned).

Fig. 5.4 is a k-letter DFA, and we simply illustrate the definition of k-letter DFA as follows.

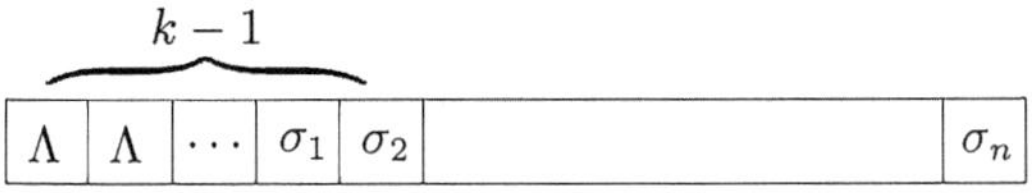

Figure 5.4 k-letter DFA.

A k-letter DFA is a five-tuple $(Q, Q_{acc}, q_0, \Sigma, \gamma)$. Here, Q is a finite set of states; $Q_{acc} \subseteq Q$ is a set of accepting states; $q_0 \in Q$ is the initial state; Σ is the input alphabet; $\gamma : Q \times \Gamma^k \to Q$ is the transition function; $\Gamma = \{\Lambda\} \cup \Sigma$, where Λ represents blank-mark and Γ^k are all strings with length k on Γ.

The computational process of k-letter DFA is as follows: for input string $x = \sigma_1\sigma_2 \cdots \sigma_n \in \Sigma^*$, machine starts to scan $k - 1$ Λ and σ_1 when the initial state is q_0 (with k-th tape head pointing to σ_1). Based on these k symbols, the machine transmits to a new state, and k tape heads move to the next squares on the right in parallel. At that time, k tape heads point to $k - 2$ Λ, σ_1, and σ_2, respectively. It will continue working until k-th tape head points to σ_n and the state is also updated. If the state is accepting, then x is accepted by the machine, otherwise x is rejected.

The definition of k-letter 1QFA is given as follows.

Definition 5.13. A k-letter 1QFA $\mathcal{A}$ is a five-tuple

$$\mathcal{A} = (Q, Q_{acc}, |\psi_0\rangle, \Sigma, \mu).$$

Here,

- Q is the set of quantum basis states;
- $Q_{acc} \subseteq Q$ is the set of accepting basis states;
- $|\psi_0\rangle$ is the initial state;

- Σ is a finite input alphabet;
- μ is a mapping: For any $w \in (\{\Lambda\} \cup \Sigma)^k$, $\mu(w)$ is an unitary matrix on $\mathbb{C}^{|Q|}$.

Remark 5.8. The tape head of k-letter 1QFA is the same as the tape head of k-letter DFA. When $k = 1$, a 1-letter 1QFA is an MO-1QFA that has been introduced before.

Denote $\bar{\mu}$ as the mapping from Σ^* to the set of unitary matrices $|Q| \times |Q|$. $\bar{\mu}$, derived from μ, is defined as follows: For any $x = \sigma_1 \cdots \sigma_m \in \Sigma^*$,

$$\bar{\mu}(x) = \begin{cases} \mu(\Lambda^{k-m}\sigma_1\sigma_2\cdots\sigma_m)\cdots\mu(\Lambda^{k-2}\sigma_1\sigma_2)\mu(\Lambda^{k-1}\sigma_1), & m < k, \\ \mu(\sigma_{m-k+1}\sigma_{m-k+2}\cdots\sigma_m)\cdots\mu(\Lambda^{k-2}\sigma_1\sigma_2)\mu(\Lambda^{k-1}\sigma_1), & m \geq k. \end{cases} \tag{5.40}$$

Let P_{acc} be the projectors of the subspace that is a tensor product of Q_{acc}. Then the probability of $\mathcal{A}$ accepting x is

$$\mathrm{P}_{\mathcal{A}}(x) = ||P_{acc}\bar{\mu}(x)|\psi_0\rangle||^2. \tag{5.41}$$

Here is an example of 2-letter 1QFA.

Example 5.4. [21] Let $\mathcal{A} = (Q, Q_{acc}, |\psi_0\rangle, \Sigma, \mu)$. Here, $Q = \{q_0, q_1\}$, $Q_{acc} = q_1$, $|\psi_0\rangle = |q_0\rangle = \begin{bmatrix} 1 \\ 0 \end{bmatrix}$, $\Sigma = \{a, b\}$, $\mu(\Lambda b) = \mu(bb) = \begin{bmatrix} 1 & 0 \\ 0 & 1 \end{bmatrix}$, $\mu(\Lambda a) = \mu(ab) = \mu(ba) = \begin{bmatrix} 0 & 1 \\ 1 & 0 \end{bmatrix}$. $\mathcal{A}$ can exactly recognize $(a+b)^*b$.

The language $(a+b)^*b$ cannot be recognized by MM-1QFA and MO-1QFA with bounded error [13]. Therefore we have some languages, which can not be recognized by MM-1QFA and MO-1QFA with bounded error, and can be recognized by the multi-letter 1QFA with bounded error.

What are the differences in the language recognitional abilities in k-letter 1QFA for different k? In fact, for any $k = 1, 2, \cdots$, it is a proper subset relationship that $L(\mathrm{QFA}_k) \subset L(\mathrm{QFA}_{k+1})$, where $L(\mathrm{QFA}_k)$ represents the class of languages recognized by k-letter 1QFA [22].

We give the following results regarding the equivalence decidability and minimization of multi-letter 1QFA.

Theorem 5.19. [23] *Any* k_1-letter 1QFA *and* k_2-letter 1QFA *on alphabet* Σ *are equivalent if and only if they are* $(n^2m^{k-1} - m^{k-1} + k)$*-equivalent. Here,* $k = \max(k_1, k_2)$, $n = n_1 + n_2$, n_i $(i = 1, 2)$ *is the number of quantum basis states in* Q_i, $m = |\Sigma|$. *Additionally, there exists an algorithm whose time complexity is* $O(m^{2k-1}n^8 + km^kn^6)$ *to decide whether* $\mathcal{A}_1$ *and* $\mathcal{A}_2$ *are equivalent.*

Theorem 5.20. [23] *The state minimization problem for multi-letter* 1QFA *is decidable.*

Regarding comparisons with the state complexity of 1QFAC, we give the following results.

Proposition 5.3. [23] *For any $m \geq 2$ and any $z = z_1 z_2 \cdots z_n$, the regular language $L_z(m) = \{w \mid w \in \Sigma^* z_1 \Sigma^* z_2 \Sigma^* \cdots \Sigma^* z_n,\ |w| = km,\ k = 1, 2, \cdots\}$ cannot be recognized by multi-letter* 1QFA. *However, there exists a* 1QFAC *$\mathcal{A}_m$ with $n+1$ classical states and 2 quantum basis states to recognize $L_z(m)$ with one-sided error ϵ, where ϵ is arbitrary positive number. Additionally, the minimized* DFA *that can recognize $L_z(m)$ has $m(n+1)$ states.*

Exercises

5.1. Given an MO-1QFA, for any $q_1, q_2 \in Q$ and any $\sigma \in \Sigma$, prove the equation

$$\sum_{p \in Q} \delta(q_1, \sigma, p)^* \delta(q_2, \sigma, p) = \begin{cases} 1, & q_1 = q_2, \\ 0, & q_1 \neq q_2, \end{cases}$$

is equivalent to $U(\sigma)$ being a unitary matrix, where $U(\sigma)(j, i) = \delta(q_i, \sigma, q_j)$, $U(\sigma)(j, i)$ is the element located at the j-th row and i-th column of $U(\sigma)$.

5.2. Given an MO-1QFA $M = (Q, \Sigma, \delta, q_0, F)$. Here, $Q = \{q_0, q_1\}$, $F = \{q_1\}$, $\Sigma = \{a\}$, and let q_0 be the initial state. $\delta(q_0, a, q_0) = \frac{1}{\sqrt{2}}$, $\delta(q_1, a, q_0) = \frac{1}{\sqrt{2}}$, $\delta(q_0, a, q_1) = \frac{1}{\sqrt{2}}$, $\delta(q_1, a, q_1) = -\frac{1}{\sqrt{2}}$.

(1) Calculate $U(a)$.

(2) Calculate $\mathrm{P}_M(aa)$.

5.3. Provide an example of non-reversible languages.

5.4. Provide an example to illustrate that the class of reversible languages is a proper subclass of regular languages.

5.5. Given an MM-1QFA,

$$\begin{aligned}
Q &= \{q_0, q_1, q_{acc}, q_{rej}\}, \\
\Sigma &= \{a\},\ Q_{acc} = \{q_{acc}\},\ Q_{rej} = \{q_{rej}\}, \\
U(a)|q_0\rangle &= \frac{1}{2}|q_0\rangle + \frac{1}{\sqrt{2}}|q_1\rangle + \frac{1}{2}|q_{acc}\rangle, \\
U(a)|q_1\rangle &= \frac{1}{2}|q_0\rangle - \frac{1}{\sqrt{2}}|q_1\rangle + \frac{1}{2}|q_{acc}\rangle,
\end{aligned}$$

$$U(\$)|q_0\rangle = |q_{acc}\rangle,$$
$$U(\$)|q_1\rangle = |q_{rej}\rangle.$$

Calculate $P_A(aa\$)$.

5.6. Prove that MM-1QFA can simulate MO-1QFA (i.e., given any MO-1QFA, construct an MM-1QFA such that they have same accepting probability for any input string).

5.7. Based on Theorem 5.10, prove $\{a, b\}^*a$ cannot be recognized by MM-1QFA with bounded error.

5.8. Explain what conditions will make a 1QFAC $\mathcal{A}$ become an MO-1QFA? And what conditions will make it become a DFA?

5.9. Suppose $\mathcal{V} = l_2(Q) \times \mathbb{R} \times \mathbb{R}$ is a Hilbert space, and denote $\mathcal{B} = \{v \in \mathcal{V} \mid ||v|| \leq 1\}$. For any $(\psi, p_1, p_2) \in \mathcal{V}$, define its norm as $||(\psi, p_1, p_2)|| = \frac{||\psi||_2 + |p_1| + |p_2|}{2}$. Prove: If $A \subseteq \mathcal{B}$, and there exists a real number $\xi > 0$ such that $||v - v'|| > \xi$ for any $v, v' \in A$, then A is a finite set.

5.10. Prove: There exists a constant $c > 0$ such that $||T_x v - T_x v'|| \leq c||v - v'||$ for any $x \in \Gamma^*$ and any $v, v' \in \mathcal{B}$, where the definition of $||\cdot||$ is the same as previous.

5.2 Two-way quantum finite automata

Unlike 1QFA, the tape head of two-way quantum finite automata (2QFA) can move to the left, to the right, or remain stationary. 2QFA cannot only recognize all regular languages, but also some context-free and non-context-free languages within linear time. We give the following formal definition of 2QFA.

Definition 5.14. A 2QFA $\mathcal{A}$ is a six-tuple

$$\mathcal{A} = (Q, \Sigma, q_0, Q_{acc}, Q_{rej}, \delta).$$

Here,

- Σ is a finite input alphabet;
- Q is a finite set of states;
- $q_0 \in Q$ is the initial state;
- $Q_{acc} \in Q$ and $Q_{rej} \in Q$ are accepting state and rejecting state, respectively, and $Q_{acc} \cap Q_{rej} = \varnothing$;

- $\delta : Q \times \Gamma \times Q \times \{\leftarrow, \downarrow, \rightarrow\} \to \mathbb{C}$ is the transition function, where $\Gamma = \Sigma \cup \{\#, \$\}$ is the tape alphabet of $\mathcal{A}$. # and \$, which do not belong to Σ, can represent a left end-mark and a right end-mark, respectively. $\leftarrow, \downarrow, \rightarrow$ represent moving to the next square on the left, remaining stationary, and moving to the next square on the right, respectively. δ satisfies that: For any $q_1, q_2 \in Q$, any $\sigma, \sigma_1, \sigma_2 \in \Gamma$, any $d \in \{\leftarrow, \downarrow, \rightarrow\}$:
  (1) Local probability and the condition of orthogonality:

$$\sum_{q',d} \delta(q_1, \sigma, q', d)^* \delta(q_2, \sigma, q', d) = \begin{cases} 1, & q_1 = q_2, \\ 0, & q_1 \neq q_2. \end{cases} \tag{5.42}$$

  (2) The condition of separability I:
  $\sum_{q'} (\delta(q_1, \sigma_1, q', \rightarrow)^* \delta(q_2, \sigma_2, q', \downarrow) + \delta(q_1, \sigma_1, q', \downarrow)^* \delta(q_2, \sigma_2, q', \leftarrow)) = 0.$
  (3) The condition of separability II:
  $\sum_{q'} \delta(q_1, \sigma_1, q', \rightarrow)^* \delta(q_2, \sigma_2, q', \leftarrow) = 0.$

Remark 5.9. The previous three conditions are equivalent to the evolution process of $\mathcal{A}$ satisfying unitarity.

Any regular language can be exactly recognized by a 2QFA [13]. In fact, 2QFA are two-way reversible finite automata if all the amplitudes for transitions are either 0 or 1. In addition, any DFA can be simulated by a two-way reversible finite automaton (denoted as 2RFA).

Proposition 5.4. *For any* DFA $\mathcal{A}$, *there exists a two-way reversible finite automaton* $\mathcal{M}$ *satisfies that: For any* $w \in \Sigma^*$, *if* $\mathcal{A}$ *accepts* w, *then* $\mathcal{M}$ *accepts* w *within* $O(|w|)$ *steps; if* $\mathcal{A}$ *does not accept* w, *then* $\mathcal{M}$ *rejects* w *within* $O(|w|)$ *steps.*

Corollary 5.1. *For any regular language* L, *there exists a* 2RFA *to exactly recognize* L.

Remark 5.10. Since the languages recognized by *two-way deterministic finite automata* 2DFA are also regular, any 2DFA can be simulated by a 2RFA.

Let us continue to see the transition function δ of 2QFA $\mathcal{A}$. For convenience, we use -1, 0, and 1 to represent the directions $\leftarrow$, $\downarrow$, and $\rightarrow$, respectively. $\delta(q, \sigma, q', d)$ refers to the amplitude of the transition where the machine locating in the state q, scans the symbol σ, and will transform to the state q' with its tape head in direction d. When the length of the string on the input tape is n, a configuration of $\mathcal{A}$ can be described as (q, k), where

$q \in Q$ denotes the current state and $k \in \mathbb{Z}_n$ indicates the position that the tape head points to.

It can be seen that the total number of configurations in $\mathcal{A}$ is $n|Q|$. Therefore all configurations can be described by the Hilbert space that is a tensor product of C_n, where $C_n = Q \times \mathbb{Z}_n = \{|q_i\rangle \otimes |k\rangle \mid q_i \in Q, k \in \mathbb{Z}_n\}$. Then, arbitrary state $|\psi\rangle$ can be given by $|\psi\rangle = \sum_{c \in C_n} \alpha_c |c\rangle$, where $\langle\psi|\psi\rangle = 1$. We denote x as tape string, and let $x(k)$ be the k-th symbol of x ($k = 0, 1, \cdots, |x| - 1$). Then δ can induce a unitary operator U_δ^x such that

$$U_\delta^x |q, k\rangle = \sum_{q', d} \delta(q, x(k), q', d)|q', k + d(\text{mod } |x|)\rangle \tag{5.43}$$

for any $(q, k) \in C_{|x|}$.

Proposition 5.5. *For any x, U_δ^x is an unitary operator if and only if δ satisfies the three conditions in the definition of* 2QFA.

In 2QFA, if we can represent the transition function δ in a special form, then the three conditions of δ are easier to be verified. For any $\sigma \in \Sigma$, let the unitary operator $V_\sigma : l_2(Q) \to l_2(Q)$ such that

$$\delta(q, \sigma, q', d) = \begin{cases} \langle q'|V_\sigma|q\rangle, & D(q') = d, \\ 0, & D(q') \neq d, \end{cases} \tag{5.44}$$

where $D : Q \to \{-1, 0, 1\}$. Then δ satisfies the three conditions in the definition of 2QFA if and only if

$$\sum_{q'} (\langle q'|V_\sigma|q_1\rangle)^* (\langle q'|V_\sigma|q_2\rangle) = \begin{cases} 1, & q_1 = q_2, \\ 0, & q_1 \neq q_2, \end{cases} \tag{5.45}$$

for any $\sigma \in \Gamma$.

The definition of accepting and rejecting probabilities for a 2QFA $\mathcal{A}$ on any input string $w \in \Sigma^*$ is similar to that of an MM-1QFA. Denote the tape string as $x = \#w\$$. Then when the machine scans a symbol of x each time, we will apply U_δ^x:

$$U_\delta^x |q, k\rangle = \sum_{q', d} \delta(q, x(k), q', d)|q', k + d(\text{mod } |x|)\rangle.$$

After that, we perform a measurement with the projectors corresponding to $\{E_{acc}, E_{rej}, E_{non}\}$. Here, $E_{acc} = \text{span}(Q_{acc} \times \mathbb{Z}_{|x|})$, $E_{rej} = \text{span}(Q_{rej} \times \mathbb{Z}_{|x|})$, and $E_{non} = \text{span}(Q_{non} \times \mathbb{Z}_{|x|})$.

Example 5.5. For any natural number N, a 2QFA is given by

$$M_N = (Q, \Sigma, \delta, q_0, Q_{acc}, Q_{rej}).$$

Here,

- $\Sigma = \{a, b\}$;
- $Q = \{q_0, q_1, q_2, q_3\} \cup \{r_{j,k} \mid 1 \leq j \leq N, 0 \leq k \leq \max(j, N-j+1)\} \cup \{s_j \mid 1 \leq j \leq N\}$;
- $Q_{acc} = \{s_N\}$, $Q_{rej} = \{q_3\} \cup \{s_j \mid 1 \leq j < N\}$;
- $\delta(q, \sigma, q', d) = \begin{cases} \langle q'|V_\sigma|q\rangle, & D(q') = d, \\ 0, & D(q') \neq d, \end{cases}$

  where the definitions of D and V_σ are as follows:

$$V_\#|q_0\rangle = |q_0\rangle, \qquad V_\$|q_0\rangle = |q_3\rangle,$$
$$V_\#|q_1\rangle = |q_3\rangle, \qquad V_\$|q_2\rangle = \frac{1}{\sqrt{N}}\sum_{j=1}^{N}|r_{j,0}\rangle,$$
$$V_\#|r_{j,0}\rangle = \frac{1}{\sqrt{N}}\sum_{l=1}^{N}\exp\left(\frac{2\pi i}{N}jl\right)|s_l\rangle,$$
$$V_a|q_0\rangle = |q_0\rangle, \qquad V_b|q_0\rangle = |q_1\rangle,$$
$$V_a|q_1\rangle = |q_2\rangle, \qquad V_b|q_2\rangle = |q_2\rangle,$$
$$V_a|q_2\rangle = |q_3\rangle,$$
$$V_a|r_{j,0}\rangle = |r_{j,j}\rangle,\ 1 \leq j \leq N,$$
$$V_a|r_{j,k}\rangle = |r_{j,k-1}\rangle,\ 1 \leq k \leq j,\ 1 \leq j \leq N,$$
$$V_b|r_{j,0}\rangle = |r_{j,N-j+1}\rangle,\ 1 \leq j \leq N,$$
$$V_b|r_{j,k}\rangle = |r_{j,k-1}\rangle,\ 1 \leq k \leq N-j+1,\ 1 \leq j \leq N.$$
$$D(q_0) = +1, \qquad D(r_{j,0}) = -1,\ 1 \leq j \leq N,$$
$$D(q_1) = -1, \qquad D(r_{j,k}) = 0,\ 1 \leq j \leq N,\ k \neq 0,$$
$$D(q_2) = +1, \qquad D(s_j) = 0,\ 1 \leq j \leq N,$$
$$D(q_3) = 0.$$

Proposition 5.6. *Suppose M_N is a* 2QFA *in Example 5.5. For any positive integer N, if $x \in \{a^n b^n \mid n \geq 1\}$, then M_N accepts x with probability* 1*; if $x \notin \{a^n b^n \mid n \geq 1\}$, then M_N rejects x with probability at least $1 - \frac{1}{N}$, and both cases terminate within $O(N|x|)$ steps.*

Proof. We divide the proof into two parts. First, M_N rejects any input that does not conform to the form $x = a^u b^v$ $(u, v \geq 1)$. For any input $x \in \{a, b\}^*$, if a or b are not contained in x, then it is easy to verify that M_N transforms directly to state q_3 and rejects x; if x contains substring ba, then M_N also transforms to q_3 and rejects x.

Second, if $x = a^u b^v$ $(u, v \geq 1)$, then M_N checks whether $u = v$. It will reject the case where $u \neq v$ with a certain probability or accept the case where $u = v$ with probability 1.

Actually, after the tape head scanning \$, the state will be $\frac{1}{\sqrt{N}}\sum_{j=1}^{N}|r_{j,0}\rangle$. Then the tape head moves to the left and locates on b. When the current state is $|r_{j,0}\rangle$ the tape head performs $N-j+2$ operations for each symbol b, and then it moves to the left with the state $|r_{j,0}\rangle$; when it moves to the input symbol a with state $|r_{j,0}\rangle$ the tape head performs $j+1$ operations for each symbol a. Therefore the machine with state $|r_{j,0}\rangle$ totally performs operations $(N-j+2)v+(j+1)u$ times from the rightmost b to the leftmost #. When $j \neq j'$, $(N-j+2)v+(j+1)u=(N-j'+2)v+(j'+1)u$ if and only if $u=v$.

When $u=v$, all $|r_{j,0}\rangle$ $(j=1,\cdots,N)$ reach # simultaneously. Since for $l=1,2,\cdots N-1$, we have

$$\sum_{j=1}^{N}\exp\left(\frac{2\pi i}{N}jl\right)=\frac{\exp(\frac{2\pi i}{N}l)-\exp(\frac{2\pi i}{N}l)}{1-\exp(\frac{2\pi i}{N}l)}=0, \tag{5.46}$$

then

$$\frac{1}{N}\sum_{j=1}^{N}\exp\left(\frac{2\pi i}{N}jl\right)=\begin{cases}1, & l=N,\\ 0, & l=1,2,\cdots,N-1.\end{cases} \tag{5.47}$$

The current state is

$$V_{\#}\left(\frac{1}{\sqrt{N}}\sum_{j=1}^{N}|r_{j,0}\rangle\right)=\frac{1}{N}\sum_{l=1}^{N}\sum_{j=1}^{N}\exp\left(\frac{2\pi i}{N}jl\right)|s_l\rangle=|s_N\rangle. \tag{5.48}$$

Therefore the machine accepts $a^n b^n$ with probability 1 after measurement.

When $u \neq v$, each $|r_{j,0}\rangle$ reaches # with different steps, and the machine positions as the state $|r_{j,0}\rangle$ with probability $\frac{1}{N}$. Starting from b at the rightmost, the state will evolve to $V_{\#}|r_{j,0}\rangle$ after arriving at #. The probability of obtaining the accepting state after measurement is $\frac{1}{N}$. Therefore the probability of machine accepting $a^u b^v$ (when $u \neq v$) is $\frac{1}{N}$, and the probability of rejecting is $1-\frac{1}{N}$. Additionally, the number of operations that tape head performs is $O(N|w|)$. □

To sum up, we have the following theorem.

Theorem 5.21. *Language* $L_{eq}=\{a^n b^n \mid n \in \mathbb{N}\}$ *can be recognized by* 2QFA *with one-side error within linear time.*

Exercises

5.11. A 2QFA $M=(Q,\Sigma,\delta,q_0,Q_{acc},Q_{rej})$ is well formed if and only if for any $\sigma,\sigma_1,\sigma_2 \in \Sigma$ and any $q_1,q_1 \in Q$ the following conditions hold:

(1) $\sum_{q',d}\delta(q_1,\sigma,q',d)^*\delta(q_2,\sigma,q',d)=\begin{cases}1, & q_1=q_2,\\ 0, & q_1\neq q_2.\end{cases}$

(2) $\sum_{q'}(\delta(q_1,\sigma_1,q',1)^*\delta(q_2,\sigma_2,q',0)+\delta(q_1,\sigma_1,q',0)^*\delta(q_2,\sigma_2,q',-1))=0.$

(3) $\sum_{q'}\delta(q_1,\sigma_1,q',1)^*\delta(q_2,\sigma_2,q',-1)=0.$

For any input w, denote tape string as $x=\#w\$$. Then δ can induce an operator U_δ^x on $\mathcal{H}_{|x|}$:

$$U_\delta^x|q,k\rangle=\sum_{q',d}\delta(q,x(k),q',d)|q',k+d(\text{mod }|x|)\rangle.$$

Prove: U_δ^x is unitary if and only if M is well formed.

5.12. For any $\sigma\in\Gamma$, let the linear operator $V_\sigma: l_2(Q)\to l_2(Q)$, $D: Q\to\{-1,0,1\}$, and define $\delta(q,\sigma,q',d)=\begin{cases}\langle q'|V_\sigma|q\rangle, & D(q')=d,\\ 0, & D(q')\neq d.\end{cases}$

Prove: M is well formed if and only if

$$\sum_{q'}(\langle q'|V_\sigma|q_1\rangle)^*\langle q'|V_\sigma|q_2\rangle=\begin{cases}1, & q_1=q_2,\\ 0, & q_1\neq q_2,\end{cases}$$

for any $\sigma\in\Gamma$.

5.3 Two-way finite automata with quantum and classical states

In the 2QFA introduced earlier, their tape heads are quantum states, which are entangled with the control states, making the physical implementation relatively complex. Therefore in this section the main goal is to investigate the computational power of 2QFA where their tape heads are controlled by classical states. If this type of model still possesses strong computational capabilities, it would have significant theoretical and practical application value.

In 2002, Ambainis and Watrous [24] first introduced a class of models known as *two-way quantum finite automata with quantum and classical states* (2QCFA). 2QCFA can recognize the language $L_{eq}=\{a^nb^n\mid n\in\mathbb{N}\}$ within polynomial time, and it can also recognize the palindromic language $L_{pal}=\{x\in\{a,b\}^*\mid x=x^R\}$, which cannot be recognized by two-way DFA or two-way probabilistic finite automata. The definition of 2QCFA is described as follows.

Definition 5.15. A 2QCFA $\mathcal{M}$ is a nine-tuple:

$$\mathcal{M} = (Q, S, \Sigma, \Theta, \delta, q_0, s_0, S_{acc}, S_{rej}),$$

where

- Q and S are finite sets of states (divided into quantum states and classical states);
- Σ is a finite input alphabet;
- Θ and δ are two state transition functions;
- $q_0 \in Q$ is the initial quantum state;
- $s_0 \in S$ is the initial classical state;
- S_{acc}, $S_{rej} \subseteq S$ are classical accepting states and rejecting states, respectively.

Denote $\Gamma = \Sigma \cup \{¢, \$\}$ as the tape alphabet, where ¢ as well as \$ that do not belong to Σ, are left end-marked and right end-marked, respectively. In the following, we continue to illustrate the computational process of this model.

Function Θ illustrates the evolution of quantum states in $\mathcal{M}$: For any $(s, \sigma) \in S\backslash(S_{acc} \cup S_{rej}) \times \Gamma$, $\Theta(s, \sigma)$ represents an unitary transformation or an orthogonal measurement.

Function δ illustrates the evolution of classical states. If $\Theta(s, \sigma)$ is an unitary transformation, then $\delta(s, \sigma) \in S \times \{-1, 0, 1\}$ represents transitioning to a new classical state and specifying the movement direction of the tape head; if $\Theta(s, \sigma)$ is a measurement, then $\delta(s, \sigma)$ is a mapping from the set of all possible measurement results to $S \times \{-1, 0, 1\}$ (also specifying the new classical state as well as the movement direction of the tape head). In addition, the tape head does not move left when it points to ¢ and does not move right when it points to \$.

For any input $x = x_1x_2 \cdots x_n$, the operational process of 2QCFA $\mathcal{M}$ is as follows. The initial classical state of $\mathcal{M}$ is s_0, and the initial quantum state is $|q_0\rangle$. The input tape is $¢x_1x_2 \cdots x_n\$$, and the tape head of $\mathcal{M}$ points to ¢ (denote the square as 0, and the squares to its right are sequentially denoted as $1, 2, \cdots, n+1$). After scanning each tape symbol σ, the quantum part will first evolve according to $\Theta(s, \sigma)$, where s and σ are classical state and tape symbol, respectively. Then the classical state as well as the tape head position will be changed according to $\delta(s, \sigma)$. If $\mathcal{M}$ attains a classical accepting state or rejecting state within its operation, it will correspondingly accept or reject the input string and halt.

When $\Theta(s, \sigma)$ is a measurement, it will obtain a random measurement result. At this point, the transition of classical states in $\mathcal{M}$ is also random. For any input x, we can obtain the accepting probability $P_{acc}(x)$ and rejecting probability $P_{rej}(x)$.

Next, we will prove that 2QCFA can recognize palindromic language L_{pal}.

Theorem 5.22. *For any $\epsilon > 0$, there exists a 2QCFA $\mathcal{M}$ recognizing $L_{pal} = \{x \in \{a, b\}^* \mid x = x^R\}$ with one-side error ϵ.*

First, we define unitary operators U_a and U_b as

$U_a|q_0\rangle = \frac{4}{5}|q_0\rangle - \frac{3}{5}|q_1\rangle$, $U_a|q_1\rangle = \frac{3}{5}|q_0\rangle + \frac{4}{5}|q_1\rangle$, $U_a|q_2\rangle = |q_2\rangle$.

$U_b|q_0\rangle = \frac{4}{5}|q_0\rangle - \frac{3}{5}|q_2\rangle$, $U_b|q_1\rangle = |q_1\rangle$, $U_b|q_2\rangle = \frac{3}{5}|q_0\rangle + \frac{4}{5}|q_2\rangle$.

We illustrate the operational process of 2QCFA $\mathcal{M}$ (we can construct $\mathcal{M}$ according to its computational process).

The algorithm of $\mathcal{M}$ can be illustrated as follows:

For any input $x = x_1 x_2 \cdots x_n$, $\mathcal{M}$ repeats the following process:

Let the tape head of $\mathcal{M}$ point to x_1 and set the current state as $|q_0\rangle$. Then repeat step (I).

(I) If the current symbol that tape head points to is not \$, then $\mathcal{M}$ applies the unitary operator U_{x_i} to the current quantum state, and the tape head moves to the next square on the right, where x_i is the current symbol that tape head points to. Otherwise, the tape head moves to ¢ and repeats step (II).

(II) If the current symbol that tape head points to is not \$, then $\mathcal{M}$ applies the unitary operator $U_{x_i}^{-1}$ to the current quantum state, and the tape head moves to the next square on the right. If the current symbol that tape head points to is \$, then $\mathcal{M}$ will measure the quantum state. And if the measurement result is q_0, then $\mathcal{M}$ will reject x; otherwise, set $b = 0$ and repeat step (III).

(III) If the current symbol that tape head points to is not ¢, then the machine will perform the following operations: Flip a coin k times, and set $b = 1$ if at least one of the flips makes the coin face up. After flipping the coin k times, the tape head will move to the square on the left. If the tape head points to ¢, then $\mathcal{M}$ will run the step (IV).

(IV) If $b = 0$, then $\mathcal{M}$ accepts x.

To prove that 2QCFA can recognize L_{pal}, we need the following basic results.

Suppose

$$A = \begin{bmatrix} 4 & 3 & 0 \\ -3 & 4 & 0 \\ 0 & 0 & 5 \end{bmatrix}, \ B = \begin{bmatrix} 4 & 0 & 3 \\ 0 & 5 & 0 \\ -3 & 0 & 4 \end{bmatrix}. \tag{5.49}$$

$f : \mathbb{Z}^3 \to \mathbb{Z}$ is given by $f(u) = 4u[1] + 3u[2] + 3u[3]$ for any $u \in \mathbb{Z}^3$, and $K \subseteq \mathbb{Z}^3$ is given by

$$K = \{u \in \mathbb{Z}^3 \mid u[1] \not\equiv 0(\text{mod } 5), f(u) \not\equiv 0(\text{mod } 5), u[2] \cdot u[3] \equiv 0(\text{mod } 5)\}. \tag{5.50}$$

Lemma 5.3. *If $u \in K$, then $Au \in K$ as well as $Bu \in K$.*

Proof. In the following content, we will prove that $Au \in K$ can be derived from $u \in K$; it is similar to $Bu \in K$. Let $u = (a, b, c)^T$. Then $Au = (4a + 3b, -3a + 4b, 5c)^T$. It is obvious that $(Au)[2](Au)[3] \equiv 0(\text{ mod } 5)$, so we only need to prove that $(Au)[1] \not\equiv 0(\text{mod } 5)$ and $f(Au) \not\equiv 0(\text{mod } 5)$.

Due to $u \in K$, we have

$$a \not\equiv 0(\text{mod } 5), \tag{5.51}$$

$$f(u) = 4a + 3b + 3c \not\equiv 0(\text{mod } 5), \tag{5.52}$$

and $b \equiv 0(\text{mod } 5)$ or $c \equiv 0(\text{mod } 5)$.

Let $b \equiv 0(\text{mod } 5)$. Then we have $(Au)[1] \equiv 4a(\text{mod } 5)$ and

$$f(Au) = 4(4a + 3b) + 3(-3a + 4b) + 3(5c) \equiv 2a(\text{mod } 5). \tag{5.53}$$

Therefore according to Eq. (5.51), we have $(Au)[1] \not\equiv 0(\text{mod } 5)$ and $f(Au) \not\equiv 0(\text{mod } 5)$.

Let $c \equiv 0(\text{mod } 5)$. Then

$$(Au)[1] = 4a + 3b \tag{5.54}$$

$$\equiv 4a + 3b + 3c(\text{mod } 5) \tag{5.55}$$

$$\equiv f(u)(\text{mod } 5) \tag{5.56}$$

and

$$f(Au) = 4(4a + 3b) + 3(-3a + 4b) + 3(5c) \tag{5.57}$$

$$\equiv 2a + 4b(\text{mod } 5) \tag{5.58}$$

$$\equiv 3(4a + 3b + 3c)(\text{mod } 5) \tag{5.59}$$

$$\equiv 3f(u)(\text{mod } 5). \tag{5.60}$$

Therefore according to Eq. (5.52), we have $(Au)[1] \not\equiv 0(\text{mod } 5)$ and $f(Au) \not\equiv 0(\text{mod } 5)$. □

Lemma 5.4. *Let $u \in \mathbb{Z}^3$ such that $u = Av = Bw$, where $v, w \in \mathbb{Z}^3$. Then $u \notin K$.*

Proof. Set $u = Av = Bw$, where $u, v, w \in \mathbb{Z}^3$, so $A^{-1}u, B^{-1}u \in \mathbb{Z}^3$. We have $u[2] \equiv 0(\text{mod } 5)$ according to $(B^{-1}u)[2] \in \mathbb{Z}$, and $4u[1] - 3u[2] \equiv 0(\text{mod } 25)$ according to $(A^{-1}u)[1] \in \mathbb{Z}$. Above all, with $u[1] \equiv 0(\text{mod } 5)$, we have $u \notin K$. □

Lemma 5.5. *Suppose $u = Y_1^{-1} \cdots Y_n^{-1} X_n \cdots X_1 (1, 0, 0)^T$, where $X_j, Y_j \in \{A, B\}$. If $X_j = Y_j$ $(j = 1, 2, \cdots, n)$, then $u[2]^2 + u[3]^3 = 0$; if there exists a $j \in \{1, 2, \cdots, n\}$ such that $X_j \neq Y_j$, then $u[2]^2 + u[3]^2 > 25^{-n}$.*

Proof. If $X_j = Y_j$ for any $1 \leq j \leq n$, then it is obvious that $u = (1, 0, 0)^T$. Therefore $u[2]^2 + u[3]^2 = 0$.

If there exists a j with $X_j \neq Y_j$, then we have $||u|| = 1$ since $5^{-1}X_j$ and $5Y_j^{-1}$ are unitary for any j. We know that $25^n u$ is an integer. Therefore to prove the lemma, we only need to prove $u \neq \pm(1, 0, 0)^T$. Since $|u[1]| < 1$, we have $|u[1]| \leq 1 - 25^{-n}$ and

$$u[2]^2 + u[3]^2 = 1 - u[1]^2 \geq 1 - (1 - 25^{-n})^2 > 25^{-n}. \tag{5.61}$$

Let k be the maximum value of the subscript such that $X_k \neq Y_k$. Denote $X_k = A$ and $Y_k = B$ without loss of generality. Suppose $v = X_{k-1} \cdots X_1 (1, 0, 0)^T$ and $w = Y_{k-1} \cdots Y_1 (1, 0, 0)^T$. Since $(1, 0, 0)^T \in K$, we have $Av, Bw \in K$ according to Lemma 5.3; we have $Av \neq Bw$ according to Lemma 5.4 (because there exists a contradiction between $Av = Bw$ and $Av, Bw \in K$). Since $X_j = Y_j$ for any $j > k$, we have

$$Y_n \cdots Y_1 (1, 0, 0)^T \neq X_n \cdots X_1 (1, 0, 0)^T, \tag{5.62}$$

and

$$u = Y_1^{-1} \cdots Y_n^{-1} X_n \cdots X_1 (1, 0, 0)^T \tag{5.63}$$

$$\neq (1, 0, 0)^T. \tag{5.64}$$

Similarly, $u \neq (-1, 0, 0)^T$ because of $(-1, 0, 0)^T \in K$. Consequently, we have

$$Y_n \cdots Y_1 (-1, 0, 0)^T \neq X_n \cdots X_1 (1, 0, 0)^T. \tag{5.65}$$

□

Lemma 5.6. *In the operational step* (I) *of* $\mathcal{M}$ *in Theorem 5.22, after scanning* x_n *and applying* U_{x_n}, *let the quantum state evolve to* $\sum_{i=0}^{2} \alpha_i |q_i\rangle$. *Then*

$$(\alpha_0, \alpha_1, \alpha_2)^T = U_{x_n} \cdots U_{x_1}(1, 0, 0)^T \tag{5.66}$$
$$= 5^{-n} X_n \cdots X_1(1, 0, 0)^T, \tag{5.67}$$

where $X_j \in \{A, B\}$ $(j = 1, 2, \cdots, n)$. *When* $x_j = a$, $X_j = A$; *when* $x_j = b$, $X_j = B$.

Lemma 5.7. *In the operational step* (II) *of* $\mathcal{M}$ *in Theorem 5.22, after scanning* x_n *and applying* U_{x_n}, *let the quantum state evolve to* $\sum_{i=0}^{2} \beta_i |q_i\rangle$. *Then*

$$(\beta_0, \beta_1, \beta_2)^T = U_{x_n}^{-1} U_{x_{n-1}}^{-1} \cdots U_{x_1}^{-1} U_{x_n} U_{x_{n-1}} \cdots U_{x_1}(1, 0, 0)^T. \tag{5.68}$$

The probability of rejecting is $P_{rej} = \beta_1^2 + \beta_2^2$, *where it satisfies: If* $x = x^R$, *then* $P_{rej} = 0$; *if* $x \neq x^R$, *then* $P_{rej} > \frac{1}{25^n}$.

Lemma 5.8. *In the operational step* (III) *of* $\mathcal{M}$ *in Theorem 5.22, after scanning* x_1, *the probability of* $b = 0$ *is* $P_{acc} = \frac{1}{2^{k(n+1)}}$.

Lemma 5.9. *After the continuous operation of* $\mathcal{M}$, *the probabilities of rejecting and accepting will be*

$$\sum_{j \geq 0} (1 - P_{acc})^j (1 - P_{rej})^j P_{rej} = \frac{P_{rej}}{P_{acc} + P_{rej} - P_{acc} P_{rej}}, \tag{5.69}$$

$$\sum_{j \geq 0} (1 - P_{acc})^j (1 - P_{rej})^{j+1} P_{acc} = \frac{P_{acc} - P_{acc} P_{rej}}{P_{acc} + P_{rej} - P_{acc} P_{rej}}, \tag{5.70}$$

respectively.

Proof. We can prove the lemma according to the operational steps (I), (II), and (III) of $\mathcal{M}$. □

According to the previous lemma, when $x = x^R$, $p_{rej} = 0$, the probability of accepting is 1; when $x \neq x^R$, combining

$$\frac{P_{rej}}{P_{acc} + P_{rej} - P_{acc} P_{rej}} > 1 - \epsilon, \tag{5.71}$$

$$P_{acc} = \frac{1}{2^{k(n+1)}}, \tag{5.72}$$

and

$$P_{rej} > \frac{1}{25^n}, \tag{5.73}$$

we know that the probability of rejecting is larger than $1 - \epsilon$ when $k \geq \max\{-\log \epsilon, \log 25\}$.

2QCFA can also recognize $L_{eq} = \{a^n b^n \mid n \in \mathbb{N}\}$.

Theorem 5.23. *For any $\epsilon > 0$, there exists a 2QCFA $\mathcal{M}$ recognizing $\{a^n b^n \mid n \in \mathbb{N}\}$ with one-side error ϵ, and the expected time complexity of $\mathcal{M}$ halting is $O(|x|^4)$.*

First, we illustrate the operational process of $\mathcal{M}$, and we can construct $\mathcal{M}$ according to the process of the algorithm.

For any input $x = x_1 x_2 \cdots x_n \in \{a, b\}^*$, $\mathcal{M}$ has the following computational process.

$\mathcal{M}$ first checks whether x is in the form of $a^* b^*$, if it does not satisfy, then the string is rejected; otherwise, it repeats the following process:

(I) The tape head moves to x_1, with the quantum state $|q_0\rangle$. If tape head points to a, then we apply a unitary transformation U_α to the quantum state (rotate α); if the tape head points to b, then we apply a unitary transformation $U_{-\alpha}$ to the quantum state. Next, the tape head moves to the next square on the right. After scanning x_n and applying an unitary transformation to the quantum state, if the measurement result is not $|q_0\rangle$, then $\mathcal{M}$ rejects x; otherwise, $\mathcal{M}$ performs step (II).

(II) Perform the following steps twice:
move the tape head to the first input symbol x_1, and repeatedly perform step (III).

(III) If the tape head does not point to ¢ or \$, then $\mathcal{M}$ performs the following operations:
Flip a coin, if it faces up, the tape head moves to the right; otherwise, the tape head moves to the left.

If both cases of the previous process finish with the tape heads pointing to \$, then flip a coin k times. If all results face up, then machine $\mathcal{M}$ accepts x.

Now we briefly illustrate the proof of the previous theorem and provide a detailed proof.

We consider a 2QCFA $\mathcal{M}$ with two quantum basic states $|q_0\rangle$ and $|q_1\rangle$. $|q_0\rangle$ is the initial quantum state of $\mathcal{M}$. When $\mathcal{M}$ scans a, the quantum state is rotated with $\alpha = \sqrt{2}\pi$. When $\mathcal{M}$ scans b, the quantum state is rotated with $-\alpha$. When the tape head of $\mathcal{M}$ finishes scanning the last symbol, we will perform a measurement to the quantum state. If the result is $|q_1\rangle$, then the input string is rejected; otherwise, $\mathcal{M}$ repeats the earlier processes.

If the number of a is equal to the number of b, then $|q_0\rangle$ can be finally obtained; otherwise, the final state is the superposition of $|q_0\rangle$ and $|q_1\rangle$. Additionally, the amplitude of $|q_1\rangle$ is sufficiently large. Therefore we can obtain q_1 with high probability after repeating the previous process multi-times. In fact, repeating $O(n^2)$ times can ensure to obtain q_1 at least once with high probability.

We also need to consider the halting problem of $\mathcal{M}$ for the input $x \in \{a^n b^{n'} \mid n, n' \in N\}$. We periodically execute a subroutine that accepts the input with a small probability $\frac{c}{n^2}$. If $x \notin L_{eq}$, then the accepting probability has almost no impact on the whole process (since the probability is much smaller than the probability of obtaining q_1 after measurement).

Lemma 5.10. *If input is $x = a^n b^{n'}$ with $n \neq n'$, then the probability of $\mathcal{M}$ rejecting input string after operational step (I) is at least $\frac{1}{2(n-n')^2}$.*

Proof. According to

$$U_a = \begin{bmatrix} \cos\sqrt{2}\pi & -\sin\sqrt{2}\pi \\ \sin\sqrt{2}\pi & \cos\sqrt{2}\pi \end{bmatrix}, \tag{5.74}$$

and

$$U_b = \begin{bmatrix} \cos(-\sqrt{2}\pi) & -\sin(-\sqrt{2}\pi) \\ \sin(-\sqrt{2}\pi) & \cos(-\sqrt{2}\pi) \end{bmatrix}, \tag{5.75}$$

we know that after the machine scanning input $a^n b^{n'}$, the initial state $|q_0\rangle$ will evolve to superposition state $\cos(\sqrt{2}(n-n')\pi)|q_0\rangle + \sin(\sqrt{2}(n-n')\pi)|q_1\rangle$. The probability of obtaining $|q_1\rangle$ is $\sin^2(\sqrt{2}(n-n')\pi)$.

Suppose k is the integer closest to $\sqrt{2}(n-n')$ and let $\sqrt{2}(n-n') > k$ (the other case is symmetrical). Then

$$k \leq \sqrt{2(n-n')^2 - 1}$$

and

$$\sqrt{2}(n-n') - k > \frac{1}{2\sqrt{2}(n-n')}.$$

Since

$$0 < \sqrt{2}(n - n') - k < \frac{1}{2},$$

and

$$\sin(\pi x) \geq 2x$$

for any $x \in [0, \frac{1}{2}]$, we have

$$\begin{aligned} \sin^2(\sqrt{2}(n - n')\pi) &= \sin^2((\sqrt{2}(n - n') - k)\pi) & (5.76)\\ &\geq 4(\sqrt{2}(n - n') - k)^2 & (5.77)\\ &\geq 4\left(\frac{1}{2\sqrt{2}(n - n')}\right)^2 & (5.78)\\ &= \frac{1}{2(n - n')^2}. & (5.79) \end{aligned}$$

□

Lemma 5.11. *The probability of $\mathcal{M}$ accepting the input after executing step* (II) *is* $\frac{1}{2^k(n + n' + 1)^2}$ *(the proof is left as an exercise).*

Lastly, we complete the proof of Theorem 5.23 as follows.

Proof. First, the probability of rejecting after performing step (II) each time is $\frac{1}{2^k(n + n' + 1)^2}$. In the step (III), we set $k = 1 + \lceil \log \epsilon^{-1} \rceil$. If $x = a^n b^n$, then we always obtain $|q_0\rangle$ after the step (I). After executing step (II) cn^2 times the probability of $\mathcal{M}$ accepting input string will be

$$1 - \left(1 - \frac{1}{2^k(n + n' + 1)^2}\right)^{cn^2}. \tag{5.80}$$

If $x = a^n b^{n'}$ with $n \neq n'$, then the probability of $\mathcal{M}$ rejecting the input string after step (I) is

$$P_{rej} > \frac{1}{2(n - n')^2}, \tag{5.81}$$

and the probability of rejecting after step (II) is

$$P_{acc} = \frac{1}{2^k(n + n' + 1)^2} \tag{5.82}$$

$$\leq \frac{\epsilon}{2(n+n'+1)^2}. \tag{5.83}$$

Due to the repeated execution of the algorithm the final rejecting probability is

$$\sum_{k\geq 0}(1-\mathrm{P}_{acc})^k(1-\mathrm{P}_{rej})^k\mathrm{P}_{rej} = \frac{\mathrm{P}_{rej}}{\mathrm{P}_{acc}+\mathrm{P}_{rej}-\mathrm{P}_{acc}\mathrm{P}_{rej}} \tag{5.84}$$

$$> \frac{\mathrm{P}_{rej}}{\mathrm{P}_{acc}+\mathrm{P}_{rej}} \tag{5.85}$$

$$> \frac{\frac{1}{2}}{\frac{1}{2}+\frac{\epsilon}{2}} \tag{5.86}$$

$$= \frac{1}{1+\epsilon} \tag{5.87}$$

$$> 1-\epsilon. \tag{5.88}$$

In the following, we analyze the time complexity of $\mathcal{M}$: After each conclusion of step (I) and step (II) the probability of accepting or rejecting is at least $\frac{c}{(n+n')^2}$. Therefore for the previous two cases ($x = a^n b^n$ or $x = a^n b^{n'}$ $(n \neq n')$), the expected number of iterations for $\mathcal{M}$ is $O((n+n')^2)$. Additionally, the time complexities of step (I) and step (II) are $O((n+n'))$ and $O((n+n')^2)$, respectively. Therefore the expected executive time of $\mathcal{M}$ is at most $O((n+n')^4)$. □

With certain computational abilities, 2QCFA can simulate arbitrary query algorithms (the definition of query algorithms can be learned from the section of quantum query model).

Theorem 5.24. *The computation of a query algorithm $\mathcal{A}$ for a Boolean function $f: \{0,1\}^n \to \{0,1\}$ can be simulated by a 2QCFA $\mathcal{M}$. Furthermore, if $\mathcal{A}$ uses t queries and l quantum basis states, then $\mathcal{M}$ needs $O(l)$ quantum basis states as well as $O(n^2)$ classical states, and the time complexity of $\mathcal{M}$ is $O(tn)$.*

Proof. Denote O_x as the query operator in $\mathcal{A}$, let U_k $(k = 0, 1, \cdots, t)$ be the unitary operators, and denote $\{M_0, M_1\}$ as the measurement operators. Then the idea of $\mathcal{M}$ simulating is given as follows. The input of $\mathcal{M}$ is same as the input of $\mathcal{A}$, whose tape is ¢x\$ with $x = x_1 \cdots x_n$. The quantum basis states of $\mathcal{M}$ are $|0\rangle$ and $|i, b, w\rangle$ $(i = 0, 1, \cdots, n)$. The classical states are $s_{k,i}$ (k represents the k-th scanning, and i denotes that the tape head is located in the i-th square, where ¢ is the 0-th square). The initial quantum state of

$\mathcal{M}$ is $|0\rangle$ and the initial classical state is s_0. When $\mathcal{M}$ first scans symbol $¢$, we apply $\Theta(s_0, ¢)$, that is, $\Theta(s_0, ¢)|0\rangle = U_0|\psi_s\rangle$. Here, $|\psi_s\rangle$ is the initial state of $\mathcal{A}$ and the transformation of classical states as well as the moving of tape head are $\delta(s_0, ¢) = (s_{1,1}, 1)$.

$\mathcal{M}$ will scan $¢x\$$ from the left to the right t times. During the k-th scanning ($k < t$), if it scans symbol \$, then it applies $\Theta(s_{k,n+1}, \$) = U_k$ to the quantum state while keeping the classical state unchanged, and the tape head moves to the left. The moving will continue until the tape head goes back to $¢$ and $\mathcal{M}$ will start the $k+1$-th time's scanning. In other words, $\delta(s_{k,n+1}, \sigma) = (s_{k,n+1}, -1)$ $(\sigma \in \{0, 1\})$, $\delta(s_{k,n+1}, ¢) = (s_{k+1,1}, 1)$. If it scans $\sigma = 0$ or 1, then it applies

$$\Theta(s_{k,i}, \sigma)|i, b, w\rangle = |i, b \oplus \sigma, w\rangle, \Theta(s_{k,i}, \sigma)|u, b, w\rangle = |u, b, w\rangle, \;\; u \neq i,$$

and moves to the right, that is, $\delta(s_{k,i}, \sigma) = (s_{k,i+1}, 1)$. During the t-th time's scanning, if it scans \$, then it applies U_t and measures the quantum state with $\{M_0, M_1\}$. Finally, $\mathcal{M}$ will reject the input if the outcome is 0; otherwise, it will accept the input.

We can prove that

$$\Theta(s_{k,n}, x_n)\Theta(s_{k,n-1}, x_{n-1}) \cdots \Theta(s_{k,1}, x_1) = O_x. \tag{5.89}$$

Therefore for any input x, it is clear that the probability of $\mathcal{A}(x) = 1$ is equal to the probability of $\mathcal{M}$ accepting x and the probability of $\mathcal{A}(x) = 0$ is equal to the probability of $\mathcal{M}$ rejecting x. Also, $\mathcal{M}$ has $O(l)$ quantum basis states, $O(n^2)$ classical states and has performed $O(tn)$ steps. □

Exercises

5.13. For X_i defined in Lemma 5.6, prove: $U_{x_n}^{-1}U_{x_{n-1}}^{-1} \cdots U_{x_1}^{-1}U_{x_n}U_{x_{n-1}} \cdots U_{x_1}(1, 0, 0)^T = X_n^{-1}X_{n-1}^{-1} \cdots X_1^{-1}X_nX_{n-1} \cdots X_1(1, 0, 0)^T$.

5.14. Compute the time complexity of 2QCFA recognizing the palindromic language in Theorem 5.22.

5.15. According to this section, give a 2QCFA that recognizes $L_{pal} = \{x \mid x = x^R, x \in \{a, b\}^*\}$ with one-side error.

5.16. According to this section, give a 2QCFA that recognizes $L_{eq} = \{a^nb^n \mid n \in \mathbb{N}\}$ with one-side error.

5.17. Prove: In Theorem 5.23, the probability of 2QCFA (that recognizes language $L_{eq} = \{a^nb^n \mid n \in \mathbb{N}\}$) accepting input string at the (II)-th step is $\dfrac{1}{2^k(n + n' + 1)^2}$.

5.4 Quantum pushdown automata

Similar to classical pushdown automata, there are also quantum pushdown automata in quantum computing models. Quantum pushdown automata were first studied by Golovkins [25], Gudder [26], Qiu [27], and Nakanish [28]. These different definitions of quantum pushdown automata are is a little complicated. Let us first review the classical pushdown automata (PDA).

Definition 5.16. A classical pushdown automaton is a seven-tuple

$$\mathcal{A} = (Q, \Sigma, \Gamma, \delta, q_0, Z_0, F),$$

where

- Q is a finite set of states;
- Σ is a finite input alphabet;
- Γ is a finite stack alphabet;
- $q_0 \in Q$ is the initial state;
- $Z_0 \in \Gamma$ is the initial symbol of stack;
- $F \subseteq Q$ is a set of accepting states;
- $\delta : Q \times (\Sigma \cup \{\epsilon\}) \times \Gamma \to \mathcal{P}(Q \times \Gamma^*)$ is the transition function, where $\mathcal{P}(X)$ denotes the power set of X.

The initial state of PDA is q_0, and Z_0 is the initial symbol in the stack. Suppose PDA is located on the state q at a certain moment and the symbol at the top of stack is Z. Then, for any $(p, \gamma) \in \delta(q, a, Z)$ with $\gamma \in \Gamma^*$, PDA will transform to state p and the symbol at the top of the stack will be replaced by a string γ (there may have more than one possible value of (p, γ), which reflects the non-determinism of PDA) according to the input symbol a (a can be ϵ, which represents the machine does not scan the symbol in the input string). Let w be the input. If w is represented as $w = w_1 w_2 \cdots w_m$, where $w_i \in \Sigma \cup \{\epsilon\}$, and after sequentially scanning $w_1 w_2 \cdots w_m$, there exists a branch (due to the non-determinism of the PDA) such that it eventually obtains an accepting state, then PDA accepts the string. The class of languages recognized by PDA is identical to the class of context-free languages (CFL). As we know, the class of regular languages is a proper subset of the class of CFL.

Example 5.6. Here is a PDA that recognizes $\{0^n 1^n \mid n \geq 1\}$:

$$\mathcal{A} = (Q = \{q_0, q_1, q_2\}, \Sigma = \{0, 1\}, \Gamma = \{0, 1, Z_0\}, \delta, q_0, Z_0, F = \{q_2\}),$$

where δ is defined as

$$\delta(q_0, 0, \gamma) = \{(q_0, 0\gamma)\}, \gamma \in \Gamma, \tag{5.90}$$

$$\delta(q_0, 1, 0) = \delta(q_1, 1, 0) = \{(q_1, \epsilon)\}, \tag{5.91}$$

$$\delta(q_1, \epsilon, Z_0) = \{(q_2, \epsilon)\}. \tag{5.92}$$

If $\mathcal{A}$ locates on an undefined part, then it will reject the input string.

The operational process of $\mathcal{A}$ is given as follows. When the state is q_0, if 0 is scanned, $\mathcal{A}$ replaces the symbol γ on the top of the stack with 0γ, which is equivalent to pushing 0 into the stack; if 1 is scanned, it transforms to state q_1 and pops 0 (on the top of the stack) out of the stack. When the state is q_1, if the input symbol 1 is scanned, then the machine pops 0 (on the top of the stack) out of the stack. Finally, if the symbol on the top of the stack is Z_0, then the machine transforms to the accepting state q_2. To sum up, $\mathcal{A}$ can recognize the language $\{0^n1^n \mid n \geq 1\}$.

There are different versions of definitions for quantum pushdown automata. We first introduce one of them [29].

Definition 5.17. A q quantum pushdown automaton (qQPDA) is a six-tuple $\mathscr{A} = (Q, \Sigma, \Gamma, \delta, S, Q_f)$, where

- Q is a finite set of states;
- Σ is a finite alphabet;
- Γ is a finite stack alphabet;
- $S = \{(p_i, \alpha_i, c_i) \mid p_i \in Q, \alpha_i \in \Gamma^*, c_i \in \mathbb{C}, i = 1, \cdots, k\}$;
- $Q_f \subseteq Q$ is the final state;
- δ is a mapping from $Q \times \Gamma^* \times \Sigma \times Q \times \Gamma^*$ to $\mathbb{C}$ and it satisfies the following conditions: For any $\sigma \in \Sigma$ and any $(p_1, \gamma_1), (p_2, \gamma_2) \in Q \times \Gamma^*$,

  (I) $\delta(p_1, \gamma_1, \sigma, p_2, \gamma_2)$ is nonzero only if there exists a $t \in \Gamma$ such that $t\gamma_1 = \gamma_2$ or $\gamma_1 = t\gamma_2$ or $\gamma_1 = \gamma_2$.

  (II) $$\sum_{q \in Q, \gamma \in \Gamma^*} \delta(p_1, \gamma_1, \sigma, q, \gamma)\delta(p_2, \gamma_2, \sigma, q, \gamma)^* = \begin{cases} 1, & (p_1, \gamma_1) = (p_2, \gamma_2), \\ 0, & \text{else.} \end{cases}$$

  (III) $$\sum_{p \in Q, \gamma \in \Gamma^*} \delta(p, \gamma, \sigma, p_1, \gamma_1)\delta(p, \gamma, \sigma, p_2, \gamma_2)^* = \begin{cases} 1, & (p_1, \gamma_1) = (p_2, \gamma_2), \\ 0, & \text{else.} \end{cases}$$

Definition 5.18. The probability that qQPDA $\mathscr{A}$ accepts input string w is

$$f_{\mathscr{A}}(w) = \begin{cases} \sum_{q_n \in Q_f, \gamma_n \in \Gamma^*} \left| \sum_{(p_i,\alpha_i,c_i)\in S} c_i \sum_{q_1,\cdots,q_{n-1}\in Q, \gamma_1,\cdots,\gamma_{n-1}\in\Gamma^*} \delta(p_i,\alpha_i,\sigma_1,q_1,\gamma_1) \times \delta(q_1,\gamma_1,\sigma_2,q_2,\gamma_1) \times \cdots \times \delta(q_{n-1},\gamma_{n-1},\sigma_n,q_n,\gamma_n) \right|^2, & w \in \Sigma^* \backslash \{\epsilon\}, \\ \sum_{i\in S_f} |c_i|^2, & w = \epsilon, \end{cases}$$

where $S_f = \{i \mid (p_i, \alpha_i, c_i) \in S, p_i \in Q_f\}$. Additionally, if $S_f = \varnothing$, then $f_{\mathscr{A}} = 0$.

Remark 5.11. According to the condition (II) in Definition 5.17, $f_{\mathscr{A}}(w) \in [0, 1]$ for any $w \in \Sigma^*$.

Furthermore, we define quantum pushdown automata equivalent to the qQPDA based on the work of Moore and Crutchfield [1].

Definition 5.19. A quantum pushdown automaton (QPDA) is a five-tuple

$$\mathcal{M} = (H_Q \otimes H_\Gamma, \Sigma, |S_{init}\rangle, U, H_{accept}),$$

where

- H_Q is a finite-dimensional Hilbert space with the orthonormal basis Q;
- H_Γ is an infinite-dimensional Hilbert space with the orthonormal basis equivalent to Γ^*;
- Σ is the input alphabet;
- $|S_{init}\rangle \in H_Q \otimes H_\Gamma$ is the initial unit vector;
- $H_{accept} = \text{span}\{|q\rangle \otimes |\gamma\rangle \mid q \in Q_{accept}, \gamma \in \Gamma^*\}$, where $Q_{accept} \subseteq Q$;
- $U : \Sigma \cup \{\epsilon\} \to \mathscr{U}(H_Q \otimes H_\Gamma)$ satisfies: For any $\sigma \in \Sigma$, any $(q_1, \gamma_1), (q_2, \gamma_2) \in Q \times \Gamma^*$, the transition amplitude $\langle q_2|\langle\gamma_2|U(\sigma)|q_1\rangle|\gamma_1\rangle$ is nonzero only if there exists $t \in \Gamma$ such that $t\gamma_1 = \gamma_2$ or $\gamma_1 = t\gamma_2$ or $\gamma_1 = \gamma_2$, where $\mathscr{U}(H_Q \otimes H_\Gamma)$ represents the space spanned by the unitary operators acting on $H_Q \otimes H_\Gamma$.

The probability of $\mathcal{M}$ accepting string w is

$$f_{\mathcal{M}}(w) = ||P(H_{accept})U(w)|S_{init}\rangle||^2,$$

where $P(H_{accept})$ is the projector that projects states onto the space generated by H_{accept}. The language recognized by $\mathcal{M}$ is defined as $\{w \in \Sigma^* \mid f_{\mathcal{M}}(w) > 0\}$.

Remark 5.12. In the previous definition, if we take $H_{accept} = \text{span}\{|q\rangle \otimes |\epsilon\rangle \mid q \in Q_{accept}\}$, then $\mathcal{M}$ corresponds to the MO-QPDA defined by Moore and Crutchfield [1]. If the definition of MO-QPDA does not require all transformations to be unitary, it is referred to as a generalized MO-QPDA. The relationship between the language recognition abilities of MO-QPDA and classical PDA is still not fully understood.

Theorem 5.25. *QPDA and qQPDA are equivalent, that is,*

- *For any* QPDA $\mathcal{M} = (H_Q \otimes H_\Gamma, \Sigma, |S_{init}\rangle, U, H_{accept})$, *there exists a* qQPDA $\mathscr{A}$ *such that for any* $w \in \Sigma^*$, *then we have* $f_{\mathscr{A}}(w) = f_{\mathcal{M}}(w)$.
- *For any* qQPDA $\mathscr{A} = (Q, \Sigma, \Gamma, \delta, S, Q_f)$, *there exists a* QPDA $\mathcal{M}$ *such that for any* $w \in \Sigma^*$, *then we have* $f_{\mathscr{A}}(w) = f_{\mathcal{M}}(w)$.

5.5 Quantum grammars

Quantum grammars are closely related to quantum pushdown automata. We will first introduce classical context-free grammars and regular grammars, and then proceed to quantum regular grammars and quantum context-free grammars.

5.5.1 Context-free grammars and regular grammars

We begin by presenting the definition of classical context-free grammars (CFG).

Definition 5.20. A context-free grammar can be represented as a four-tuple

$$G = (V, \Sigma, S, P),$$

where

- V is a finite set of variables;
- Σ is a finite set of terminal symbols;
- $S \in V$ is the start variable;
- $P \subseteq \{A \to \beta \mid A \in V, \beta \in (V \cup \Sigma)^*\}$ is a finite set of productions.

$\alpha, \beta \in (V \cup \Sigma)^*$, a derivation chain $\alpha \overset{*}{\Rightarrow} \beta$ is a sequence of strings of the form $\alpha \Rightarrow \alpha_1 \Rightarrow \cdots \Rightarrow \beta$ ($\alpha_i \in (V \cup \Sigma)^*$), where each step replaces a variable with a substring according to a production rule. For example, given the production rules $\{A \to 0A, A \to 1\}$, the sequence $0AA \Rightarrow 00AA \Rightarrow 001A$ is a derivation chain for $0AA \overset{*}{\Rightarrow} 001A$. The language generated by a CFG G is defined as $L(G) = \{w \in \Sigma^* \mid S \overset{*}{\Rightarrow} w\}$, and the set of all languages generated by CFG is called the set of context-free languages (CFL).

Example 5.7. The language $\{0^n1^n \mid n \geq 0\}$ can be generated by the context-free grammar $(V=\{S\}, \Sigma=\{0,1\}, S, P=\{S \to 0S1, S \to \epsilon\})$.

A regular grammar is a special form of context-free grammar that can generate regular languages.

Definition 5.21. A context-free grammar $G=(V,\Sigma,S,P)$ is called a regular grammar if all productions are in the form $A \to aB$ or $A \to \epsilon$ $(A, B \in V, a \in \Sigma)$.

In fact, regular grammars are closely related to non-deterministic finite automata (NFA). NFA and DFA are equivalent, except that in an NFA, each state can transfer to multiple states after reading a character, and whether the input string is accepted depends on whether there is a branch that reaches an accepting state. The class of languages recognized by NFA is called the set of regular languages.

A regular grammar can be seen as an equivalent definition of an NFA: each variable in the regular grammar corresponds to a state, and the transition function is defined as $\delta(A, a) = \{B \mid A \to aB \in P\}$, with the accepting set being $\{A \mid A \to \epsilon \in P\}$. Conversely, a DFA or NFA can also be described by a corresponding regular grammar. Therefore the class of languages generated by regular grammar is the regular language.

5.5.2 Quantum regular grammars

Similarly, we can define quantum regular grammars.

Definition 5.22. A quantum regular grammar can be represented as a four-tuple

$$G=(V,\Sigma,V_0,P),$$

where

- V is a finite set of variables;
- Σ is a finite set of terminal symbols;
- $V_0=\{(v_i,c_i) \mid v_i \in V, c_i \in \mathbb{C}, i=1,2,\cdots,k\}$, where $\sum_{i=1}^{k}|c_i|^2=1$;
- $P \subseteq \{v \to \beta \mid v \in V, \beta \in (V \cup \Sigma)^*\}$ is a finite set of productions, where each production $v \to \beta$ has an amplitude $c(v \to \beta)$, and only productions of the form $v \to \sigma u$ or $v \to \epsilon$ $(v, u \in V, \sigma \in \Sigma)$ have nonzero amplitudes. Additionally, $c(v \to \epsilon) \in \{0,1\}$ and c satisfies

$$\sum_{u \in V} c(v \to au)c(v' \to au)^* = \begin{cases} 1, & \text{if } v=v', \\ 0, & \text{if } v \neq v'. \end{cases} \tag{5.93}$$

Next, we define the languages generated by a quantum regular grammars. Suppose $w = \sigma_1\sigma_2 \cdots \sigma_m \in \Sigma^*$, then the sequence

$$v_i, \sigma_1 v^{(1)}, \sigma_1\sigma_2 v^{(2)}, \cdots, \sigma_1\sigma_2\cdots\sigma_m v^{(m)}, \sigma_1\sigma_2\cdots\sigma_m$$

is called a derivation of w, where v_i comes from V_0, and $v^{(j)} \in V$, $j = 1, 2, \cdots, m$. Since the last step uses the production $v^{(m)} \to \epsilon$, we call it a $v^{(m)}$-type derivation of w and define its amplitude as $c(v_i \to \sigma_1 v^{(1)})c(v^{(1)} \to \sigma_2 v^{(2)}) \cdots c(v^{(m)} \to \epsilon)$. Denote $c_{v^{(m)}}(w)$ as the sum of the amplitudes of all $v^{(m)}$-type derivations of w, that is,

$$c_{v^{(m)}}(w) = \sum_{i=1}^{k} c_i \sum_{v^{(1)},\cdots,v^{(m-1)} \in V} c(v_i \to \sigma_1 v^{(1)})c(v^{(1)} \to \sigma_2 v^{(2)}) \cdots c(v^{(m)} \to \epsilon). \tag{5.94}$$

The acceptance probability of w, denoted as $f_G(w)$, is defined as

$$f_G(w) = \sum_{c(v \to \epsilon)=1} |c_v(w)|^2. \tag{5.95}$$

Just as the language generated by a classical regular grammar is equivalent to the language recognized by a DFA, quantum regular grammars have a similar relationship with MO-1QFA.

Theorem 5.26. *For any quantum regular grammar G, there exists an* MO-1QFA $\mathcal{A}$ *such that for any* $w \in \Sigma^*$, *the acceptance probability of* w *by* $\mathcal{A}$ *is equal to* $f_G(w)$. *Conversely, for any* MO-1QFA $\mathcal{A}$, *there exists a quantum regular grammar* G *such that for any* $w \in \Sigma^*$, *the acceptance probability of* w *by* $\mathcal{A}$ *is equal to* $f_G(w)$.

Proof. Let $(Q, \Sigma, \delta, q_0, F)$ be an MO-1QFA. First, it should be noted that although in the definition of MO-1QFA, $q_0 \in Q$ is required, the capability of MO-1QFA does not change if we relax this requirement to allow q_0 to be a quantum superposition state. In this case, there exists a new set of vectors Q' such that a new $q_0' \in Q'$ as the initial state, and we can easily show that $(Q', \Sigma, \delta', q_0', F)$ is also an MO-1QFA equivalent to $(Q, \Sigma, \delta, q_0, F)$ by means of appropriately defining it. We will use this definition of MO-1QFA with an initial state being a quantum superposition.

Given a quantum regular grammar $G = (V, \Sigma, V_0, P)$, we construct an "equivalent" MO-1QFA $\mathcal{A} = (Q, \Sigma, \delta, q_0, F)$, where $Q = \{|v\rangle \mid v \in V\}$, $|q_0\rangle = \sum_{(v_i,c_i)} c_i|v_i\rangle$, for any $|v_1\rangle, |v_2\rangle \in Q$, $\sigma \in \Sigma$, $\delta(v_1, \sigma, v_2) = c(v_1 \to \sigma v_2)$, and $F = \{v \mid c(v \to \epsilon) = 1\}$. By the definition of MO-1QFA, for any $w = \sigma_1\sigma_2\cdots\sigma_m \in \Sigma^*$, the acceptance probability of w by $\mathcal{A}$ is

$$||P_{acc}U(\sigma_m)U(\sigma_{m-1})\cdots U(\sigma_1)|q_0\rangle||^2 \tag{5.96}$$

$$= \sum_{v^{(m)}\in F}\left|\sum_{i=1}^{k} c_i \sum_{v^{(1)},\cdots,v^{(m-1)}\in V} \delta(v_i,\sigma_1,v^{(1)})\delta(v^{(1)},\sigma_2,v^{(2)})\cdots\delta(v^{(m-1)},\sigma_m,v^{(m)})\right|^2 \tag{5.97}$$

$$= \sum_{c(v^{(m)}\to\epsilon)=1}\left|\sum_{i=1}^{k} c_i \sum_{v^{(1)},\cdots,v^{(m-1)}\in V} c(v_i\to\sigma_1 v^{(1)})c(v^{(1)}\to\sigma_2 v^{(2)})\cdots c(v^{(m)}\to\epsilon)\right|^2 \tag{5.98}$$

$$= \sum_{c(v^{(m)}\to\epsilon)=1} |c_{v^{(m)}}(w)|^2 \tag{5.99}$$

$$= f_G(w). \tag{5.100}$$

Therefore the acceptance probability of w by $\mathcal{A}$ is $f_G(w)$. Similarly, given an MO-1QFA $\mathcal{A} = (Q, \Sigma, \delta, q_0, F)$, we can construct an "equivalent" quantum regular grammar. The proof is completed. □

5.5.3 * Quantum context-free grammars

Finally, we introduce quantum context-free grammars (QCFG).

Definition 5.23. [1] A quantum context-free grammar can be represented as a five-tuple

$$G = (V, \Sigma, S, P, \{c_i \mid 1 \le i \le n\}),$$

where

- V is a finite set of variables;
- Σ is a finite set of terminal symbols;
- $S \in V$ is the start variable;
- $P \subseteq \{A \to \beta \mid A \in V, \beta \in (V \cup \Sigma)^*\}$ is a finite set of productions;
- For any $A \to \beta \in P$, there are n amplitudes $c_k(A \to \beta) \in \mathbb{C}$, $1 \le k \le n$, where n is the dimension of the grammar.

For any $\alpha, \beta \in (V \cup \Sigma)^*$, we define the k amplitudes of a derivation chain that derives $\alpha \overset{*}{\Rightarrow} \beta$ to be c_k, whose value is the product of the k-th amplitude of the production used at each step in the chain. Define $c_k(\alpha \overset{*}{\Rightarrow} \beta)$ as the sum of the k-th amplitude of all derivation chains from α to β. The k-th amplitude of a string $w \in \Sigma^*$ is defined as $c_k(w) = c_k(S \overset{*}{\Rightarrow} w)$, and we denote $f_G(w) = \sum_{k=1}^{n} |c_k(w)|^2$. The language generated by G is defined as $L(G) = \{w \in \Sigma^* \mid f_G(w) > 0\}$.

The set of all languages generated by QCFGs is called quantum context-free languages (QCFL). The class of languages recognized by generalized MO-QPDA is the same as QCFL [29]. Furthermore, we know that QCFL $\neq$ CFL, as the language $L = \{a^i b^j c^k \mid i = j \text{ or } j = k, \text{ and } i = j = k \text{ does not hold}\} \in$ QCFL but $L \notin$ CFL [29].

Theorem 5.27. [29] *For any* QCFG G, *there exists generalized* MO-QPDA $\mathcal{M}$ *such that for any* $w \in \Sigma^*$, $f_{\mathcal{M}}(w) = f_G(w)$. *Conversely, for any generalized* MO-QPDA $\mathcal{M}$, *there exists* QCFG G *such that for any* $w \in \Sigma^*$, $f_G(w) = f_{\mathcal{M}}(w)$.

The QCFG that satisfies certain conditions can be transformed into a QCFG that satisfies the Greibach normal form.

Definition 5.24. A QCFG $G = (V, \Sigma, S, P, \{c_i \mid 1 \leq i \leq n\})$ is said to satisfy the Greibach normal form if only the productions of form $v \rightarrow a\gamma$ ($v \in V$, $a \in \Sigma$, $\gamma \in V^*$) have nonzero amplitudes.

Definition 5.25. A QCFG $G = (V, \Sigma, S, P, \{c_i \mid 1 \leq i \leq n\})$ is said to be terminating if all infinite derivation trees (i.e., infinite derivation chains of the form $S \Rightarrow \alpha_1 \Rightarrow \cdots \Rightarrow \alpha_m \Rightarrow \cdots$) have amplitude 0.

Theorem 5.28. *For any terminating* QCFG G_1, *there exists a* QCFG G_2 *that satisfies the* Greibach *normal form such that for any* $w \in \Sigma^*$, $f_{G_1}(w) = f_{G_2}(w)$.

Exercises

5.18. Prove that the language $\{xy \mid x, y \in \{0, 1\}^*, |x| = |y| \text{ and } x \neq y^R\}$ is a context-free language ($|x|$ denotes the length of x, y^R denotes the reverse of y).

5.19. Given any DFA $\mathcal{A}$, construct a regular grammar G such that $L(G)$ is the language recognized by $\mathcal{A}$.

5.20. Let L be the language over the alphabet $\{0\}$ such that $L = \{0^{3n} \mid n \in \mathbb{N}\}$. Provide a quantum regular grammar G that satisfies Definition 5.22 such that $\forall w \in L, f(w) = 1$, and $\forall w \notin L, f(w) = 0$.

Questions

5.21. How can QCFG be restricted to make it equivalent to MO-QPDA?

5.6 Quantum Turing machines

Since one theoretical model of modern computers is Turing machines, Turing machines are a core theory in the field of computation. Before introducing QTMs, let us first recall deterministic Turing machines.

Definition 5.26. A deterministic Turing machine is defined as a five-tuple

$$\mathcal{D} = (Q, \Sigma, \delta, q_0, q_f),$$

where

- Σ is a finite alphabet, with the blank symbol $B \in \Sigma$ representing an empty character;
- Q is a finite set of states, and $q_0 \in Q$ is the initial state;
- $q_f \in Q$ is the halting state ($q_0 \neq q_f$);
- $\delta : Q \times \Sigma \rightarrow \Sigma \times Q \times \{L, R\}$ is the transition function, where L and R represent moving left and right, respectively.

Next, we further introduce the configuration of deterministic Turing machines. A configuration contains the content of the tape, the position and the state of the head. Let $c \rightarrow_{\mathcal{M}} c'$ denote that the current configuration c becomes c' after one step of operation (i.e., according to the action defined by δ). Here, we assume the tape is two-way infinite.

The initial configuration is as follows: the head is at position 0, and the state is q_0, referred to as the start configuration. For the input $x = x_0x_1 \cdots x_n \in (\Sigma - \{B\})^*$, $x_0, x_1, \cdots, x_n$ are respectively at positions $0, 1, 2, \cdots, n$, and the rest are all blank. If $\mathcal{M}$ enters the accepting state q_f, then $\mathcal{M}$ halts. The runtime of $\mathcal{M}$ is defined as the number of steps $\mathcal{M}$ takes to enter q_f. If $\mathcal{M}$ halts, the output string is formed from the leftmost non-blank character to the rightmost non-blank character (if all are blank, the output is the empty string). If $\mathcal{M}$ halts for all input strings, it computes a function from $(\Sigma - B)^*$ to Σ^*.

The QTM is introduced as follows.

Definition 5.27. A QTM is defined as a seven-tuple

$$\mathcal{M} = (Q, \Sigma, \delta, B, q_0, q_a, q_r),$$

where

- Σ is a finite input alphabet;
- $B \in \Sigma$ is the blank symbol;

- Q is a finite set of states, with $\{q_0, q_a, q_r\} \subseteq Q$ (q_0, q_a, q_r are distinct and represent the initial, accepting, and rejecting states, respectively);
- δ is the quantum transition function: $\delta : Q \times \Sigma \times \Sigma \times Q \times \{L, R\} \to \mathbb{C}$.

A QTM has a two-way infinite tape with each cell labeled by an integer from $\mathbb{Z}$. A configuration of $\mathcal{M}$ is represented by $|q\rangle|\tau\rangle|i\rangle$, where q represents the current state, $\tau \in \Sigma^{\mathbb{Z}}$ represents the current string on the tape, and $i \in \mathbb{Z}$ represents the position of the head. A configuration containing the initial (or final) state is called an initial (or final) configuration.

The definition of a generalized QTM is similar to that of a QTM, except that the head movement direction is in $\{L, N, R\}$ (N represents the head staying stationarily).

Let $C_{\mathcal{M}}$ denote the set of all configurations of $\mathcal{M}$. Thus $\mathcal{H}_{C_{\mathcal{M}}} = l_2(C_{\mathcal{M}})$ is a Hilbert space with an orthonormal basis consisting of $C_{\mathcal{M}}$. The operator $U_{\mathcal{M}}$ on $l_2(C_{\mathcal{M}})$ can be defined by δ as follows:

$$\forall |c\rangle \in C_{\mathcal{M}}, \quad U_{\mathcal{M}}|c\rangle = \sum_{|c'\rangle \in C_{\mathcal{M}}} a(c, c')|c'\rangle, \tag{5.101}$$

where $a(c, c')$ is the amplitude for evolving from configuration c to c' determined by δ. The following theorem gives the necessary and sufficient condition for $U_{\mathcal{M}}$ to be a unitary operator on $l_2(C_{\mathcal{M}})$.

Theorem 5.29. *$U_{\mathcal{M}}$ is a unitary operator if and only if the following conditions are satisfied:*

(1) $\forall (p, \sigma) \in Q \times \Sigma$,
$\sum_{(\sigma', q, d) \in \Sigma \times Q \times \{R, L\}} |\delta(p, \sigma, \sigma', q, d)|^2 = 1.$

(2) $\forall (p_1, \sigma_1), (p_2, \sigma_2) \in Q \times \Sigma$, *with* $(p_1, \sigma_1) \neq (p_2, \sigma_2)$,
$\sum_{(\sigma, q, d) \in \Sigma \times Q \times \{R, L\}} \delta(p_1, \sigma_1, \sigma, q, d)^* \delta(p_2, \sigma_2, \sigma, q, d) = 0.$

(3) $\forall (p_1, \sigma_1, \sigma_1'), (p_2, \sigma_2, \sigma_2') \in Q \times \Sigma \times \Sigma$,
$\sum_{q \in Q} \delta(p_1, \sigma_1, \sigma_1', q, R)^* \delta(p_2, \sigma_2, \sigma_2', q, L) = 0.$

Example 5.8. Let $\mathcal{M} = (\Sigma = \{1\}, Q = \{q_0, q_1\}, \delta, B, q_0)$ be a QTM (ignoring the accepting and rejecting states), where

$$\begin{aligned}
\delta(q_0, B, 1, q_1, R) &= 1, \\
\delta(q_0, 1, 1, q_0, R) &= 1, \\
\delta(q_1, B, B, q_1, R) &= 1, \\
\delta(q_1, 1, B, q_0, R) &= 1,
\end{aligned}$$

and the undefined parts of δ are all 0. It can be verified that δ satisfies the conditions in Theorem 5.29.

Next, we define the runtime of QTMs.

Definition 5.28. For any input $x \in \Sigma^*$, if QTM $\mathcal{M}$ reaches a superposition of configurations containing at least one final configuration after T steps from the initial configurations, and no final configuration is present before T steps, then the runtime of $\mathcal{M}$ for x is T.

The QTMs are more complicated in definition compared with deterministic Turing machines, but they can simulate deterministic Turing machines since any deterministic Turing machine can be transformed into an equivalent reversible Turing machine [30], and reversible Turing machines can be simulated by QTMs.

Definition 5.29. Any reversible Turing machine is a deterministic Turing machine where each configuration c' has at most one predecessor configuration c that can directly lead to c'.

For example, the QTM defined in Example 5.8 can be considered as a deterministic Turing machine and is also a reversible Turing machine.

Theorem 5.30. *Any reversible Turing machine can be simulated by a* QTM.

Proof. The proof can be found in [31]. We can directly construct a QTM $\mathcal{M}$ with the same transition function as the reversible Turing machines. By the definition of reversible Turing machines, the operator $U_{\mathcal{M}}$ derived from the transition function of $\mathcal{M}$ is unitary (i.e., it satisfies Theorem 5.29). □

Given a Turing machine that can solve a particular problem, we might wonder: if there is a Turing machine capable of simulating any other Turing machine, can it solve all the problems that any Turing machine can solve? In fact, such a Turing machine is called a universal Turing machine, and both universal deterministic Turing machines and universal QTMs exist.

Definition 5.30. In full generality, for any input x, a QTM M produces a sample from a probability distribution over configurations. We say that a machine M' simulates M if for any input x, it allows an observer to sample from this distribution. Alternatively, we say that M' simulates M with accuracy ϵ if it allows an observer to sample from a distribution that is within ϵ total variation distance of this distribution.

Theorem 5.31. *There exists a QTM $\mathcal{M}$ such that for any QTM $\mathcal{M}'$, any $\epsilon > 0$, and any $T \in \mathbb{N}$, $\mathcal{M}$ can simulate $\mathcal{M}'$ within polynomial time concerning T and $\frac{1}{\epsilon}$ with an error no greater than ϵ.*

What problems can a Turing machine solve? What relationships do these problems have? These problems are some of the most fundamental questions in computer science. We present definitions and relationships in classical and quantum computing complexity classes.

Definition 5.31. The complexity classes P, BPP, PSPACE, EQP, and BQP are defined as follows:

- P: The class of languages recognized by deterministic Turing machines in polynomial time.
- BPP: The class of languages recognized by probabilistic Turing machines with bounded error in polynomial time.
- PSPACE: The class of languages recognized by a deterministic Turing machine using polynomial space.
- EQP: The class of languages recognized exactly by QTM in polynomial time.
- BQP: The class of languages recognized by QTM with bounded error in polynomial time.

In the following, we present the inclusion relationships and a diagram illustrating these relationships (Fig. 5.5).

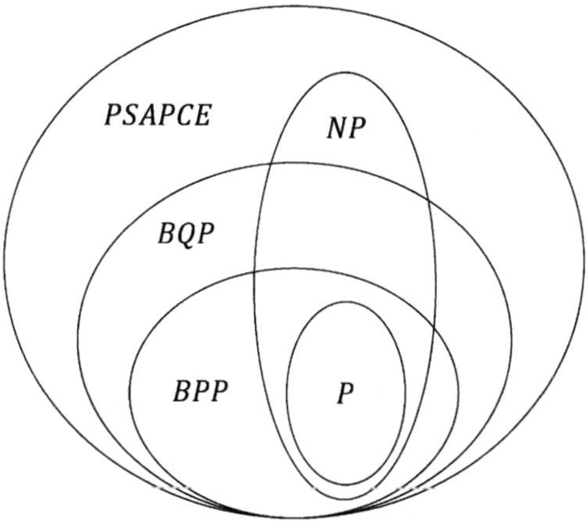

Figure 5.5 Relationships between computational complexity classes.

Theorem 5.32.

$$1.\quad \mathrm{P} \subseteq \mathrm{EQP}. \tag{5.102}$$

$$2.\quad \mathrm{P} \subseteq \mathrm{BPP} \subseteq \mathrm{BQP} \subseteq \mathrm{PSPACE}. \tag{5.103}$$

Exercises

5.22. Prove Theorem 5.29, where a linear operator U on an infinite-dimensional space is defined to be unitary if:

(1) For any vector $|c\rangle$ in the space, $\| U|c\rangle \| = \| |c\rangle \|$;
(2) U is surjective.

5.23. Provide and prove a theorem similar to Theorem 5.29 for generalized QTM.

5.7 Quantum circuits

5.7.1 Quantum gates

First, we discuss the simplest quantum gates—single-qubit gates. Single-qubit gates have been briefly introduced in Chapter 1, and we will now discuss them in greater depth. All single-qubit gates can be represented by 2×2 unitary matrices, among which Pauli matrices are particularly important:

$$X \equiv \begin{bmatrix} 0 & 1 \\ 1 & 0 \end{bmatrix}, \quad Y \equiv \begin{bmatrix} 0 & -i \\ i & 0 \end{bmatrix}, \quad Z \equiv \begin{bmatrix} 1 & 0 \\ 0 & -1 \end{bmatrix}. \tag{5.104}$$

Three other fundamental single-qubit quantum gates are Hadamard gate (denoted as H), phase gate (denoted as S), and $\frac{\pi}{8}$ gate (denoted as T):

$$H = \frac{1}{\sqrt{2}} \begin{bmatrix} 1 & 1 \\ 1 & -1 \end{bmatrix}, \quad S = \begin{bmatrix} 1 & 0 \\ 0 & i \end{bmatrix}, \tag{5.105}$$

$$T = \begin{bmatrix} 1 & 0 \\ 0 & e^{i\frac{\pi}{4}} \end{bmatrix} = e^{i\frac{\pi}{8}} \begin{bmatrix} e^{-i\frac{\pi}{8}} & 0 \\ 0 & e^{i\frac{\pi}{8}} \end{bmatrix}, \tag{5.106}$$

where $H = \frac{X+Z}{\sqrt{2}}$ and $S = T^2$.

From Pauli matrices, we can derive three types of unitary matrices that represent rotation matrices about x, y, and z axes on the Bloch sphere:

$$R_x(\theta) \equiv e^{-i\theta X/2} = \cos\frac{\theta}{2} I - i \sin\frac{\theta}{2} X = \begin{bmatrix} \cos\frac{\theta}{2} & -i\sin\frac{\theta}{2} \\ -i\sin\frac{\theta}{2} & \cos\frac{\theta}{2} \end{bmatrix}, \tag{5.107}$$

$$R_y(\theta) \equiv e^{-i\theta Y/2} = \cos\frac{\theta}{2} I - i \sin\frac{\theta}{2} Y = \begin{bmatrix} \cos\frac{\theta}{2} & -\sin\frac{\theta}{2} \\ \sin\frac{\theta}{2} & \cos\frac{\theta}{2} \end{bmatrix}, \tag{5.108}$$

$$R_z(\theta) \equiv e^{-i\theta Z/2} = \cos\frac{\theta}{2}I - i\sin\frac{\theta}{2}Z = \begin{bmatrix} e^{-i\theta/2} & 0 \\ 0 & e^{i\theta/2} \end{bmatrix}. \tag{5.109}$$

Any unitary matrix acting on a single qubit can be expressed in various ways as a combination of rotation matrices and a global phase factor. The following theorem provides a very useful representation of single-qubit gates.

Theorem 5.33 (Z-Y decomposition of single-qubit gates). *Suppose U is a single-qubit gate, then there exist real numbers α, β, γ, and δ such that*

$$U = e^{i\alpha} R_z(\beta) R_y(\gamma) R_z(\delta). \tag{5.110}$$

Proof. Since U is unitary, that is, the rows and columns of U are orthogonal, there exist real numbers α, β, γ, and δ such that

$$U = \begin{bmatrix} e^{i(\alpha-\beta/2-\delta/2)}\cos\gamma/2 & -e^{i(\alpha-\beta/2+\delta/2)}\sin\gamma/2 \\ e^{i(\alpha+\beta/2-\delta/2)}\sin\gamma/2 & e^{i(\alpha+\beta/2+\delta/2)}\cos\gamma/2 \end{bmatrix} \tag{5.111}$$

$$= e^{i\alpha} \begin{bmatrix} e^{-i\beta/2} & 0 \\ 0 & e^{i\beta/2} \end{bmatrix} \begin{bmatrix} \cos\frac{\gamma}{2} & -\sin\frac{\gamma}{2} \\ \sin\frac{\gamma}{2} & \cos\frac{\gamma}{2} \end{bmatrix} \begin{bmatrix} e^{-i\delta/2} & 0 \\ 0 & e^{i\delta/2} \end{bmatrix}. \tag{5.112}$$

□

Corollary 5.2. *Suppose U is a single-qubit gate, then there exist unitary matrices A, B, C satisfying $ABC = I$ and a real number α, such that $U = e^{i\alpha}AXBXC$.*

Proof. Let $A \equiv R_z(\beta)R_y(\frac{\gamma}{2})$, $B \equiv R_y(-\frac{\gamma}{2})R_z(-\frac{\delta+\beta}{2})$, $C \equiv R_z(\frac{\delta-\beta}{2})$. Notice that

$$ABC = R_z(\beta)R_y(\frac{\gamma}{2}) \cdot R_y(-\frac{\gamma}{2})R_z(-\frac{\delta+\beta}{2}) \cdot R_z(\frac{\delta-\beta}{2}) = I. \tag{5.113}$$

Since $X^2 = I$, using the result of Exercise 5.26, we have

$$XBX = XR_y(-\frac{\gamma}{2})XXR_z(-\frac{\delta+\beta}{2})X = R_y(\frac{\gamma}{2})R_z(\frac{\delta+\beta}{2}). \tag{5.114}$$

Therefore

$$AXBXC = R_z(\beta)R_y(\frac{\gamma}{2})R_y(\frac{\gamma}{2})R_z(\frac{\delta+\beta}{2})R_z(\frac{\delta-\beta}{2}) \tag{5.115}$$

$$= R_z(\beta)R_y(\gamma)R_z(\delta). \tag{5.116}$$

So, by Theorem 5.33, $U = e^{i\alpha}AXBXC$ and $ABC = I$. □

An n-qubit gate can be represented by a $2^n \times 2^n$ unitary matrix. For any n-qubit gate, we have the following theorem.

Theorem 5.34. [32] *Any n-qubit gate can be implemented by a circuit consisting of $O(n^2 4^n)$ single-qubit gates and* CNOT gates.

Thus any quantum gate can be implemented using single-qubit gates and CNOT gates.

5.7.2 Polynomial-time simulation of QTM

The definition of the transition function of QTM is relatively complex, while quantum circuits are more intuitive. When designing quantum algorithms, researchers often use quantum circuits to describe them. A natural question is: what are the relationships between quantum circuits and QTM? Yao [33] first proved that quantum circuits can simulate generalized QTM in polynomial time. Molina and Watrous [34] later further improved this simulation. Next, we introduce Molina and Watrous' results.

Let the state of a QTM M be $Q = \{1, \ldots, m\}$, with an initial state p_0, and let the tape alphabet be $\Gamma = \{0, \ldots, k-1\}$. The transition function is given by $\delta : Q \times \Gamma \times Q \times \Gamma \times \{-1, +1\} \to \mathbb{C}$.

Define the function $T : \mathbb{Z} \to \Gamma$, where $T(j)$ represents the tape character at position j on the tape of QTM M. Given a function $T : \mathbb{Z} \to \Gamma$, $i \in \mathbb{Z}$, and a tape character $a \in \Gamma$, define

$$T_{i,a}(j) = \begin{cases} a, & \text{if } j = i, \\ T(j), & \text{if } j \neq i. \end{cases} \tag{5.117}$$

Furthermore, define the operator

$$U_\delta |p, i, T\rangle = \sum_{q,a,D} \delta(p, T(i), q, a, D) |q, i + D, T_{i,a}\rangle. \tag{5.118}$$

We will prove that quantum circuits can simulate M running for t steps, where t is given in advance. During t steps of operation by M, the information in $2t+1$ cells at most on the tape can be changed. Therefore we can assume that the tape of M has only $N = 2t+1$ cells. In addition, we define the following concepts:

(1) Let the set of indices for the tape be $\mathbb{Z}_N = \{0, 1, \ldots, N-1\}$, and the initial position of the head is at index t.

(2) Define a finite-dimensional Hilbert space $\mathcal{H}_N$, with a basis consisting of vectors of the form $|p, i, T\rangle$, where $p \in Q$, $i \in \mathbb{Z}_N$. At this point, the function T is as $T : \mathbb{Z}_N \to \Gamma$.

(3) Let the unitary operator derived from the transition function δ be $U_{\delta,N} \in \mathrm{L}(\mathcal{H}_N)$, where $\mathrm{L}(\mathcal{H}_N)$ represents the space of all linear operators acting on $\mathcal{H}_N$.

Since the proof is rather complex, we still need some definitions and theorems as groundwork. Let $\mathcal{X}$, $\mathcal{Y}$, and $\mathcal{Z}$ be Hilbert spaces. Denote $\mathrm{U}(\mathcal{X} \otimes \mathcal{Y} \otimes \mathcal{Z})$ as the set of all unitary operators acting on the Hilbert space $\mathcal{X} \otimes \mathcal{Y} \otimes \mathcal{Z}$, and $\mathrm{D}(\mathcal{X} \otimes \mathcal{Y} \otimes \mathcal{Z})$ as the set of all density operators acting on the Hilbert space $\mathcal{X} \otimes \mathcal{Y} \otimes \mathcal{Z}$. The definition of a causal operator is given as follows.

Definition 5.32. Suppose $\mathcal{X}$, $\mathcal{Y}$, and $\mathcal{Z}$ are Hilbert spaces. Let $\mathcal{U} \in \mathrm{U}(\mathcal{X} \otimes \mathcal{Y} \otimes \mathcal{Z})$ be a unitary operator, and let $\mathcal{V}$ be a subspace of $\mathcal{X} \otimes \mathcal{Y} \otimes \mathcal{Z}$. For any ρ, if $\sigma \in \mathrm{D}(\mathcal{X} \otimes \mathcal{Y} \otimes \mathcal{Z})$ with $\mathrm{im}(\rho) \subseteq \mathcal{V}$, $\mathrm{im}(\sigma) \subseteq \mathcal{V}$, and $\mathrm{Tr}_z(\rho) = \mathrm{Tr}_z(\sigma)$, it holds that

$$\mathrm{Tr}_{y \otimes z}(\mathcal{U} \rho \mathcal{U}^\dagger) = \mathrm{Tr}_{y \otimes z}(\mathcal{U} \sigma \mathcal{U}^\dagger), \tag{5.119}$$

then $\mathcal{U}$ is called a $\mathcal{Y} \to \mathcal{X}$ causal operator acting on $\mathcal{V}$, where $\mathrm{im}(\rho)$ denotes the image space of ρ.

Let $\mathrm{Proj}(\mathcal{H})$ denote the set of all projection operators acting on the Hilbert space $\mathcal{H}$, and $\mathrm{L}(\mathcal{H})$ denote the set of all linear operators acting on $\mathcal{H}$. We denote $[A, B] = AB - BA$. Causal operators have the following properties.

Theorem 5.35. [34] *Suppose $\mathcal{X}$, $\mathcal{Y}$, and $\mathcal{Z}$ are Hilbert spaces. Let $\{\Delta_1, \ldots, \Delta_n\} \subseteq \mathrm{Proj}(\mathcal{X} \otimes \mathcal{Y})$ and $\{\Lambda_1, \ldots, \Lambda_n\} \subseteq \mathrm{Proj}(\mathcal{Z})$ be orthogonal sets of nonzero projection operators and denote Π by*

$$\Pi = \sum_{k=1}^{n} \Delta_k \otimes \Lambda_k. \tag{5.120}$$

If $\mathcal{U} \in \mathrm{U}(\mathcal{X} \otimes \mathcal{Y} \otimes \mathcal{Z})$ is a $\mathcal{Y} \to \mathcal{X}$ causal operator acting on $\mathrm{im}(\Pi)$, then for every operator $X \in \mathrm{L}(\mathcal{X})$, there exists an operator $W \in \mathrm{L}(\mathcal{X} \otimes \mathcal{Y})$ such that

$$\Pi \mathcal{U}^\dagger (X \otimes \mathbb{1}_{y \otimes z}) \mathcal{U} \Pi = \Pi (W \otimes \mathbb{1}_z) \Pi. \tag{5.121}$$

Moreover, if X is unitary and $[\mathcal{U}^\dagger (X \otimes \mathbb{1}_{y \otimes z}) \mathcal{U}, \Pi] = 0$, then W is also unitary.

Quantum circuits do not directly simulate QTM M, and this means that quantum states of quantum circuits are not completely identical to the quantum states describing the configurations of M, but rather there is a correspondence. First, we describe a formulation of quantum states of quantum circuits, and then provide a correspondence between quantum circuit states and configurations of M.

Let M run for t steps, and denote $N = 2t + 1$. Define registers $\mathrm{S}_0, \cdots, \mathrm{S}_{N-1}$ and $\mathrm{T}_0, \cdots, \mathrm{T}_{N-1}$. Each register S_i contains elements from $\{-m, \cdots, m\}$, and each register T_i contains elements from the set $\Gamma = \{0, \ldots, k-1\}$. If S_i is 0, it indicates that the head of QTM M is not on the cell with index i of the tape. If the element of S_i is $p \in \{1, \ldots, m\}$, it indicates that the head of QTM M is on the cell with index i of the tape, and M is currently in state p.

The basis states of quantum circuit simulating M in the evolution process of quantum states are denoted as

$$(\mathrm{S}_0, \mathrm{T}_0), \ldots, (\mathrm{S}_{N-1}, \mathrm{T}_{N-1}). \tag{5.122}$$

For each $i \in \mathbb{Z}_N$, denote $\mathcal{S}_i$ and $\mathcal{T}_i$ as the Hilbert spaces corresponding to registers S_i and T_i, respectively. Define the Hilbert space $\mathcal{K}_N$ as

$$\mathcal{K}_N = (\mathcal{S}_0 \otimes \mathcal{T}_0) \otimes \cdots \otimes (\mathcal{S}_{N-1} \otimes \mathcal{T}_{N-1}). \tag{5.123}$$

For each configuration (p, i, T) of QTM M with a tape of length N, the corresponding registers are

$$(0, T(0)), \cdots, (p, T(i)), \cdots, (0, T(N-1)), \tag{5.124}$$

that is, the state of the i-th register is p, while the rest are in state 0. Denote this mapping by f, that is,

$$f(p, i, T) = (0, T(0)), \cdots, (p, T(i)), \cdots, (0, T(N-1)). \tag{5.125}$$

Define the operator $A \in \mathrm{U}(\mathcal{H}_N, \mathcal{K}_N)$ as

$$A = \sum_{(p,i,T)} |f(p, i, T)\rangle\langle p, i, T|, \tag{5.126}$$

which maps the configurations of M to the corresponding quantum states in the quantum circuit.

Furthermore, it can be observed that $A^\dagger$ maps the quantum states of the quantum circuit onto the configurations of M. By observing the operator

$AU_{\delta,N}A^\dagger$, $A^\dagger$ first maps the quantum state of the quantum circuit to the configuration of M, and then $U_{\delta,N}$ evolves the current configuration of M by one step. Finally, A maps the evolved Turing machine configuration to the quantum state of the quantum circuit. Thus $AU_{\delta,N}A^\dagger$ can be used as an operator for a quantum circuit simulating M running one step. However, $AU_{\delta,N}A^\dagger$ is not unitary. In fact, we only need to construct a unitary operator W such that for any $|x\rangle \in \mathrm{im}(A)$,

$$W|x\rangle = AU_{\delta,N}A^\dagger|x\rangle. \tag{5.127}$$

For simplicity, we denote $\mathcal{U} = U_{\delta,N}$ from now on.

Since the initial configuration of M is specified as $|p_0, t, T\rangle$, the corresponding input state of the quantum circuit is $|f(p_0, t, T)\rangle$. We will now describe how to construct the operator W step by step.

First, define the reversible transformation

$$F|p\rangle = |-p\rangle, \tag{5.128}$$

where $p \in \{-m, \ldots, m\}$. For each index $i \in \mathbb{Z}_N$, define F_i as

$$F_i = \prod_{j=0}^{i-1}(\mathbb{1}_{\mathcal{S}_j} \otimes \mathbb{1}_{\mathcal{T}_j})(F \otimes \mathbb{1}_{\mathcal{T}_i}) \prod_{j=i+1}^{N-1}(\mathbb{1}_{\mathcal{S}_j} \otimes \mathbb{1}_{\mathcal{T}_j}), \tag{5.129}$$

where $\mathbb{1}_{\mathcal{S}_j}$ and $\mathbb{1}_{\mathcal{T}_j}$ are the identity operators on Hilbert spaces $\mathcal{S}_j$ and $\mathcal{T}_j$, respectively. It can be seen that F_i applies F to register S_i and applies identity operators to the remaining registers.

Define the unitary operators

$$V = A\mathcal{U}A^\dagger + (\mathbb{1} - AA^\dagger), \tag{5.130}$$

$$W = (F_0 \cdots F_{N-1})V^\dagger(F_0 \cdots F_{N-1})V. \tag{5.131}$$

It can be seen that $V|_{im(A)} = A\mathcal{U}A^\dagger|_{im(A)}$ (meaning that V acts the same as $A\mathcal{U}A^\dagger$ on $im(A)$), while on $im(A)^\perp$, V and $V^\dagger$ are identity transformations.

Detailed proofs of these two problems are as follows:

(1) Let $\mathrm{im}(A) = \{Ax \mid x \in \mathcal{H}_N\}$. To prove $V|_{\mathrm{im}(A)} = A\mathcal{U}A^\dagger|_{\mathrm{im}(A)}$, we need to show $\mathbb{I} - AA^\dagger|_{\mathrm{im}(A)} = \mathcal{O}$. Since A is an isometry, for any $x, y \in \mathcal{H}_N$, we have $(x, y) = (Ax, Ay) = (x, A^\dagger Ay)$. Therefore for any $x, y \in \mathcal{H}_N$, $(x, (A^\dagger A - I_{\mathcal{H}_N})y) = 0$ holds. Specifically, by choosing $x = (A^\dagger A - I_{\mathcal{H}_N})y$, we know for any $y \in \mathcal{H}_N$, $(A^\dagger A - I_{\mathcal{H}_N})y = \mathbf{0}$. Hence, $A^\dagger A = I_{\mathcal{H}_N}$.

This implies $(\mathbb{I} - AA^\dagger)Ax = Ax - Ax = \mathbf{0}$.

(2) To prove that on $\text{im}(A)^\perp$, V and $V^\dagger$ are identity transformations, we need to show that $(AUA^\dagger - AA^\dagger)|_{\text{im}(A)^\perp} = \mathcal{O}$ and $(AU^\dagger A^\dagger - AA^\dagger)|_{\text{im}(A)^\perp} = \mathcal{O}$.

Let $\text{im}(A) = \{Ax \mid x \in \mathcal{H}_N\}$. For any $y \in \text{im}(A)^\perp$, $x \in \mathcal{H}_N$, we have $(Ax, y) = (x, A^\dagger y) = 0$, which implies $A^\dagger y = \mathbf{0}$. It follows that $y \in \ker(A^\dagger)$ and we have $\text{im}(A)^\perp \subset \ker(A^\dagger)$.

From this, we conclude that $(AUA^\dagger - AA^\dagger)|_{\text{im}(A)^\perp} = \mathcal{O}$ and $(AU^\dagger A^\dagger - AA^\dagger)|_{\text{im}(A)^\perp} = \mathcal{O}$.

It follows that $F_0 \cdots F_{N-1}$ maps $im(A)$ to $im(A)^\perp$ (and maps $im(A)^\perp$ to $im(A)$), so the operator

$$(F_0 \cdots F_{N-1}) V^\dagger (F_0 \cdots F_{N-1})$$

is the identity on $im(A)$. Therefore $V|_{im(A)} = W|_{im(A)}$, which means that W satisfies Eq. (5.127).

It follows that

$$V^\dagger (F_0 F_1 \cdots F_{N-1}) V = (V^\dagger F_0 V)(V^\dagger F_1 V) \cdots (V^\dagger F_{N-1} V). \tag{5.132}$$

Let $k_0, k_1, \cdots, k_{N-1}$ be any permutation of $0, 1, \cdots, N-1$. Then

$$F_{k_0} \cdots F_{k_{N-1}} = F_0 \cdots F_{N-1}, \tag{5.133}$$

$$V^\dagger (F_{k_0} \cdots F_{k_{N-1}}) V = (V^\dagger F_{k_0} V) \cdots (V^\dagger F_{k_{N-1}} V). \tag{5.134}$$

To minimize the complexity of constructing W, we employ a "localization" technique. We will prove that each operator $V^\dagger F_i V$ can be implemented by a quantum circuit with a smaller number of quantum gates.

Consider the given registers $(\mathrm{S}_{i-1}, \mathrm{T}_{i-1})$, $(\mathrm{S}_i, \mathrm{T}_i)$, $(\mathrm{S}_{i+1}, \mathrm{T}_{i+1})$, restricted to registers in the basis state of $\text{im}(A)$. For a given $i \in \mathbb{Z}_N$, define

$$X = (\mathrm{S}_i, \mathrm{T}_i), \tag{5.135}$$

$$Y = (\mathrm{S}_{i-1}, \mathrm{T}_{i-1}, \mathrm{S}_{i+1}, \mathrm{T}_{i+1}), \tag{5.136}$$

and Z to be the set of registers $(\mathrm{S}_0, \mathrm{T}_0), \ldots, (\mathrm{S}_{N-1}, \mathrm{T}_{N-1})$ excluding X and Y.

Let $\mathcal{X}$, $\mathcal{Y}$, $\mathcal{Z}$ be the Hilbert spaces corresponding to X, Y, Z, respectively. For each $a \in \{0, 1\}$, define $\Delta_a \in \text{Proj}(\mathcal{X} \otimes \mathcal{Y})$ as the projection operator onto the space tensor formed by the standard basis (X, Y), where registers S_{i-1}, S_i, S_{i+1} contain a nonzero values. Similarly, define $\Lambda_a \in \text{Proj}(\mathcal{Z})$, where registers $\mathrm{S}_0, \cdots, S_{i-2}, \mathrm{S}_{i+2}, \cdots, S_{N-1}$ contain a nonzero values.

Define the projection operator

$$\Pi = \Delta_0 \otimes \Lambda_1 + \Delta_1 \otimes \Lambda_0. \tag{5.137}$$

Since the registers in X, Y, Z contain only one nonzero value, it can be seen that $\mathrm{im}(\Pi)$ is the space spanned by all possible (X, Y, Z). And exactly one of the registers $S_0, \cdots, S_{N-1}$ contains a nonzero value.

It can be verified that V is a $Y \rightarrow X$ causal operator acting on the subspace $\mathrm{im}(\Pi)$. Therefore by Theorem 5.35, there exists a unitary operator $G \in \mathrm{U}(\mathcal{X} \otimes \mathcal{Y})$ such that

$$\Pi(G \otimes \mathbb{1}_{\mathcal{Z}})\Pi = \Pi V^{\dagger}((F \otimes \mathbb{1}) \otimes \mathbb{1}_{\mathcal{Y}\otimes\mathcal{Z}}) V \Pi. \tag{5.138}$$

Combining Eqs. (5.131), (5.132), and (5.138), we can construct W using $O(N)$ numbers of G and the operators $F_0 \cdots F_{N-1}$, as illustrated in Fig. 5.6.

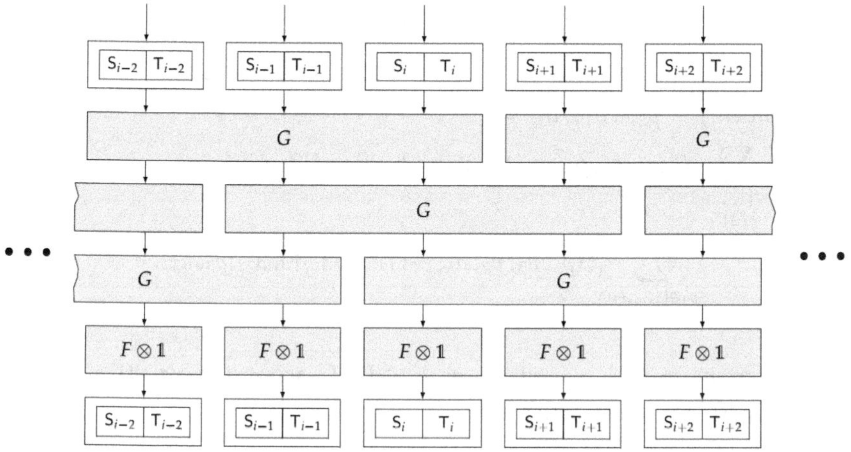

Figure 5.6 Construction of *W*.

W can simulate one step of the Turing machine M. Thus simulating M for t steps requires t's W with series connection. Next, we analyze the gates' complexity of W.

$S_i \in \{-m, \cdots, m\}$, so each S_i can be represented using $\log_2\lceil 2m+1 \rceil = \log_2\lceil 2|Q|+1 \rceil$ qubits. $T_i \in \{0, \cdots, k-1\}$, so each T_i can be represented using $\log_2\lceil k \rceil = \log_2\lceil |\Gamma| \rceil$ qubits. G acts on $3(\log_2\lceil 2m+1 \rceil + \log_2\lceil k \rceil)$ qubits and, therefore, by Theorem 5.34, G can be implemented using

$\mathrm{Poly}(|Q|, |\Gamma|)$ basic gates, and F can be implemented using $\mathrm{Poly}(|Q|)$ basic gates, where $\mathrm{Poly}(|Q|, |\Gamma|)$ represents a polynomial in $|Q|$ and $|\Gamma|$. Since each W contains $O(N)$ numbers of G and N numbers of F, a single W can be implemented using $O(N) \cdot \mathrm{Poly}(|Q|, |\Gamma|)$ basic gates. Therefore the t's W in the entire circuit can be implemented using $tO(N) \cdot \mathrm{Poly}(|Q|, |\Gamma|) = \mathrm{Poly}(|Q|, |\Gamma|, t)$ basic gates. This proves that quantum circuits can simulate QTM in polynomial time.

Finally, we describe the specific action of G based on Eq. (5.138).

(1) For $p_1, p_2, p_3 \in \{1, \ldots, m\}$, $a_1, a_2, a_3 \in \Gamma$, G acts as the identity on $|0, a_1\rangle|p_2, a_2\rangle|0, a_3\rangle$, $|-p_1, a_1\rangle|0, a_2\rangle|0, a_3\rangle$, $|0, a_1\rangle|0, a_2\rangle|-p_3, a_3\rangle$. Similarly, for the standard basis state of the form

$$|q_1, a_1\rangle|q_2, a_2\rangle|q_3, a_3\rangle, \tag{5.139}$$

G does not change its action, where q_1, q_2, and q_3 have two or three nonzero values.

(2) For $p_2 \in \{1, \ldots, m\}$, $a_1, a_2, a_3 \in \Gamma$, G acts on $|0, a_1\rangle|-p_2, a_2\rangle|0, a_3\rangle$ as follows:

$$\begin{aligned} &G|0, a_1\rangle|-p_2, a_2\rangle|0, a_3\rangle = \\ &\sum_{\substack{p_1 \in \{1,\ldots,m\} \\ b_1 \in \Gamma}} (\delta(p_1, b_1, p_2, a_1, +1))^*|p_1, b_1\rangle|0, a_2\rangle|0, a_3\rangle \\ &\quad + \sum_{\substack{p_3 \in \{1,\ldots,m\} \\ b_3 \in \Gamma}} (\delta(p_3, b_3, p_2, a_3, -1))^*|0, a_1\rangle|0, a_2\rangle|p_3, a_3\rangle. \end{aligned} \tag{5.140}$$

(3) For $p_1, p_3 \in \{1, \ldots, m\}$, $a_1, a_2, a_3 \in \Gamma$, G acts on $|p_1, a_1\rangle|0, a_2\rangle|0, a_3\rangle$ and $|0, a_1\rangle|0, a_2\rangle|p_3, a_3\rangle$ as follows:

$$\begin{aligned} &G|p_1, a_1\rangle|0, a_2\rangle|0, a_3\rangle = \\ &\sum_{\substack{q_2 \in \{1,\ldots,m\} \\ b_1 \in \Gamma}} \delta(p_1, a_1, q_2, b_1, +1)|0, b_1\rangle|-q_2, a_2\rangle|0, a_3\rangle \\ &\quad + \sum_{\substack{q_1 \in \{1,\ldots,m\} \\ r_0 \in \{1,\ldots,m\} \\ b_1 \in \Gamma, c_1 \in \Gamma}} \delta(p_1, a_1, r_0, c_1, -1)(\delta(q_1, b_1, r_0, c_1, -1))^*|q_1, b_1\rangle|0, a_2\rangle|0, a_3\rangle \end{aligned} \tag{5.141}$$

and

$$G|0, a_1\rangle|0, a_2\rangle|p_3, a_3\rangle = \sum_{\substack{q_2\in\{1,\dots,m\}\\ b_3\in\Gamma}} \delta(p_3, a_3, q_2, b_3, -1)|0, a_1\rangle|-q_2, a_2\rangle|0, b_3\rangle$$
$$+ \sum_{\substack{q_3\in\{1,\dots,m\}\\ r_4\in\{1,\dots,m\}\\ b_3\in\Gamma, c_3\in\Gamma}} \delta(p_3, a_3, r_4, c_3, +1)(\delta(q_3, b_3, r_4, c_3, +1))^*|0, a_1\rangle|0, a_2\rangle|q_3, b_3\rangle. \tag{5.142}$$

So, the proof of QTMs simulated by quantum circuits has been finished. Then, a further question may be how to construct and design a concrete and more practical universal quantum circuit.

Exercises

5.24. Let x be a real number and let A be a normal matrix such that $A^2 = I$. Prove that

$$\exp(iAx) = \cos(x)I + i\sin(x)A, \tag{5.143}$$

and use this result to verify Eqs. (5.107) and (5.109).

5.25. Prove that Hadamard gate H can be expressed as a product of R_x, R_z, and some $e^{i\varphi}$.

5.26. Prove that $XYX = -Y$ and further derive that $XR_y(\theta)X = R_y(-\theta)$.

5.27. Explain why any single-qubit gate can be written in the form of Eq. (5.109).

5.28. (Single-qubit X-Y decomposition) Replace R_z with R_x and provide a decomposition similar to Theorem 5.33.

5.29. In Corollary 5.2, if $U = H$, provide A, B, C, and α.

5.30. Prove that

$$HXH = Z; \quad HYH = -Y; \quad HZH = X. \tag{5.144}$$

5.31. Prove that V is a causal operator from $\mathcal{Y}$ to $\mathcal{X}$ acting on the subspace $\mathrm{im}(\Pi)$, where V is defined in Eq. (5.130), Π is defined in Eq. (5.137), and $\mathcal{Y}$, $\mathcal{X}$ are Hilbert spaces.

5.32. Derive Eq. (5.140) from Eq. (5.138).

5.33. Derive Eq. (5.141) from Eq. (5.138).

5.34. Derive Eq. (5.142) from Eq. (5.138).

5.8 Summary

In this chapter, we have focused on introducing quantum computation models from a viewpoint more related to computer science. We began with the most fundamental model of quantum computation's 1QFA. This model does not have a stronger recognition capability compared with DFA or PFA, but it offers significant advantages in terms of state complexity for recognizing certain languages. As state complexity is a crucial aspect of automata theory, 1QFA have promising applications, such as in the simulation of quantum discrete event systems [35]. For further details on quantum automata, one can refer to the surveys by Ambainis and Yakaryilmaz et al. [36,37]. As for discussions on equivalence and minimization of quantum automata, [38] provides more details.

Second, we have introduced 2QFA. These automata are more complex in definitions, but they can recognize meaningful non-regular languages, albeit with some challenges for constructing techniques.

Third, we have introduced quantum pushdown automata in terms of several different definitions and discussed their relationships. Also, quantum grammars and their equivalence to quantum finite automata and quantum pushdown automata have been briefly presented.

Subsequently, we have described an important computational model in quantum computing—quantum circuits. Quantum circuits are the most commonly used model for studying quantum algorithms, as they intuitively represent the quantum computation process. One measure of the complexity of a circuit is the number of basic gates, which we also briefly introduced.

Lastly, we have dealt with QTMs. Similar to how classical Turing machines serve as the theoretical model for classical computers, QTMs can be thought of as the theoretical model of quantum computers. Although its definition is more complex and less intuitive, this chapter proved that quantum circuits can simulate QTMs in polynomial time, providing a theoretical foundation for studying quantum algorithms using intuitive quantum circuits.

Automata theory based on quantum logic can be regarded as another approach to exploring quantum computational models [39–42], from which fundamental differences between quantum and classical computation are also discovered in the light of other points of view.

Finally, it is worth mentioning that both quantum discrete evemt systems and learning QFA via queries initiated by Qiu [35,43] are two new research subjects for QFA and we would like to study these problems in future.

References

[1] C. Moore, J. Crutchfield, Quantum automata and quantum grammars, Theoretical Computer Science 237 (1) (2000) 275–306.

[2] A. Bertoni, M. Carpentieri, Regular languages accepted by quantum automata, Information and Computation 165 (2) (2001) 174–182.

[3] A. Brodsky, N. Pippenger, Characterizations of 1-way quantum finite automata, SIAM Journal on Computing 31 (5) (2002) 1456–1478.

[4] A. Bertoni, M. Carpentieri, Analogies and differences between quantum and stochastic automata, Theoretical Computer Science 262 (1) (2001) 69–81.

[5] V. Blondel, E. Jeandel, P. Koiran, et al., Decidable and undecidable problems about quantum automata, SIAM Journal on Computing 34 (6) (2005) 1464–1473.

[6] L.Z. Li, D.W. Qiu, Determining the equivalence for one-way quantum finite automata, Theoretical Computer Science 403 (1) (2008) 42–51.

[7] J.E. Hopcroft, R. Motwani, J.D. Ullman, Introduction to automata theory, languages, and computation, SIGACT News 32 (1) (2001) 60–65.

[8] J. Hopcroft, An nlogn algorithm for minimizing states in a finite automaton, in: Z. Kohavi, A. Paz (Eds.), Theory of Machines and Computations, Academic Press, 1971, pp. 189–196.

[9] A. Paz, Introduction to probabilistic automata, Discrete Mathematics 3 (4) (1971) 406–407.

[10] D.W. Qiu, L.Z. Li, X.F. Zou, et al., Multi-letter quantum finite automata: decidability of the equivalence and minimization of states, Acta Informatica 48 (5–6) (2011) 271–290.

[11] C. Mereghetti, B. Palano, S. Cialdi, et al., Photonic realization of a quantum finite automaton, Physical Review Research 2 (1) (2020) 013089.

[12] A. Ambainis, R. Freivalds, 1-way quantum finite automata: strengths, weaknesses and generalizations, in: Proceedings of the 39th Annual Symposium on Foundations of Computer Science, IEEE, 1998, pp. 332–341.

[13] A. Kondacs, J. Watrous, On the power of quantum finite state automata, in: Proceedings of the 38th IEEE Conference on Foundations of Computer Science, 1997, pp. 66–75.

[14] A. Ambainis, A. Nayak, A. Ta-Shma, et al., Dense quantum coding and quantum finite automata, Journal of the ACM 49 (4) (2002) 496–511.

[15] P. Mateus, D.W. Qiu, L.Z. Li, On the complexity of minimizing probabilistic and quantum automata, Information and Computation 218 (2012) 36–53.

[16] D.W. Qiu, L.Z. Li, P. Mateus, et al., Exponentially more concise quantum recognition of non-RMM regular languages, Journal of Computer and System Sciences 81 (2) (2015) 359–375.

[17] L. Xiao, D. Qiu, State complexity of one-way quantum finite automata together with classical states, Journal of Computer and System Sciences 154 (2025) 103659.

[18] A. Bertoni, C. Mereghetti, B. Palano, Quantum computing: 1-way quantum automata, in: Developments in Language Theory, Springer Berlin Heidelberg, Berlin, Heidelberg, 2003, pp. 1–20.

[19] C. Mereghetti, B. Palano, Quantum finite automata with control language, RAIRO – Theoretical Informatics and Applications 40 (2) (2006) 315–332.

[20] J. Hromkovic, One-way multihead deterministic finite automata, Acta Informatica 19 (4) (1983) 377–384.

[21] A. Belovs, A. Rosmanis, J. Smotrovs, Multi-letter reversible and quantum finite automata, in: Developments in Language Theory, Springer Berlin Heidelberg, 2007, pp. 60–71.

[22] D.W. Qiu, S. Yu, Hierarchy and equivalence of multi-letter quantum finite automata, Theoretical Computer Science 410 (30) (2009) 3006–3017.

[23] D.W. Qiu, L.Z. Li, X.F. Zou, et al., Multi-letter quantum finite automata: decidability of the equivalence and minimization of states, Acta Informatica 48 (5) (2011) 271–290.
[24] A. Ambainis, J. Watrous, Two-way finite automata with quantum and classical states, Theoretical Computer Science 287 (1) (2002) 299–311.
[25] M. Golovkins, Quantum pushdown automata, in: International Conference on Current Trends in Theory and Practice of Computer Science, 2000, pp. 336–346.
[26] S. Gudder, Quantum computers, International Journal of Theoretical Physics 39 (9) (2000) 2151–2177.
[27] D.W. Qiu, Automata theory based on quantum logic: reversibilities and pushdown automata, Theoretical Computer Science 386 (1) (2007) 38–56.
[28] M. Nakanishi, Quantum pushdown automata with garbage tape, International Journal of Foundations of Computer Science 29 (3) (2018) 425–446.
[29] D. Qiu, M. Ying, Characterizations of quantum automata, Theoretical Computer Science 312 (2–3) (2004) 479–489.
[30] C. Bennett, Logical reversibility of computation, IBM Journal of Research and Development 17 (6) (1973) 525–532.
[31] E. Bernstein, U. Vazirani, Quantum complexity theory, in: Proceedings of the Twenty-Fifth Annual ACM Symposium on Theory of Computing, 1993, pp. 11–20.
[32] M.A. Nielsen, I.L. Chuang, Quantum Computation and Quantum Information: 10th Anniversary Edition, Cambridge University Press, 2010.
[33] A. Chi-Chih Yao, Quantum circuit complexity, in: Proceedings of the 1993 IEEE 34th Annual Foundations of Computer Science, 1993, pp. 352–361.
[34] A. Molina, J. Watrous, Revisiting the simulation of quantum Turing machines by quantum circuits, Proceedings of the Royal Society A 475 (2226) (2019) 20180767.
[35] D.W. Qiu, Supervisory control of quantum discrete event systems, arXiv:2104.09753, 2021.
[36] A. Ambainis, A. Yakaryılmaz, Automata and quantum computing, arXiv:1507.01988, 2015.
[37] A.S. Bhatia, A. Kumar, Quantum finite automata: survey, status and research directions, arXiv:1901.07992, 2019.
[38] L. Li, D. Qiu, Quantum Finite Automata: Equivalence and Minimization, Zhejiang University Press, 2019.
[39] M. Ying, Automata theory based on quantum logic (I), International Journal of Theoretical Physics 39 (4) (2000) 985–995.
[40] M. Ying, Automata theory based on quantum logic II, International Journal of Theoretical Physics 39 (11) (2000) 2545–2557.
[41] D. Qiu, Automata theory based on quantum logic: some characterizations, Information and Computation 190 (2) (2004) 179–195.
[42] D. Qiu, Some notes on automata theory based on quantum logic, Science in China, Series E 37 (6) (2007) 723–737.
[43] D. Qiu, Learning quantum finite automata with queries, Mathematical Structures in Computer Science 34 (2) (2024) 128–146.

CHAPTER 6

Quantum algorithms[*]

In this chapter, we introduce a number of fundamental quantum algorithms and clarify their connection with classical probabilistic algorithms. We focus on describing quantum query algorithms, so the general form of quantum query model is presented. First, in Section 6.1, we provide a rough description of the basic processes of probabilistic and quantum algorithms, which helps in understanding their fundamental relationship. Then, in Section 6.2, we introduce the quantum query model, upon which many quantum algorithms are based. In Section 6.3, we further present the relationship between exact query complexity and the polynomial degree of partial Boolean functions. Then, in the subsequent sections, we provide detailed discussions on Deutsch's algorithm, Deutsch–Jozsa algorithm, Simon's algorithm, quantum phase estimation algorithm, Shor's algorithm, Grover's algorithm, and the quantum amplitude amplification technique. Additionally, we give an overview of HHL algorithm, Variational Quantum Eigensolver (VQE), and Quantum Approximate Optimization Algorithm (QAOA).

6.1 Basic relationships between probabilistic and quantum algorithms

In this section, we analyze and compare probabilistic and quantum computation models, from which we derive the fundamental relationship between probabilistic and quantum algorithms.

First, consider the probabilistic computation model shown in Fig. 6.1, which describes a transition from one state to three states. Let the initial state be 0, and in the first step, the system transfers to state i $(i = 0, 1, 2)$ with probability $p_{0,i}$. In the second step, state i transfers to state j $(j = 0, 1, 2)$ with probability $q_{i,j}$.

It follows from the properties of probability that $\sum_{i=0}^{2} p_{0,i} = 1$ and $\sum_{j=0}^{2} q_{i,j} = 1$ $(i = 0, 1, 2)$. Thus the probability of obtaining state j after the second step

[*] This book has a companion website hosting complementary materials. Visit this URL to access it: https://www.elsevier.com/books-and-journals/book-companion/9780443277047.

Theoretical Foundations of Quantum Computing
https://doi.org/10.1016/B978-0-44-327704-7.00011-6

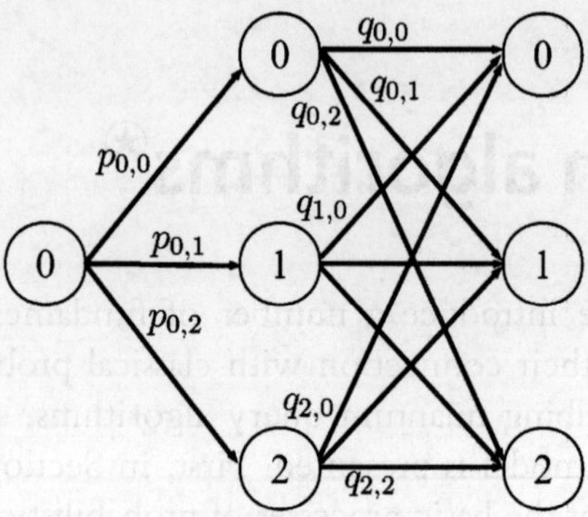

Figure 6.1 Basic probabilistic computation model.

is given by

$$p(j) = \sum_{i=0}^{2} p_{0,i} q_{i,j}. \tag{6.1}$$

In the quantum computation model shown in Fig. 6.2, let the initial state be $|0\rangle$. In the first step, the amplitude for transitioning to state $|i\rangle$ is $\alpha_{0,i}$ $(i = 0, 1, 2)$ via unitary evolution. In the second step, another unitary evolution takes state $|i\rangle$ to state $|j\rangle$ with amplitude $\beta_{i,j}$ $(i, j = 0, 1, 2)$. If a measurement is made after each step, the probability of obtaining state $|j\rangle$ after the second step is

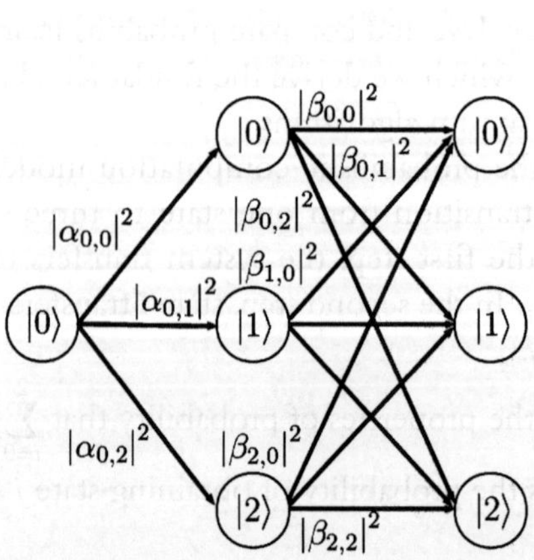

Figure 6.2 Quantum basic evolutionary model with measuring after each step.

$$p(j) = \sum_{i=0}^{2} |\alpha_{0,i}|^2 |\beta_{i,j}|^2 = \sum_{i=0}^{2} |\alpha_{0,i}\beta_{i,j}|^2. \tag{6.2}$$

In the quantum computation model shown in Fig. 6.3, if there is no measurement after the first step and only measurement is performed after the second step, the probability of obtaining state j is

$$p(j) = \left| \sum_{i=0}^{2} \alpha_{0,i}\beta_{i,j} \right|^2. \tag{6.3}$$

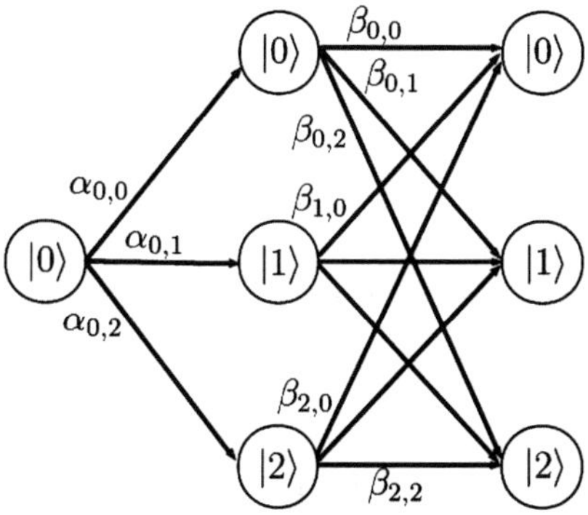

Figure 6.3 Quantum basic evolutionary model with measuring only after the second step.

Note that the probabilities obtained from the earlier two quantum computation models differ due to the difference in measurement operations during the computation process. Exercise 6.3 shows that, under certain transition amplitudes, the probabilities from these two models can be significantly different.

In the probabilistic computation model described by Fig. 6.1, for any $i = 0, 1, 2$, we have $\sum_{j=0}^{2} q_{i,j} = 1$, so $[q_{i,j}]$ forms a stochastic matrix. It is easy to see that for any unitary matrix $U = [u_{i,j}]$, $S_U = [|u_{i,j}|^2]$ forms a stochastic matrix; however, not every stochastic matrix $S = [s_{i,j}]$ has a unitary matrix $U_S = [u_{i,j}]$ such that $[|u_{i,j}|^2] = [s_{i,j}]$. Nevertheless, it can be proven that any probabilistic computation model with M states can be simulated by a quantum computation model with M^2 states, where M auxiliary states are added. The simulation process involves applying a unitary operator to the combined system and then measuring and discarding the auxiliary states.

In this section, we observe that quantum computation model can be regarded as a generalization of probabilistic computation model. Probabilistic model is a special case of quantum model under certain measurement conditions. Generally, classical probabilistic algorithms can be efficiently simulated by quantum algorithms. However, no general method currently exists for designing classical probabilistic algorithms that can efficiently simulate general quantum systems. In subsequent sections, we will also see that for certain problems, quantum algorithms are more powerful than any known classical probabilistic algorithms.

Exercises

6.1. Specify the calculation process of the probabilities for each resulting state in the probabilistic and two quantum computation models discussed in this section.

6.2. Can a quantum computation model with two measurements be simulated by a model with a single measurement? Provide a proof or a counterexample.

6.3. The following exercises illustrate the differences in results between the two quantum computation models discussed in this section.

(1) Provide a set of complex numbers α_i such that $\sum_{i=0}^{N-1} |\alpha_i|^2 = 1$ and $\left|\sum_{i=0}^{N-1} \alpha_i\right|^2 = 0$.

(2) Provide a set of complex numbers β_i such that $\sum_{i=0}^{N-1} |\beta_i|^2 = \frac{1}{N}$ and $\left|\sum_{j=0}^{N-1} \beta_j\right|^2 = 1$.

6.4. Consider how to use a quantum computation model to simulate a probabilistic computation model. Generally, how can a classical probabilistic algorithm be simulated by a quantum algorithm?

6.5. In Fig. 6.1, the transition probabilities $q_{i,j}$ of the classical probabilistic algorithm form a 3×3 stochastic matrix, where for any j, $\sum_{i=1}^{3} q_{i,j} = 1$.

(1) Prove that for any unitary matrix $U = [u_{i,j}]$, the matrix $S = [|u_{i,j}|^2]$ is a stochastic matrix.

(2) Prove that not all stochastic matrices can be constructed from a unitary

matrix U as described in (1).
(3) Prove that any probabilistic computation model with M states can be simulated by a quantum computational model with M^2 states, where M auxiliary states are added. Hint: The simulation process involves applying a unitary operator to the combined system and then measuring and discarding the auxiliary states.

6.2 Quantum query model

In this section, we describe a general form of the quantum query model, which primarily serves to compute Boolean functions $f:\{0,1\}^n \to \{0,1\}$. Many quantum algorithms are built upon the quantum query model described in this section, so these algorithms are some concretizations of the quantum query model.

A quantum query model $\mathcal{A}$ is composed of a query operator O_x and a series of unitary operators $U_0, U_1, \cdots, U_T$, where $x = x_1x_2\cdots x_n \in \{0,1\}^n$. When O_x and $U_0, U_1, \cdots, U_T$ are determined, the quantum query model is instantiated as a quantum query algorithm to compute a Boolean function $f:\{0,1\}^n \to \{0,1\}$. The initial state of a quantum query algorithm is an m-qubit quantum state $|0\rangle^{\otimes m}$. For any $x \in \{0,1\}^n$, the query operator O_x satisfies

$$O_x : |i, b, w\rangle \to |i, b \oplus x_i, w\rangle, \tag{6.4}$$

$$O_x : |0, b, w\rangle \to |0, b, w\rangle, \tag{6.5}$$

where $i \in \{1, 2, 3, \cdots, n\}$, $b \in \{0,1\}$, and $|w\rangle$ is a set of auxiliary qubit states.

The quantum query model $\mathcal{A}$ starts from the initial state $|0\rangle^{\otimes m}$ and applies the operators O_x and U_i $(i = 0, 1, \cdots, T)$ alternately, resulting in the final state $|\psi_f\rangle$, that is,

$$|\psi_f\rangle = U_T O_x U_{T-1} O_x \cdots O_x U_0 |0\rangle^{\otimes m}. \tag{6.6}$$

We can specify a measurement using $\{|0\rangle\langle 0|, |1\rangle\langle 1|\}$ on the first qubit of $|\psi_f\rangle$. The probability of measuring outcome 1 is given by

$$p(x) = \left\| (|1\rangle\langle 1| \otimes I_{m-1}) |\psi_f\rangle \right\|^2. \tag{6.7}$$

If for any $x \in \{0,1\}^n$, we have $|p(x) - f(x)| \le \epsilon < \frac{1}{2}$, then we say that $\mathcal{A}$ computes f with error ϵ. If $\epsilon \in [0, \frac{1}{2})$, we say that $\mathcal{A}$ computes f with bounded error; specifically, if $\epsilon = 0$, $\mathcal{A}$ computes f exactly. The number of times the quantum query model $\mathcal{A}$ queries O_x, denoted by T, is the query complexity of $\mathcal{A}$.

Let $Q_E(f)$, $Q_\epsilon(f)$, and $Q(f)$ denote the query complexities for computing f exactly, with error ϵ, and with bounded error, respectively, which are the minimum number of queries required.

6.3 Query complexity and polynomial degree

The query complexity for any Boolean function f in the query model has a certain relationship with the degree of multilinear polynomials. To illustrate this relationship, we first introduce some definitions related to multilinear polynomials.

Definition 6.1. The general form of a multilinear polynomial is given by

$$p(x_1, \cdots, x_i, \cdots, x_n) = \sum_{S \subseteq [n]} c_S \prod_{i \in S} x_i, \tag{6.8}$$

where $c_S \in \mathbb{C}$.

Definition 6.2. The degree of the previous multilinear polynomial is defined as

$$\deg(p) = \max\{|S| \mid c_S \neq 0\}. \tag{6.9}$$

Definition 6.3. Let f be a partial Boolean function mapping domain D to $\{0, 1\}$, where $D \subseteq \{0, 1\}^n$. For $0 \leq \epsilon < \frac{1}{2}$, a real multilinear polynomial p is said to approximate f with error ϵ if the following two conditions are satisfied:

$$\begin{aligned} &(1) \quad |p(x) - f(x)| \leq \epsilon, \forall x \in D, \\ &(2) \quad 0 \leq p(x) \leq 1, \forall x \in \{0, 1\}^n. \end{aligned}$$

When $\epsilon = 0$, p is said to represent f.

Definition 6.4. Let $\widetilde{\deg}_\epsilon(f)$ denote the approximate degree of f with error ϵ, which is the minimum degree among all real multilinear polynomials that approximate f with error ϵ.

Definition 6.5. For $D = \{0, 1\}^n$ and $\epsilon = 0$, let $\deg(f)$ denote $\widetilde{\deg}_0(f)$, and it is called the degree of the Boolean function f.

Definition 6.6. Suppose f and g are Boolean functions. If f and g are equivalent under permutation of input variables, negation, or negation of output variables, then f and g are said to be equivalent.

Definition 6.7. For any given $x \in D \subseteq \{0,1\}^n$, and for any $y \in \{0,1\}^n$, if $|x| = |y|, f(y)$ is defined, and $f(x) = f(y)$, then f is called a symmetric partial Boolean function, where $|x|$ denotes the Hamming weight of x.

Given a symmetric partial Boolean function $f(x)$, it can be described using the vector $(b_0, b_1, \cdots, b_n) \in \{0, 1, *\}^{n+1}$, where $f(x) = b_{|x|}$, and b_k is the value of $f(x)$ when $|x| = k$; if $b_{|x|} = *$, then $f(x)$ is undefined.

Example 6.1. For the symmetric partial Boolean function $f(x) = b_{|x|}$, the following functions are equivalent:

- $(b_0, b_1, \cdots, b_n)$,
- $(b_n, b_{n-1}, \cdots, b_0)$,
- $(\bar{b}_0, \bar{b}_1, \cdots, \bar{b}_n)$,
- $(\bar{b}_n, \bar{b}_{n-1}, \cdots, \bar{b}_0)$.

With these definitions in mind, we present some important theorems.

Theorem 6.1. *Let $\mathcal{A}$ be a quantum query algorithm that makes T queries. Then there exists a set of n-variable complex-valued multilinear polynomials $\alpha_i(x)$ with degree at most T, such that for any $x \in \{0,1\}^n$, the final state of $\mathcal{A}$ is $\sum_{i \in \{0,1\}^m} \alpha_i(x)|i\rangle$.*

Proof. We use mathematical induction on the number of queries. When $T = 0$, $|\psi_f\rangle$ is $U_0|00\cdots 0\rangle$, which is clearly a polynomial of degree 0. Suppose after k queries and applying U_k, the state is $\sum_{z \in \{0,1\}^m} \alpha_z(x)|z\rangle$, where $\alpha_z(x)$ is a multilinear polynomials of degree at most k. Note that

$$O_x(\alpha_{i,0,w}(x)|i, 0, w\rangle + \alpha_{i,1,w}(x)|i, 1, w\rangle) \tag{6.10}$$

$$= \begin{cases} \alpha_{i,0,w}(x)|i, 0, w\rangle + \alpha_{i,1,w}(x)|i, 1, w\rangle, & x_i = 0 \\ \alpha_{i,1,w}(x)|i, 0, w\rangle + \alpha_{i,0,w}(x)|i, 1, w\rangle, & x_i = 1 \end{cases} \tag{6.11}$$

$$= ((1 - x_i)\alpha_{i,0,w}(x) + x_i\alpha_{i,1,w}(x))|i, 0, w\rangle + (x_i\alpha_{i,0,w}(x) + (1 - x_i)\alpha_{i,1,w}(x))|i, 1, w\rangle, \tag{6.12}$$

where both $(1 - x_i)\alpha_{i,0,w}(x) + x_i\alpha_{i,1,w}(x)$ and $x_i\alpha_{i,0,w}(x) + (1 - x_i)\alpha_{i,1,w}(x)$ are multilinear polynomials of degree at most $k + 1$. Since the action of U_{k+1} does not change the degree, the proof is completed. □

Theorem 6.2. [1] *For any partial Boolean function f on D, if $\deg(f) \leq d$, then there exists a real-value multilinear polynomial q representing f such that*

$$q(x) = c_0 + \sum_{i=1}^{d} c_i V_i, \tag{6.13}$$

where $c_i \in \mathbb{R}$ $(0 \leq i \leq d)$, and $V_i = \sum_{j_1 j_2 \cdots j_i \in \{1,2,\cdots,n\}^i} x_{j_1} x_{j_2} \cdots x_{j_i}$ $(1 \leq i \leq d)$ with $j_1, j_2, \ldots, j_i$ being distinct.

Theorem 6.3. [1] *For any partial Boolean function f, $Q_\epsilon(f) \geq \frac{1}{2}\widetilde{\deg}_\epsilon(f)$.*

Corollary 6.1. $Q_E(f) \geq \dfrac{\deg(f)}{2}$.

Proof. Since there exists an exact quantum query algorithm with query complexity $Q_E(f)$ that computes f, it follows that the algorithm derives a multilinear polynomial $p(x)$, that is,

$$p(x) = \sum_i |\alpha_i(x)|^2 = f(x). \tag{6.14}$$

Since

$$\deg(f) = \deg(p) \leq 2Q_E(f), \tag{6.15}$$

it follows that

$$Q_E(f) \geq \frac{\deg(f)}{2}. \tag{6.16}$$

□

Here are examples of symmetric partial Boolean functions of degrees 1 and 2, demonstrating some applications of these theorems.

Example 6.2. For $n > 1$, let $f : \{0,1\}^n \to \{0,1\}$ be a symmetric partial Boolean function, then:

(1) **The following functions have degree 2:**

$$f_{n,k}^{(1)}(x) = \begin{cases} 0, & |x| = 0, \\ 1, & |x| = k, \end{cases} \tag{6.17}$$

$$f_{n,k}^{(2)}(x) = \begin{cases} 0, & |x| = 0, \\ 1, & |x| = k \text{ or } |x| = k+1, \end{cases} \tag{6.18}$$

$$f_{n,l}^{(3)}(x) = \begin{cases} 0, & |x| = 0 \text{ or } |x| = n, \\ 1, & |x| = l, \end{cases} \tag{6.19}$$

$$f_{n}^{(4)}(x) = \begin{cases} 0, & |x| = 0 \text{ or } |x| = n, \\ 1, & |x| = \lfloor \frac{n}{2} \rfloor \text{ or } |x| = \lceil \frac{n}{2} \rceil, \end{cases} \tag{6.20}$$

where $n-1 \geq k \geq \lfloor \frac{n}{2} \rfloor$ and $\lceil \frac{n}{2} \rceil \geq l \geq \lfloor \frac{n}{2} \rfloor$.
(2) $\deg(f_{n,n}^{(1)}(x)) = 1$, where $f_{n,n}^{(1)}(x)$ is defined as $f_{n,k}^{(1)}(x)$ in (1) when $k = n$.

Exercises

6.6. Prove that the multilinear polynomial representation of any Boolean function exists and is unique.

6.7. Let $f : \{0,1\}^2 \to \{0,1\}$ and $f(x) = x_1 \oplus x_2$. Design an exact quantum query algorithm (with one query) to compute f.

6.4 Deutsch's algorithm

Deutsch's algorithm [2] is the first quantum algorithm. Although this algorithm is simple, it embodies the basic ideas of quantum parallelism and quantum coherence, and also demonstrates the fundamental process of quantum algorithms. We first introduce the Deutsch problem: Given a Boolean function $f : \{0,1\} \to \{0,1\}$, determine whether f is a constant function (i.e., $f(0) \oplus f(1) = 0$) or a balanced function (i.e., $f(0) \oplus f(1) = 1$) by querying the value of f.

A classical deterministic algorithm to solve the Deutsch problem must query both function values $f(0)$ and $f(1)$ to calculate $f(0) \oplus f(1)$, thereby determining whether f is balanced or constant. In other words, the classical deterministic algorithm requires 2 queries to solve the Deutsch problem. We will observe that Deutsch's algorithm only requires a single query to determine whether f is constant or balanced.

Before presenting the idea of designing Deutsch's algorithm, we make some preparations in advance.

From the definition of CNOT gate, we have

$$\text{CNOT}|i\rangle|j\rangle = |i\rangle|i \oplus j\rangle, \quad i, j = 0, 1. \tag{6.21}$$

Thus

$$\text{CNOT}|0\rangle\left(\frac{|0\rangle - |1\rangle}{\sqrt{2}}\right) = |0\rangle\left(\frac{|0\rangle - |1\rangle}{\sqrt{2}}\right), \tag{6.22}$$

$$\mathrm{CNOT}|1\rangle\left(\frac{|0\rangle-|1\rangle}{\sqrt{2}}\right)=|1\rangle\left(\frac{|1\rangle-|0\rangle}{\sqrt{2}}\right). \tag{6.23}$$

From Eqs. (6.22) and (6.23), we obtain

$$\mathrm{CNOT}|b\rangle\left(\frac{|0\rangle-|1\rangle}{\sqrt{2}}\right)=(-1)^b|b\rangle\left(\frac{|0\rangle-|1\rangle}{\sqrt{2}}\right), \quad b=0,1, \tag{6.24}$$

and

$$\mathrm{CNOT}\left(\frac{|0\rangle+|1\rangle}{\sqrt{2}}\right)\left(\frac{|0\rangle-|1\rangle}{\sqrt{2}}\right)=\left(\frac{|0\rangle-|1\rangle}{\sqrt{2}}\right)\left(\frac{|0\rangle-|1\rangle}{\sqrt{2}}\right). \tag{6.25}$$

More generally,

$$\mathrm{CNOT}\,(\alpha_0|0\rangle+\alpha_1|1\rangle)\left(\frac{|0\rangle-|1\rangle}{\sqrt{2}}\right)=(\alpha_0|0\rangle-\alpha_1|1\rangle)\left(\frac{|0\rangle-|1\rangle}{\sqrt{2}}\right). \tag{6.26}$$

Let the function $f:\{0,1\}\to\{0,1\}$ be queried using a unitary transformation U_f of 2 qubits, that is, for $x\in\{0,1\}$ and $y\in\{0,1\}$, we have

$$U_f|x\rangle|y\rangle=|x\rangle|y\oplus f(x)\rangle, \tag{6.27}$$

which can be verified to be unitary.

The circuit for implementing U_f is shown in Fig. 6.4.

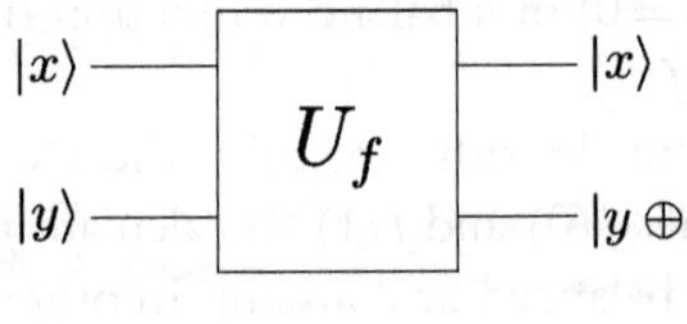

Figure 6.4 Two qubit U_f gate.

According to the definition of U_f, we have

$$U_f|x\rangle\left(\frac{|0\rangle-|1\rangle}{\sqrt{2}}\right)=|x\rangle\left(\frac{|0\oplus f(x)\rangle-|1\oplus f(x)\rangle}{\sqrt{2}}\right) \tag{6.28}$$

$$=|x\rangle(-1)^{f(x)}\left(\frac{|0\rangle-|1\rangle}{\sqrt{2}}\right). \tag{6.29}$$

Thus

$$U_f\,(\alpha_0|0\rangle+\alpha_1|1\rangle)\left(\frac{|0\rangle-|1\rangle}{\sqrt{2}}\right) \tag{6.30}$$

$$= \left((-1)^{f(0)}\alpha_0|0\rangle + (-1)^{f(1)}\alpha_1|1\rangle\right)\left(\frac{|0\rangle - |1\rangle}{\sqrt{2}}\right). \tag{6.31}$$

The circuit of the Deutsch's algorithm is shown in Fig. 6.5.

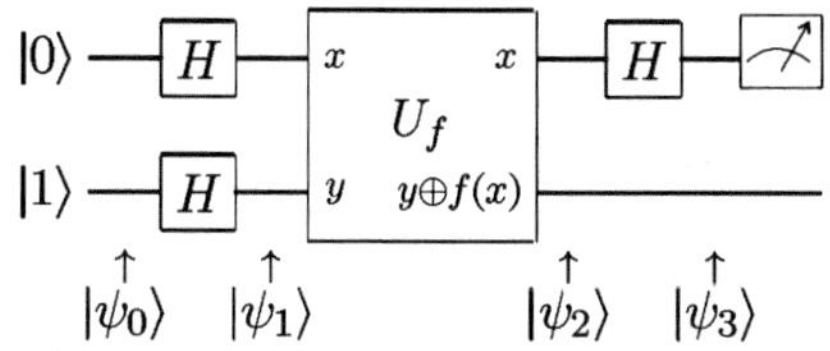

Figure 6.5 Deutsch's algorithm circuit.

The process of Deutsch's algorithm is described as follows.

Algorithm 1: Deutsch's algorithm.

Input: Black box U_f.

Output: Output 0 if f is constant; output 1 if f is balanced.

Set initial state $|\psi_0\rangle = |0\rangle|1\rangle$.

$|\psi_1\rangle = H^{\otimes 2}|\psi_0\rangle = \frac{|0\rangle+|1\rangle}{\sqrt{2}}\frac{|0\rangle-|1\rangle}{\sqrt{2}}$.

$|\psi_2\rangle = U_f|\psi_1\rangle = \begin{cases} \pm\frac{|0\rangle+|1\rangle}{\sqrt{2}}\frac{|0\rangle-|1\rangle}{\sqrt{2}}, & f(0)=f(1), \\ \pm\frac{|0\rangle-|1\rangle}{\sqrt{2}}\frac{|0\rangle-|1\rangle}{\sqrt{2}}, & f(0)\neq f(1). \end{cases}$

$|\psi_3\rangle = (H\otimes I)|\psi_2\rangle = \begin{cases} \pm|0\rangle|-\rangle, & f(0)=f(1), \\ \pm|1\rangle|-\rangle, & f(0)\neq f(1). \end{cases}$

Measure the first qubit using $\{|0\rangle\langle 0|, |1\rangle\langle 1|\}$.

As we can see, Deutsch's algorithm requires only a single application of the U_f gate, which means it queries the function f only once to determine whether f is constant or balanced. Compared with the best classical algorithm, it requires two queries to f, and thus this demonstrates the advantage of quantum algorithms in reducing the number of queries compared with classical deterministic algorithms.

Exercises

6.8. Prove that $H^{\otimes n}|x\rangle = \frac{1}{\sqrt{2^n}} \sum_{z\in\{0,1\}^n} (-1)^{x\cdot z}|z\rangle$, where $x \in \{0, 1\}^n$.

6.9. In Deutsch's algorithm, if U_f is treated as a single-qubit operator $\hat{U}_{f(x)}$, then $\frac{|0\rangle-|1\rangle}{\sqrt{2}}$ is an eigenstate of $\hat{U}_{f(x)}$, and the corresponding eigenvalue provides the solution to the Deutsch problem. Suppose we cannot directly prepare this eigenstate. If the second qubit in Deutsch's algorithm is initialized to $|0\rangle$, please show that the probability of obtaining the correct solution is $\frac{3}{4}$. Furthermore, please show that the algorithm can determine the correct solution with a confidence probability of $\frac{1}{2}$.

6.5 Deutsch–Jozsa algorithm

The Deutsch–Jozsa problem [3] is an extension of the Deutsch problem. The Deutsch–Jozsa problem is a promise problem. Given a function $f : \{0, 1\}^n \to \{0, 1\}$, f is either a constant function (all input values produce the same output) or a balanced function (half of the input values produce 0, and the other half produce 1). The goal of the Deutsch–Jozsa problem is to determine whether f is constant or balanced with as few queries to f as possible.

The circuit of Deutsch–Jozsa algorithm is shown in Fig. 6.6.

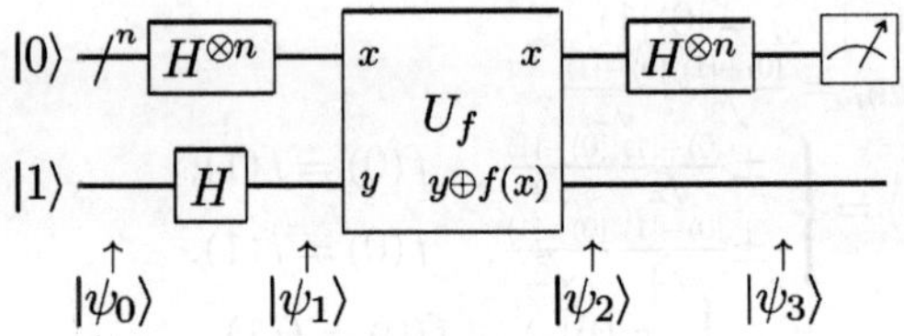

Figure 6.6 The circuit of Deutsch–Jozsa algorithm.

Deutsch–Jozsa algorithm is as follows.

Algorithm 2: Deutsch–Jozsa algorithm.

Input: Black box U_f.
Output: Output 0^n if f is constant; output a value different from 0^n if f is balanced.

Set the initial state $|\psi_0\rangle = |0\rangle^{\otimes n}|1\rangle = |0^n\rangle|1\rangle$.

$|\psi_1\rangle = H^{\otimes(n+1)}|\psi_0\rangle = \frac{1}{\sqrt{2^n}} \sum_{x\in\{0,1\}^n} |x\rangle|-\rangle$.

$|\psi_2\rangle = U_f|\psi_1\rangle = \frac{1}{\sqrt{2^n}} \sum_{x\in\{0,1\}^n} (-1)^{f(x)}|x\rangle|-\rangle$.

$|\psi_3\rangle = (H^{\otimes n} \otimes I)|\psi_2\rangle = \sum_{z\in\{0,1\}^n} \sum_{x\in\{0,1\}^n} \frac{(-1)^{x\cdot z+f(x)}}{2^n}|z\rangle|-\rangle$.

Measure the first n qubits.

Note that in step 4 of the algorithm, if $f(x)$ is a constant function, the amplitude of $|0^n\rangle|-\rangle$ is given by

$$\sum_{x\in\{0,1\}^n} \frac{(-1)^{x\cdot 0^n+f(x)}}{2^n} = \sum_{x\in\{0,1\}^n} \frac{(-1)^{f(x)}}{2^n} = \sum_{x\in\{0,1\}^n} \frac{(-1)^{f(0^n)}}{2^n} = (-1)^{f(0^n)}. \quad (6.32)$$

It follows that the probability of measuring $|0^n\rangle|-\rangle$ is 1, and we have

$$|\psi_3\rangle = (-1)^{f(0^n)}|0^n\rangle|-\rangle. \quad (6.33)$$

If $f(x)$ is a balanced function, the amplitude of $|0^n\rangle|-\rangle$ is

$$\sum_{x\in\{0,1\}^n} \frac{(-1)^{x\cdot 0^n+f(x)}}{2^n} = \sum_{x\in\{0,1\}^n} \frac{(-1)^{f(x)}}{2^n} = 0. \quad (6.34)$$

Thus we have

$$|\psi_3\rangle = \sum_{z\in\{0,1\}^n, z\neq 0^n} \sum_{x\in\{0,1\}^n} \frac{(-1)^{x\cdot z+f(x)}}{2^n}|z\rangle|-\rangle. \quad (6.35)$$

By means of the analysis of step 4 of Deutsch–Jozsa algorithm, if the measurement result in step 5 is $|0\rangle^{\otimes n}$, then f is a constant function; otherwise, f is a balanced function. Deutsch–Jozsa algorithm requires only a single application of the U_f gate, that is, a single query to the function f, to determine whether f is constant or balanced.

If we use a classical deterministic algorithm, it is easy to see that the optimal number of queries to solve the Deutsch–Jozsa problem is $2^{n-1}+1$. Therefore, compared with the classical deterministic algorithm, the quantum algorithm has an exponential advantage in query complexity.

If we allow some error probability in determining the type of f, that is, using a classical probabilistic algorithm, we can design a classical probabilistic algorithm with 2 queries that determines whether f is constant or balanced with a correctness probability of at least $\frac{2}{3}$. Furthermore, using $O(n)$ queries, a classical probabilistic algorithm can determine whether f is constant or balanced with a correctness probability of $1-\frac{1}{2^n}$. Therefore if some error probability for the Deutsch–Jozsa problem is acceptable, the query complexity difference between classical probabilistic algorithms and quantum algorithms are a constant factor. Moreover, if we need to control the error probability below ϵ, a classical probabilistic algorithm requires $O(\log(\frac{1}{\epsilon}))$ queries to f. Thus for solving the Deutsch–Jozsa problem, quantum algorithms still have a certain advantage over classical probabilistic algorithms.

In fact, we can also consider the Deutsch–Jozsa problem from another perspectives. According to the definition of symmetric partial Boolean functions, the Deutsch–Jozsa problem can be equivalently described as a symmetric partial Boolean function

$$\mathrm{DJ}_N^0(x) = \begin{cases} 0, & |x| \in \{0, N\}, \\ 1, & |x| = \frac{N}{2}, \end{cases} \tag{6.36}$$

where $N = 2^n$.

Jozsa, Mitchison, and Montanaro [4] generalized the previous problem (i.e., Eq. (6.36)) to

$$\mathrm{DJ}_N^1(x) = \begin{cases} 0, & |x| \in \{0, 1, N-1, N\}, \\ 1, & |x| = \frac{N}{2}, \end{cases} \tag{6.37}$$

and proved that an upper bound of exact quantum query complexity concerning DJ_N^1 is 2 but did not discuss its lower bound.

The work of Qiu et al. [1] further generalized the previous problem (i.e., Eq. (6.37)) to

$$\mathrm{DJ}_N^k(x) = \begin{cases} 0, & |x| \in \{0, 1, \cdots, k, N-k, N-k+1, \cdots, N\}, \\ 1, & |x| = \frac{N}{2}, \end{cases} \tag{6.38}$$

where $0 \le k < \frac{N}{2}$, and proved that the exact quantum query complexity of DJ_N^k is

$$Q_E(\mathrm{DJ}_N^k) = k + 1. \tag{6.39}$$

Exercises

6.10. Prove that a classical probabilistic algorithm can determine whether f is constant or balanced with a correctness probability of at least $\frac{2}{3}$ using 2 queries.

6.11. Design a probabilistic algorithm that makes $O(k)$ queries and determines whether f is constant or balanced with a correctness probability of at least $1 - \frac{1}{2^k}$.

6.6 Simon's algorithm

Simon's algorithm [5] was proposed by Simon in 1994 and is the first algorithm to demonstrate an exponential speedup of quantum algorithms over classical probabilistic algorithms, making it significant in the history of quantum computing. We first introduce the Simon problem: Suppose there is a function $f : \{0, 1\}^n \to \{0, 1\}^m$, where f satisfies: there exists a string $s = s_1 s_2 \cdots s_n \in \{0, 1\}^n$ with $s \neq 0^n$, such that for any $x, y \in \{0, 1\}^n, f(x) = f(y)$ if and only if $x = y$ or $x = y \oplus s$. We have access to a black box that allows us to query the value of f, and the goal is to find s using as few queries to f as possible.

Remark 6.1. Here, we consider the domain $\{0, 1\}^n$ of the function f as the vector space $\mathbb{Z}_2^n$ over the finite field $\mathbb{Z}_2$, and the operation $\oplus$ is the vector addition in the vector space $\mathbb{Z}_2^n$. It can also be viewed as a bitwise XOR of two n-bit binary strings.

The query complexity of the Simon problem using classical probabilistic algorithms has an exponential lower bound [5].

Theorem 6.4. *Any classical probabilistic algorithm solving the Simon problem has a query complexity of* $\Omega(\sqrt{2^n})$.

Proof. We provide a more detailed proof based on reference [6]. Suppose there exists a classical probabilistic algorithm $\mathcal{A}$ that makes T queries to solve the Simon problem, such that for any valid function f, the probability of success is at least $\frac{2}{3}$.

Suppose the input strings of algorithm $\mathcal{A}$ for T queries to the function f are $x_1, x_2, x_3, \ldots, x_T$, respectively. Let the function values for these queries be $f(x_1), f(x_2), f(x_3), \ldots, f(x_T)$ correspondingly, where $x_1, x_2, x_3, \ldots, x_T$ are all distinct.

If there exists $1 \leq i < j \leq T$ such that $f(x_i) = f(x_j)$, then we say that a collision has occurred among the T queries, and x_i and x_j form a collision pair. According to the definition of the Simon problem, $s = x_i \oplus x_j$ is the solution.

It is proved below that for smaller T, the probability that these T queries will not collide will be close to 1. According to the definition of the Simon problem, it can be obtained that the probability that $x_1, x_2, x_3, \cdots, x_{k-1}$ have no collision is greater than or equal to $1 - \dfrac{k-1}{2^n - (k-1)}$.

Based on the previous analysis, the probability that $x_1, x_2, x_3, \cdots, x_T$ have no collision is

$$\begin{aligned}
&\mathrm{P}[\text{No collision in } x_1, x_2, x_3, \cdots, x_T] && (6.40)\\
&= \prod_{k=2}^{T} \mathrm{P}[\text{No collision in } x_1, \cdots, x_k | \text{No collision in } x_1, \cdots, x_{k-1}] && (6.41)\\
&\geq \prod_{k=2}^{T} \left(1 - \frac{k-1}{2^n - (k-1)}\right) && (6.42)\\
&\geq 1 - \sum_{k=2}^{T} \frac{k-1}{2^n - (k-1)} && (6.43)\\
&\geq 1 - \frac{T^2}{2^n - T}. && (6.44)
\end{aligned}$$

Notice that the earlier derivation from Eq. (6.42) to Eq. (6.43) utilizes the property that $a > 0$ and $b > 0$ imply $(1-a)(1-b) = 1 - a - b + ab > 1 - (a+b)$.

Eq. (6.44) is greater than or equal to $\frac{2}{3}$, that is,

$$1 - \frac{T^2}{2^n - T} \geq \frac{2}{3}$$

if and only if

$$\frac{-1 - \sqrt{1 + 12 \cdot 2^n}}{6} \leq T \leq \frac{-1 + \sqrt{1 + 12 \cdot 2^n}}{6}.$$

Since $T > 0$, it can be seen that the probability of success is less than $\frac{1}{3}$ if and only if

$$T \leq \frac{-1 + \sqrt{1 + 12 \cdot 2^n}}{6}.$$

Consequently, to make the probability of success greater than or equal to $\frac{2}{3}$,

$$T \geq \frac{-1 + \sqrt{1 + 12 \cdot 2^n}}{6}$$

is a necessary condition. □

For the Simon problem, Cai and Qiu [7] proved the following result.

Theorem 6.5. *Any classical deterministic algorithm for solving the Simon problem requires $\Omega(\sqrt{2^n})$ queries.*

In particular, the upper bound on the query complexity of any classical deterministic algorithms for solving the Simon problem is also the same as the lower bound on the query complexity of any classical probabilistic algorithm [7,8].

Theorem 6.6. *There exists a classical deterministic algorithm to solve the Simon problem with a query complexity of $O(\sqrt{2^n})$.*

Proof. Let $k = \lfloor \frac{n}{2} \rfloor$. Then query the function values for all strings in the form of $u0^{n-k}$ ($u \in \{0, 1\}^k$), and then query the function values for all strings in the form of $0^k v$ ($v \in \{0, 1\}^{n-k}$).

Since any s can be split into two parts, that is, the first k bits and the last $n-k$ bits, there exist $a \in \{0, 1\}^k$, $b \in \{0, 1\}^{n-k}$ such that $a0^{n-k} \oplus 0^k b = s$. Thus after $2^k + 2^{n-k} = 2^{\lfloor \frac{n}{2} \rfloor} + 2^{\lceil \frac{n}{2} \rceil}$ queries at most as described previously, a collision pairs $a0^{n-k}$ and $0^k b$ can be found inevitably, and then the two elements are executed $\oplus$ operations on $\mathbb{Z}_2^n$ to find s.

Therefore, there exists a classical deterministic algorithm with query complexity $O(\sqrt{2^n})$ for solving the Simon problem. □

The Simon problem is the first to demonstrate the exponential speedup advantage of quantum algorithms over classical probabilistic algorithms. Simon first gave a quantum algorithm for solving the Simon problem with a query complexity of $O(n)$, but the algorithm might not obtain s, that is, it has a certain error rate. Later Brassard and other scholars [9] gave exact query algorithms with the same query complexity, but the methods are more complicated. Cai and Qiu [7] utilized quantum amplitude amplification to give an exact quantum query algorithm solving the Simon problem within the same query complexity $O(n)$.

Before presenting Simon's algorithm, we do some preparatory work. First, according to

$$H^{\otimes n}|x\rangle = \frac{1}{\sqrt{2^n}} \sum_{z \in \{0,1\}^n} (-1)^{x \cdot z}|z\rangle, \tag{6.45}$$

we obtain

$$H^{\otimes n}\left(\frac{|0\rangle^{\otimes n} + |s\rangle}{\sqrt{2}}\right) = \frac{1}{\sqrt{2^{n+1}}} \sum_{z \in \{0,1\}^n} (1 + (-1)^{s \cdot z})|z\rangle. \tag{6.46}$$

To introduce Simon's algorithm, we need a definition as follows.

Definition 6.8. For $s \in \{0,1\}^n$, denote $s^\perp = \{z \in \{0,1\}^n \mid s \cdot z = 0\}$, $S = \{0^n, s\}$, $S^\perp = \{z \in \{0,1\}^n \mid \forall s \in S, s \cdot z = 0\}$, where $s \cdot z = \sum_{i=1}^{n} s_i \cdot z_i \bmod 2$.

Due to

$$\dim(S) + \dim(S^\perp) = \dim(\mathbb{Z}_2^n) = n, \tag{6.47}$$

$$\dim(S) = 1, \tag{6.48}$$

we have

$$\dim(S^\perp) = \dim(s^\perp) = n - 1. \tag{6.49}$$

According to Eq. (6.46) and definition of $s^\perp$, it follows that

$$H^{\otimes n}\left(\frac{|0\rangle^{\otimes n} + |s\rangle}{\sqrt{2}}\right) = \frac{1}{\sqrt{2^{n-1}}}\sum_{z \in s^\perp} |z\rangle. \tag{6.50}$$

For any $x, y \in \{0,1\}^n$ with $s = x \oplus y$, the following proposition holds.

Proposition 6.1. $H^{\otimes n}\left(\frac{|x\rangle+|y\rangle}{\sqrt{2}}\right) = \frac{1}{\sqrt{2^{n-1}}}\sum_{z \in s^\perp}(-1)^{x \cdot z}|z\rangle$, *where* $s = x \oplus y$.

Proof.

$$H^{\otimes n}\left(\frac{|x\rangle + |y\rangle}{\sqrt{2}}\right) \tag{6.51}$$

$$= H^{\otimes n}\left(\frac{|x\rangle + |x \oplus s\rangle}{\sqrt{2}}\right) \tag{6.52}$$

$$= \frac{1}{\sqrt{2^{n+1}}}\sum_{z \in \{0,1\}^n}(-1)^{x \cdot z}|z\rangle + \frac{1}{\sqrt{2^{n+1}}}\sum_{z \in \{0,1\}^n}(-1)^{(x \oplus s) \cdot z}|z\rangle \tag{6.53}$$

$$= \frac{1}{\sqrt{2^{n+1}}}\sum_{z \in \{0,1\}^n}(-1)^{x \cdot z}[1 + (-1)^{s \cdot z}]|z\rangle \tag{6.54}$$

$$= \frac{1}{\sqrt{2^{n-1}}}\sum_{z \in s^\perp}(-1)^{x \cdot z}|z\rangle. \tag{6.55}$$

□

After the previous preparation, we are ready to describe Simon's algorithm specifically below. The black box regarding f is defined as

$$U_f : |x\rangle|b\rangle \to |x\rangle|b \oplus f(x)\rangle.$$

Algorithm 3: Simon's algorithm.

Input: Black Box U_f.

Output: The string s such that $f(x) = f(x \oplus s)$.

1 Set $i = 1$.

2 Prepare quantum state $|\psi_0\rangle = (H^{\otimes n}|0^n\rangle)|0^m\rangle = \frac{1}{\sqrt{2^n}} \sum_{x \in \{0,1\}^n} |x\rangle|0^m\rangle$.

3 $|\psi_1\rangle = U_f|\psi_0\rangle = \frac{1}{\sqrt{2^n}} \sum_{x \in \{0,1\}^n} |x\rangle|f(x)\rangle$.

4 Measure the second register.

5 Apply $H^{\otimes n}$ on the first register.

6 Measure the first register to get the measuring result w_i.

7 If $\dim(\mathrm{span}\{w_1, w_2, \cdots, w_i\}) = n - 1$, go to step 8, otherwise increase i by 1 and return to step 2.

8 Solving the system of equation $\{w_j \cdot s = 0 | 1 \leq j \leq i\}$ yields the unique nonzero solution s.

9 Return s.

Fig. 6.7 is a circuit diagram of Simon's algorithm.

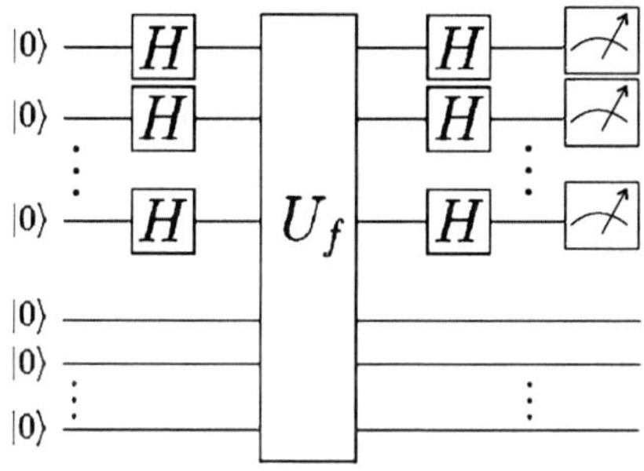

Figure 6.7 Circuit diagram of Simon's algorithm.

Next, we analyze the previous algorithm.

After returning to Step 3 of Simon's algorithm, the state can be written as

$$|\psi_1\rangle = \frac{1}{\sqrt{2^{n-1}}} \sum_{x \in I} \frac{1}{\sqrt{2}} (|x\rangle + |x \oplus s\rangle)|f(x)\rangle, \tag{6.56}$$

where $I \subseteq \{0, 1\}^n$, and for any $x, y \in I$, we have $x \oplus y \neq s$, thus $|I| = 2^{n-1}$.

In step 4, measuring the second register gives an $f(x)$ and the state of the first register is

$$\frac{1}{\sqrt{2}}(|x\rangle + |x \oplus s\rangle).$$

In step 5, the state after Hadamard transformation $H^{\otimes n}$ acting on the first register is

$$\frac{1}{\sqrt{2^{n-1}}} \sum_{z \in s^{\perp}} (-1)^{x \cdot z} |z\rangle |f(x)\rangle. \tag{6.57}$$

In step 6, after the measurement, the resulting state $w_i \in s^{\perp}$. If step 7 yields

$$\dim(\text{span}\{w_1, w_2, \cdots, w_i\}) = n - 1,$$

then $\text{span}\{w_1, w_2, \cdots, w_i\} = s^{\perp}$. Step 8 yields the unique solution, that is, nonzero string s (using Gaussian elimination).

Theorem 6.7. *In Simon's algorithm mentioned earlier, the expectation value of the number of queries required to U_f for finding a solution s does not exceed $n+1$.*

Proof. It is known that $\dim(s^{\perp}) = n - 1$, and w_i obtained from each run of Simon's algorithm is a vector randomly selected from $s^{\perp}$ with equal probability. Denote $V_i = \text{span}\{w_1, w_2, \cdots, w_i\}$, $i \geq 1$.

Next, we define a set of random variables $\{X_j\}$ which represent the required number of times to obtain a space with j dimensions. Then, the random variable X_j takes the value $m(j)$ if the smallest k satisfying $\dim(V_k) = j$ $(1 \leq k)$ is $m(j)$ during a single run of Simon's algorithm. At this point, X_{n-1} denotes the smallest subscript $m(j)$ such that $\dim(V_{m(j)}) = n - 1$, and hence $V_{m(j)} = s^{\perp}$. X_{n-1} is thus equal to the number of queries to U_f for finding the solution s in one run of Simon's algorithm. We next prove that $E(X_{n-1}) \leq n + 1$.

Define $Y_1 = X_1$ and $Y_j = X_j - X_{j-1} (j > 1)$. Then there is $X_j = Y_1 + Y_2 + \cdots + Y_j$. By additivity of expectation, there is

$$E(X_j) = E(Y_1 + Y_2 + \cdots + Y_j) = E(Y_1) + E(Y_2) + \cdots + E(Y_j).$$

Consider further the meaning of Y_t $(1 \leq t < n)$. Y_t can be understood as the number of randomly selecting a vector in $s^{\perp}$ that makes V_i grow into a linear space of dimension t if the current $V_i = \text{span}\{w_1, w_2, \cdots, w_i\}$ is dimension $t - 1$. Since both $s^{\perp}$ and V_i are subspaces of $\mathbb{Z}_2^n$ and $|s^{\perp}| = 2^{n-1}$, $|V_i| = 2^{t-1}$, w is randomly selected from $s^{\perp}$ such that $\text{span}\{w_1, w_2, \cdots, w_i, w\}$

has a dimension larger than $\text{span}\{w_1, w_2, \cdots, w_i\}$. Therefore the probability of selecting such w equals the probability that w is not in the space V_i,

$$1 - \frac{|V_i|}{|s^{\perp}|} = 1 - \frac{2^{t-1}}{2^{n-1}} = \frac{2^{n-1} - 2^{t-1}}{2^{n-1}}. \tag{6.58}$$

It can be seen that Y_t obeys the geometric distribution

$$Ge\left(\frac{2^{n-1} - 2^{t-1}}{2^{n-1}}\right).$$

Thus

$$E(Y_t) = \frac{1}{\frac{2^{n-1}-2^{t-1}}{2^{n-1}}} = \frac{2^{n-1}}{2^{n-1} - 2^{t-1}}. \tag{6.59}$$

So, we have

$$E(X_{n-1}) = \sum_{t=1}^{n-1} E(Y_t) \tag{6.60}$$

$$= \sum_{t=1}^{n-1} \frac{2^{n-1}}{2^{n-1} - 2^{t-1}} \tag{6.61}$$

$$= \sum_{t=1}^{n-1} \left(1 + \frac{2^{t-1}}{2^{n-1} - 2^{t-1}}\right) \tag{6.62}$$

$$= n - 1 + \sum_{t=1}^{n-1} \frac{2^{t-1}}{2^{n-1} - 2^{t-1}} \tag{6.63}$$

$$\leq n - 1 + \sum_{t=1}^{n-1} \frac{2^{t-1} + 2^{t-1}}{2^{n-1} - 2^{t-1} + 2^{t-1}} \tag{6.64}$$

$$= n - 1 + \sum_{t=1}^{n-1} \frac{2^t}{2^{n-1}} \tag{6.65}$$

$$= n - 1 + \frac{\sum_{t=1}^{n-1} 2^t}{2^{n-1}} \tag{6.66}$$

$$= n - 1 + \frac{2^n - 2}{2^{n-1}} \tag{6.67}$$

$$< n - 1 + \frac{2^n}{2^{n-1}} = n + 1. \tag{6.68}$$

□

In fact, if finding s with a certain error rate is allowed, we can fix the upper bound on the number of times for finding w_i in the algorithm. In fact, if $n+3$ is the upper bound on the number of times i, then we have the following theorem.

Theorem 6.8. *For $n>3$, in Simon's algorithm, if $n+3$ repetitions are used to find w_i, then the probability of finding s is at least $\frac{2}{3}$.*

Proof. Denote $V_i = \text{span}\{w_1, w_2, \cdots, w_i\}$ with $1 \le i \le n+3$, and denote $V_0 = \{\mathbf{0}\}$.

For $0 \le i \le n-2$, by assuming that the current $w_1, w_2, \cdots, w_i$ are linearly independent, there are $\dim(V_i) = i$ and $|V_i| = 2^i$. The probability that $w_1, w_2, \cdots, w_i, w_{i+1}$ are linearly independent after randomly selecting the vector w_{i+1} from $s^{\perp}$ is

$$1 - \frac{|V_i|}{|s^{\perp}|} = 1 - \frac{2^i}{2^{n-1}}. \tag{6.69}$$

It can be seen that $w_1, w_2, \cdots, w_{n-4}$ are linearly independent (i.e., $\dim(V_{n-4}) = n-4$) with probability:

$$\begin{aligned}
\text{P}[\dim(V_{n-4}) = n-4] &= \prod_{t=0}^{n-5} \text{P}[\dim(V_{t+1}) = t+1 \,|\, \dim(V_t) = t] && (6.70)\\
&= \prod_{t=0}^{n-5}\left(1 - \frac{2^t}{2^{n-1}}\right) && (6.71)\\
&> 1 - \sum_{t=0}^{n-5} \frac{2^t}{2^{n-1}} && (6.72)\\
&= 1 - \frac{\sum_{t=0}^{n-5} 2^t}{2^{n-1}} && (6.73)\\
&= 1 - \frac{2^{n-4}-1}{2^{n-1}} && (6.74)\\
&> 1 - \frac{2^{n-4}}{2^{n-1}} && (6.75)\\
&= \frac{7}{8}. && (6.76)
\end{aligned}$$

Notice that the inequality (6.72) derived previously utilizes the property that when $a>0$, $b>0$, we have

$$(1-a)(1-b) = 1 - a - b + ab \tag{6.77}$$

$$> 1 - (a + b). \tag{6.78}$$

If $\dim(V_{n-4}) = n - 4$, then the probability that both w_{n-3} and w_{n-2} are in space V_{n-4} is

$$\left(\frac{|V_{n-4}|}{|s^{\perp}|}\right)^2 = \left(\frac{2^{n-4}}{2^{n-1}}\right)^2 = \left(\frac{1}{8}\right)^2 = \frac{1}{64}, \tag{6.79}$$

and therefore the probability of $\dim(V_{n-2}) > \dim(V_{n-4}) = n - 4$ is $1 - \frac{1}{64} = \frac{63}{64}$.

With the prerequisite of $\dim(V_{n-2}) > n - 4$, we can prove that the probability of $\dim(V_n) > n - 3$ is $\frac{15}{16}$. In fact, if $\dim(V_{n-2}) = n - 2$, then naturally $\dim(V_n) \geq \dim(V_{n-2}) = n - 3$; if $\dim(V_{n-2}) = n - 3$, then the probability that both w_{n-1}, w_n are in V_{n-2} is

$$\left(\frac{|V_{n-2}|}{|s^{\perp}|}\right)^2 = \left(\frac{2^{n-3}}{2^{n-1}}\right)^2 = \frac{1}{16}. \tag{6.80}$$

Therefore, the probability of $\dim(V_n) > n - 3$ is $1 - \frac{1}{16} = \frac{15}{16}$.

Similarly, with the prerequisite of $\dim(V_n) > n - 3$, we can prove that the probability of $\dim(V_{n+3}) = n - 1$ is $\frac{7}{8}$. In fact, if $\dim(V_n) = n - 1$, then naturally $\dim(V_n) \geq \dim(V_{n+2}) = n - 1$; if $\dim(V_n) = n - 2$, then the probability that both $w_{n+1}, w_{n+2}, w_{n+3}$ are in V_n is

$$\left(\frac{2^{n-2}}{2^{n-1}}\right)^3 = \frac{1}{8}, \tag{6.81}$$

that is, the probability of $\dim(V_{n+3}) = n - 1$ is $1 - \frac{1}{8} = \frac{7}{8}$.

Consequently, after the algorithm performs $n+3$ rounds, the probability that $\dim(V_{n+3}) = n - 1$ is

$$\frac{7}{8} \times \frac{63}{64} \times \frac{15}{16} \times \frac{7}{8} > \frac{2}{3}. \tag{6.82}$$

□

Furthermore, it has been shown by Cai and Qiu [7] that algorithms can be devised to find s exactly without increasing the query complexity. The main idea is that the state of the first register is not measured immediately after applying $H^{\otimes n}$ on the first register in step 5. Instead of measuring the state of the first register immediately after applying $H^{\otimes n}$ in step 5, the idea is to run the quantum amplitude amplification algorithm and then to measure the first register again so that the result w_i is linearly independent of the $\{w_1, w_2, \cdots, w_{i-1}\}$ measured before. This avoids $w_i \in \text{span}\{w_1, w_2, \cdots, w_{i-1}\}$ and keeps the dimensionality of $\text{span}\{w_1, w_2, \cdots, w_i\}$ increasing and ultimately finding s.

For Simon problem, Koiran et al. [10] proved a lower bound on its quantum query complexity of $\Omega(n)$.

Theorem 6.9. *Given $0 \leq \epsilon < 1/2$, any quantum algorithm for solving Simon problem with probability of error no higher than ϵ requires at least $\Omega(n)$ queries.*

Finally, we have the following theorem concerning quantum query complexity versus classical query complexity of the Simon problem.

Theorem 6.10. *The quantum query complexity of the Simon problem is $\Theta(n)$, while the classical randomized query complexity and the classical deterministic query complexity of the problem are both $\Theta(\sqrt{2^n})$.*

We briefly describe the generalized Simon problem below.

Generalized Simon problem: Suppose there is a function $f: \{0, 1\}^n \to X$, where X is a finite set and satisfies $f(x) = f(y)$ if and only if $x \oplus y \in S$, where S is a subspace of $\mathbb{Z}_2^n$. We have a black box that can query the values of function f, and we require that the number of queries be as small as possible to find a set of bases $s_1, s_2, \cdots, s_m \in S$ ($\dim(S) = m$). It is not difficult to generalize the quantum algorithm for solving the Simon problem to obtain a quantum algorithm for solving the generalized Simon problem, and the query complexity of the generalized quantum algorithm for solving the generalized Simon problem is $\Theta(n - k)$. The upper and lower bounds on the classical query complexity of the generalized Simon problem currently derived are not yet tight. In other words, this problem has not yet been fully solved [11].

Exercises

6.12. Compute the probability of $\{w_1, w_2, \cdots, w_{k-1}\}$ being linearly independent in the proof of Theorem 6.7 and show that the probability is greater than $1 - \frac{1}{2^{n-k}}$.

Questions

6.13. Is step 4 of Simon's algorithm necessary? Please justify it.

6.7 Quantum Fourier transform

In this section, we introduce quantum Fourier transform, an important tool in designing quantum algorithms. Denote $|\phi_j\rangle = \frac{1}{\sqrt{2^m}} \sum_{k=0}^{2^m-1} \omega^{jk}|k\rangle$, where $\omega = e^{2\pi i/2^m}$, we have

$$
\begin{aligned}
\langle\phi_j|\phi_{j'}\rangle =& (\frac{1}{\sqrt{2^m}} \sum_{k=0}^{2^m-1} \omega^{-jk}\langle k|)(\frac{1}{\sqrt{2^m}} \sum_{k'=0}^{2^m-1} \omega^{j'k'}|k'\rangle) && (6.83)\\
=& \frac{1}{2^m} \sum_{k=0}^{2^m-1} \sum_{k'=0}^{2^m-1} \omega^{-jk}\omega^{j'k'}\langle k|k'\rangle && (6.84)\\
=& \frac{1}{2^m} \sum_{k=0}^{2^m-1} \omega^{-jk}\omega^{j'k} && (6.85)\\
=& \frac{1}{2^m} \sum_{k=0}^{2^m-1} \omega^{(j'-j)k} && (6.86)\\
=& \frac{1}{2^m} \sum_{k=0}^{2^m-1} (\omega^{j'-j})^k && (6.87)\\
=& \begin{cases} 1, & j=j', \\ 0, & j\neq j'. \end{cases} && (6.88)
\end{aligned}
$$

Remark 6.2. When $j \neq j'$, we have

$$\frac{1}{2^m} \sum_{k=0}^{2^m-1} (\omega^{j'-j})^k = \frac{\omega^{(j'-j)2^m} - 1}{2^m(\omega^{j'-j} - 1)} = \frac{1-1}{2^m(\omega^{j'-j} - 1)} = 0.$$

Therefore, $\{|\phi_j\rangle : j = 0, 1, 2, \cdots, 2^m - 1\}$ constitute a set of orthonormal basis. Define transform F as $F|j\rangle = |\phi_j\rangle$, $j = 0, 1, 2, \cdots, 2^m - 1$, then F is a unitary transform. In fact, $F = \sum_{j=0}^{2^m-1} |\phi_j\rangle\langle j|$. More specifically, F can be expressed as a matrix:

$$F = \frac{1}{\sqrt{2^m}} \begin{bmatrix} 1 & 1 & 1 & \cdots & 1 \\ 1 & \omega & \omega^2 & \cdots & \omega^{2^m-1} \\ 1 & \omega^2 & \omega^4 & \cdots & \omega^{2(2^m-1)} \\ \vdots & \vdots & \vdots & \ddots & \vdots \\ 1 & \omega^{2^m-1} & \omega^{2(2^m-1)} & \cdots & \omega^{(2^m-1)^2} \end{bmatrix}. \quad (6.89)$$

Quantum Fourier transform F, denoted as QFT_{2^m}, is described as follows:

$$\mathrm{QFT}_{2^m}|j\rangle = \frac{1}{\sqrt{2^m}}\sum_{k=0}^{2^m-1} e^{2\pi ijk/2^m}|k\rangle \tag{6.90}$$

$$= \frac{1}{\sqrt{2^m}}\sum_{k=0}^{2^m-1} \omega_{2^m}^{jk}|k\rangle, \tag{6.91}$$

where $\omega_N = e^{2\pi i/N}$.

On the other hand, for the inverse transform of QFT_{2^m}, that is, the quantum Fourier inverse transform, is denoted as $\mathrm{QFT}_{2^m}^{\dagger}$.

In the following, we discuss the quantum circuit realization of quantum Fourier transform [12].

Express j and k in binary form as

$$j = j_{m-1}j_{m-2}\cdots j_0,\ k = k_{m-1}k_{m-2}\cdots k_0, \tag{6.92}$$

and define

$$\widetilde{\mathrm{QFT}}_{2^m}|j\rangle = \frac{1}{\sqrt{2^m}}\sum_{k=0}^{2^m-1} \omega_{2^m}^{jk}|k_0k_1\cdots k_{m-1}\rangle. \tag{6.93}$$

(If $\widetilde{\mathrm{QFT}}_{2^m}$ can be implemented, the result of QFT_{2^m} can be obtained by flipping the order of the outputs or relabeling them.)

One can construct $\widetilde{\mathrm{QFT}}_{2^m}$ by using induction on m. Considering the simple case with $m = 1$, we have

$$\widetilde{\mathrm{QFT}}_{2^m}|j\rangle = \frac{1}{\sqrt{2}}\sum_{k=0}^{1} \omega_2^{jk}|k\rangle = \frac{1}{\sqrt{2}}|0\rangle + \frac{1}{\sqrt{2}}(-1)^j|1\rangle = H|j\rangle. \tag{6.94}$$

It can be seen that $\widetilde{\mathrm{QFT}}_{2^m}$ at $m = 1$ is a Hadamard transform, which can be realized with just one Hadamard gate.

For $m \geq 1$, assuming that one already has a circuit realizing $\widetilde{\mathrm{QFT}}_{2^m}$, one has the following circuit diagram (Fig. 6.8) realizing $\widetilde{\mathrm{QFT}}_{2^{m+1}}$:

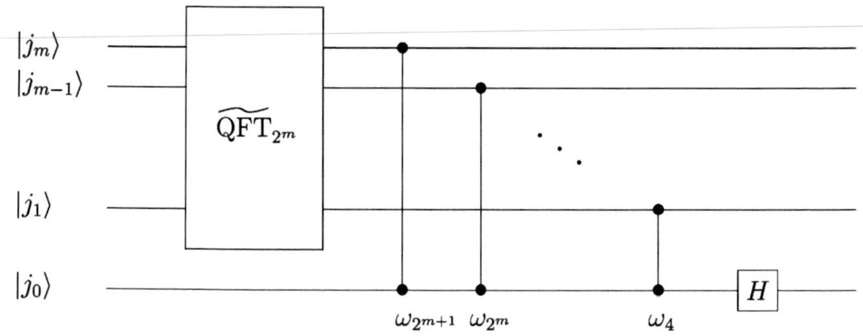

Figure 6.8 Quantum Fourier transform.

Now we further explain how Fig. 6.8 concretely implements $\widetilde{\mathrm{QFT}}_{2^{m+1}}$. Denote that

$$\widetilde{\mathrm{QFT}}_{2^{m+1}}|j_m j_{m-1}\cdots j_0\rangle = \frac{1}{\sqrt{2^{m+1}}}\sum_{k=0}^{2^{m+1}-1}\omega_{2^{m+1}}^{jk}|k_0k_1\cdots k_m\rangle, \tag{6.95}$$

where $j' = j_m j_{m-1}\cdots j_1 = \lfloor \frac{j}{2} \rfloor$, $k' = k_{m-1}k_{m-2}\cdots k_0 = k - k_m 2^m$. Then $|j\rangle = |j'\rangle|j_0\rangle$, and

$$\widetilde{\mathrm{QFT}}_{2^m}|j'\rangle|j_0\rangle = \frac{1}{\sqrt{2^m}}\sum_{k'=0}^{2^m-1}\omega_{2^m}^{j'k'}|k'_0k'_1\cdots k'_{m-1}\rangle|j_0\rangle. \tag{6.96}$$

The following states are obtained through a series of controlled phase shift transforms:

$$\frac{1}{\sqrt{2^m}}\sum_{k'=0}^{2^m-1}\omega_{2^m}^{j'k'}\omega_{2^{m+1}}^{j_0k'_0}\omega_{2^m}^{j_0k'_1}\cdots\omega_4^{j_0k'_{m-1}}|k'_0k'_1\cdots k'_{m-1}\rangle|j_0\rangle. \tag{6.97}$$

Since $\omega_N = \omega_{Nr}^r$ holds for any r, the previous equation is equal to

$$\frac{1}{\sqrt{2^m}}\sum_{k'=0}^{2^m-1}\omega_{2^{m+1}}^{2j'k'+j_0k'_0+j_0(2k'_1)+\cdots+j_0(2^{m-1}k'_{m-1})}|k'_0k'_1\cdots k'_{m-1}\rangle|j_0\rangle \tag{6.98}$$

$$=\frac{1}{\sqrt{2^m}}\sum_{k'=0}^{2^m-1}\omega_{2^{m+1}}^{2j'k'+j_0(k'_0+2k'_1+\cdots+2^{m-1}k'_{m-1})}|k'_0k'_1\cdots k'_{m-1}\rangle|j_0\rangle \tag{6.99}$$

$$=\frac{1}{\sqrt{2^m}}\sum_{k'=0}^{2^m-1}\omega_{2^{m+1}}^{2j'k'+j_0k'}|k'_0k'_1\cdots k'_{m-1}\rangle|j_0\rangle \tag{6.100}$$

$$=\frac{1}{\sqrt{2^m}}\sum_{k'=0}^{2^m-1}\omega_{2^{m+1}}^{(2j'+j_0)k'}|k_0'k_1'\cdots k_{m-1}'\rangle|j_0\rangle \tag{6.101}$$

$$=\frac{1}{\sqrt{2^m}}\sum_{k'=0}^{2^m-1}\omega_{2^{m+1}}^{jk'}|k_0'k_1'\cdots k_{m-1}'\rangle|j_0\rangle. \tag{6.102}$$

Finally, the following state is obtained after the Hadamard gate in the circuit diagram is applied:

$$\frac{1}{\sqrt{2^{m+1}}}\sum_{k'=0}^{2^m-1}\sum_{k_m=0}^{1}\omega_{2^{m+1}}^{jk'}(-1)^{k_m j_0}|k_0'k_1'\cdots k_{m-1}'\rangle|k_m\rangle. \tag{6.103}$$

Due to

$$\omega_{2^{m+1}}^{j(2^m k_m)}=\omega_2^{jk_m}=e^{\frac{2\pi ijk_m}{2}}=(e^{\pi i})^{k_m j}=(-1)^{k_m j}=(-1)^{k_m j_0}, \tag{6.104}$$

Eq. (6.103) equals

$$\frac{1}{\sqrt{2^{m+1}}}\sum_{k'=0}^{2^m-1}\sum_{k_m=0}^{1}\omega_{2^{m+1}}^{jk'+j(2^m k_m)}|k_0'k_1'\cdots k_{m-1}'\rangle|k_m\rangle \tag{6.105}$$

$$=\frac{1}{\sqrt{2^{m+1}}}\sum_{k'=0}^{2^m-1}\sum_{k_m=0}^{1}\omega_{2^{m+1}}^{j(k'+2^m k_m)}|k_0'k_1'\cdots k_{m-1}'\rangle|k_m\rangle \tag{6.106}$$

$$=\frac{1}{\sqrt{2^{m+1}}}\sum_{k=0}^{2^{m+1}-1}\omega_{2^{m+1}}^{jk}|k_0k_1\cdots k_m\rangle. \tag{6.107}$$

In the following, we analyze the time complexity of quantum Fourier transform, that is, the number of elementary quantum gates required to realize quantum Fourier transform. Let $g(m)$ be the number of elementary quantum gates to realize $\widetilde{\mathrm{QFT}}_{2^m}$, then $g(1)=1$ and $g(m+1)=g(m)+(m+1)$. Therefore, $g(m)=\sum_{j=1}^{m} j=\binom{m+1}{2}=O(m^2)$. Notice that currently, the fastest classical algorithm known for implementing the discrete Fourier transform is the fast Fourier transform algorithm, which has a time complexity of $O(m2^m)$. Thus the essential advantage of quantum algorithms over classical algorithms is also reflected in the realization of the discrete Fourier transform.

Exercises

6.14. Prove

$$\frac{1}{\sqrt{2^m}}\sum_{k'=0}^{2^m-1}\omega_{2^{m+1}}^{2j'k'+j_0k_0'+j_0(2k_1')+\cdots+j_0(2^{m-1}k_{m-1}')}|k_0'k_1'\cdots k_{m-1}'\rangle|j_0\rangle$$
$$=\frac{1}{\sqrt{2^m}}\sum_{k'=0}^{2^m-1}\omega_{2^{m+1}}^{jk'}|k_0'k_1'\cdots k_{m-1}'\rangle|j_0\rangle.$$

Furthermore, after the Hadamard gate applying on $|j_0\rangle$, we have

$$\frac{1}{\sqrt{2^{m+1}}}\sum_{k=0}^{2^{m+1}-1}\omega_{2^{m+1}}^{jk}|k_0k_1\cdots k_m\rangle.$$

6.15. Quantum Fourier transform QFT on the computable basis $|0\rangle,\ldots,$ $|N-1\rangle$ is defined as a linear operator applying on the ground states, defined as follows:

$$|j\rangle\to\frac{1}{\sqrt{N}}\sum_{k=0}^{N-1}e^{2\pi ijk/N}|k\rangle.$$

Prove that QFT is unitary.

6.16. Compute quantum Fourier transform acts on the n quantum bit states $|00\cdots0\rangle$ and $|11\cdots1\rangle$, respectively.

6.17. Design a quantum circuit realizing the inverse quantum Fourier transform.

6.8 Quantum phase estimation

Let U be a $2^n\times2^n$ unitary matrix with corresponding eigenvectors $|\psi_1\rangle,\cdots,|\psi_N\rangle$ $(N=2^n)$ and corresponding eigenvalues $e^{2\pi i\theta_1},\cdots,e^{2\pi i\theta_N}$, with $\theta_i\in[0,1)$, $i=1,2,\cdots,N$, that is,

$$U|\psi_j\rangle=e^{2\pi i\theta_j}|\psi_j\rangle,\tag{6.108}$$

for $j\in\{1,2,\cdots,N\}$, then

$$\langle\psi_j|\psi_k\rangle=\begin{cases}1, & j=k,\\ 0, & j\neq k,\end{cases}\tag{6.109}$$

where $j, k \in \{1, \cdots, N\}$.

The phase estimation problem can be described as follows: given the unitary operator U and $|\psi\rangle$ as the eigenvector of U, that is, $U|\psi\rangle = e^{2\pi i\theta}|\psi\rangle$, the goal is to estimate and output $\theta \in [0, 1)$.

Suppose U is a unitary transform applied on n qubits, with m being a positive integer. Let $\Lambda_m(U)$ denote the unitary transform applying on $m+n$ qubits, defined as

$$\Lambda_m(U)|k\rangle|\phi\rangle = |k\rangle(U^k|\phi\rangle), \tag{6.110}$$

where $k \in \{0, \cdots, 2^m - 1\}$ and $|\phi\rangle$ is an n-bit quantum state.

We can solve the phase estimation problem with the help of the quantum Fourier transform introduced in the previous section. In the following, we describe the specific process of quantum phase estimation, as shown in Fig. 6.9.

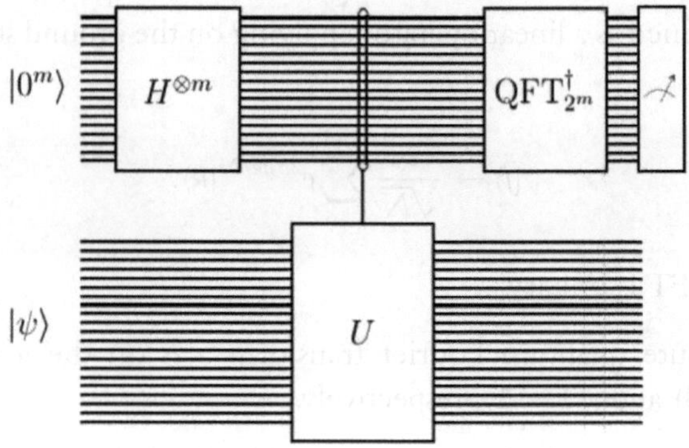

Figure 6.9 Quantum phase estimation.

The quantum phase estimation algorithm (Algorithm 4) is analyzed by two cases.

Case 1: There exists $j \in \{0, 1, 2, \cdots, 2^m - 1\}$ such that $\theta = \frac{j}{2^m}$. At this point, the state in Step 4 of the quantum phase estimation algorithm is

$$\frac{1}{\sqrt{2^m}}\sum_{k=0}^{2^m-1} e^{2\pi ik\theta}|k\rangle = \frac{1}{\sqrt{2^m}}\sum_{k=0}^{2^m-1} e^{2\pi ik\frac{j}{2^m}}|k\rangle \tag{6.111}$$

$$= \frac{1}{\sqrt{2^m}}\sum_{k=0}^{2^m-1} \omega^{jk}|k\rangle \tag{6.112}$$

$$= |\phi_j\rangle. \tag{6.113}$$

Algorithm 4: Quantum phase estimation.

Input: The black box U and its feature vector $|\psi\rangle$.

Output: θ satisfying $U|\psi\rangle = e^{2\pi i\theta}|\psi\rangle$.

1 Set the Initial State as $|\Phi_0\rangle = |0^m\rangle|\psi\rangle$.

2 $|\Phi_1\rangle = (H^{\otimes m} \otimes I)|\Phi_0\rangle = \frac{1}{\sqrt{2^m}} \sum_{k=0}^{2^m-1} |k\rangle|\psi\rangle$.

3 $|\Phi_2\rangle = \Lambda_m(U)|\Phi_1\rangle = \frac{1}{\sqrt{2^m}} \sum_{k=0}^{2^m-1} |k\rangle(U^k|\psi\rangle) = \frac{1}{\sqrt{2^m}} \sum_{k=0}^{2^m-1} |k\rangle e^{2\pi ik\theta}|\psi\rangle = (\frac{1}{\sqrt{2^m}} \sum_{k=0}^{2^m-1} e^{2\pi ik\theta}|k\rangle)|\psi\rangle$.

4 Ignoring the n qubits of the second register, we get $\frac{1}{\sqrt{2^m}} \sum_{k=0}^{2^m-1} e^{2\pi ik\theta}|k\rangle$.

5 Perform the inverse quantum Fourier transform $\mathrm{QFT}^\dagger_{2\mathrm{m}}$ on the m quantum bits of the first register.

6 Measure m qubits of the first register to get j.

7 Return $\theta = \frac{j}{2^m}$.

It can be seen that $\mathrm{QFT}^\dagger_{2^m}|\phi_j\rangle = |j\rangle, j \in \{0, 1, 2, \cdots, 2^m - 1\}$. This gives j exactly, and thus gives θ without error.

Case 2: For any $j \in \{0, 1, 2, \cdots, 2^m - 1\}$, there is $\theta \neq \frac{j}{2^m}$.

In step 5, after applying $\mathrm{QFT}^\dagger_{2^m}$, the state is

$$\mathrm{QFT}^\dagger_{2^m}\left(\frac{1}{\sqrt{2^m}} \sum_{k=0}^{2^m-1} e^{2\pi ik\theta}|k\rangle\right) \tag{6.114}$$

$$=\frac{1}{\sqrt{2^m}} \sum_{k=0}^{2^m-1} e^{2\pi ik\theta}\mathrm{QFT}^\dagger_{2^m}\left(|k\rangle\right) \tag{6.115}$$

$$=\frac{1}{\sqrt{2^m}} \sum_{k=0}^{2^m-1} e^{2\pi ik\theta} \frac{1}{\sqrt{2^m}} \sum_{j=0}^{2^m-1} e^{-2\pi ijk/2^m}|j\rangle \tag{6.116}$$

$$=\frac{1}{2^m} \sum_{k=0}^{2^m-1} \sum_{j=0}^{2^m-1} e^{2\pi ik(\theta-j/2^m)}|j\rangle \tag{6.117}$$

$$=\sum_{j=0}^{2^m-1} \left(\frac{1}{2^m} \sum_{k=0}^{2^m-1} e^{2\pi ik(\theta-j/2^m)}\right)|j\rangle. \tag{6.118}$$

Therefore the probability of obtaining j is

$$\mathrm{P}_j = \left| \frac{1}{2^m} \sum_{k=0}^{2^m-1} e^{2\pi i k(\theta - j/2^m)} \right|^2, \tag{6.119}$$

where $j \in \{0, \cdots, 2^m - 1\}$.

Since $e^{2\pi i k(\theta - j/2^m)} \neq 1 \; (j \in \{0, 1, 2, \cdots, 2^m - 1\})$, it is easy to get

$$\mathrm{P}_j = \frac{1}{2^{2m}} \left| \frac{e^{2\pi i(2^m\theta - j)} - 1}{e^{2\pi i(\theta - j/2^m)} - 1} \right|^2. \tag{6.120}$$

In the following, we prove that P_j is relatively larger for $\frac{j}{2^m} \approx \theta$, but P_j is smaller for $\frac{j}{2^m}$ more differing from θ.

For the closest θ to $\frac{j}{2^m}$, denote $\theta - \frac{j}{2^m} = \epsilon$, then $|\epsilon| \leq 2^{-(m+1)}$. Suppose

$$a = \left| e^{2\pi i(2^m\theta - j)} - 1 \right| = \left| e^{2\pi i \epsilon 2^m} - 1 \right|, \tag{6.121}$$

$$b = \left| e^{2\pi i(\theta - \frac{j}{2^m})} - 1 \right| = \left| e^{2\pi i \epsilon} - 1 \right|. \tag{6.122}$$

Then

$$\mathrm{P}_j = \frac{1}{2^{2m}} \frac{a^2}{b^2}. \tag{6.123}$$

To compute a lower bound on P_j, we can refer to Figs. 6.10 and 6.11.

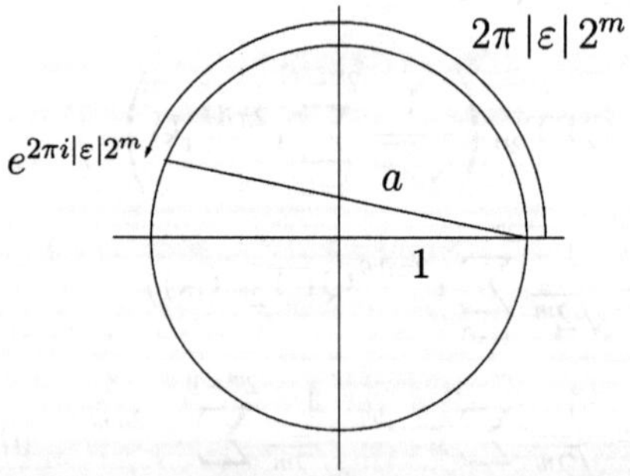

Figure 6.10 Lower bound on the probability of quantum phase estimation (1).

As shown in Fig. 6.10, it can be shown that the arc length divided by the chord length between $e^{2\pi i|\epsilon|2^m}$ and 1 is less than or equal to $\frac{\pi}{2}$ on the unit circle in the complex plane, and the arc length between $e^{2\pi i|\epsilon|2^m}$ and 1 is $2\pi|\epsilon|2^m$, and the chord length is a, so there is $\frac{2\pi|\epsilon|2^m}{a} \le \frac{\pi}{2}$, which in turn gives $a \ge 4|\epsilon|2^m$.

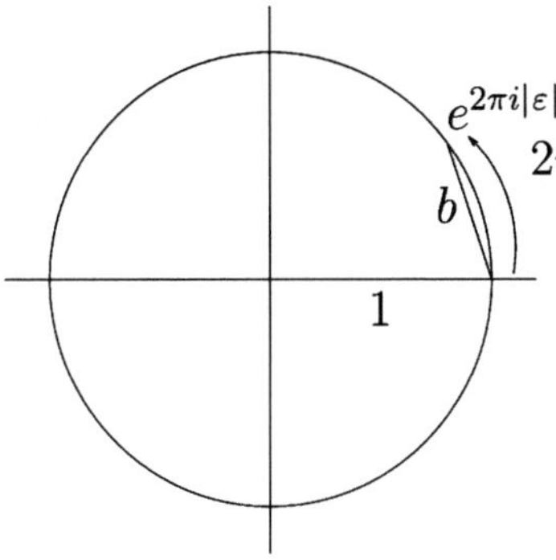

Figure 6.11 Lower bound on the probability of quantum phase estimation (2).

As shown in Fig. 6.11, it is easy to see that the arc length between $e^{2\pi i|\epsilon|}$ and 1 is greater than equal to the chord length on the unit circle in the complex plane, while the arc length between $e^{2\pi i|\epsilon|}$ and 1 is $2\pi|\epsilon|$ and the chord length is b, so there is a $2\pi|\epsilon| \ge b$.

Furthermore, we have

$$P_j \ge \frac{1}{2^{2m}}\frac{16|\epsilon|^2 2^{2m}}{4\pi^2|\epsilon|^2} = \frac{4}{\pi^2} > 0.4, \tag{6.124}$$

so, the closest $\frac{j}{2^m}$ to θ can be obtained with greater probability.

On the other hand, suppose $e^{2\pi i\theta} = e^{2\pi i(\frac{j}{2^m}+\epsilon)}$, where $\frac{t}{2^m} \le |\epsilon| \le \frac{1}{2}$ (t is some positive integer). In this case, according to Eq. (6.123) and the trigonometric inequality, we have

$$a = \left|e^{2\pi i\epsilon 2^m} - 1\right| \le \left|e^{2\pi i\epsilon 2^m}\right| + |-1| = 2. \tag{6.125}$$

As is analyzed before, we have $\frac{2\pi|\epsilon|}{b} \le \frac{\pi}{2}$, and thus $b \ge 4|\epsilon|$.

Therefore, we have

$$P_j \le \frac{4}{2^{2m}4^2|\epsilon|^2} = \frac{1}{2^{2m}4|\epsilon|^2} \le \frac{1}{2^{2m}4t^2 2^{-2m}} = \frac{1}{4t^2}. \tag{6.126}$$

So, the probability of obtaining $\frac{j}{2^m}$ with a large difference from θ is small.

6.9 * Detailed probabilistic analyses of quantum phase estimation

In this section, we generalize the previous quantum Fourier transform applying on orthonormal basis of dimension 2^m to the general quantum Fourier transform applying on orthonormal basis of arbitrary dimension, and give theorems and more detailed analyses related to the probabilities of different results from quantum phase estimation algorithms [13].

We start with some definitions as follows.

Definition 6.9. For any $M \geq 1$, $0 \leq x < M$, define the quantum Fourier transform

$$\mathrm{QFT}_M : |x\rangle \to \frac{1}{\sqrt{M}} \sum_{y=0}^{M-1} e^{2\pi i x y/M} |y\rangle. \tag{6.127}$$

Definition 6.10. For any positive integer M and real number ω with $0 \leq \omega < 1$, denote

$$|S_M(\omega)\rangle = \frac{1}{\sqrt{M}} \sum_{y=0}^{M-1} e^{2\pi i \omega y} |y\rangle. \tag{6.128}$$

Then for $0 \leq x \leq M-1$, we have

$$\mathrm{QFT}_M |x\rangle = |S_M(x/M)\rangle. \tag{6.129}$$

Definition 6.11. For any real number ω_0 and ω_1, denote

$$d(\omega_0, \omega_1) = \min_{z \in \mathbb{Z}} |z + \omega_1 - \omega_0|. \tag{6.130}$$

Then we have the following lemmas.

Lemma 6.1. *For* $0 \leq \omega_0 < 1$ *and* $0 \leq \omega_1 < 1$, *denote* $\Delta = d(\omega_0, \omega_1)$. *If* $\Delta = 0$, *then*

$$|\langle S_M(\omega_0) | S_M(\omega_1) \rangle|^2 = 1; \tag{6.131}$$

otherwise

$$|\langle S_M(\omega_0) | S_M(\omega_1) \rangle|^2 = \frac{\sin^2(M\Delta\pi)}{M^2 \sin^2(\Delta\pi)}. \tag{6.132}$$

Proof. According to Definition 6.10,

$$|\langle S_M(\omega_0)|S_M(\omega_1)\rangle|^2 = \left|\left(\frac{1}{\sqrt{M}}\sum_{y=0}^{M-1} e^{-2\pi i\omega_0 y}\langle y|\right)\left(\frac{1}{\sqrt{M}}\sum_{y=0}^{M-1} e^{2\pi i\omega_1 y}|y\rangle\right)\right|^2 \tag{6.133}$$

$$= \frac{1}{M^2}\left|\sum_{y=0}^{M-1} e^{2\pi i(\omega_1-\omega_0)y}\right|^2. \tag{6.134}$$

First, we know $-1 < \omega_1 - \omega_0 < 1$. Considering

$$\Delta = d(\omega_0, \omega_1) = \min_{z\in\mathbb{Z}}\{|z + \omega_1 - \omega_0|\}, \tag{6.135}$$

we discuss its value in four cases.

Case 1: When $-1 < \omega_1 - \omega_0 < -\frac{1}{2}$, we have

$$\Delta = |1 + \omega_1 - \omega_0| = 1 + \omega_1 - \omega_0. \tag{6.136}$$

Thus we have

$$e^{2\pi i(\omega_1-\omega_0)y} = e^{2\pi i(\omega_1-\omega_0)y}e^{2\pi iy} = e^{2\pi i(1+\omega_1-\omega_0)y} = e^{2\pi i\Delta y}. \tag{6.137}$$

Case 2: When $-\frac{1}{2} \le \omega_1 - \omega_0 < 0$, we have $\Delta = |0 + \omega_1 - \omega_0| = \omega_0 - \omega_1$. Therefore

$$\left|\sum_{y=0}^{M-1} e^{2\pi i(\omega_1-\omega_0)y}\right|^2 = \left(\sum_{y=0}^{M-1} e^{-2\pi i(\omega_1-\omega_0)y}\right)\left(\sum_{y=0}^{M-1} e^{2\pi i(\omega_1-\omega_0)y}\right) \tag{6.138}$$

$$= \left(\sum_{y=0}^{M-1} e^{2\pi i\Delta y}\right)\left(\sum_{y=0}^{M-1} e^{-2\pi i\Delta y}\right) \tag{6.139}$$

$$= \left|\sum_{y=0}^{M-1} e^{2\pi i\Delta y}\right|^2. \tag{6.140}$$

Case 3: When $0 \le \omega_1 - \omega_0 < \frac{1}{2}$, we have

$$\Delta = |0 + \omega_1 - \omega_0| = \omega_1 - \omega_0. \tag{6.141}$$

As a result,

$$e^{2\pi i(\omega_1-\omega_0)y} = e^{2\pi i\Delta y}. \tag{6.142}$$

Case 4: When $\frac{1}{2} \le \omega_1 - \omega_0 < 1$, we have

$$\Delta = |-1 + \omega_1 - \omega_0| = 1 - \omega_1 + \omega_0. \tag{6.143}$$

Consequently, we obtain

$$\left|\sum_{y=0}^{M-1} e^{2\pi i(\omega_1-\omega_0)y}\right|^2 = \left(\sum_{y=0}^{M-1} e^{-2\pi i(\omega_0-\omega_1)y}\right)\left(\sum_{y=0}^{M-1} e^{2\pi i(\omega_0-\omega_1)y}\right) \tag{6.144}$$

$$= \left|\sum_{y=0}^{M-1} e^{2\pi i(\omega_0-\omega_1)y}\right|^2 \tag{6.145}$$

$$= \left|\sum_{y=0}^{M-1} e^{2\pi i(1-\omega_1+\omega_0)y}\right|^2 \tag{6.146}$$

$$= \left|\sum_{y=0}^{M-1} e^{2\pi i\Delta y}\right|^2. \tag{6.147}$$

Summarizing the four cases, we have

$$|\langle S_M(\omega_0)|S_M(\omega_1)\rangle|^2 = \frac{1}{M^2}\left|\sum_{y=0}^{M-1} e^{2\pi i(\omega_1-\omega_0)y}\right|^2 \tag{6.148}$$

$$= \frac{1}{M^2}\left|\sum_{y=0}^{M-1} e^{2\pi i\Delta y}\right|^2 \tag{6.149}$$

$$= \begin{cases} 1, & \Delta = 0; \\ \frac{\sin^2(M\Delta\pi)}{M^2\sin^2(\Delta\pi)}, & \Delta \neq 0. \end{cases} \tag{6.150}$$

□

Suppose ω is a real number with $0 \le \omega < 1$, and M a positive integer. x is an integer with $0 \le x < M$, and k is an integer greater than 1. Then define

$$\Delta_x = d(\omega, \frac{x}{M}) = \min_{z\in\mathbb{Z}}\left\{\left|z + \frac{x}{M} - \omega\right|\right\}. \tag{6.151}$$

For any x, let $z_x \in \mathbb{Z}$ such that

$$\Delta_x = \left|z_x + \frac{x}{M} - \omega\right|. \tag{6.152}$$

We have the following lemma.

Lemma 6.2. *Suppose* $S_1 = \{x|z_x + \frac{x}{M} - \omega > \frac{k}{M}\}$ *and* $S_2 = \{x| - (z_x + \frac{x}{M} - \omega) > \frac{k}{M}\}$. *Then for any* $x_1, x_2 \in S_1$, $x'_1, x'_2 \in S_2$ *with* $x_1 \neq x_2$, $x'_1 \neq x'_2$, *there exist* $t_{(x_1,x_2)}, t'_{(x'_1,x'_2)} \in \mathbb{Z}\backslash\{0\}$ *such that* $\Delta_{x_1} - \Delta_{x_2} = \frac{1}{M} \cdot t_{(x_1,x_2)}$ *and* $\Delta_{x'_1} - \Delta_{x'_2} = \frac{1}{M} \cdot t'_{(x'_1,x'_2)}$.

Proof. For any $x_1, x_2 \in S_1$, and $x_1 \neq x_2$, we have

$$\Delta_{x_1} - \Delta_{x_2} = (z_{x_1} + \frac{x_1}{M} - \omega) - (z_{x_2} + \frac{x_2}{M} - \omega) \tag{6.153}$$

$$= \frac{1}{M} \cdot (M(z_{x_1} - z_{x_2}) + x_1 - x_2). \tag{6.154}$$

Since $-(M-1) \leq x_1 - x_2 \leq (M-1)$ and $x_1 - x_2 \neq 0$, $z_{x_1} - z_{x_2} \in \mathbb{Z}$, it follows that $M(z_{x_1} - z_{x_2}) + x_1 - x_2$ are nonzero integers. Denote $t_{(x_1,x_2)} = M(z_{x_1} - z_{x_2}) + x_1 - x_2$, and this gives $\Delta_{x_1} - \Delta_{x_2} = \frac{1}{M} \cdot t_{(x_1,x_2)}$. Similarly, for any $x'_1, x'_2 \in S_2$, and $x'_1 \neq x'_2$, there exists $t'_{(x'_1,x'_2)} \in \mathbb{Z}\backslash\{0\}$ such that $\Delta_{x'_1} - \Delta_{x'_2} = \frac{1}{M} \cdot t'_{(x'_1,x'_2)}$. □

Now we further give and prove the following theorem.

Theorem 6.11. *Let X be the discrete random variable associated with the measurement obtained by measuring* $\mathrm{QFT}_M^{-1}|S_M(\omega)\rangle$ *in the computational basis. If* $M\omega$ *is an integer, then* $\mathrm{P}(X = M\omega) = 1$; *otherwise,*

$$\mathrm{P}(X = x) = \frac{\sin^2(M\Delta_x\pi)}{M^2\sin^2(\Delta_x\pi)} \leq \frac{1}{(2M\Delta_x)^2}, \tag{6.155}$$

where $0 \leq \omega < 1$, *M is a positive integer, x is an integer and satisfies* $0 \leq x \leq M-1$. *For any* $k > 1$, *there is*

$$\mathrm{P}(d(X/M, \omega) \leq k/M) \geq 1 - \frac{1}{2(k-1)}; \tag{6.156}$$

when $k = 1$, $M \geq 2$, *we have*

$$\mathrm{P}(d(X/M, \omega) \leq 1/M) \geq \frac{8}{\pi^2}. \tag{6.157}$$

Proof. First,

$$\mathrm{P}(X = x) = |\langle x|\mathrm{QFT}^{-1}|S_M(\omega)\rangle|^2 \tag{6.158}$$

$$= |(\mathrm{QFT}|x\rangle)^\dagger|S_M(\omega)\rangle|^2 \tag{6.159}$$

$$= |\langle S_M(x/M)|S_M(\omega)\rangle|^2. \tag{6.160}$$

Then, by utilizing Lemma 6.1, if $M\omega$ is integer, we have

$$\mathrm{P}(X = M\omega) = |\langle S_M(M\omega/M)|S_M(\omega)\rangle|^2 \tag{6.161}$$
$$= |\langle S_M(\omega)|S_M(\omega)\rangle|^2 \tag{6.162}$$
$$= 1. \tag{6.163}$$

If $M\omega$ is not integer, it follows that $0 < \Delta_x \le \frac{1}{2}$, due to $0 \le \omega < 1$, M being a positive integer, and x being an integer with $0 \le x \le M - 1$,

Since $\sin^2(M\Delta_x\pi) \le 1$, we have

$$\mathrm{P}(X = x) = \frac{\sin^2(M\Delta_x\pi)}{M^2 \sin^2(\Delta_x\pi)} \le \frac{1}{M^2 \sin^2(\Delta_x\pi)}. \tag{6.164}$$

According to $\sin(\frac{\pi}{2}t) \ge t$, where $0 < t \le 1$, with $\Delta_x = \frac{t}{2}$, it follows that $\sin(\pi\Delta_x) \ge 2\Delta_x$, where $0 < \Delta_x \le \frac{1}{2}$. Therefore

$$\mathrm{P}(X = x) \le \frac{1}{M^2 \sin^2(\Delta_x\pi)} \le \frac{1}{(2M\Delta_x)^2}. \tag{6.165}$$

In the following, we further prove the remainder by using Eq. (6.165). Denote

$$A = \{x \mid \Delta_x > \frac{k}{M}\}, \tag{6.166}$$

$$S_1 = \{x \mid z_x + \frac{x}{M} - \omega > \frac{k}{M}\}, \tag{6.167}$$

$$S_2 = \{x \mid -(z_x + \frac{x}{M} - \omega) > \frac{k}{M}\}, \tag{6.168}$$

then we have

$$\mathrm{P}(d(X/M, \omega) \le k/M) \tag{6.169}$$
$$= 1 - \mathrm{P}(d(X/M, \omega) > k/M) \tag{6.170}$$
$$= 1 - \sum_{x \in A} \mathrm{P}(X = x) \tag{6.171}$$
$$= 1 - \left(\sum_{x \in S_1} \mathrm{P}(X = x) + \sum_{x \in S_2} \mathrm{P}(X = x) \right) \tag{6.172}$$
$$\ge 1 - \left(\sum_{x \in S_1} \frac{1}{(2M\Delta_x)^2} + \sum_{x \in S_2} \frac{1}{(2M(\Delta_x))^2} \right) \tag{6.173}$$

$$\geq 1 - \left(\sum_{j=k}^{\infty} \frac{1}{4M^2(\frac{j}{M})^2} + \sum_{j=k}^{\infty} \frac{1}{4M^2(\frac{j}{M})^2} \right) \tag{6.174}$$

$$= 1 - 2\sum_{j=k}^{\infty} \frac{1}{4M^2(\frac{j}{M})^2} \tag{6.175}$$

$$= 1 - \sum_{j=k}^{\infty} \frac{1}{2j^2} \tag{6.176}$$

$$\geq 1 - \sum_{j=k}^{\infty} \frac{1}{2j(j-1)} \tag{6.177}$$

$$= 1 - \sum_{j=k}^{\infty} \left(\frac{1}{2(j-1)} - \frac{1}{2j} \right) \tag{6.178}$$

$$= 1 - \frac{1}{2(k-1)}, \tag{6.179}$$

where inequality (6.174) is verified as follows: according to Lemma 6.2, for $x_1, x_2 \in S_1$, we have $\Delta_{x_1} - \Delta_{x_2} = \frac{1}{M} \cdot t_{(x_1,x_2)}$ for $t_{(x_1,x_2)} \in \mathbb{Z} \backslash \{0\}$. Notice that for $j_1, j_2 \geq k$, we have

$$\min_{j_1,j_2} \left| \frac{j_1}{M} - \frac{j_2}{M} \right| = \frac{1}{M} \leq \min_{x_1,x_2} \{\Delta_{x_1} - \Delta_{x_2}\},$$

and $\min_{j \geq k} j/M < \min_x \Delta_x$. Then we can find a bijection $f(j) = \Delta_{x_j}$ such that $j/M < \Delta_{x_j}$. By replacing Δ_{x_j} with $f^{-1}(\Delta_{x_j})/M$, we have obtained that inequality (6.174) holds.

The last part of the theorem is proved below. Since $M\omega$ is not an integer, one can set $M\omega = \lfloor M\omega \rfloor + \epsilon_1 = \lceil M\omega \rceil - \epsilon_2$, where $0 < \epsilon_1 < 1$, $0 < \epsilon_2 < 1$ and $\epsilon_1 + \epsilon_2 = 1$.

When $X = \lfloor M\omega \rfloor = M\omega - \epsilon_1$, we have

$$d(X/M, \omega) = \min_{z \in \mathbb{Z}} \{|z + \omega - \frac{X}{M}|\} \tag{6.180}$$

$$= \min_{z \in \mathbb{Z}} \{|z + \omega - \frac{M\omega - \epsilon_1}{M}|\} \tag{6.181}$$

$$= \min_{z \in \mathbb{Z}} \{|z + \frac{\epsilon_1}{M}|\}. \tag{6.182}$$

Since $M \geq 2$, $0 < \epsilon_1 < 1$, $0 < \frac{\epsilon_1}{M} < \frac{1}{2}$, we have

$$\min_{z \in \mathbb{Z}} \{|z + \frac{\epsilon_1}{M}|\} = |0 + \frac{\epsilon_1}{M}| = \frac{\epsilon_1}{M} \leq \frac{1}{M}. \tag{6.183}$$

Similarly, when $X = \lceil M\omega \rceil = M\omega + \epsilon_2$, there is $d(X/M, \omega) \leq 1/M$; and when $X = \lfloor M\omega \rfloor - l$ or $X = \lceil M\omega \rceil + l$, there is $d(X/M, \omega) > 1/M$ where l is a positive integer. Therefore, it can be seen that

$$\mathrm{P}(d(X/M, \omega) \leq 1/M) = \mathrm{P}(X = \lfloor M\omega \rfloor) + \mathrm{P}(X = \lceil M\omega \rceil). \tag{6.184}$$

Denote $\Delta' = d(\frac{\lfloor M\omega \rfloor}{M}, \omega)$. Due to

$$d(\frac{\lfloor M\omega \rfloor}{M}, \omega) + d(\frac{\lceil M\omega \rceil}{M}, \omega) = \frac{\epsilon_1 + \epsilon_2}{M} = \frac{1}{M}, \tag{6.185}$$

we have

$$\begin{aligned} \mathrm{P}(d(X/M, \omega) \leq 1/M) &= \mathrm{P}(X = \lfloor M\omega \rfloor) + \mathrm{P}(X = \lceil M\omega \rceil) & (6.186)\\ &= \frac{\sin^2(M\Delta'\pi)}{M^2 \sin^2(\Delta'\pi)} + \frac{\sin^2(M(\frac{1}{M} - \Delta')\pi)}{M^2 \sin^2((\frac{1}{M} - \Delta')\pi)}, & (6.187) \end{aligned}$$

where $0 \leq \Delta' \leq 1/M$.

In view of

$$f(\Delta') = \frac{\sin^2(M\Delta'\pi)}{M^2 \sin^2(\Delta'\pi)} + \frac{\sin^2(M(\frac{1}{M} - \Delta')\pi)}{M^2 \sin^2((\frac{1}{M} - \Delta')\pi)}, \tag{6.188}$$

it can be checked that when $0 < \Delta' < \frac{1}{2M}$,

$$f'(\Delta') < 0; \tag{6.189}$$

when $\Delta' = \frac{1}{2M}$, we have

$$f'(\Delta') = 0; \tag{6.190}$$

when $\frac{1}{2M} < \Delta' < \frac{1}{M}$, we have

$$f'(\Delta') > 0. \tag{6.191}$$

Thus $f(\Delta')$ attains at the minimum value on $(0, \frac{1}{M})$, that is, $f(\frac{1}{2M})$.

Therefore

$$\begin{aligned} &\mathrm{P}(d(X/M, \omega) \leq 1/M) & (6.192)\\ =&\frac{\sin^2(M\Delta'\pi)}{M^2 \sin^2(\Delta'\pi)} + \frac{\sin^2(M(\frac{1}{M} - \Delta')\pi)}{M^2 \sin^2((\frac{1}{M} - \Delta')\pi)} & (6.193)\\ \geq&\frac{\sin^2(\frac{\pi}{2})}{M^2 \sin^2(\frac{\pi}{2M})} + \frac{\sin^2(\frac{\pi}{2})}{M^2 \sin^2(\frac{\pi}{2M})} & (6.194) \end{aligned}$$

$$\geq \frac{4}{\pi^2} + \frac{4}{\pi^2} \tag{6.195}$$

$$= \frac{8}{\pi^2}. \tag{6.196}$$

□

Theorem 6.11 more accurately quantifies that quantum phase estimation can estimate $\frac{X}{M}$ that is closer to ω with high probability.

6.10 Shor's factorization algorithm

Shor's factorization algorithm was proposed by Peter Shor [14] in 1994. Shor's factorization algorithm provides an exponential speedup in time complexity over the best-known classical algorithms for factorization problems and solving discrete logarithmic problems, which is one of the most important advances in the history of quantum computing. In this section, we present Shor's factorization algorithm for factorizing large integers in detail.

Shor's factorization algorithm is well known for its challenge in today's widely used RSA cryptosystem, a public-key cryptosystem widely used in the field of information security for encrypting information and digital authentication. The security of RSA is based on the fact that it is difficult for computers to factorize large integers. That is, there is no known classical algorithm that can factorize n-bit integers in polynomial time about n. If an algorithm is found that can factor n-digit integers in polynomial time with respect to n, the very foundations of RSA security will be shaken, posing a serious threat to the information security of government and industries, where the RSA algorithm is widely used today. Therefore, Shor's design of a quantum algorithm that can efficiently factorize large integers has aroused great interest in quantum computing and inspired governments and industries to explore the potential of quantum computing. At the same time, Shor's factorization algorithm has also stimulated researches on post-quantum cryptography.

Before presenting Shor's factorization algorithm, we introduce some basics of number theory involved in Shor's algorithm.

Let a, b, N be integers with $N \geq 1$, and denote by $N|(a-b)$ as $a \equiv b \pmod{N}$, meaning the remainders of a and b modulo N are equivalent.

Denote $\mathbb{Z}_N^* = \{a \in \mathbb{Z}_N \mid \gcd(a, N) = 1\}$, where $\mathbb{Z}_N = \{0, \cdots, N-1\}$.

The Euler function is defined as $\varphi(N) = |\mathbb{Z}_N^*|$.

In fact, for any $a \in \mathbb{Z}_N^*$, there exists a unique element $b \in \mathbb{Z}_N^*$ such that $ab \equiv 1 \pmod{N}$, and b is referred to as the inverse of a in the sense of the modulo N, which is notated as $a^{-1} \pmod{N}$ for convenience.

Theorem 6.12. *(Euler's theorem) For any integers $a > 0$ and $N \geq 2$, there is $a^{\varphi(N)} \equiv 1 \pmod{N}$ when $\gcd(a, N) = 1$.*

For any $a \in \mathbb{Z}_N^*$, the order of a in $\mathbb{Z}_N^*$ is the smallest positive integer r satisfying $a^r \equiv 1 \pmod{N}$. By Euler's theorem, it follows that for any $a \in \mathbb{Z}_N^*$ there exists an order and the order of a is a divisor of $\varphi(N)$.

The order problem is a key problem in factorization problems, and we begin with the order problem below.

Definition 6.12. Order-finding problem:

Input: positive integers $N \geq 2$ and $a \in \mathbb{Z}_N^*$.

Output: the order of a in $\mathbb{Z}_N^*$, that is, the smallest positive integer r satisfying $a^r \equiv 1 \pmod{N}$.

The time complexity of the fastest classical algorithm known to solve the order problem is exponential time with respect to $\log(N)$ (the number of bits in N). An intuitive classical algorithm is to compute the power of a modulo N one by one until 1 is obtained, with a time complexity of $O(N)$, which is exponential time with respect to $\log(N)$.

We next describe how to solve the order problem using quantum phase estimation.

Denote $n = \lceil \log(N) \rceil$. For any $a \in \mathbb{Z}_N^*$, define an n-qubit transform M_a as

$$M_a|x\rangle = |ax \pmod{N}\rangle, \ x \in \mathbb{Z}_N \tag{6.197}$$

(define $M_a|x\rangle = |x\rangle$, $N \leq x < 2^n$). For any $0 \leq x < N$, we have

$$\begin{aligned} M_{a^{-1}} M_a|x\rangle &= M_{a^{-1}}|ax \pmod{N}\rangle & (6.198)\\ &= |a^{-1}ax \pmod{N}\rangle & (6.199)\\ &= |x \pmod{N}\rangle & (6.200)\\ &= |x\rangle, & (6.201) \end{aligned}$$

and for any $N \leq x < 2^n$, we have

$$\begin{aligned} M_{a^{-1}} M_a|x\rangle &= M_{a^{-1}}|x\rangle & (6.202)\\ &= |x\rangle. & (6.203) \end{aligned}$$

Thus $M_{a^{-1}}M_a = I$.

Let r be the order of a in $\mathbb{Z}_N^*$. Then the following $|\psi_0\rangle$ is the eigenvector of M_a (for convenience and clarity, (mod N) is omitted on the right-hand side of the kets in the equation below):

$$|\psi_0\rangle = \frac{1}{\sqrt{r}}(|1\rangle + |a\rangle + |a^2\rangle + \cdots + |a^{r-1}\rangle). \tag{6.204}$$

In fact,

$$M_a|\psi_0\rangle = M_a\left(\frac{1}{\sqrt{r}}(|1\rangle + |a\rangle + |a^2\rangle + \cdots + |a^{r-1}\rangle)\right) \tag{6.205}$$

$$= \frac{1}{\sqrt{r}}(M_a|1\rangle + M_a|a\rangle + M_a|a^2\rangle + \cdots + M_a|a^{r-1}\rangle) \tag{6.206}$$

$$= \frac{1}{\sqrt{r}}(|a\rangle + |a^2\rangle + |a^3\rangle + \cdots + |a^r\rangle) \tag{6.207}$$

$$= \frac{1}{\sqrt{r}}(|a\rangle + |a^2\rangle + \cdots + |a^{r-1}\rangle + |1\rangle) \tag{6.208}$$

$$= |\psi_0\rangle. \tag{6.209}$$

It can be seen that $|\psi_0\rangle$ is an eigenvector of M_a, corresponding to eigenvalue 1.

Denote

$$|\psi_1\rangle = \frac{1}{\sqrt{r}}(|1\rangle + \omega_r^{-1}|a\rangle + \omega_r^{-2}|a^2\rangle + \cdots + \omega_r^{-(r-1)}|a^{r-1}\rangle), \tag{6.210}$$

where $\omega_r = e^{2\pi i/r}$. Then

$$M_a|\psi_1\rangle = \omega_r|\psi_1\rangle. \tag{6.211}$$

Generally, $\forall 0 \leq j < r$, denote

$$|\psi_j\rangle = \frac{1}{\sqrt{r}}(|1\rangle + \omega_r^{-j}|a\rangle + \omega_r^{-2j}|a^2\rangle + \cdots + \omega_r^{-j(r-1)}|a^{r-1}\rangle) \tag{6.212}$$

$$= \frac{1}{\sqrt{r}}\sum_{k=0}^{r-1}\omega_r^{-jk}|a^k\rangle, \tag{6.213}$$

where

$$M_a|\psi_j\rangle = \omega_r^j|\psi_j\rangle. \tag{6.214}$$

Since r is unknown, $|\psi_j\rangle$ $(0 \leq j < r)$ is not known, either. However, we notice

$$|1\rangle \equiv \frac{1}{\sqrt{r}} \sum_{k=0}^{r-1} |\psi_k\rangle. \tag{6.215}$$

Therefore, by using the quantum phase estimation algorithm, we have the quantum circuit for order finding as shown in Fig. 6.12.

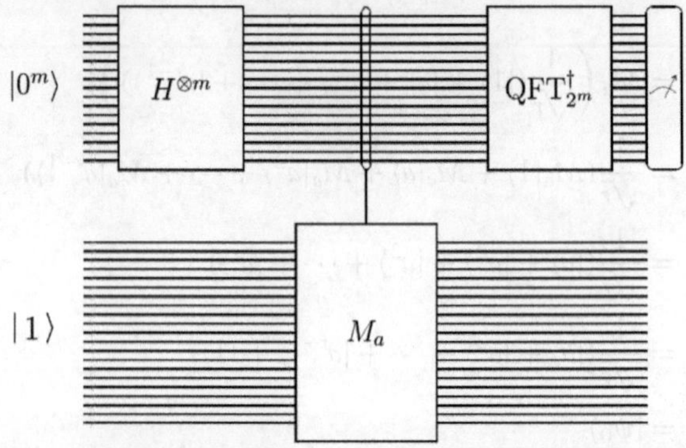

Figure 6.12 Quantum circuit diagram for order finding.

The order-finding algorithm is presented as Algorithm 5.

Analyze the quantum states from step 4 to step 6 in the order-finding algorithm as follows:

$$|\psi_1\rangle = (H^{\otimes m} \otimes I)|0^m\rangle|1\rangle \tag{6.216}$$

$$= \frac{1}{\sqrt{2^m}} \sum_{l=0}^{2^m-1} |l\rangle|1\rangle, \tag{6.217}$$

$$|\psi_2\rangle = \Lambda_m(M_a)|\Phi_1\rangle \tag{6.218}$$

$$= \frac{1}{\sqrt{2^m}} \sum_{l=0}^{2^m-1} |l\rangle M_a^l|1\rangle \tag{6.219}$$

$$= \frac{1}{\sqrt{2^m}} \sum_{l=0}^{2^m-1} |l\rangle M_a^l \left(\frac{1}{\sqrt{r}} \sum_{k=0}^{r-1} |\psi_k\rangle \right) \tag{6.220}$$

$$= \frac{1}{\sqrt{2^m}} \sum_{l=0}^{2^m-1} |l\rangle \frac{1}{\sqrt{r}} \sum_{k=0}^{r-1} M_a^l|\psi_k\rangle \tag{6.221}$$

Algorithm 5: Order-finding algorithm.

Input: Composite number $N \geq 2$, a positive integer a satisfying $\gcd(a, N) = 1$, $m = \lceil 2\log(N) \rceil + 1$.

Output: r such that $a^r = 1 \pmod N$.

1 Set $i = 1$.
2 Prepare the initial state $|\psi_0\rangle = |0^m\rangle|1\rangle$.
3 $|\psi_1\rangle = (H^{\otimes m} \otimes I)|\psi_0\rangle$.
4 $|\psi_2\rangle = \Lambda_m(M_a)|\psi_1\rangle$.
5 $|\psi_3\rangle = (\mathrm{QFT}^\dagger_{2^m} \otimes I)|\psi_2\rangle$.
6 Measure the first register of $|\psi_3\rangle$ to get j_i.
7 Use the continued fraction algorithm to find two integers x_i and y_i that satisfy $\left|\frac{x_i}{y_i} - \frac{j_i}{2^m}\right| < \frac{1}{2^m}$. If the continued fraction algorithm cannot find integers x_i and y_i that satisfy the requirement, skip to step 3.
8 Compute the least common multiple $r = \mathrm{lcm}(y_1, y_2, \ldots, y_i)$.
9 Verify that $a^r \mod N$ is 1, if so output r and the algorithm ends; otherwise make i increase by 1 and jump to step 3.

$$= \frac{1}{\sqrt{2^m}} \sum_{l=0}^{2^m-1} |l\rangle \frac{1}{\sqrt{r}} \sum_{k=0}^{r-1} w_r^{kl} |\psi_k\rangle \tag{6.222}$$

$$= \frac{1}{\sqrt{2^m}} \sum_{l=0}^{2^m-1} |l\rangle \frac{1}{\sqrt{r}} \sum_{k=0}^{r-1} e^{\frac{2\pi ikl}{r}} |\psi_k\rangle \tag{6.223}$$

$$= \frac{1}{\sqrt{r}} \sum_{k=0}^{r-1} \left(\frac{1}{\sqrt{2^m}} \sum_{l=0}^{2^m-1} e^{\frac{2\pi ikl}{r}} |l\rangle \right) |\psi_k\rangle, \tag{6.224}$$

$$|\psi_3\rangle = (\mathrm{QFT}^\dagger_{2^m} \otimes I)|\Phi_2\rangle \tag{6.225}$$

$$= \frac{1}{\sqrt{r}} \sum_{k=0}^{r-1} \left(\mathrm{QFT}^\dagger_{2^m} \left(\frac{1}{\sqrt{2^m}} \sum_{l=0}^{2^m-1} e^{\frac{2\pi ikl}{r}} |l\rangle \right) \right) (I|\psi_k\rangle) \tag{6.226}$$

$$= \frac{1}{\sqrt{r}} \sum_{k=0}^{r-1} \left(\frac{1}{\sqrt{2^m}} \sum_{l=0}^{2^m-1} e^{\frac{2\pi ikl}{r}} \left(\mathrm{QFT}^\dagger_{2^m} |l\rangle \right) \right) |\psi_k\rangle \tag{6.227}$$

$$= \frac{1}{\sqrt{r}} \sum_{k=0}^{r-1} \left(\frac{1}{\sqrt{2^m}} \sum_{l=0}^{2^m-1} e^{\frac{2\pi ikl}{r}} \left(\frac{1}{\sqrt{2^m}} \sum_{j=0}^{2^m-1} e^{-\frac{2\pi ilj}{2^m}} |j\rangle \right) \right) |\psi_k\rangle \tag{6.228}$$

$$=\frac{1}{\sqrt{r}}\sum_{k=0}^{r-1}\left(\frac{1}{2^m}\sum_{j=0}^{2^m-1}\sum_{l=0}^{2^m-1}e^{2\pi il\left(\frac{k}{r}-\frac{j}{2^m}\right)}|j\rangle\right)|\psi_k\rangle. \tag{6.229}$$

At step 6 of the order-finding algorithm, measure the first register to get

$$\frac{j}{2^m}\approx\frac{k}{r}\quad (k\in\{0,\cdots,r-1\}). \tag{6.230}$$

More precisely, the probability of j being obtained after measuring in step 6:

$$\mathrm{P}_j=\frac{1}{r}\sum_{k=0}^{r-1}\left|\frac{1}{2^m}\sum_{l=0}^{2^m-1}e^{2\pi il(k/r-j/2^m)}\right|^2. \tag{6.231}$$

Intuitively, the order-finding algorithm randomly selects a $k\in\{0,\cdots,r-1\}$ and returns an approximation $\frac{k}{r}$ of $\frac{j}{2^m}$.

According to the continued fractions algorithm, for any $\alpha\in(0,1)$ and $N\geq 2$, there exists at most one fraction $\frac{x}{y}$ that satisfies $0\leq x,y<N$, $y\neq 0$, $\gcd(x,y)=1$ and $\left|\alpha-\frac{x}{y}\right|\leq\frac{1}{2N^2}$. The time complexity of the continued fraction algorithm is $O((\log N)^3)$.

Therefore, after the measurements in step 6 of the order-finding algorithm, we can use the continued fraction algorithm to find $\frac{x}{y}$ that satisfies $0\leq x,y<2^m$, $y\neq 0$, $\gcd(x,y)=1$, and

$$\left|\frac{j}{2^m}-\frac{x}{y}\right|\leq\frac{1}{2\times 2^m}\leq\frac{1}{2N^2}\leq\frac{1}{2r^2}. \tag{6.232}$$

This gives us $\frac{x}{y}$ as the approximated value of $\frac{k}{r}$.

If $\gcd(k,r)>1$, then it can be known that r is a multiple of y (although r is not found out). It can be seen that, assuming that $y_1,y_2,\cdots,y_T$ are obtained after repeating T times, r is a multiple of them. By taking the least common multiple of $y_1,y_2,\cdots,y_T$ according to the knowledge of number theory, r can be obtained with high probability.

The key to factorization problem is order finding. Based on the previous quantum order-finding algorithm, we can give Shor's factorization algorithm (Algorithm 6).

Remark 6.3. The probability that r is even and $a^{\frac{r}{2}}+1$ is not divided exactly by N is at least $\frac{1}{2}$.

Algorithm 6: Shor's factorization algorithm.

Input: Composite number $N \geq 2$ $(N = p_1^{k_1} \cdots p_m^{k_m})$.
Output: Factorization of N by u and v $(N = uv,\ u > 1,\ v > 1)$.

Repeat
  For any $a \in \{2, \cdots, N-1\}$.
  Compute $d = \gcd(a, N)$.
  If $d \geq 2$ then
    Return $u = d$ and $v = N/d$.
  Else
    Find the order r of a in $\mathbb{Z}_N^*$.
    If r is even, then
      Compute $x = a^{\frac{r}{2}} - 1 \pmod{N}$.
      Compute $d = \gcd(x, N)$.
      If $d \geq 2$ then
        Return $u = d$ and $v = N/d$.
until finish.

Exercises

6.18. Prove: for any $a \in \mathbb{Z}_N^*$, there exists a unique $b \in \mathbb{Z}_N^*$ such that $ab \equiv 1 \pmod{N}$.

6.19. Find the order of 3 modulo 7 and compute $3^{2021} \pmod{7}$.

6.20. Find the order of $5 \pmod{21}$.

6.21. For any $a \in \mathbb{Z}_N^*$, define the transformation M_a of n-qubit as

$$M_a|x\rangle = |ax \pmod{N}\rangle,\ x \in \mathbb{Z}_N,$$
$$M_a|x\rangle = |x \pmod{N}\rangle,\ N \leq x < 2^n.$$

Prove that M_a is a unitary operator.

6.22. Prove: $|1\rangle = \frac{1}{\sqrt{r}} \sum_{k=0}^{r-1} |\psi_k\rangle$.

6.23. Prove: for any $0 \leq j < r$, $M_a|\psi_j\rangle = \omega_r^j |\psi_j\rangle$.

6.11 Shor's discrete logarithm algorithm

Shor's factorization algorithm poses a significant threat to RSA algorithms whose security is based on the difficulty of solving the large number factorization problems, but not all public-key cryptographic algorithms rely on the difficulty of solving the large number factorization problems. In fact, the security of a number of public-key cryptography algorithms currently in use is based on the difficulty of solving the discrete logarithm problem in the multiplicative group over a finite field or in the additive group of points on an elliptic curve. Shor [14] also devised a quantum algorithm that can efficiently solve discrete logarithms in $\mathbb{Z}_N^*$, which can also be further generalized to solve discrete logarithm problems in other groups.

In this section, we first describe the discrete logarithm problem in $\mathbb{Z}_N^*$. Suppose that two numbers a, b and the order r of a in $\mathbb{Z}_N^*$ are known, where b satisfies $b = a^t (\bmod\ N)$ and t is an unknown integer in $\{0, 1, 2, \cdots, r-1\}$. The discrete logarithm problem is to find the integer t.

A common classical algorithm for solving the discrete logarithm problem is the baby-step giant-step algorithm, which can solve the discrete logarithm problem in $\mathbb{Z}_N^*$ with $O(\sqrt{N})$, which is an exponential time complexity with respect to the length of the digits of N.

Let us specify the quantum algorithm for solving the earlier discrete logarithm problem from now on. Denote $m = \lceil \log_2(r) + 1 \rceil$. Follow the notation in the previous section and define M_a as the unitary operator that implements the following operations:

$$M_a : |s\rangle \to |sa\ (\bmod\ N)\rangle, 0 \le s < N; \tag{6.233}$$

also define M_b as the unitary operator that realizes the following operations:

$$M_b : |s\rangle \to |sb\ (\bmod\ N)\rangle, 0 \le s < N. \tag{6.234}$$

For convenience and clarity of algorithmic analyses, we assume that r is prime. With some more complex analyses, it can be verified that Shor's discrete logarithm algorithm is actually applicable to the case of r being a composite number.

It can be verified that $|\psi_j\rangle = \frac{1}{\sqrt{r}} \sum_{k=0}^{r-1} \omega_r^{-jk} |a^k\rangle$ defined in the previous section are simultaneously the eigenvectors of M_a and M_b, with corresponding eigenvalues $\omega_r^j = e^{2\pi i \frac{j}{r}}$ and $\omega_r^{jt} = e^{2\pi i \frac{jt}{r}}$, respectively.

The key idea of Shor's discrete logarithmic algorithm is to apply quantum phase estimation algorithm twice to estimate $\frac{j}{r}$ and $\frac{jt\ (\bmod\ r)}{r}$ with sufficient accuracy. Since we already know r, it is different from the previous section, and without using the continued fraction algorithm we can derive $\frac{j}{r}$ and $\frac{jt\ (\bmod\ r)}{r}$ with an estimated phase error of at most $\frac{1}{2r}$.

It is not hard to find that the probability that the j derived is equal to 0 is $\frac{1}{r}$. In the case of $j \neq 0$, the multiplicative inverse of j modulo r exists certainly, so we can find t by the following equation:

$$t = j^{-1} jt \pmod r = (j \pmod r)^{-1} (jt \pmod r) (\mathrm{mod} r). \tag{6.235}$$

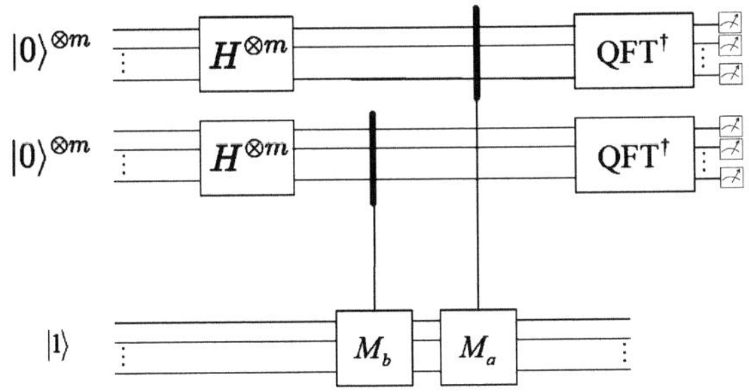

Figure 6.13 Quantum circuit diagram for Shor's discrete logarithmic algorithm.

The circuit in Fig. 6.13 maps the input state $|0\rangle^{\otimes m}|0\rangle^{\otimes m}|\psi_j\rangle$ to the output state $|\widetilde{\frac{j}{r}}\rangle|\widetilde{\frac{jt}{r}}\rangle|\psi_j\rangle$. Therefore, for the input state $|0\rangle^{\otimes m}|0\rangle^{\otimes m}|1\rangle = |0\rangle^{\otimes m}|0\rangle^{\otimes m}(\frac{1}{\sqrt{r}}\sum_{j=0}^{r-1}|\psi_j\rangle)$ the output of the circuit is

$$\frac{1}{\sqrt{r}} \sum_{j=0}^{r-1} |\widetilde{\frac{j}{r}}\rangle |\widetilde{\frac{jt}{r}}\rangle |\psi_j\rangle. \tag{6.236}$$

According to quantum phase estimation the measurement of the first register is x and the measurement of the second register is y. By Theorem 6.11, we have

$$\mathrm{P}(d(X/M, \omega) \leq 1/M) \geq \frac{8}{\pi^2}, \tag{6.237}$$

where $0 \leq \omega < 1$, M is integer and $M \geq 2$.

Suppose $X = x$, $M = 2^m$, $\omega = \frac{j}{r}$, then we have

$$\mathrm{P}\left(d\left(\frac{x}{2^m}, \frac{j}{r}\right) \leq \frac{1}{2^m}\right) \geq \frac{8}{\pi^2}. \tag{6.238}$$

For $\left|\frac{x}{2^m} - \frac{j}{r}\right| \leq \frac{1}{2^m}$, then $m \geq 1$ and

$$\left|\frac{j}{r} - \frac{x}{2^m}\right| = \left|\frac{x}{2^m} - \frac{j}{r}\right| \leq \frac{1}{2^m} \leq \frac{1}{2}. \tag{6.239}$$

Therefore, $d(\frac{x}{2^m}, \frac{j}{r}) = \min_{z\in\mathbb{Z}}\left\{\left|z + \frac{j}{r} - \frac{x}{2^m}\right|\right\} = \left|0 + \frac{j}{r} - \frac{x}{2^m}\right| = \left|\frac{x}{2^m} - \frac{j}{r}\right|$, and

$$P\left(\left|\frac{x}{2^m} - \frac{j}{r}\right| \le \frac{1}{2^m}\right) = P\left(d\left(\frac{x}{2^m}, \frac{j}{r}\right) \le \frac{1}{2^m}\right) \tag{6.240}$$

$$\ge \frac{8}{\pi^2}. \tag{6.241}$$

Similarly, it can be obtained that

$$P\left(\left|\frac{y}{2^m} - \frac{jt \text{ (mod } r)}{r}\right| \le \frac{1}{2^m}\right) \tag{6.242}$$

$$= P\left(d\left(\frac{y}{2^m}, \frac{jt \text{ (mod } r)}{r}\right) \le \frac{1}{2^m}\right) \tag{6.243}$$

$$\ge \frac{8}{\pi^2}. \tag{6.244}$$

So the probability that x and y both satisfy

$$\left|\frac{x}{2^m} - \frac{j}{r}\right| \le \frac{1}{2^m} \tag{6.245}$$

and

$$\left|\frac{y}{2^m} - \frac{jt \text{ (mod } r)}{r}\right| \le \frac{1}{2^m} \tag{6.246}$$

is at least $(\frac{8}{\pi^2})^2$.

In this case, we have

$$\left|\frac{xr}{2^m} - j\right| \le \frac{r}{2^m} \tag{6.247}$$

and

$$\left|\frac{yr}{2^m} - jt \text{ (mod } r)\right| \le \frac{r}{2^m}. \tag{6.248}$$

Furthermore, since $m = \lceil \log_2(r) + 1 \rceil$, we have $\frac{r}{2^m} \le \frac{1}{2}$. So, we can round off $\frac{xr}{2^m}$ and $\frac{yr}{2^m}$ to the nearest integers to obtain j and jt (mod r), respectively, and then we use Eq. (6.235) to find t.

Shor's discrete logarithm algorithm is described in Algorithm 7.

In Shor's discrete logarithmic algorithm, the number of basic gates used is ploy($\log_2(N)$), and its probability of success is

$$\frac{r-1}{r}\left(\frac{8}{\pi^2}\right)^2 = \frac{64(r-1)}{\pi^4 r} > 0.657\frac{r-1}{r}. \tag{6.249}$$

Algorithm 7: Shor's discrete logarithm algorithm.

Input: The composite number $N \geq 2$, a positive integer a satisfying $\gcd(a, N) = 1$, a positive integer b satisfying $b = a^t$ (t is an unknown integer), and order r of a modulo N.

Output: t such that $a^t = b \pmod{N}$.

1 Set $m = \lceil \log_2(r) + 1 \rceil$.

2 Prepare initial state $|0^m\rangle|0^m\rangle|1\rangle$.

3 $|\psi_1\rangle = (H^{\otimes m} \otimes H^{\otimes m} \otimes I)|\psi_0\rangle$.

4 With the second register as the control register and the third register as the target register, apply $\Lambda_m(M_b)$ gate on $|\psi_1\rangle$ to obtain $|\psi_2\rangle$.

5 With the first register as the control register and the third register as the target register, apply $\Lambda_m(M_a)$ gate on $|\psi_2\rangle$ to obtain $|\psi_3\rangle$.

6 $|\psi_4\rangle = (\mathrm{QFT}^\dagger_{2^m} \otimes \mathrm{QFT}^\dagger_{2^m} \otimes I)|\psi_3\rangle$.

7 Measure the first two registers of $|\psi_4\rangle$ to obtain an estimated value $\frac{j}{r}$ of $\frac{x}{2^m}$ and an estimated value $\frac{jt \pmod{r}}{r}$ of $\frac{y}{2^m}$ ($j \in \{0, 1, \ldots, r-1\}$).

8 Round off $\frac{xr}{2^m}$ and $\frac{yr}{2^m}$ to get integers $\tilde{x}$ and $\tilde{y}$, respectively. If $\tilde{x}$ is 0, the algorithm fails; otherwise, compute $\tilde{t} = \tilde{y}\tilde{x}^{-1} \bmod r$. Verify that if there is $b = a^{\tilde{t}} \bmod N$, then the algorithm succeeds and outputs $\tilde{t}$; otherwise the algorithm fails.

Exercises

6.24. Prove that if a unitary operator U satisfies $U^r = I$, then any eigenvalue e of U must satisfy $e^r = 1$.

6.25. Prove that in Eq. (6.234), the operator M_b has an eigenvalue $\omega_r^{jt} = e^{2\pi i \frac{jt}{r}}$ corresponding to the eigenvector $|\psi_j\rangle$.

6.12 Hidden subgroup algorithm

In this section, we will further introduce the hidden subgroup problem and the corresponding quantum algorithm. In fact, Simon's problem, the order-finding problem and discrete logarithm problem studied earlier can be all thought of as special cases of the hidden subgroup problem. First, we give a definition of the hidden subgroup problem [15].

Definition 6.13. (Hidden subgroup problem) Let $f: G \rightarrow X$ be a function mapping a group G to a finite set X, and assume there exists a subgroup S

of G such that for any $x, y \in G, f(x) = f(y)$ if and only if $xS = yS$. The goal is to find the subgroup S.

A number of problems discussed before can be redescribed in the framework of the hidden subgroup problem as follows.

Example 6.3. Deutsch problem: $G = \mathbb{Z}_2$, $X = \{0, 1\}$. If f is a balanced function, then $S = \{0\}$; if f is a constant function, then $S = \{0, 1\}$.

Example 6.4. Generalized Simon problem: $G = \mathbb{Z}_2^n$, $X = \{0, 1\}^m$, where $m \geq n - k$, $k = \dim(S)$. S is a subgroup of $\mathbb{Z}_2^n$, and $f(x) = f(y) \Leftrightarrow x \oplus y \in S$. When $S = \{0, s\}$, it is Simon problem.

Example 6.5. Order-finding problem: $G = \mathbb{Z}$, X is a finite group H, and r to be discovered is the order of $a \in H$. The goal is to find the hidden subgroup $S = r\mathbb{Z}$, and then the generator of S can derive r.

Example 6.6. Period-finding problem of functions: $G = \mathbb{Z}$, X is a set, and r to be discovered is the period of function f. The goal is to find the hidden subgroup $S = r\mathbb{Z}$, and then the generator of S can derive the period r.

Example 6.7. Discrete logarithm problem in general groups: $G = \mathbb{Z}_r \times \mathbb{Z}_r$, and X is a finite group H, with elements a and b in H such that $a^r = 1$ and $b = a^k$. Consider function $f(x_1, x_2) = a^{x_1} b^{x_2}$, then $f(x_1, x_2) = f(y_1, y_2)$ if and only if

$$(x_1, x_2) - (y_1, y_2) \in \{(-tk, t) | t \in \{1 - r, 2 - r, \ldots, r - 1\}\}. \tag{6.250}$$

Finding the generator $(-k, 1)$ of S will give the discrete logarithm k.

Example 6.8. Hidden linear function problem: $G = \mathbb{Z} \times \mathbb{Z}$. For a positive integer N, suppose g is a permutation of $\mathbb{Z}_N$, and h a function from $\mathbb{Z} \times \mathbb{Z}$ to $\mathbb{Z}_N$ defined as $h(x, y) = (x + ay) \bmod N$. Consider function

$$f(x_1, x_2) = g(h(x_1, x_2)) = g((x_1 + ax_2) \bmod N), \tag{6.251}$$

then $f(x_1, x_2) = f(y_1, y_2)$ if and only if $(x_1, x_2) - (y_1, y_2) \in \{(-ta, t) \mid t \in \mathbb{Z}\}$. Finding the generator $(-a, 1)$ of S will result in the hidden coefficient a.

Example 6.9. Self-shift-equivalent polynomial problem: Given a polynomial p with l variables, where variables $X_1, X_2, \ldots, X_l$ take values in the finite field $\mathbb{F}_q$. The function f maps $(a_1, a_2, \ldots, a_l) \in \mathbb{F}_q^l$ to $p(X_1 - a_1, X_2 -$

$a_2, \ldots, X_l - a_l)$, and f is constant on cosets of a subgroup S of $\mathbb{F}_q^l$, where S is the self-shift polynomial set of p.

Example 6.10. Abelian stabilizer problem: X is a finite set, and G is a group composed of functions on the finite set X, that is, every element in G is a function that maps X to X. For any two elements $a, b \in G$, we have $a(b(x)) = (ab)(x)$, $\forall x \in X$. For a particular element $x \in X$, all elements $a \in G$ that satisfy $a(x) = x$ form a subgroup. This subgroup is called the Abelian stabilizer of x with respect to G, denoted as $St_G(x)$. Let $f_x : G \rightarrow X$ satisfy $f_x(g) = g(x)$ for any $g \in G$, then the hidden subgroup of function f_x is $St_G(x)$.

Example 6.11. General graph automorphism problem: S_n denotes the symmetric group on n elements (equivalent to permutation group of $\{1, 2, \ldots, n\}$). Let $\mathbf{G}$ denote a graph with n vertices labeled $1, 2, \ldots, n$. For any permutation $\sigma \in S_n$, function $f_{\mathbf{G}}$ maps S_n to the set of graphs with n vertices and satisfies $f_{\mathbf{G}}(\sigma) = \sigma(\mathbf{G})$, where $\sigma(\mathbf{G})$ is the graph obtained by permuting the vertex labels of $\mathbf{G}$ according to σ. Then the hidden subgroup of function $f_{\mathbf{G}}$ is the automorphism group of $\mathbf{G}$.

Remark 6.4. A group is called Abelian if and only if for any two elements a and b in the group, $ab = ba$, that is, group operation is commutative.

Note that in the general graph automorphism problem earlier, group S_n is non-Abelian. Currently, there exist quantum algorithms that can efficiently solve hidden subgroup problems for finite Abelian groups and some special non-Abelian groups. However, for many non-Abelian subgroup problems, no effective quantum algorithms have been designed yet.

Next, we introduce a quantum hidden subgroup algorithm for general finite Abelian groups. Before presenting a detailed process of the quantum hidden subgroup algorithm, we first generalize some related properties and propositions of Simon's algorithm.

In Simon's algorithm, we use transformation $H^{\otimes k}$, which is a special case of tensor product of quantum Fourier transform $\mathrm{QFT}_N^{\otimes k}$. More generally, this transformation can be further generalized as

$$\mathrm{QFT}_{N_1, N_2, N_3, \ldots, N_k} = \mathrm{QFT}_{N_1} \otimes \mathrm{QFT}_{N_2} \otimes \mathrm{QFT}_{N_3} \otimes \cdots \otimes \mathrm{QFT}_{N_k}, \quad (6.252)$$

where QFT_{N_i} acts on the space $\mathcal{H}_{N_i}$. $\mathrm{QFT}_{N_1, N_2, N_3, \ldots, N_k}$ acts on the space $\mathcal{H}_{N_1} \otimes \mathcal{H}_{N_2} \otimes \mathcal{H}_{N_3} \otimes \cdots \otimes \mathcal{H}_{N_k}$.

Based on the definition of quantum Fourier transform in Eq. (6.90), we can verify that

$$
\begin{aligned}
&\mathrm{QFT}_{N_1,N_2,N_3,\ldots,N_k}|x_1\rangle|x_2\rangle|x_3\rangle\cdots|x_k\rangle \\
&=\frac{1}{\sqrt{N_1N_2N_3\cdots N_k}}\sum_{\substack{(y_1,y_2,y_3,\ldots,y_k)\\ \in\mathbb{Z}_{N_1}\times\mathbb{Z}_{N_2}\\ \times\mathbb{Z}_{N_3}\times\cdots\times\mathbb{Z}_{N_k}}} e^{2\pi i\left(\frac{x_1y_1}{N_1}+\frac{x_2y_2}{N_2}+\frac{x_3y_3}{N_3}+\cdots+\frac{x_ky_k}{N_k}\right)}|y_1\rangle|y_2\rangle|y_3\rangle\cdots|y_k\rangle.
\end{aligned} \tag{6.253}
$$

If $N_1 = N_2 = N_3 = \cdots = N_k = N$, then the expression earlier can be simplified as

$$
\mathrm{QFT}_N^{\otimes k}|\mathbf{x}\rangle = \frac{1}{\sqrt{N^k}}\sum_{\mathbf{y}\in\mathbb{Z}_N^k} e^{\frac{2\pi i}{N}\mathbf{x}\cdot\mathbf{y}}|\mathbf{y}\rangle, \tag{6.254}
$$

where $\mathbf{x}\cdot\mathbf{y} = \left(\sum_{i=1}^{k} x_iy_i\right) \bmod N$.

Let S be a subgroup of $\mathbb{Z}_N^k$, and denote

$$
|S\rangle = \frac{1}{\sqrt{|S|}}\sum_{\mathbf{s}\in S}|\mathbf{s}\rangle, \tag{6.255}
$$

$S^{\perp} = \{\mathbf{t} \mid \mathbf{t}\cdot\mathbf{s} = 0, \forall \mathbf{s}\in S\}$. Then the following equation holds:

$$
\mathrm{QFT}_N^{\otimes k}|S\rangle = \frac{1}{\sqrt{|S^{\perp}|}}\sum_{\mathbf{t}\in S^{\perp}}|\mathbf{t}\rangle, \tag{6.256}
$$

In fact, we can verify Eq. (6.256) in detail as follows:

$$
\mathrm{QFT}_N^{\otimes k}|S\rangle \tag{6.257}
$$

$$
=\frac{1}{\sqrt{|S|N^k}}\sum_{\mathbf{t}\in\mathbb{Z}_N^k}\sum_{\mathbf{s}\in S} e^{\frac{2\pi i}{N}\mathbf{s}\cdot\mathbf{t}}|\mathbf{t}\rangle \tag{6.258}
$$

$$
=\frac{1}{\sqrt{|S|N^k}}\sum_{\mathbf{t}\in S^{\perp}}\sum_{\mathbf{s}\in S} e^{\frac{2\pi i}{N}\mathbf{s}\cdot\mathbf{t}}|\mathbf{t}\rangle + \frac{1}{\sqrt{|S|N^k}}\sum_{\mathbf{t}\in\mathbb{Z}_N^k\backslash S^{\perp}}\sum_{\mathbf{s}\in S} e^{\frac{2\pi i}{N}\mathbf{s}\cdot\mathbf{t}}|\mathbf{t}\rangle \tag{6.259}
$$

$$
=\frac{1}{\sqrt{|S|N^k}}\sum_{\mathbf{t}\in S^{\perp}}\sum_{\mathbf{s}\in S} e^{0}|\mathbf{t}\rangle + \frac{1}{\sqrt{|S|N^k}}\sum_{\mathbf{t}\in\mathbb{Z}_N^k\backslash S^{\perp}}\sum_{\mathbf{s}\in S} e^{\frac{2\pi i}{N}\mathbf{s}\cdot\mathbf{t}}|\mathbf{t}\rangle \tag{6.260}
$$

$$
=\frac{|S|}{\sqrt{|S|N^k}}\sum_{\mathbf{t}\in S^{\perp}}|\mathbf{t}\rangle + \frac{1}{\sqrt{|S|N^k}}\sum_{\mathbf{t}\in\mathbb{Z}_N^k\backslash S^{\perp}}\sum_{\mathbf{s}\in S} e^{\frac{2\pi i}{N}\mathbf{s}\cdot\mathbf{t}}|\mathbf{t}\rangle \tag{6.261}
$$

$$=\sqrt{\frac{|S|}{N^k}}\sum_{\mathbf{t}\in S^\perp}|\mathbf{t}\rangle+\frac{1}{\sqrt{|S|N^k}}\sum_{\mathbf{t}\in\mathbb{Z}_N^k\setminus S^\perp}\sum_{\mathbf{s}\in S}e^{\frac{2\pi i}{N}\mathbf{s}\cdot\mathbf{t}}|\mathbf{t}\rangle. \tag{6.262}$$

Since $\dim(S)+\dim(S^\perp)=\dim(\mathbb{Z}_N^k)$, we have $N^{\dim(S)}\cdot N^{\dim(S^\perp)}=N^{\dim(\mathbb{Z}_N^k)}$, that is, $|S|\cdot|S^\perp|=N^k$. Therefore

$$\mathrm{QFT}_N^{\otimes k}|S\rangle \tag{6.263}$$

$$=\frac{1}{\sqrt{|S^\perp|}}\sum_{\mathbf{t}\in S^\perp}|\mathbf{t}\rangle+\frac{1}{\sqrt{|S|N^k}}\sum_{\mathbf{t}\in\mathbb{Z}_N^k\setminus S^\perp}\sum_{\mathbf{s}\in S}e^{\frac{2\pi i}{N}\mathbf{s}\cdot\mathbf{t}}|\mathbf{t}\rangle. \tag{6.264}$$

Since the norm of both $\mathrm{QFT}_N^{\otimes k}|S\rangle$ and $\frac{1}{\sqrt{|S^\perp|}}\sum_{\mathbf{t}\in S^\perp}|\mathbf{t}\rangle$ is 1, we know

$$\frac{1}{\sqrt{|S|N^k}}\sum_{\mathbf{t}\in\mathbb{Z}_N^k\setminus S^\perp}\sum_{\mathbf{s}\in S}e^{\frac{2\pi i}{N}\mathbf{s}\cdot\mathbf{t}}|\mathbf{t}\rangle \tag{6.265}$$

is a zero vector. Therefore

$$\mathrm{QFT}_N^{\otimes k}|S\rangle=\frac{1}{\sqrt{|S^\perp|}}\sum_{\mathbf{t}\in S^\perp}|\mathbf{t}\rangle. \tag{6.266}$$

Furthermore, for any $\mathbf{b}\in\mathbb{Z}_N^k$, denote

$$|\mathbf{b}+S\rangle=\frac{1}{\sqrt{|S|}}\sum_{\mathbf{s}\in S}|\mathbf{b}+\mathbf{s}\rangle, \tag{6.267}$$

then the following equation holds:

$$\mathrm{QFT}_N^{\otimes k}|\mathbf{b}+S\rangle=\frac{1}{\sqrt{|S^\perp|}}\sum_{\mathbf{t}\in S^\perp}e^{\frac{2\pi i}{N}\mathbf{b}\cdot\mathbf{t}}|\mathbf{t}\rangle. \tag{6.268}$$

More generally, for any Abelian group $G=\mathbb{Z}_{N_1}\times\mathbb{Z}_{N_2}\times\mathbb{Z}_{N_3}\times\cdots\times\mathbb{Z}_{N_k}$ and any subgroup $S\leq G$, similarly denote

$$|S\rangle=\frac{1}{\sqrt{|S|}}\sum_{\mathbf{s}\in S}|\mathbf{s}\rangle. \tag{6.269}$$

Additionally, for any $\mathbf{b}\in G$, denote

$$|\mathbf{b}+S\rangle=\frac{1}{\sqrt{|S|}}\sum_{\mathbf{s}\in S}|\mathbf{b}+\mathbf{s}\rangle. \tag{6.270}$$

Correspondingly, we also generalize $S^{\perp}$ to represent $\{\mathbf{t} \mid (\sum_{i=1}^{k} \frac{t_i s_i}{N_i}) \equiv 0 \pmod 1, \forall \mathbf{s} \in S\}$, and then the following equality can be verified:

$$\mathrm{QFT}^{\dagger}_{N_1,N_2,N_3,\ldots,N_k}|\mathbf{b}+S\rangle = \frac{1}{\sqrt{|S^{\perp}|}} \sum_{\mathbf{t} \in S^{\perp}} e^{-2\pi i (\sum_{i=1}^{k} \frac{t_i b_i}{N_i})} |\mathbf{t}\rangle. \tag{6.271}$$

To describe quantum algorithm for finite Abelian hidden subgroups more conveniently, we assume that QFT_N can be implemented efficiently for any N. If the prime factorization of $\prod_{i=1}^{k} N_i$ is $\prod_{i=1}^{l} p_i^{n_i}$, denote $n = \sum_{i=1}^{l} n_i$. A quantum hidden subgroup algorithm for finite Abelian groups is described in Algorithm 8.

Algorithm 8: Quantum algorithm for finite Abelian hidden subgroup.

Input: Oracle U_f (Let the Hilbert space that U_f acts on be $\mathcal{H}_X$).
Output: A basis for generating the hidden subgroup S.

1 Let $i = 1$.
2 Prepare the quantum state
$|0\rangle|0\rangle|0\rangle \cdots |0\rangle|0\rangle \in \mathcal{H}_{N_1} \otimes \mathcal{H}_{N_2} \otimes \mathcal{H}_{N_3} \otimes \cdots \otimes \mathcal{H}_{N_k} \otimes \mathcal{H}_X$.
3 Apply unitary transformation $\mathrm{QFT}_{N_1,N_2,N_3,\ldots,N_k}$ on the first k registers.
4 Let U_f act on the quantum state from step 3, obtaining
$\frac{1}{\sqrt{|G|}} \sum_{\mathbf{x} \in G} |\mathbf{x}\rangle|f(\mathbf{x})\rangle$.
5 Measure the second register.
6 Apply unitary transformation $\mathrm{QFT}^{-1}_{N_1,N_2,N_3,\ldots,N_k}$ on the first k registers.
7 Measure the first register to obtain $t_{i1}, \ldots, t_{ik}$, and let
$w_i = (t_{i1}/N_1, \ldots, t_{ik}/N_k)$.
8 If $i \geq n+4$, proceed to step 9, otherwise increase i by 1 and return to step 2.
9 Solve the system of equations $\mathbf{W}x^T = \mathbf{0}^T \pmod 1$ to obtain the generators $\mathbf{g}_1, \mathbf{g}_2, \ldots$ of the subgroup S, where $\mathbf{W}$ is the matrix with w_i as its ith row.
10 Output $\mathbf{g}_1, \mathbf{g}_2, \ldots$.

Note that group G can be partitioned into cosets $\mathbf{y} + S$ with respect to the hidden subgroup S. We can express the state after step 4 of the hidden subgroup algorithm as a sum of these cosets:

$$\frac{\sqrt{|S|}}{\sqrt{|G|}} \sum_{\mathbf{y} \in G/S} |\mathbf{y} + S\rangle |f(\mathbf{y})\rangle. \tag{6.272}$$

The measurement in step 5 of the hidden subgroup algorithm makes the first k registers collapse into a random state $|\mathbf{y} + S\rangle$. According to Eq. (6.271), the inverse quantum Fourier transform in step 6 transforms the state into a uniform superposition of the elements of $S^{\perp}$. Then $\mathbf{w}_1, \mathbf{w}_2, \mathbf{w}_3, \cdots, \mathbf{w}_{n+3}, \mathbf{w}_{n+4}$ will generate $S^{\perp}$ with a high probability. In this case, solving the system of equations can give all the generators of S in ploy(n) time complexity. We have the following theorem.

Theorem 6.13. *The group* $\langle \mathbf{w}_1, \mathbf{w}_2, \mathbf{w}_3, \cdots, \mathbf{w}_{n+3}, \mathbf{w}_{n+4}\rangle$ *generated by* $\mathbf{w}_i$ *is a subgroup of* $S^{\perp}$. *Moreover, the probability of* $\langle \mathbf{w}_1, \mathbf{w}_2, \mathbf{w}_3, \cdots, \mathbf{w}_{n+3}, \mathbf{w}_{n+4}\rangle = S^{\perp}$ *is at least* $\frac{2}{3}$.

We get the following corollary.

Corollary 6.2. *The probability of* $\langle \mathbf{g}_1, \mathbf{g}_2, \cdots\rangle = S$ *is at least* $\frac{2}{3}$, *which means that we can obtain the hidden subgroup* S *of* f *through* $\langle \mathbf{g}_1, \mathbf{g}_2, \cdots\rangle$ *with a high probability.*

We can check all $\mathbf{g}_i$ to see whether $f(\mathbf{g}_i) = f(\mathbf{0})$. Thus by computing f $n + O(1)$ times, we can check whether $\langle \mathbf{g}_1, \mathbf{g}_2, \cdots\rangle = S$.

Therefore, we can summarize the following theorem.

Theorem 6.14. *There exists a bounded-error quantum algorithm to solve the finite Abelian hidden subgroup problem to find* S *of* f, *by means of* $O(\log(N))$ *queries to* f *and* $O(\log^3(N))$ *classical elementary operations.*

Exercises

6.26. Prove Eq. (6.253).

6.27. Prove Eq. (6.256).

6.28. Prove Eq. (6.268).

6.29. Prove Eq. (6.271).

6.13 Grover's algorithm

In this section, we introduce Grover's algorithm, which was proposed by Grover [16] in 1996 and is one of the most important algorithms in the history of quantum computing. Grover's algorithm is a widely used quantum algorithm that provides polynomial speedup over the best-known classical algorithm.

Though Grover's algorithm does not provide exponential speedup like Shor's algorithm, it requires less structure of the problem, giving it potential to be applied to many problems. For example, when searching for a specific element in an unstructured database, a classical deterministic algorithm must traverse all elements in the database, whereas Grover's algorithm provides a quadratic speedup over the classical approach, which is a significant advantage.

Before explaining Grover's algorithm in detail, we introduce some basic concepts. Let $f: \{0,1\}^n \to \{0,1\}$ be a Boolean function, and define a reversible transformation B_f:

$$B_f|x\rangle|y\rangle = |x\rangle|y \oplus f(x)\rangle, \tag{6.273}$$

where $x \in \{0,1\}^n$, $y \in \{0,1\}$. The goal is to find $x \in \{0,1\}^n$ such that $f(x) = 1$, or make sure that no such x exists (i.e., when $f(x) \equiv 0$).

Assume there is exactly one x such that $f(x) = 1$. The complexity of a classical deterministic query algorithm in the worst case is $\Theta(2^n)$; for probabilistic queries, we assume the error of k queries is less than ϵ, and the probability of not finding the answer after k queries is $1 - \frac{k}{2^n} \leq \epsilon$. Therefore, $k \geq (1-\epsilon)2^n$, that is, $k = \Omega(2^n)$.

Now we describe Grover's algorithm. First, we define unitary operators U_f and $U_0^{\perp}$ as follows:

$$U_f|x\rangle = (-1)^{f(x)}|x\rangle, \tag{6.274}$$

$$U_0^{\perp}|x\rangle = \begin{cases} |x\rangle, & x = 0^n, \\ -|x\rangle, & x \neq 0^n, \end{cases} \tag{6.275}$$

where $x \in \{0,1\}^n$.

The quantum circuit of Grover's algorithm is shown in Fig. 6.14.

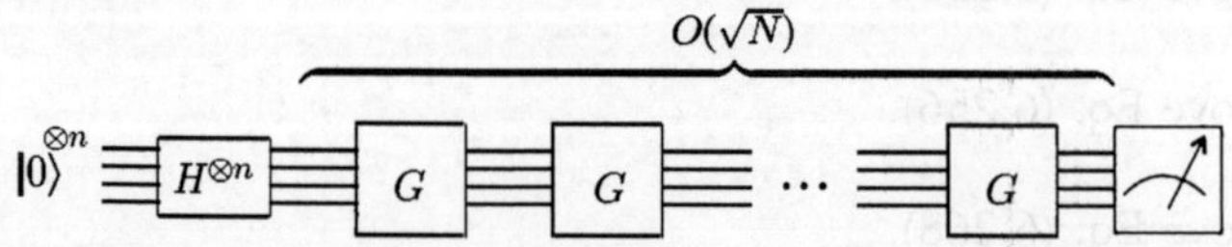

Figure 6.14 Quantum circuit of Grover's algorithm.

Grover's algorithm is described as follows:

Algorithm 9: Grover's algorithm.

Input: Oracle U_f, where $|\{x \in \{0,1\}^n \mid f(x)=1\}| = a \geq 1$ is a small number.

Output: $x \in \{0,1\}^n$ such that $f(x)=1$.

1 $|\psi_0\rangle = H^{\otimes n}|0\rangle^{\otimes n} = \frac{1}{\sqrt{2^n}} \sum_{x\in\{0,1\}^n} |x\rangle$.

2 Apply G operator $\left\lfloor \frac{\pi}{4}\sqrt{\frac{2^n}{a}} \right\rfloor$ times to $|\psi_0\rangle$, where $G = H^{\otimes n} U_0^{\perp} H^{\otimes n} U_f$.

3 Measure the result.

Next, we analyze Grover's algorithm. First, we introduce some notation:

$$A = \{x \in \{0,1\}^n \mid f(x) = 1\}, \tag{6.276}$$

$$B = \{x \in \{0,1\}^n \mid f(x) = 0\}, \tag{6.277}$$

$$|A\rangle = \frac{1}{\sqrt{a}} \sum_{x\in A} |x\rangle, \tag{6.278}$$

$$|B\rangle = \frac{1}{\sqrt{b}} \sum_{x\in B} |x\rangle. \tag{6.279}$$

After the first step of Grover's algorithm, we have

$$H^{\otimes n}|0\rangle^{\otimes n} = \sqrt{\frac{a}{N}}|A\rangle + \sqrt{\frac{b}{N}}|B\rangle \triangleq |h\rangle, \tag{6.280}$$

where $a = |A|$, $b = |B|$, and $N = 2^n$. Furthermore, it is easy to see

$$U_0^{\perp} = 2|0^n\rangle\langle 0^n| - I, \tag{6.281}$$

thus

$$H^{\otimes n} U_0^{\perp} H^{\otimes n} = H^{\otimes n}(2|0^n\rangle\langle 0^n| - I)H^{\otimes n} \tag{6.282}$$

$$= 2|h\rangle\langle h| - I. \tag{6.283}$$

Therefore, we have

$$G|A\rangle = H^{\otimes n} U_0^{\perp} H^{\otimes n} U_f |A\rangle \tag{6.284}$$

$$= (I - 2|h\rangle\langle h|)(-U_f)|A\rangle \tag{6.285}$$

$$= (I - 2|h\rangle\langle h|)|A\rangle \tag{6.286}$$

$$= |A\rangle - 2\sqrt{\frac{a}{N}}\left(\sqrt{\frac{a}{N}}|A\rangle + \sqrt{\frac{b}{N}}|B\rangle\right) \tag{6.287}$$

$$= \left(1 - \frac{2a}{N}\right)|A\rangle - \frac{2\sqrt{ab}}{N}|B\rangle. \tag{6.288}$$

Similarly, we have

$$G|B\rangle = \frac{2\sqrt{ab}}{N}|A\rangle - \left(1 - \frac{2b}{N}\right)|B\rangle. \tag{6.289}$$

We can express the transformation of G on $|A\rangle$ and $|B\rangle$ in matrix form as follows:

$$M = \begin{bmatrix} -(1-\frac{2b}{N}) & -\frac{2\sqrt{ab}}{N} \\ \frac{2\sqrt{ab}}{N} & 1-\frac{2a}{N} \end{bmatrix} \tag{6.290}$$

$$= \begin{bmatrix} \frac{b-a}{N} & -\frac{2\sqrt{ab}}{N} \\ \frac{2\sqrt{ab}}{N} & \frac{b-a}{N} \end{bmatrix} \tag{6.291}$$

$$= \begin{bmatrix} \sqrt{\frac{b}{N}} & -\sqrt{\frac{a}{N}} \\ \sqrt{\frac{a}{N}} & \sqrt{\frac{b}{N}} \end{bmatrix}^2. \tag{6.292}$$

Denote $\sin\theta = \sqrt{\frac{a}{N}}$, $\cos\theta = \sqrt{\frac{b}{N}}$, and then we have

$$R_{2\theta} = \begin{bmatrix} \cos\theta & -\sin\theta \\ \sin\theta & \cos\theta \end{bmatrix}^2 = \begin{bmatrix} \sqrt{\frac{b}{N}} & -\sqrt{\frac{a}{N}} \\ \sqrt{\frac{a}{N}} & \sqrt{\frac{b}{N}} \end{bmatrix}^2 = M. \tag{6.293}$$

It is evident that G performs a 2θ rotation on vectors in span$\{|A\rangle, |B\rangle\}$, where $\theta = \sin^{-1}\sqrt{\frac{a}{N}}$.

Since $|h\rangle = \cos\theta|B\rangle + \sin\theta|A\rangle$, after k iterations of G, the state $G^k|h\rangle$ becomes

$$\cos((2k+1)\theta)|B\rangle + \sin((2k+1)\theta)|A\rangle. \tag{6.294}$$

Our goal is to make $\sin((2k+1)\theta) \approx 1$, which implies $(2k+1)\theta \approx \frac{\pi}{2}$, thus $k \approx \frac{\pi}{4\theta} - \frac{1}{2}$. If the number of target states $a \geq 1$ and a is relatively small, then $\theta = \sin^{-1}\sqrt{\frac{a}{N}} \approx \sqrt{\frac{a}{N}}$, and $k = \left\lfloor \frac{\pi}{4}\sqrt{\frac{N}{a}} \right\rfloor$. The success probability of Grover's algorithm is

$$\sin^2\left(\left(2\left\lfloor\frac{\pi}{4}\sqrt{\frac{N}{a}}\right\rfloor+1\right)\sin^{-1}\left(\sqrt{\frac{a}{N}}\right)\right). \tag{6.295}$$

Remark 6.5. If the number of targets a is large, meaning target elements have a high proportion, then a classical algorithm that randomly selects the target can find it with a high probability, and Grover's algorithm is not necessary.

Specifically, if $a=1$, then $\theta=\sin^{-1}\sqrt{\frac{1}{N}}\approx\frac{1}{\sqrt{N}}$, and $k=\left\lfloor\frac{\pi}{4}\sqrt{N}\right\rfloor$, with success probability

$$\sin^2\left(\left(2\left\lfloor\frac{\pi}{4}\sqrt{N}\right\rfloor+1\right)\sin^{-1}\left(\sqrt{\frac{1}{N}}\right)\right). \tag{6.296}$$

Exercises

6.30. In 2^n elements, if there are $s\geq 1$ target elements and we only need to find one, what is the probability of success after k iterations?

6.31. Prove that in Grover's algorithm, we have

$$G^k|h\rangle=\sin\left((2k+1)\theta\right)|A\rangle+\cos\left((2k+1)\theta\right)|B\rangle. \tag{6.297}$$

6.32. Prove that the operator $2|h\rangle\langle h|-I$ acting on a state $\sum_k\alpha_k|k\rangle$ results in the following state:

$$\sum_k[-\alpha_k+2\langle\alpha\rangle]|k\rangle,$$

where $\langle\alpha\rangle\equiv\sum_k\frac{\alpha_k}{N}$ is the average of α_k.

6.14 Quantum amplitude amplification

In this section, we introduce quantum amplitude amplification algorithm [13]. Quantum amplitude amplification algorithm is a generalization of Grover's algorithm, whose basic idea is that for quantum algorithm with a low success probability, its probability can be improved by running quantum amplitude amplification algorithm multiple times and using some additional auxiliary operations. Like Grover's algorithm, quantum amplitude amplification algorithm is not constrained by structure of the problem, so it has a certain generality and is expected to demonstrate potential in a wide range of problems. Moreover, this section can deepen the understanding of Grover's algorithm introduced in the previous section.

Let $f:\{0,1\}^n \to \{0,1\}$ be a Boolean function, and denote the sets $X_g = \{x \in \{0,1\}^n | f(x) = 1\}$ and $X_b = \{x \in \{0,1\}^n | f(x) = 0\}$.

For any quantum algorithm $\mathcal{A}$, let

$$\mathcal{A}|0^m\rangle = |\psi\rangle \tag{6.298}$$

$$= \sum_x \alpha_x |x\rangle |\text{junk}(x)\rangle \tag{6.299}$$

$$= \sum_{x\in X_g} \alpha_x |x\rangle |\text{junk}(x)\rangle + \sum_{x\in X_b} \alpha_x |x\rangle |\text{junk}(x)\rangle, \tag{6.300}$$

where X_g represents the set of desired elements, X_b represents the set of undesired elements, and $|\text{junk}(x)\rangle$ represents the auxiliary state.

Denote

$$P_g = \sum_{x\in X_g} |\alpha_x|^2, \tag{6.301}$$

$$P_b = \sum_{x\in X_b} |\alpha_x|^2 = 1 - P_g, \tag{6.302}$$

where P_g represents the success probability of algorithm $\mathcal{A}$ and P_b represents the failure probability of algorithm $\mathcal{A}$.

Let

$$|\psi_g\rangle = \sum_{x\in X_g} \frac{\alpha_x}{\sqrt{P_g}} |x\rangle |\text{junk}(x)\rangle, \tag{6.303}$$

$$|\psi_b\rangle = \sum_{x\in X_b} \frac{\alpha_x}{\sqrt{P_b}} |x\rangle |\text{junk}(x)\rangle, \tag{6.304}$$

then

$$|\psi\rangle = \sqrt{P_g}|\psi_g\rangle + \sqrt{P_b}|\psi_b\rangle \tag{6.305}$$

$$= \sin\theta |\psi_g\rangle + \cos\theta |\psi_b\rangle, \tag{6.306}$$

where $0 < \theta < \frac{\pi}{2}$.

Let

$$Q = \mathcal{A}U_0^{\perp}\mathcal{A}^{-1}U_f \quad (6.307)$$

$$= U_{\psi}^{\perp}U_f, \quad (6.308)$$

where

$$U_0^{\perp} = 2|0^n\rangle\langle 0^n| - I, \quad (6.309)$$

$$U_f|x\rangle = (-1)^{f(x)}|x\rangle, \quad (6.310)$$

$$U_{\psi}^{\perp} = \mathcal{A}U_0^{\perp}\mathcal{A}^{-1} \quad (6.311)$$

$$= 2|\psi\rangle\langle\psi| - I. \quad (6.312)$$

Hence,

$$U_{\psi}^{\perp}|\psi\rangle = |\psi\rangle. \quad (6.313)$$

For a vector $|\phi\rangle$ that satisfies $\langle\phi|\psi\rangle = 0$, that is, $|\phi\rangle$ orthogonal to $|\psi\rangle$, we have

$$U_{\psi}^{\perp}|\phi\rangle = -|\phi\rangle. \quad (6.314)$$

Thus $U_{\psi}^{\perp}$ leaves the vector $|\psi\rangle$ unchanged, while flipping vectors orthogonal to $|\psi\rangle$.

Denote

$$|\bar{\psi}\rangle = \cos\theta|\psi_g\rangle - \sin\theta|\psi_b\rangle, \quad (6.315)$$

thus $\langle\psi|\bar{\psi}\rangle = 0$.

We can refer to Fig. 6.15 to further understand quantum amplitude amplification algorithm.

As shown in Fig. 6.15, we can regard $|\psi\rangle$ as a vector in Cartesian plane constructed by $|\psi_g\rangle$ and $|\psi_b\rangle$ as basis vectors. The angle between $|\psi\rangle$ and $|\psi_b\rangle$ is θ, our goal is to increase θ as close as possible to $\frac{\pi}{2}$ so that the probability of measuring elements from $|\psi_g\rangle$ is maximized. Further analyses are as follows:

$$U_f|\psi\rangle = -\sin\theta|\psi_g\rangle + \cos\theta|\psi_b\rangle \quad (6.316)$$

$$= \cos 2\theta|\psi\rangle - \sin 2\theta|\bar{\psi}\rangle, \quad (6.317)$$

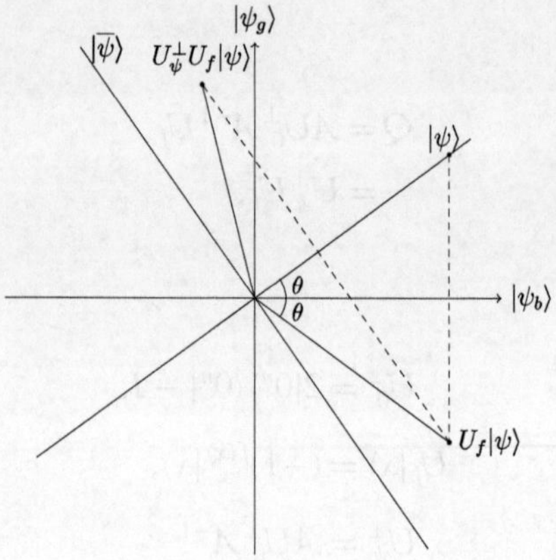

Figure 6.15 Quantum amplitude amplification.

$$Q|\psi\rangle = U_\psi^\perp U_f|\psi\rangle \tag{6.318}$$
$$= \cos 2\theta|\psi\rangle + \sin 2\theta|\bar{\psi}\rangle \tag{6.319}$$
$$= \cos 3\theta|\psi_b\rangle + \sin 3\theta|\psi_g\rangle \tag{6.320}$$
$$= \cos((2+1)\theta)|\psi_b\rangle + \sin((2+1)\theta)|\psi_g\rangle, \tag{6.321}$$

$$Q^k|\psi\rangle = \cos((2k+1)\theta)|\psi_b\rangle + \sin((2k+1)\theta)|\psi_g\rangle. \tag{6.322}$$

As analyzed earlier, the effect of applying U_f to $|\psi\rangle$ is to reflect $|\psi\rangle$ to a position symmetric with $|\psi_b\rangle$, and the effect of applying Q to $|\psi\rangle$, that is, applying $U_\psi^\perp$ to $U_f|\psi\rangle$, is to reflect $U_f|\psi\rangle$ to a position symmetric with $|\psi\rangle$. The total effect is to rotate $|\psi\rangle$ counterclockwise by an angle of 2θ. Therefore, after applying Q to $|\psi\rangle$ for k times, the effect is to rotate $|\psi\rangle$ counterclockwise by an angle of $2k\theta$. We can calculate the required number of rotation k based on the value of θ so that the rotated angle $(2k+1)\theta$ is as close as possible to $\frac{\pi}{2}$.

Algorithm 10 shows the description of quantum amplitude amplification algorithm.

It can be seen that Grover's algorithm is a special case of quantum amplitude amplification algorithm when $\mathcal{A} = H^{\otimes n}$.

Exercises

6.33. Let U_f be a black box implementing $U_f : |x\rangle|b\rangle \mapsto |x\rangle|b \oplus f(x)\rangle$.

(*a*) Suppose $f : \{0,1\}^n \to \{0,1\}$, and the unitary operator A defined as $A|00\ldots0\rangle = \sum_x \alpha_x|x\rangle|\text{junk}(x)\rangle$ with the probability of measuring a good string x upon $A|00\ldots0\rangle$ being $\frac{1}{4}$.

Algorithm 10: Quantum amplitude amplification algorithm.

Input: Quantum algorithm $\mathcal{A}$ with a success probability P_g, and oracle U_f.

Output: $x \in \{0, 1\}^n$ such that $f(x) = 1$.

1 $|\psi_0\rangle = \mathcal{A}|0\rangle^{\otimes n}$.

2 Perform $\left\lfloor \dfrac{\pi}{4\arcsin(\sqrt{P_g})} \right\rfloor$ iterations of $Q = \mathcal{A}U_0^{\perp}\mathcal{A}^{-1}U_f$ on $|\psi_0\rangle$.

3 Measure to obtain the result.

Show how to find with certainty the unique x satisfying $f(x) = 1$ for only one application to U_f.

(*b*) Suppose $f : \{0, 1\}^n \to \{0, 1\}$, and the unitary operator A defined as $A|00\ldots0\rangle = \sum_x \alpha_x|x\rangle|\text{junk}(x)\rangle$ with the probability of measuring a good string x upon $A|00\ldots0\rangle$ being $\frac{1}{2}$.

Show how to find with certainty an x satisfying $f(x) = 1$ for only one application to U_f.

(*c*) Suppose $f : \{0, 1\}^n \to \{0, 1\}$, and the unitary operator A defined as $A|00\ldots0\rangle = \sum_x \alpha_x|x\rangle|\text{junk}(x)\rangle$ with the probability of measuring a good string x upon $A|00\ldots0\rangle$ being $\mathrm{P} > 0$.

Show that if we know P we can define a circuit that finds a solution to $f(x)$ with certainty using $O\left(\frac{1}{\sqrt{\mathrm{P}}}\right)$ applications of U_f.

6.15 Quantum amplitude estimation

In Grover's algorithm, it is necessary to know the number of target elements in advance to determine the number of iterations for Grover's operator G. Similarly, in quantum amplitude amplification, the success probability of algorithm $\mathcal{A}$ must be known in advance. This section introduces quantum amplitude estimation algorithm [13], which can find the target element with high probability even when the success probability of algorithm $\mathcal{A}$ is unknown. Due to the difficulty of this section, it can be considered as optional learning part.

Definition 6.14. Let Boolean function be $f : \{0, 1\}^n \to \{0, 1\}$, denote

$$\mathcal{H} = \text{span}\{|x\rangle | x \text{ is a preimage of } f\}, \tag{6.323}$$

$$\mathcal{H}_{\mathcal{G}} = \text{span}\{|x\rangle | f(x) = 1\}, \tag{6.324}$$

$$\mathcal{H}_{\mathcal{B}} = \text{span}\{|x\rangle | f(x) = 0\}. \tag{6.325}$$

If there exists a measurement-free quantum algorithm $\mathcal{A}$ such that $\mathcal{A}|0^n\rangle = |\Psi\rangle \in \mathcal{H}$, then $|\Psi\rangle$ can be written as

$$|\Psi\rangle = |\Psi_1\rangle + |\Psi_0\rangle, \tag{6.326}$$

where

$$|\Psi_1\rangle = \sum_{x:f(x)=1} \alpha_x |x\rangle, \tag{6.327}$$

$$|\Psi_0\rangle = \sum_{x:f(x)=0} \alpha_x |x\rangle. \tag{6.328}$$

Let

$$a = \langle \Psi_1 | \Psi_1 \rangle = \sin^2 \theta_a, \tag{6.329}$$

where $0 < a < 1$, $0 \leq \theta_a \leq \frac{\pi}{2}$.

Recall the following unitary operators:

$$Q = \mathcal{A} U_0^{\perp} \mathcal{A}^{-1} U_f,$$
$$U_0^{\perp} = 2|0^n\rangle\langle 0^n| - I,$$
$$U_f|x\rangle = (-1)^{f(x)}|x\rangle,$$
$$Q = U_\Psi^{\perp} U_f, \text{ where } U_\Psi^{\perp} = \mathcal{A} U_0^{\perp} \mathcal{A}^{-1}.$$

Then operator Q can be represented with the basis $\{|\Psi_0\rangle, |\Psi_1\rangle\}$ as the following matrix:

$$\begin{pmatrix} 1-2a & -2a \\ 2-2a & 1-2a \end{pmatrix}. \tag{6.330}$$

The eigenvalues of matrix (6.330) are

$$\begin{aligned} \lambda_{\pm} &= 1 - 2a \pm \sqrt{4a^2 - 4a} \\ &= \cos(2\theta) \pm i\sin(2\theta) \\ &= e^{\pm i2\theta}. \end{aligned} \tag{6.331}$$

The corresponding eigenvectors are

$$|\Psi_{\pm}\rangle = \frac{1}{\sqrt{2}} \left(\frac{1}{\sqrt{a}} |\Psi_1\rangle \pm \frac{i}{\sqrt{1-a}} |\Psi_0\rangle \right). \tag{6.332}$$

So, we have

$$Q|\Psi_{\pm}\rangle = e^{\pm i2\theta_a}|\Psi_{\pm}\rangle, \tag{6.333}$$

$$\begin{aligned}\mathcal{A}|0^n\rangle &= |\Psi\rangle & (6.334)\\ &= \frac{-i}{\sqrt{2}}\left(e^{i\theta_a}|\Psi_+\rangle - e^{-i\theta_a}|\Psi_-\rangle\right), & (6.335)\\ Q^j|\Psi\rangle &= \frac{-i}{\sqrt{2}}\left(e^{(2j+1)i\theta_a}|\Psi_+\rangle - e^{-(2j+1)i\theta_a}|\Psi_-\rangle\right) & (6.336)\\ &= \frac{1}{\sqrt{a}}\sin((2j+1)\theta_a)|\Psi_1\rangle + \frac{1}{\sqrt{1-a}}\cos((2j+1)\theta_a)|\Psi_0\rangle. & (6.337)\end{aligned}$$

Let $(2j+1)\theta_a \approx \frac{\pi}{2}$, then $j = \lfloor \frac{\pi}{4\theta_a} \rfloor$. When a is small, $\theta_a = \arcsin\sqrt{a} \approx \sqrt{a}$, thus $j = \lfloor \frac{\pi}{4\theta_a} \rfloor \approx \lfloor \frac{\pi}{4\sqrt{a}} \rfloor$.

To calculate an appropriate value of j such that the probability of obtaining x with $f(x) = 1$ is maximized, we consider the following two cases:

(I) When a is known, calculate j based on the value of a.

(II) When a is unknown, use quantum phase estimation to estimate a and then compute j.

Detailed discussions are as follows:

(I) When a is known, calculate θ_a from $\sin^2\theta_a = a$. According to $(2j+1)\theta_a \approx \frac{\pi}{2}$, we have $j = \lfloor \frac{\pi}{4\theta_a} \rfloor$. The following theorem holds.

Theorem 6.15. [17] *Let $\mathcal{A}$ be a measurement-free quantum algorithm, and let $f : \{0,1\}^n \to \{0,1\}$ be a Boolean function. Suppose that the success probability of performing $\mathcal{A}$ is $a > 0$. Let $m = \lfloor \frac{\pi}{4\theta_a} \rfloor$, where $\sin^2\theta_a = a$, $0 < \theta_a \leq \frac{\pi}{2}$. After measuring $Q^m\mathcal{A}|0\rangle$, the probability of obtaining a good result x with $f(x) = 1$ is at least* $\max(1-a, a)$, *where $m = \lfloor \frac{\pi}{4\theta_a} \rfloor$.*

(II) When a is unknown, first we provide the following proposition.

Proposition 6.2. *Let $a = \sin^2(\theta_a)$, $\tilde{a} = \sin^2(\tilde{\theta}_a)$, where $0 \leq \theta_a, \tilde{\theta}_a \leq 2\pi$, then*

$$|\tilde{\theta}_a - \theta_a| \leq \epsilon \Rightarrow |\tilde{a} - a| \leq 2\epsilon\sqrt{a(1-a)} + \epsilon^2. \quad (6.338)$$

Proof. Denote $\Delta\theta_a = \tilde{\theta}_a - \theta_a$ and $f(\theta_a) = \sin^2\theta_a$. By using the second-order Taylor series, we have

$$f(\theta_a + \Delta\theta_a) = f(\theta_a) + f'(\theta_a)\Delta\theta_a + \frac{1}{2}f''(\xi)(\Delta\theta_a)^2 \quad (6.339)$$

where $\xi \in (\theta_a, \tilde{\theta}_a)$. Since $f'(\theta_a) = \sin(2\theta_a)$ and $f''(\theta_a) = 2\cos(2\theta_a)$, with $|f''(\xi)| \leq 2$, we further obtain:

$$|\tilde{a} - a| = |f'(\theta_a)\Delta\theta_a + \frac{1}{2}f''(\xi)(\Delta\theta_a)^2| \quad (6.340)$$

$$\leq |\sin(2\theta_a)||\Delta\theta_a| + |\cos(2\xi)||\Delta\theta_a|^2. \tag{6.341}$$

Due to $|\Delta\theta_a| \leq \epsilon$, $|\sin(2\theta_a)| = 2\sqrt{a(1-a)}$, and $|\cos(2\xi)| \leq 1$, the following inequality holds:

$$|\tilde{a} - a| \leq 2\epsilon\sqrt{a(1-a)} + \epsilon^2. \tag{6.342}$$

□

Therefore, when a is fixed, we have $|\tilde{a} - a| = O(|\widetilde{\theta}_a - \theta_a|)$. Next, we consider how to obtain $\widetilde{\theta}_a$ as close as possible to θ_a.

Algorithm 11 describes quantum amplitude estimation algorithm.

Algorithm 11: Quantum amplitude estimation algorithm.

Input: Quantum algorithm $\mathcal{A}$ without measurement.

Output: Estimate $\tilde{a}$ for a.

1 $|\psi_0\rangle = |0^m\rangle\mathcal{A}|0^n\rangle$.

2 $|\psi_1\rangle = (\text{QFT}_{2^m} \otimes I)|\psi_0\rangle$.

3 $|\psi_2\rangle = \Lambda_{2^m}(Q)|\psi_1\rangle$.

4 $|\psi_3\rangle = (\text{QFT}^{\dagger}_{2^m} \otimes I)|\psi_2\rangle$.

5 Measure the first register of m qubits, and get $|y\rangle$.

6 Output $\tilde{a} = \sin^2(\pi \frac{y}{2^m})$.

The circuit diagram of the algorithm is shown in Fig. 6.16.

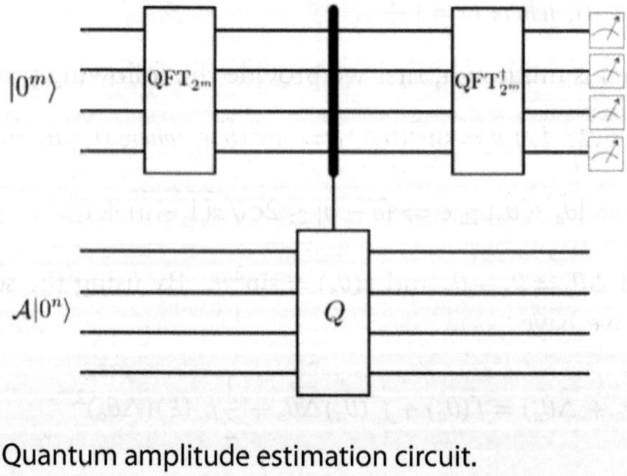

Figure 6.16 Quantum amplitude estimation circuit.

Operations of quantum amplitude estimation algorithm can be represented by the following unitary transformation:

$$(\text{QFT}^{\dagger}_{2^m} \otimes I)\Lambda_{2^m}(Q)(\text{QFT}_{2^m} \otimes I). \tag{6.343}$$

To prove the correctness of quantum amplitude estimation algorithm, we present the following theorem.

Theorem 6.16. *For any positive integer k, quantum amplitude estimation algorithm outputs* $\widetilde{a}$ $(0 \leq \widetilde{a} \leq 1)$ *such that*

$$|\widetilde{a} - a| \leq 2\pi k \frac{\sqrt{a(1-a)}}{2^m} + k^2 \frac{\pi^2}{2^{2m}} \tag{6.344}$$

with the probability P*:*

(1) *When* $k = 1$, $\mathrm{P} \geq \frac{8}{\pi^2}$;

(2) *When* $k \geq 2$, $\mathrm{P} \geq 1 - \frac{1}{2(k-1)}$.

In particular, when $a = 0$*, the probability of* $\widetilde{a} = 0$ *is* 1*; when* $a = 1$*, the probability of* $\widetilde{a} = 1$ *is* 1.

Proof. We analyze the state after each step of quantum amplitude estimation algorithm:

$|\psi_0\rangle = |0^m\rangle \mathcal{A}|0^n\rangle$.

$|\psi_1\rangle = (\mathrm{QFT}_{2^m} \otimes I)|\psi_0\rangle$.

$|\psi_2\rangle = \Lambda_{2^m}(Q)|\psi_1\rangle$.

$|\psi_3\rangle = (\mathrm{QFT}^\dagger_{2^m} \otimes I)|\psi_2\rangle$.

After step 1 of the algorithm, the state is

$$|\psi_0\rangle = |0^m\rangle \mathcal{A}|0^n\rangle \tag{6.345}$$

$$= \frac{-i}{\sqrt{2}} |0^m\rangle (e^{i\theta_a}|\Psi_+\rangle - e^{-i\theta_a}|\Psi_-\rangle). \tag{6.346}$$

After step 2 of the algorithm, by ignoring the global phase $-i$, the state is

$$|\psi_1\rangle = (\mathrm{QFT}_{2^m} \otimes I)|\psi_0\rangle \tag{6.347}$$

$$= \frac{1}{\sqrt{2^{m+1}}} \sum_{j=0}^{2^m-1} |j\rangle (e^{i\theta_a}|\Psi_+\rangle - e^{-i\theta_a}|\Psi_-\rangle). \tag{6.348}$$

After step 3 of the algorithm, the state is

$$|\psi_2\rangle = \Lambda_{2^m}(Q)|\psi_1\rangle \tag{6.349}$$

$$= \frac{1}{\sqrt{2^{m+1}}} \sum_{j=0}^{2^m-1} |j\rangle (e^{i\theta_a} e^{2ij\theta_a}|\Psi_+\rangle - e^{-i\theta_a} e^{-2ij\theta_a}|\Psi_-\rangle) \tag{6.350}$$

$$= \frac{e^{i\theta_a}}{\sqrt{2^{m+1}}} \sum_{j=0}^{2^m-1} e^{2ij\theta_a} |j\rangle|\Psi_+\rangle - \frac{e^{-i\theta_a}}{\sqrt{2^{m+1}}} \sum_{j=0}^{2^m-1} e^{-2ij\theta_a} |j\rangle|\Psi_-\rangle \tag{6.351}$$

$$= \frac{e^{i\theta_a}}{\sqrt{2}} |S_{2^m}(\frac{\theta_a}{\pi})\rangle|\Psi_+\rangle - \frac{e^{-i\theta_a}}{\sqrt{2}} |S_{2^m}(1-\frac{\theta_a}{\pi})\rangle|\Psi_-\rangle. \tag{6.352}$$

After step 4 of the algorithm, the state is

$$|\psi_3\rangle = (\mathrm{QFT}^\dagger_{2^m} \otimes I)|\psi_2\rangle \tag{6.353}$$

$$= \frac{e^{i\theta_a}}{\sqrt{2}} \mathrm{QFT}^\dagger_{2^m} |S_{2^m}(\frac{\theta_a}{\pi})\rangle|\Psi_+\rangle - \frac{e^{-i\theta_a}}{\sqrt{2}} \mathrm{QFT}^\dagger_{2^m} |S_{2^m}(1-\frac{\theta_a}{\pi})\rangle|\Psi_-\rangle. \tag{6.354}$$

After step 5 of the algorithm, measurement yields $|y\rangle$, and $\widetilde{\theta}_a = \frac{\pi y}{2^m}$. Since $\widetilde{a} = \sin^2 \widetilde{\theta}_a$, we have $\widetilde{a} = \sin^2 \frac{\pi y}{2^m}$.

By ignoring the second register, the first register is in a mixed state composed of $\mathrm{QFT}^\dagger_{2^m}|S_{2^m}(\frac{\theta_a}{\pi})\rangle$ and $\mathrm{QFT}^\dagger_{2^m}|S_{2^m}(1-\frac{\theta_a}{\pi})\rangle$ on average. Thus, the measurement outcome $|y\rangle$ could result from measuring either $\mathrm{QFT}^\dagger_{2^m}|S_{2^m}(\frac{\theta_a}{\pi})\rangle \doteq |\chi_1\rangle$ or $\mathrm{QFT}^\dagger_{2^m}|S_{2^m}(1-\frac{\theta_a}{\pi})\rangle \doteq |\chi_2\rangle$ with the same probability.

Denote $\widetilde{\theta_a^{(1)}} = \frac{\pi y}{2^m}$ and $\widetilde{\theta_a^{(2)}} = \pi - \frac{\pi y}{2^m}$.

Denote "measuring $|\chi_1\rangle$ and measuring $|\chi_2\rangle$" as Events A_1 and A_2, respectively; denote "obtaining measuring result y satisfying $|\widetilde{\theta_a^{(1)}} - \theta_a| \le \frac{k\pi}{2^m}$ and obtaining measuring result y satisfying $|\widetilde{\theta_a^{(2)}} - \theta_a| \le \frac{k\pi}{2^m}$" as Events B_1 and B_2, respectively.

Since

$$\mathrm{QFT}^\dagger_{2^m}|S_{2^m}(\frac{\theta_a}{\pi})\rangle = \sum_{k=0}^{2^m-1}\left(\frac{1}{2^m}\sum_{j=0}^{2^m-1} e^{2ij(\theta_a - \frac{\pi k}{2^m})}\right)|k\rangle, \tag{6.355}$$

and

$$\mathrm{QFT}^\dagger_{2^m}|S_{2^m}(1-\frac{\theta_a}{\pi})\rangle = \sum_{k=0}^{2^m-1}\left(\frac{1}{2^m}\sum_{j=0}^{2^m-1} e^{-2ij(\theta_a + \frac{\pi k}{2^m})}\right)|k\rangle \tag{6.356}$$

$$= \sum_{k'=1}^{2^m}\left(\frac{1}{2^m}\sum_{j=0}^{2^m-1} e^{-2ij(\theta_a - \frac{\pi k'}{2^m})}\right)|2^m - k'\rangle, \tag{6.357}$$

by Theorem 6.11, if measurement yields $|y\rangle$, when $k=1$, we have

$$\mathrm{P}(A_i B_i) = \frac{1}{2}\mathrm{P}\left(|\widetilde{\theta_a^{(i)}} - \theta_a| \le \frac{k\pi}{2^m}\right) \ge \frac{1}{2}\frac{8}{\pi^2}, \tag{6.358}$$

for $i = 1, 2$.

According to Proposition 6.2, if $|\widetilde{\theta_a^{(i)}} - \theta_a| \le \frac{k\pi}{2^m}$ for $i = 1$, or $i = 2$, we always have

$$|\tilde{a} - a| \le 2\pi k \frac{\sqrt{a(1-a)}}{2^m} + k^2 \frac{\pi^2}{2^{2m}}. \tag{6.359}$$

Consequently, when $k = 1$,

$$\mathrm{P}\left(|\tilde{a} - a| \le 2\pi k \frac{\sqrt{a(1-a)}}{2^m} + k^2 \frac{\pi^2}{2^{2m}} \right) \tag{6.360}$$

$$\ge \mathrm{P}\left(A_1 B_1 + A_2 B_2\right) \ge \frac{8}{\pi^2}; \tag{6.361}$$

when $k \ge 2$, by Theorem 6.11,

$$\mathrm{P}\left(A_i B_i\right) = \frac{1}{2} \mathrm{P}\left(|\widetilde{\theta_a^{(i)}} - \theta_a| \le \frac{k\pi}{2^m} \right) \ge \frac{1}{2}\left(1 - \frac{1}{2(k-1)}\right), \tag{6.362}$$

and similar to the above, we also have

$$\mathrm{P}\left(|\tilde{a} - a| \le 2\pi k \frac{\sqrt{a(1-a)}}{2^m} + k^2 \frac{\pi^2}{2^{2m}} \right) \ge 1 - \frac{1}{2(k-1)}. \tag{6.363}$$

Specifically, from Theorem 6.11 and Proposition 6.2, it follows that when $a = 0$, the probability of $\tilde{a} = 0$ is 1; when $a = 1$, the probability of $\tilde{a} = 1$ is also 1. □

Exercises

6.34. Define $U_f : |x\rangle|b\rangle \rightarrow |x\rangle|b \oplus f(x)\rangle$, and let $f : \{00, 01, 10, 11\} \rightarrow \{0, 1\}$ satisfy that there is a unique x such that $f(x) = 1$. Design a quantum algorithm that can find x using U_f once.

6.35. Prove:
(1) $Q|\Psi_1\rangle = (1 - 2a)|\Psi_1\rangle - 2a|\Psi_0\rangle$;
(2) $Q|\Psi_0\rangle = 2(1 - a)|\Psi_1\rangle + (1 - 2a)|\Psi_0\rangle$.

6.36. Prove: $Q|\Psi_\pm\rangle = e^{\pm i2\theta_a}|\Psi_\pm\rangle$.

6.37. Prove:
(1) $\mathcal{A}|0^n\rangle = |\Psi\rangle = \frac{-i}{\sqrt{2}}(e^{i\theta_a}|\Psi_+\rangle - e^{-i\theta_a}|\Psi_-\rangle)$;
(2) $Q^j|\Psi\rangle = \frac{-i}{\sqrt{2}}(e^{(2j+1)i\theta_a}|\Psi_+\rangle - e^{-(2j+1)i\theta_a}|\Psi_-\rangle)$;
(3) $Q^j|\Psi\rangle = \frac{1}{\sqrt{a}}\sin((2j+1)\theta_a)|\Psi_1\rangle + \frac{1}{\sqrt{1-a}}\cos((2j+1)\theta_a)|\Psi_0\rangle$.

6.16 * HHL algorithm

In this section, we introduce HHL algorithm for solving systems of linear equations. HHL algorithm was proposed by Aram W. Harrow, Avinatan Hassidim, and Seth Lloyd in 2009 [18]. When the coefficient matrix of the system is sparse and well-conditioned, HHL algorithm achieves exponential speedup over classical algorithms with respect to the dimension of the matrix The proposal of HHL algorithm has inspired the use of quantum algorithms to efficiently handle matrix operations, which can accelerate some machine learning algorithms. Therefore, the HHL algorithm has greatly contributed to the development of quantum machine learning. Since the original HHL algorithm imposes strong constraints on the coefficient matrix, there are some studies to improve HHL algorithm in academia.

Now, we introduce HHL algorithm in detail, starting by formally describing input and output of the system of linear equations. Given an $N \times N$ coefficient matrix A and an N-dimensional column vector $\vec{b}$, the goal is to solve the system $A\vec{x} = \vec{b}$ and obtain the vector $\vec{x}$.

In this section, we primarily discuss how to solve $\vec{x}$ under some restrictive conditions on coefficient matrix A, which is enough to illustrate the essence of HHL algorithm. For further details on how to solve systems of equations under relaxed constraints, error analysis, and application of HHL algorithm, we can refer to the original paper by Harrow et al. [18].

Some preprocessing is required for the problem's input. First, we need to ensure that the column vector $\vec{b}$ is normalized. We divide both coefficient matrix A and column vector $\vec{b}$ by a constant $|\vec{b}|$ to obtain A' and $\vec{b}'$, where $\vec{b}'$ is a unit vector. Thus the original problem is converted to solving $A'\vec{x} = \vec{b}'$, whose solution is the same as that of the original problem.

Next, we must ensure that the coefficient matrix A is Hermitian. If A is not Hermitian, we can define

$$C = \begin{bmatrix} 0 & A \\ A^\dagger & 0 \end{bmatrix},$$

and it is easy to see that C is Hermitian.

The original problem can then be transformed into solving $C\vec{y} = \begin{bmatrix} \vec{b} \\ 0 \end{bmatrix}$, from which we can obtain $\vec{y} = \begin{bmatrix} 0 \\ \vec{x} \end{bmatrix}$. Thus we can get a solution $\vec{x}$ of the original problem from $\vec{y}$.

Additionally, the condition number κ of the coefficient matrix is another important factor affecting matrix inversion algorithms. As the condition number κ of coefficient matrix increases, the matrix becomes nearly singular and the solution to the system becomes unstable. We call matrices with unstable solutions ill-conditioned matrices, while matrices with stable solutions are well-conditioned matrices.

After the preprocessing described earlier, we ensure that the coefficient matrix A of the system of equations is Hermitian, and that the column vector $\vec{b}$ is a unit vector. Let ϵ denote the error between the outcome $\vec{x}$ and the true solution. We further require:

(1) The order N of matrix is a power of 2, that is, $N = 2^n$.

(2) Matrix A is s-sparse and row-computable, meaning that each row of A contains at most s nonzero elements, and given a row index, these nonzero elements can be computed in $O(s)$ time. According to reference [19], we can implement unitary transformation $U = e^{iAu/T}$ by using poly(log(N)) basic gates, where u is taken as $O\left(\frac{\kappa}{\epsilon}\right)$.

(3) Matrix A has eigenvalues between $\frac{1}{\kappa}$ and 1.

Under these conditions, the time complexity of HHL algorithm is $O\left(s^2\kappa^2\log(N)/\epsilon\right)$. This time complexity is polynomial in log(N), giving it an exponential speedup over the best-known classical algorithms under the same conditions.

Given the constraints previously, suppose we have encoded classical information into a quantum state, that is, we have quantum state $|b\rangle = \sum_{i=1}^{N} b_i|i\rangle$, and controlled Hamiltonian transformation $\sum_{\tau=0}^{T-1} |\tau\rangle\langle\tau| \otimes e^{iA\tau u/T}$, where $T = 2^t$ is a parameter related to the upper bound on the eigenvalue estimation in quantum phase estimation algorithm. The quantum circuit for HHL algorithm is shown in Fig. 6.17.

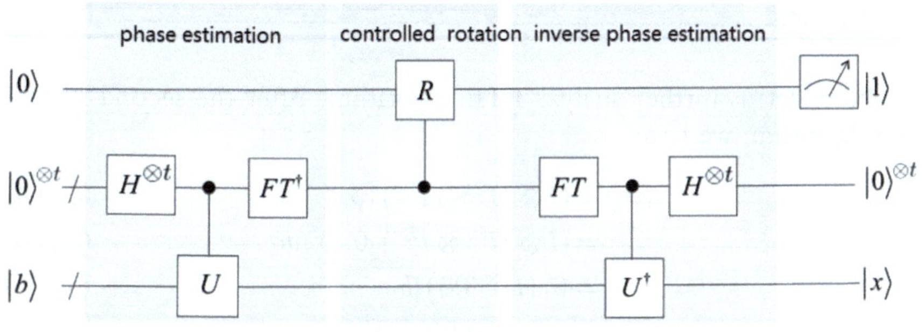

Figure 6.17 HHL algorithm.

As shown in Fig. 6.17, HHL algorithm can be divided into three main stages: phase estimation, controlled rotation, and inverse phase estimation. Qubits used in HHL algorithm can be divided into three groups, the top group containing 1 qubit, the middle group containing t qubits, and the bottom group containing n qubits.

Specific steps of HHL algorithm are listed in Algorithm 12.

Algorithm 12: HHL algorithm.

Input: Hermitian matrix A, state $|b\rangle$.

Output: State $|x\rangle$ which is the solution to the system of equations.

1 $|\psi_0\rangle = |0\rangle|0^t\rangle|b\rangle$.

2 $|\psi_1\rangle = \left(I \otimes H^{\otimes t} \otimes I^{\otimes n}\right)|\psi_0\rangle$.

3 $|\psi_2\rangle = \left(I \otimes \left(\sum_{\tau=0}^{T-1} |\tau\rangle\langle\tau| \otimes e^{iA\tau u/T}\right)\right)|\psi_1\rangle$.

4 $|\psi_3\rangle = \left(I \otimes \mathrm{QFT}_T^{\dagger} \otimes I^{\otimes n}\right)|\psi_2\rangle$.

5 Perform a controlled rotation on $|\psi_3\rangle$ to obtain $|\psi_4\rangle$, where control qubit is the second register and target qubit is the first register. The effect of controlled rotation is that, on the condition of estimating eigenvalue $\tilde{\lambda}_k$ during phase estimation stage, the state of the first register is rotated from $|0\rangle$ to $\sqrt{1 - \frac{C^2}{\tilde{\lambda}_k^2}}|0\rangle + \frac{C}{\tilde{\lambda}_k}|1\rangle$, where $C = O\left(\frac{1}{\kappa}\right)$.

6 $|\psi_5\rangle = \left(I \otimes \mathrm{QFT}_T \otimes I^{\otimes n}\right)|\psi_4\rangle$.

7 $|\psi_6\rangle = \left(I \otimes \left(\sum_{\tau=0}^{T-1} |\tau\rangle\langle\tau| \otimes e^{iA\tau u/T}\right)^{\dagger}\right)|\psi_5\rangle$.

8 $|\psi_7\rangle = \left(I \otimes H^{\otimes t} \otimes I^{\otimes n}\right)|\psi_6\rangle$.

9 Measure the first register. If measuring result is $|1\rangle$, then algorithm is successful and the solution $|x\rangle$ is obtained; if measuring result is $|0\rangle$, then algorithm needs to be re-executed and returned to the first step.

Now, let us further analyze HHL algorithm. After the second step of the algorithm, we have

$$|\psi_1\rangle = \left(I \otimes H^{\otimes t} \otimes I^{\otimes n}\right)|\psi_0\rangle \tag{6.364}$$

$$= \left(I \otimes H^{\otimes t} \otimes I^{\otimes n}\right)|0\rangle|0^t\rangle|b\rangle \tag{6.365}$$

$$= |0\rangle\left(H^{\otimes t}|0^t\rangle\right)|b\rangle \tag{6.366}$$

$$= \frac{1}{\sqrt{T}}|0\rangle\left(\sum_{\tau=0}^{T-1}|\tau\rangle\right)|b\rangle. \tag{6.367}$$

After the third step, we have

$$|\psi_2\rangle = \left(I \otimes \left(\sum_{\tau=0}^{T-1} |\tau\rangle\langle\tau| \otimes e^{iA\tau u/T}\right)\right) |\psi_1\rangle \tag{6.368}$$

$$= \left(I \otimes \left(\sum_{\tau=0}^{T-1} |\tau\rangle\langle\tau| \otimes e^{iA\tau u/T}\right)\right) \left(\frac{1}{\sqrt{T}}|0\rangle \left(\sum_{\tau'=0}^{T-1} |\tau'\rangle\right) |b\rangle\right) \tag{6.369}$$

$$= \frac{1}{\sqrt{T}}|0\rangle \left(\left(\sum_{\tau=0}^{T-1} |\tau\rangle\langle\tau| \otimes e^{iA\tau u/T}\right) \left(\sum_{\tau'=0}^{T-1} |\tau'\rangle \otimes |b\rangle\right)\right) \tag{6.370}$$

$$= \frac{1}{\sqrt{T}}|0\rangle \sum_{\tau=0}^{T-1}\sum_{\tau'=0}^{T-1} \left(|\tau\rangle\langle\tau|\tau'\rangle\right) \otimes \left(e^{iA\tau u/T}|b\rangle\right) \tag{6.371}$$

$$= \frac{1}{\sqrt{T}}|0\rangle \sum_{\tau=0}^{T-1} |\tau\rangle \left(e^{iA\tau u/T}|b\rangle\right). \tag{6.372}$$

After the fourth step, we have

$$|\psi_3\rangle = \left(I \otimes \mathrm{QFT}_T^\dagger \otimes I^{\otimes n}\right) |\psi_2\rangle \tag{6.373}$$

$$= \left(I \otimes \mathrm{QFT}_T^\dagger \otimes I^{\otimes n}\right) \left(\frac{1}{\sqrt{T}}|0\rangle \sum_{\tau=0}^{T-1} |\tau\rangle \left(e^{iA\tau u/T}|b\rangle\right)\right) \tag{6.374}$$

$$= \frac{1}{\sqrt{T}}|0\rangle \sum_{\tau=0}^{T-1} \left(\mathrm{QFT}_T^\dagger|\tau\rangle\right) \otimes \left(e^{iA\tau u/T}|b\rangle\right) \tag{6.375}$$

$$= \frac{1}{\sqrt{T}}|0\rangle \sum_{\tau=0}^{T-1} \left(\frac{1}{\sqrt{T}} \sum_{k=0}^{T-1} e^{-2\pi i\tau k/T}|k\rangle\right) \otimes \left(e^{iA\tau u/T}|b\rangle\right) \tag{6.376}$$

$$= \frac{1}{T}|0\rangle \sum_{k=0}^{T-1}\sum_{\tau=0}^{T-1} \left(e^{-2\pi i\tau k/T}|k\rangle\right) \otimes \left(e^{iA\tau u/T}|b\rangle\right) \tag{6.377}$$

$$= \frac{1}{T}|0\rangle \sum_{k=0}^{T-1} |k\rangle \sum_{\tau=0}^{T-1} e^{-2\pi i\tau k/T} \left(e^{iA\tau u/T}|b\rangle\right). \tag{6.378}$$

By noting that A is Hermitian, it can be spectrally decomposed as $A = \sum_{j=1}^{N} \lambda_j |u_j\rangle\langle u_j|$, where eigenvalues λ_j of matrix A are all real, and $|u_j\rangle$ is the eigenvector corresponding to eigenvalue λ_j. According to the previous assumptions, λ_j lies between $\frac{1}{\kappa}$ and 1. According to the spectral decomposition of A, we obtain $e^{iA\tau u/T} = \sum_{j=1}^{N} e^{i\lambda_j\tau u/T}|u_j\rangle\langle u_j|$. Under the orthonormal basis $\{|u_j\rangle\}$, $|b\rangle$ can be expressed as $|b\rangle = \sum_{j=1}^{N} \beta_j|u_j\rangle$.

Therefore, we can further simplify the state after step 4 of the algorithm as follows:

$$|\psi_3\rangle = \frac{1}{T}|0\rangle \sum_{k=0}^{T-1} |k\rangle \sum_{\tau=0}^{T-1} e^{-2\pi i \tau k/T} \left(e^{iA\tau u/T}|b\rangle\right) \tag{6.379}$$

$$= \frac{1}{T}|0\rangle \sum_{k=0}^{T-1} |k\rangle \sum_{\tau=0}^{T-1} e^{-2\pi i \tau k/T} \left(\sum_{j=1}^{N} e^{i\lambda_j \tau u/T}|u_j\rangle\langle u_j| \left(\sum_{j'=1}^{N} \beta_{j'}|u_{j'}\rangle\right)\right) \tag{6.380}$$

$$= \frac{1}{T}|0\rangle \sum_{k=0}^{T-1} |k\rangle \sum_{\tau=0}^{T-1} e^{-2\pi i \tau k/T} \left(\sum_{j=1}^{N}\sum_{j'=1}^{N} e^{i\lambda_j \tau u/T}|u_j\rangle\langle u_j|\beta_{j'}|u_{j'}\rangle\right) \tag{6.381}$$

$$= \frac{1}{T}|0\rangle \sum_{k=0}^{T-1} |k\rangle \sum_{\tau=0}^{T-1} e^{-2\pi i \tau k/T} \left(\sum_{j=1}^{N}\sum_{j'=1}^{N} e^{i\lambda_j \tau u/T}\beta_{j'}|u_j\rangle\langle u_j|u_{j'}\rangle\right) \tag{6.382}$$

$$= \frac{1}{T}|0\rangle \sum_{k=0}^{T-1} |k\rangle \sum_{\tau=0}^{T-1} e^{-2\pi i \tau k/T} \left(\sum_{j=1}^{N} e^{i\lambda_j \tau u/T}\beta_j|u_j\rangle\right) \tag{6.383}$$

$$= \frac{1}{T}|0\rangle \sum_{k=0}^{T-1} |k\rangle \sum_{\tau=0}^{T-1}\sum_{j=1}^{N} e^{(\lambda_j u - 2\pi k)i\tau/T}\beta_j|u_j\rangle \tag{6.384}$$

$$= \frac{1}{T}|0\rangle \sum_{j=1}^{N}\sum_{k=0}^{T-1} \left(\sum_{\tau=0}^{T-1} e^{(\lambda_j u/(2\pi) - k)2\pi i\tau/T}\right)\beta_j|k\rangle|u_j\rangle. \tag{6.385}$$

Note that

$$\left|\sum_{\tau=0}^{T-1} e^{(\lambda_j u/(2\pi) - k)2\pi i\tau/T}\right| \tag{6.386}$$

$$= \begin{cases} \left|\sum_{\tau=0}^{T-1} 1\right| = T, & \frac{\lambda_j u}{2\pi} = k; \\ \left|\dfrac{e^{(\lambda_j u/(2\pi)-k)2\pi i} - 1}{e^{(\lambda_j u/(2\pi)-k)2\pi i/T} - 1}\right|, & \frac{\lambda_j u}{2\pi} \neq k. \end{cases} \tag{6.387}$$

In fact, as a whole, steps 2 to 4 of the algorithm is a process of quantum phase estimation. From the analysis of quantum phase estimation algorithm, $\left|\sum_{\tau=0}^{T-1} e^{(\lambda_j u/(2\pi)-k)2\pi i\tau/T}\right|$ is large if and only if $\lambda_j \approx \frac{2\pi k}{u}$. For each eigenvalue λ_j of matrix A, the algorithm will estimate λ_j by using $\frac{2\pi k}{u}$, where

$k = 0, 1, \cdots, T-1$. The closer $\frac{2\pi k}{u}$ is to λ_j, the larger the amplitude is, which means the corresponding probability is higher. λ_j is between $\frac{1}{\kappa}$ and 1, and $u = O(\frac{\kappa}{\epsilon})$. So, we can estimate all λ_j without omission under specified precision requirement ϵ. Since the estimated eigenvalue corresponding to state $|k\rangle$ of the second register is $\frac{2\pi k}{u}$, we relabel $|k\rangle$ as $|\tilde{\lambda}_k\rangle$ to clearly indicate that the eigenvalue of the state is $\tilde{\lambda}_k = \frac{2\pi k}{u}$. Hence, $|\psi_3\rangle$ can also be written as

$$|\psi_3\rangle = \frac{1}{T}|0\rangle \sum_{j=1}^{N}\sum_{k=0}^{T-1}\left(\sum_{\tau=0}^{T-1} e^{(\lambda_j u/(2\pi)-k)2\pi i\tau/T}\right)\beta_j|\tilde{\lambda}_k\rangle|u_j\rangle. \tag{6.388}$$

In the 5th step of the algorithm, a controlled rotation gate is acted on $|\psi_3\rangle$, where the state of the first register is rotated based on the state of the second register, that is, the first register is rotated according to the estimated eigenvalue $\tilde{\lambda}_k$. After the controlled rotation, the state is

$$|\psi_4\rangle = \frac{1}{T}\sum_{j=1}^{N}\sum_{k=0}^{T-1}\left(\sum_{\tau=0}^{T-1} e^{(\lambda_j u/(2\pi)-k)2\pi i\tau/T}\right)\left(\sqrt{1-\frac{C^2}{\tilde{\lambda}_k^2}}|0\rangle + \frac{C}{\tilde{\lambda}_k}|1\rangle\right)\beta_j|\tilde{\lambda}_k\rangle|u_j\rangle, \tag{6.389}$$

where $\tilde{\lambda}_k = \frac{2\pi k}{u}$.

To illustrate the effect of the algorithm more clearly, we assume that the estimation of each λ_j is perfectly accurate, that is, for each j, there exists a k such that $\left|\sum_{\tau=0}^{T-1} e^{(\lambda_j u/(2\pi)-k)2\pi i\tau/T}\right| = T$ and $\tilde{\lambda}_k = \lambda_j$. Thus state after step 5 can be written as

$$|\psi_4\rangle = \sum_{j=1}^{N}\left(\sqrt{1-\frac{C^2}{\lambda_j^2}}|0\rangle + \frac{C}{\lambda_j}|1\rangle\right)\beta_j|\lambda_j\rangle|u_j\rangle. \tag{6.390}$$

Steps 6 to 8 of the algorithm are a process of inverse quantum phase estimation, which is the inverse of steps 2 to 4. In the state of the system after inverse quantum phase estimation process, the second register returns to its initial state and becomes disentangled from the third register, while entanglement exists between the first register and the third register. We have

$$|\psi_7\rangle = \sum_{j=1}^{N}\left(\sqrt{1-\frac{C^2}{\lambda_j^2}}|0\rangle + \frac{C}{\lambda_j}|1\rangle\right)\beta_j|0^t\rangle|u_j\rangle. \tag{6.391}$$

After measuring the first register in step 9, if the result is $|1\rangle$, then the system state will be

$$\sqrt{\frac{1}{\sum_{j=1}^{N} C^2|\beta_j|^2/|\lambda_j|^2}}\sum_{j=1}^{N}\frac{C}{\lambda_j}\beta_j|1\rangle|0^t\rangle|u_j\rangle \tag{6.392}$$

$$=|1\rangle|0^t\rangle\sqrt{\frac{1}{\sum_{j=1}^{N}|\beta_j|^2/|\lambda_j|^2}}\sum_{j=1}^{N}\frac{\beta_j}{\lambda_j}|u_j\rangle. \tag{6.393}$$

At this point, the state in the third register is

$$|x\rangle=\sqrt{\frac{1}{\sum_{j=1}^{N}|\beta_j|^2/|\lambda_j|^2}}\sum_{j=1}^{N}\frac{\beta_j}{\lambda_j}|u_j\rangle. \tag{6.394}$$

This state differs from the true solution of system $\vec{x}=A^{-1}\vec{b}=\sum_{j=1}^{N}\frac{\beta_j}{\lambda_j}\vec{u}_j$ by only a normalization factor. We can determine this normalization factor by measuring the probability of obtaining $|1\rangle$ in step 9. Thus HHL algorithm can be used to obtain the solution to systems of linear equations. Total number of qubits used in HHL algorithm is $n+t+1$, and the number of basic gates is polynomial in $\log(N)$, providing an exponential speedup in time complexity compared to the best-known classical algorithms.

The systems of linear equations play an important role in the field of science and engineering, where there are numerous situations requiring the solution of linear systems. In particular, for some complex and challenging problems, an efficient algorithm may be required to solve systems with large dimensions. Quantum algorithms for solving linear systems have the potential to play a unique role in addressing these problems.

6.17 * Variational quantum eigensolver algorithm

In this section, we discuss variational quantum eigensolver (VQE) algorithm, which was proposed by Alberto Peruzzo et al. in 2014 [20]. It is one of the earliest variational quantum algorithms. As a quantum-classical hybrid algorithm that can be implemented on noisy quantum devices, VQE is highly favored by scholars. VQE can be used to seek ground states and low-lying excited states of quantum systems, both of which are important in quantum many-body physics and quantum chemistry.

Computing ground state properties are defined as follows: for a system with Hamiltonian H, find the smallest eigenvalue E_g such that $H|\psi_g\rangle = E_g|\psi_g\rangle$, where $|\psi_g\rangle$ is the eigenvector corresponding to E_g. Though no efficient quantum algorithm has been found to prepare the ground states for general Hamiltonians, for some specific Hamiltonians, VQE can be used to find the ground states. VQE algorithm can find eigenvalues (including the smallest eigenvalue) as well as eigenvectors of a large matrix H. As a quantum-classical hybrid algorithm, the process of VQE is illustrated in Fig. 6.18.

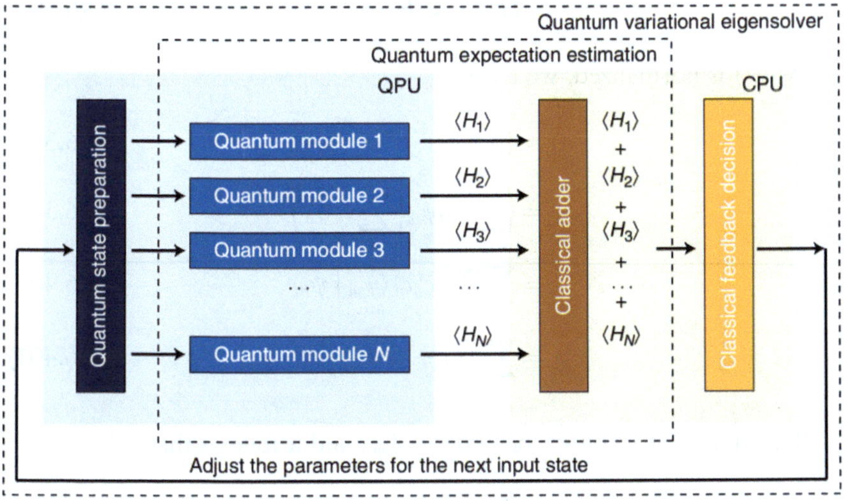

Figure 6.18 VQE algorithm.

VQE is based on variational principle in quantum mechanics. Next, we introduce variational principle. The problem of finding the minimum of Hamiltonian's expectation value is equivalent to solving Schrödinger equation, which is a second-order partial differential equation under constraint where its wave function is normalized. It is often challenging to find smooth solutions and ground state energy E_g for Schrödinger equation. However, variational principle provides an upper bound on E_g. By applying variational principle skillfully, the upper bound can be made close to exact values to a great extent. The variational principle is described below.

Theorem 6.17. *Let H be a Hamiltonian. Suppose $|\psi\rangle$ is any trial state, and E_g is the ground state energy of the system. Then we have*

$$E_g \le \langle\psi|H|\psi\rangle \equiv \langle H\rangle, \tag{6.395}$$

where $\langle H\rangle$ represents expectation value of Hamiltonian H in the state $|\psi\rangle$.

Proof. Since eigenvectors of Hamiltonian H form a complete orthonormal basis $\{|\psi_i\rangle\}$, we have

$$|\psi\rangle = \sum_n c_n |\psi_n\rangle. \tag{6.396}$$

According to eigenvalue equation of Hamiltonian H,

$$H|\psi_n\rangle = E_n |\psi_n\rangle. \tag{6.397}$$

As $|\psi\rangle$ is normalized, we have

$$1 = \langle\psi \mid \psi\rangle \tag{6.398}$$

$$= \left\langle \sum_m c_m\psi_m \middle| \sum_n c_n\psi_n \right\rangle \tag{6.399}$$

$$= \sum_m \sum_n c_m^* c_n \langle\psi_m \mid \psi_n\rangle \tag{6.400}$$

$$= \sum_n |c_n|^2. \tag{6.401}$$

The eigenvectors satisfy $\langle\psi_m \mid \psi_n\rangle = \delta_{mn}$, and it follows that

$$\langle H\rangle = \left\langle \sum_m c_m\psi_m \middle| H\sum_n c_n\psi_n \right\rangle \tag{6.402}$$

$$= \sum_m \sum_n c_m^* E_n c_n \langle\psi_m \mid \psi_n\rangle \tag{6.403}$$

$$= \sum_n E_n |c_n|^2. \tag{6.404}$$

Since ground state energy is the smallest eigenvalue, that is, $E_g \le E_n$, we have

$$\langle H\rangle \ge E_g \sum_n |c_n|^2 = E_g. \tag{6.405}$$

□

According to the proof mentioned previously, if we choose trial state $|\psi\rangle$ to be the ground state $|\psi_g\rangle$ (i.e., unit eigenvector corresponding to E_g), then the average energy of the system is $\langle H\rangle = E_g$. If trial state $|\psi\rangle$ is not the ground state, then $\langle H\rangle$ might be much larger than E_g. To solve this problem, we introduce some parameters and adjust these parameters for many times to make the trial state approach the ground state.

Besides variational principle, quantum adiabatic theorem is also used in VQE. Next, we recall quantum adiabatic theorem.

Theorem 6.18. *Suppose that Hamiltonian of a system varies with time, which is denoted as $H(t)$ $(t \leq t_f)$. At initial time, the system is in the ground state $|\psi_0(0)\rangle$ (i.e., the normalized eigenvector corresponding to the minimum eigenvalue of $H(0)$). If the system's evolution is sufficiently slow, then at the final moment t_f, the system will still be in the ground state $|\psi_0(t_f)\rangle$.*

How to use quantum adiabatic computation to calculate the ground state energy of a Hamiltonian (denoted as $H(t_f)$)? We have the following idea.

(1) At initial time, make the system's Hamiltonian sufficiently simple (denoted as $H(0)$), and the state is in the ground state of $H(0)$.

(2) Control the system so that its Hamiltonian changes with time: $H(t) = (1 - s(t))H(0) + s(t)H(t_f)$, where $s(0) = 0$ and $s(t_f) = 1$.

(3) According to the adiabatic theorem, if the system evolves slowly enough, by the time t_f, the system's Hamiltonian will be $H(t_f)$; meanwhile, the state will be in the ground state of $H(t_f)$, denoted as $|\psi_0(t_f)\rangle$.

(4) By measurement and calculation, obtain the ground state energy $\langle\psi_0(t_f)|H(t_f)|\psi_0(t_f)\rangle$ of $H(t_f)$.

Quantum adiabatic computation model and gate model are polynomial-equivalent. In the case where Hamiltonian H does not evolve with time (quantum static problem), according to Schrödinger equation, we have

$$|\psi(t_f)\rangle = e^{-\frac{iH\cdot t_f}{\hbar}}|\psi(0)\rangle, \tag{6.406}$$

where H is the Hamiltonian, $|\psi(0)\rangle$ is initial state, t_f is evolution time, and $\hbar$ is reduced Planck constant.

For the case where Hamiltonian H evolves with time (quantum dynamic problem), it is rarely solvable exactly. As we consider the case where Hamiltonian changes slowly enough, we have

$$|\psi(t_f)\rangle \approx e^{-\frac{iH(t_{n-1})\cdot(t_n - t_{n-1}) + \cdots + iH(t_0)\cdot(t_1 - t_0)}{\hbar}}|\psi(0)\rangle, \tag{6.407}$$

where $H(t_{n-1})$ and $H(t_0)$ are Hamiltonians at time t_{n-1} and t_0, respectively; $t_n = t_f$, $t_0 = 0$, and ensuring that consecutive moments are sufficiently close to each other.

Since it is necessary to ensure that consecutive moments are sufficiently close, that is, $t_i - t_{i-1}$ is sufficiently small, a large number of quantum gates is required, making the cost unaffordable. A classical optimization method can be used to optimize the parameters instead.

Detailed process of the VQE algorithm is described later, and its schematic diagram is shown in Fig. 6.18. Suppose the goal of the algorithm is to find the ground state energy E_0 (the smallest eigenvalue of Hamiltonian $H(t_f)$).

1° Construct Hamiltonian $H(t_f)$ according to chemical system, and choose a simple Hamiltonian $H(0)$ as initial Hamiltonian. Set $H(t) = (1 - s(t))H(0) + s(t)H(t_f)$, where $s(0) = 0$ and $s(t_f) = 1$.

2° Initialize $|\psi(0)\rangle$ as ground state of $H(0)$.

3° Prepare the trial state $|\psi(\overrightarrow{\theta_n})\rangle$: using the Unitary Coupled Cluster (UCC) theory and asymptotic approximation theorem, we construct a unitary operator $U(\overrightarrow{\theta_n})$ composed of some quantum gates with parameters $\overrightarrow{\theta_n}$, which transforms quantum states to $|\psi(\overrightarrow{\theta_n})\rangle = U(\overrightarrow{\theta_n})|\psi(0)\rangle$.

This step uses $U(\overrightarrow{\theta_n})$ to simulate the evolution of $|\psi(0)\rangle$ under $H(t)$, with the goal of making $|\psi(\overrightarrow{\theta_n})\rangle$ as close as possible to the ground state of $H(t_f)$.

4° By measurement and calculation, we find the expectation values of each term $\langle H_i\rangle = \langle\psi(\overrightarrow{\theta_n})|H_i|\psi(\overrightarrow{\theta_n})\rangle$. The expectation of $H(t_f)$ is obtained by summing the expectations of individual terms, given by $\langle H(t_f)\rangle = \sum_i \langle H_i\rangle$.

5° If the decrease of $\langle H(t_f)\rangle$ is less than a certain threshold, the algorithm terminates and outputs the result $\langle H(t_f)\rangle$; Otherwise, a classical optimizer (such as gradient descent) is used to optimize the parameters $\overrightarrow{\theta_n}$ to $\overrightarrow{\theta_{n+1}}$, and returns to step 3°.

In VQE, we use quantum expectation estimation algorithm to measure the energy of trial state. Quantum expectation estimation refers to the fact that the Hamiltonian of a multi-electron system can be expanded as a sum of multiple terms, namely

$$H(t_f) = \sum_{i=1}^{N} H_i. \tag{6.408}$$

Since

$$\langle H_i\rangle = \langle\psi(t_f)|H_i|\psi(t_f)\rangle, \tag{6.409}$$

after summing, we obtain

$$\langle H(t_f)\rangle = \sum_i \langle H_i\rangle. \tag{6.410}$$

Therefore, for the problem of solving system's Hamiltonian, we can first obtain the average energy of each term, and then sum these average energies to obtain the total average energy of the system. During the algorithm's execution, the measurement of each term's average energy is performed using a quantum processor; while the sum of these average energies is carried out by a classical processor.

6.18 * Quantum approximate optimization algorithm

The quantum algorithms we introduced before are mainly based on the quantum query model. In the following, we will introduce another class of quantum algorithms, the Quantum Approximate Optimization Algorithm (QAOA). The QAOA is a widely used optimization algorithm (first proposed by E. Farhi et al. [21]). This is a quantum-classical hybrid algorithm that uses quantum mechanical tools such as Hamiltonian and quantum state operation to solve the optimization problem of an objective function through a classical iterative process.

Like most approximate optimization algorithms, QAOA is not necessarily guaranteed to find the globally optimal solution of the objective function, but it will find an approximate optimal solution with a high probability. Nowadays, the underlying technology of quantum computers is in the Noisy Intermediate-Scale Quantum (NISQ) era, so QAOA may have a better chance of being implemented on a larger scale than the previous quantum query algorithms. At present, it has been found that the optimization problems in graph theory, such as the maximum cut problem and the compressed graph signal problem, can be solved by QAOA.

The basic components of QAOA are: the objective function, the initial state, the phase operator, and the mixing operator, where the general form of the objective function optimized by QAOA is as follows:

$$\max_{x\in\{0,1\}^l} C(x). \tag{6.411}$$

For a specific objective function C, we can consider a corresponding Hamiltonian H_P, which acts as follows:

$$H_P|x\rangle = C(x)|x\rangle. \tag{6.412}$$

It is not difficult to find that each quantum state $|x\rangle$ is an eigenvector of the Hamiltonian H_P with the corresponding eigenvalue $C(x)$. In this way, we transform the original optimization problem into a problem of finding the maximum eigenvalue of the Hamiltonian H_P.

To solve the maximum eigenvalue of H_P, we first define the phase operator $U_P(\gamma)$ as follows:

$$U_P(\gamma) = e^{-i\gamma H_P}, \tag{6.413}$$

where γ is a parameter. It is not difficult to find that $U_P(\gamma)$ is a kind of rotation operator in 2^l-dimensional Hilbert space.

We further define the mixed Hamiltonian as follows:

$$H_M = \sum_{i=1}^{l} X_i, \tag{6.414}$$

where X_i is the Pauli matrix X acting on the i-th qubit.

Generally, the initial state of QAOA is a uniform superposition state as follows:

$$|+\rangle^{\otimes l} = \frac{1}{\sqrt{2^l}} \sum_{x \in \{0,1\}^l} |x\rangle. \tag{6.415}$$

The k-layer QAOA operates as follows:

$$\begin{aligned} &|\psi_P(\gamma, \beta)\rangle \\ &= e^{-i\beta_k H_M} e^{-i\gamma_k H_P} e^{-i\beta_{k-1} H_M} e^{-i\gamma_{k-1} H_P} \cdots e^{-i\beta_2 H_M} e^{-i\gamma_2 H_P} e^{-i\beta_1 H_M} e^{-i\gamma_1 H_P} |+\rangle^{\otimes l}, \end{aligned} \tag{6.416}$$

where $|\psi_P(\gamma, \beta)\rangle$ is a function of the $2k$ parameters γ_i, β_i $(i = 1, 2, \ldots, k)$, and the expected value of H_P under $|\psi_P(\gamma, \beta)\rangle$,

$$C_P(\gamma, \beta) = \langle \psi_P(\gamma, \beta) | H_P | \psi_P(\gamma, \beta) \rangle \tag{6.417}$$

is also a function on the $2k$ parameters γ_i, β_i $(i = 1, 2, \ldots, k)$.

We can obtain the value of $C_P(\gamma, \beta)$ by repeatedly measuring $|\psi_P(\gamma, \beta)\rangle$ under the computational basis. Similar to the classical optimization algorithm, the optimal parameters γ_i, β_i $(i = 1, 2, \ldots, k)$ can be found by the iterative technique.

Assume that currently we run the algorithm to find a set of optimized parameters (γ^*, β^*). We can define the performance metric as follows:

$$r = \frac{\langle C^* \rangle}{C_{\max}} = \frac{\langle \psi_P(\gamma^*, \beta^*) | H_P | \psi_P(\gamma^*, \beta^*) \rangle}{C_{\max}}, \tag{6.418}$$

where $C_{\max}$ is the maximum value of the function C.

It is not difficult to conclude that after a finite number of iterations, we can obtain $0 \leq r \leq 1$. As k increases, the performance metric r of QAOA increases monotonically. As k tends to $+\infty$, QAOA will tend to find the globally optimal solution.

However, QAOA with the shallowest layer (i.e., $k = 1$) still has better performance. In general, QAOA cannot be regarded as a special case of classical optimization algorithms, but it should be regarded as a more general form of classical optimization algorithms. It can also be proved theoretically that QAOA has better running time performance than another class of quantum optimization algorithms, such as the quantum annealing algorithm [22]. Therefore, QAOA is a significant quantum-classical hybrid algorithm.

6.19 Summary

In the history of quantum computing, quantum algorithms have attracted wide-ranging attention because quantum algorithms for solving certain problems can provide polynomial or even exponential level accelerations compared to the best-known classical algorithms. In this chapter, we first discuss the relationship between quantum algorithms and classical probabilistic algorithms, then introduce related concepts and properties of the general form of quantum query model and query complexity. After that, some important quantum algorithms in the history of quantum computing are detailed.

It is hoped that this chapter stimulates the readers' interest in learning quantum algorithms, and also helps the readers understand the basic process, correctness analysis, and efficiency analysis of important quantum algorithms. These quantum algorithms introduced in this chapter mainly adopt the idea of quantum phase estimation and quantum amplitude amplification. It is also hoped that readers can master these two methods and ideas of designing quantum algorithms, and furthermore are familiar with using these two methods to design quantum algorithms to solve some practical problems. At present, there are not too many methods to design quantum algorithms, and it is expected that more readers will join the research of quantum algorithms in the future, as well as more novel quantum algorithms are going to be discovered.

Finally, we would like to mention that designing distributed quantum algorithms (for example, [23–26]) is a new subject worthy of further study.

References

[1] D.W. Qiu, S.G. Zheng, Characterizations of symmetrically partial Boolean functions with exact quantum query complexity, arXiv:1603.06505, 2016.

[2] D. Deutsch, Quantum theory, the Church-Turing principle and the universal quantum computer, Proceedings of the Royal Society of London. Series A, Mathematical and Physical Sciences 400 (1818) (1985) 97–117.

[3] D. Deutsch, R. Jozsa, Rapid solution of problems by quantum computation, Proceedings of the Royal Society of London. Series A, Mathematical and Physical Sciences 439 (1907) (1992) 553–558.

[4] A. Montanaro, R. Jozsa, G. Mitchison, On exact quantum query complexity, Algorithmica 71 (4) (2015) 775–796.

[5] D.R. Simon, On the power of quantum computation, in: Proceedings of the 35th Annual Symposium on Foundations of Computer Science, 1994, pp. 116–123.

[6] R. de Wolf, Quantum Computing, Lecture Notes, QuSoft, CWI and University of Amsterdam, 2019.

[7] G.Y. Cai, D.W. Qiu, Optimal separation in exact query complexities for Simon's problem, Journal of Computer and System Sciences 97 (2018) 83–93.

[8] A. Nayak, Deterministic algorithms for the hidden subgroup problem, arXiv:2104.14436, 2021.

[9] G. Brassard, P. Höyer, An exact quantum polynomial-time algorithm for Simon's problem, in: Proceedings of the Fifth Israeli Symposium on Theory of Computing and Systems, 1997, pp. 12–23.

[10] P. Koiran, V. Nesme, N. Portier, A quantum lower bound for the query complexity of Simon's problem, in: International Colloquium on Automata, Languages, and Programming, 2005, pp. 1287–1298.

[11] Z.G. Wu, D.W. Qiu, J.W. Tan, et al., Quantum and classical query complexities for generalized Simon's problem, Theoretical Computer Science 924 (2022) 171–186.

[12] J. Watrous, Introduction to Quantum Computing, Lecture Notes, University of Waterloo, 2005.

[13] G. Brassard, P. Hoyer, M. Mosca, et al., Quantum amplitude amplification and estimation, Contemporary Mathematics, vol. 305, 2002, pp. 53–74.

[14] P.W. Shor, Algorithms for quantum computation: discrete logarithms and factoring, in: Proceedings 35th Annual Symposium on Foundations of Computer Science, 1994, pp. 124–134.

[15] P. Kaye, R. Laflamme, M. Mosca, An Introduction to Quantum Computing, Oxford, 2006.

[16] L.K. Grover, A fast quantum mechanical algorithm for database search, in: Proceedings of the Twenty-Eighth Annual ACM Symposium on Theory of Computing, 1996, pp. 212–219.

[17] B. Michel, G. Brassard, P. Höyer, et al., Tight bounds on quantum searching, Fortschritte der Physik 46 (4–5) (1998) 493–505.

[18] A.W. Harrow, A. Hassidim, S. Lloyd, Quantum algorithm for linear systems of equations, Physical Review Letters 103 (15) (2009) 150502.

[19] D.W. Berry, G. Ahokas, R. Cleve, et al., Efficient quantum algorithms for simulating sparse Hamiltonians, Communications in Mathematical Physics 270 (2) (2006) 359–371.

[20] A. Peruzzo, J. Mcclean, P. Shadbolt, et al., A variational eigenvalue solver on a photonic quantum processor, Nature Communications 5 (4213) (2014) 1–7.

[21] E. Farhi, J. Goldstone, S. Gutmann, A quantum approximate optimization algorithm, arXiv:1411.4028, 2014.

[22] C.H. Cho, C.Y. Chen, K.C. Chen, et al., Quantum computation: algorithms and applications, Chinese Journal of Physics 72 (2021) 248–269.

[23] D.W. Qiu, L. Luo, L.G. Xiao, Distributed Grover's algorithm, Theoretical Computer Science 993 (2024) 114461.
[24] J.W. Tan, L.G. Xiao, D.W. Qiu, L. Luo, P. Mateus, Distributed quantum algorithm for Simon's problem, Physical Review A 106 (3) (2022) 032423.
[25] L.G. Xiao, D.W. Qiu, L. Luo, P. Mateus, Distributed Shor's algorithm, Quantum Information and Computation 23 (2023) 0027–0044.
[26] H. Li, D.W. Qiu, L. Luo, Distributed generalized Deutsch–Jozsa algorithm, in: Proceedings of the Thirtieth International Computing and Combinatorics Conference (COCOON), in: Lecture Notes in Computer Science, vol. 15162, Springer, Singapore, 2024, pp. 214–225.

CHAPTER 7

Quantum computational complexity[⊛]

The complexity theory of quantum computing is an important part of theoretical computer science, which describes the amount of resources such as time and space required for quantum computing, and can be used to reflect the advantages and disadvantages of quantum algorithms. First, we introduce several computational complex class notation.

Set the function $f:\mathbb{Z}^+ \to \mathbb{R}$. Denote

$$O(f(n)) = \{g \mid g \in \mathbb{R}^{\mathbb{Z}^+}, \exists c > 0, N > 0 \text{ such that } g(n) \le cf(n) \text{ for } n \ge N\}, \tag{7.1}$$

$$\Omega(f(n)) = \{g \mid g \in \mathbb{R}^{\mathbb{Z}^+}, \exists c > 0, N > 0 \text{ such that } g(n) \ge cf(n) \text{ for } n \ge N\}, \tag{7.2}$$

$$\Theta(f(n)) = O(f(n)) \cap \Omega(f(n)). \tag{7.3}$$

Given an alphabet $\Sigma = \{0, 1\}$, let $L \subseteq \Sigma^*$ be a language. If the algorithm $\mathcal{A}$ satisfies for any $x \in L$, $\mathcal{A}$ accepts x; for any $x \notin L$, $\mathcal{A}$ rejects x, then $\mathcal{A}$ is said to be able to determine the language L.

Example 7.1. Determining whether a positive integer n is prime is equivalent to determining whether the bit string representing n is in the language PRIME defined as follows:

$$\text{PRIME} = \{10, 11, 010, 011, 101, 111, \cdots\}. \tag{7.4}$$

Example 7.2. Determining whether a given graph x is 3-colorable means to decide whether the following conditions are satisfied: 1. Color any vertex of the graph x with only three colors; 2. The two vertices of any edge of graph x have different colors. This problem is equivalent to determining whether a string representing x belongs to the language 3-COLORABLE (3-COL for short, that is, the set consisting of all 3-colorable graphs).

[⊛] This book has a companion website hosting complementary materials. Visit this URL to access it: https://www.elsevier.com/books-and-journals/book-companion/9780443277047.

Theoretical Foundations of Quantum Computing
https://doi.org/10.1016/B978-0-44-327704-7.00012-8

We can represent the graph with bit string x as follows. Suppose there are n vertices $v_1, v_2, \cdots, v_n$ on the graph x, denote edges $e_1 = \{v_1, v_2\}$, $e_2 = \{v_1, v_3\}$, $\cdots$, $e_{n-1} = \{v_1, v_n\}$, $e_n = \{v_2, v_3\}$, $\cdots$, $e_{\frac{n(n-1)}{2}} = \{v_{n-1}, v_n\}$. The graph x is represented by the string $x_1x_2 \cdots x_{\frac{n(n-1)}{2}}$, where $x_j = 1$ if and only if the graph x contains the edge e_j; $x_j = 0$ if and only if the graph x does not contain the edge e_j. An example of a 3-colorable graph is given in Fig. 7.1.

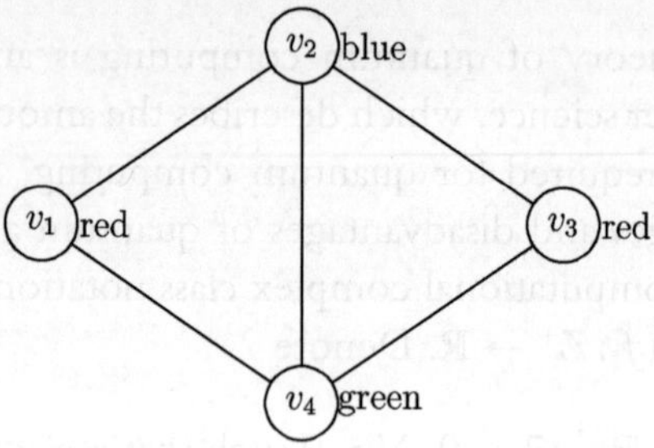

Figure 7.1 101111 ∈ 3-COL.

In the following, we give definitions and examples of some common language classes in computational complexity theory.

Definition 7.1. The language class P means that for any $L \in$ P, there exists a deterministic polynomial-time (polynomial about the length of the input strings) algorithm $\mathcal{A}$ such that for any $x \in \Sigma^*$, $\mathcal{A}$ accepts x if and only if $x \in L$.

Definition 7.2. The language class BPP means that for any $L \in$ BPP, there is a bounded-error probabilistic polynomial-time algorithm $\mathcal{A}$ such that for any $x \in \Sigma^*$, if $x \in L$, then the probability that $\mathcal{A}$ accepts x is at least $\frac{2}{3}$; if $x \notin L$, then the probability that $\mathcal{A}$ accepts x is at most $\frac{1}{3}$.

Remark 7.1. In fact, $\frac{2}{3}$ in Definition 7.2 can be changed to $\frac{1}{2} + \delta$, $\frac{1}{3}$ can be changed to $\frac{1}{2} - \delta$, where $0 < \delta < \frac{1}{2}$.

Definition 7.3. The language class BQP means that for any $L \in$ BQP, there exists a bounded-error quantum polynomial-time algorithm $\mathcal{A}$ such that for any $x \in \Sigma^*$, if $x \in L$, then the probability that $\mathcal{A}$ accepts x is at least $\frac{2}{3}$; if $x \notin L$, then the probability that $\mathcal{A}$ accepts x is at most $\frac{1}{3}$.

Definition 7.4. The language class NP means that for any $L \in$ NP, there exists a polynomial-time algorithm $\mathcal{A}(a, b)$, for any $x \in \Sigma^*$, if $x \in L$, there is an input y such that $\mathcal{A}(x, y)$ outputs "accept"; if $x \notin L$, for any input y, $\mathcal{A}(x, y)$ outputs "reject," where $|y| \leq P(|x|)$, P represents a polynomial function.

Remark 7.2. The language class NP consists of problems that are decidable in polynomial time by nondeterministic Turing machines and verifiable in polynomial time by deterministic Turing machines.

Example 7.3. Suppose the language $L = $ 3-COL. There exists a polynomial-time algorithm. For any $x \in L$, after taking y to be a 3-color coloring of x, it is sufficient to check, edge by edge, whether the two vertices of the graph x are different in color. For $x \notin L$, after arbitrarily coloring y, then checking edge by edge that at least two vertices on a connected edge have the same color. Therefore, $L \in$ NP.

Definition 7.5. NPC (NP-complete) is a subclass of NP. For any $L \in$ NPC, if L has a valid solution, then any NP problem has a valid solution. That is, for any $L' \in$ NP, there is a classical deterministic polynomial-time algorithm to compute the function: $f : \{0, 1\}^* \to \{0, 1\}^*$, for any $x \in \Sigma^*$, $x \in L'$ if and only if $f(x) \in L$.

Example 7.4. The 3-colorable problem, the traveling salesman problem (TSP), the 3-SAT problem, the circuit satisfiability (CSAT) problem, the subset sum problem are all NPC problems.

Remark 7.3. The integer factorization problem and the graph isomorphism problem are NP problems, but it is not proven whether they are NPC problems.

The 3-SAT problem is the first problem that has been proved to be NPC. Since many problems can be transformed into the 3-SAT problem, it plays a very important role in computer science. In the following, we introduce the relevant definitions.

Definition 7.6. The 3-CNF formula is a Boolean formula consisting of several clauses by conjunction, where each clause consists of 3 Boolean variables or their negation variables by disjunction.

Example 7.5. Suppose $\Phi = (a_1 \vee \overline{a_2} \vee a_3) \wedge (a_4 \vee a_5 \vee \overline{a_3}) \wedge (a_6 \vee a_7 \vee a_2)$. The set of truth assignments for this 3-CNF formula is $a_1 = 1$, $a_2 = 0$, $a_3 = 0$, $a_4 = 1$, $a_5 = 1$, $a_6 = 1$, and $a_7 = 0$.

Definition 7.7. The 3-SAT problem is to determine whether there is a set of true assignments for a 3-CNF formula.

Definition 7.8. The language class PSPACE means that for any $L \in$ PSPACE, there is a classical polynomial space algorithm $\mathcal{A}$ such that for any $x \in \Sigma^*$, $\mathcal{A}$ accepts x if and only if $x \in L$.

Remark 7.4. P $\subseteq$ BPP $\subseteq$ BQP $\subseteq$ PSPACE, P $\subseteq$ NP $\subseteq$ PSPACE.

Exercises

7.1. Prove that $f(n) \in O(g(n))$ if and only if $g(n) \in \Omega(f(n))$. Prove that $f(n) \in \Theta(g(n))$ if and only if $g(n) \in \Theta(f(n))$.

7.2. Suppose $g(n)$ is a polynomial of degree k. Prove that for any $l \geq k$, $g(n) \in O(n^l)$.

7.3. Prove that for any $k > 0$, $\log n \in O(n^k)$.

7.4. Prove that for any k, $n^k \in O(n^{\log n})$, but $n^{\log n} \notin O(n^k)$.

7.5. Prove that for any $c > 1$, $c^n \in \Omega(n^{\log n})$, but $n^{\log n} \notin \Omega(c^n)$.

7.6. Assume $e(n) \in O(f(n))$ and $g(n) \in O(h(n))$. Prove that $e(n)g(n) \in O(f(n)h(n))$.

7.1 Revisiting quantum query model

Given a Boolean function $f : \{0, 1\}^n \to \{0, 1\}$, and $N = 2^n$, define the query operator:

$$O_{\mathbf{X}} : |i\rangle|b\rangle \to |i\rangle|b \oplus X_i\rangle, \tag{7.5}$$

where $\mathbf{X} = X_0X_1 \cdots X_{N-1}$, $X_i = f(i) \in \{0, 1\}$, $0 \leq i < N$.

The search problem on the string $\mathbf{X} = X_0X_1 \cdots X_{N-1}$ refers to finding $X_j = 1$ for some $0 \leq j < N$. The decision problem on the string $\mathbf{X} = X_0X_1 \cdots X_{N-1}$ is to determine whether there exists $X_j = 1$ for some $0 \leq j < N$. In general, the search problem is no easier than the decision problem. In light of the string $\mathbf{X} = X_0X_1 \cdots X_{N-1}$, the 3-SAT problem can be redefined as follows.

Definition 7.9. Suppose Φ is a 3-SAT formula with n variables $x_1, x_2, \cdots, x_n$, $N = 2^n$. Let $0, 1, \cdots, N-1$ be N assignments of $x_1x_2 \cdots x_n$, respectively. Define the Boolean function $f_\Phi : \{0, 1\}^n \to \{0, 1\}$ as: $f_\Phi(x) = 1$ if $\Phi(x) = 1$, and $f_\Phi(x) = 0$ if $\Phi(x) = 0$, where $x = x_1x_2 \cdots x_n$. Denote $X_j = f_\Phi(j)$. Then the 3-SAT problem can be redefined as determining whether there exists $X_j = 1$ for some $0 \leq j < N$ in the string $\mathbf{X} = X_0X_1 \cdots X_{N-1}$.

In general, a quantum query model with T queries is defined as: starting from the initial state $|00\cdots0\rangle$, applying a unitary operator U_0 to get the state $U_0|00\cdots0\rangle$, followed by applying the query operator $O_{\mathbf{X}}$. After that, a unitary operator U_1 is applied, and then the query operator $O_{\mathbf{X}}$ is applied, and so on. After T queries (i.e., the query operator $O_{\mathbf{X}}$ has been used for T times), the unitary operator U_T is applied to obtain the final state $|\psi_T\rangle$, that is, $|\psi_T\rangle = U_T O_{\mathbf{X}} \cdots U_1 O_{\mathbf{X}} U_0|00\cdots0\rangle$. The result is obtained by measuring the final state $|\psi_T\rangle$.

Most of the algorithms introduced in this book belong to quantum query algorithms, such as the order-finding algorithm in Shor's algorithm. Both the quantum search algorithm and quantum amplitude amplification algorithm are also quantum query algorithms.

Given a Boolean function $F: \{0,1\}^N \to \{0,1\}$, where $N = 2^n$ for some n, a query algorithm computes $F(\mathbf{X})$ by calling $O_{\mathbf{X}}$ to query information in the string $\mathbf{X}$. The number of calls to $O_{\mathbf{X}}$ is called the query complexity of the algorithm. The minimum number of calls to $O_{\mathbf{X}}$ for any algorithm to compute F is called the query complexity of F.

The complexity of any query algorithm $\mathcal{A}$ can be represented as $Q_{\mathcal{A}} C_Q + C_{\mathcal{A}}$, where $Q_{\mathcal{A}}$ is the number of queries for $\mathcal{A}$, C_Q is the computational complexity to implement each query operation and $C_{\mathcal{A}}$ is the computational complexity for all non-query operations.

In Shor's algorithm, $Q_{\mathcal{A}} C_Q$ and $C_{\mathcal{A}}$ are polynomial-time complexities with respect to the input size, and hence the running time is polynomial. In quantum search algorithm, for Boolean function $f: \{0,1,\cdots,N-1\} \to \{0,1\}$, the upper bound on the query complexity to find a solution such that $f(x) = 1$ is $O(\sqrt{N})$. Afterward, we will prove that at least $\Omega(\sqrt{N})$ queries are required. Therefore, the query complexity of the quantum search algorithm is $\Theta(\sqrt{N})$.

In the following, we give a definition of classical query complexity for Boolean function $F: \{0,1\}^N \to \{0,1\}$, where $N = 2^n$ for some n.

Definition 7.10. The classical deterministic query complexity $D(F)$ of Boolean function F refers to the minimum number of queries required by any given classical deterministic query algorithm to compute $F(\mathbf{X})$ for any $\mathbf{X} \in \{0,1\}^N$.

The exact quantum query complexity of a Boolean function F is defined as follows:

Definition 7.11. The exact quantum query complexity $Q_E(F)$ of F refers to the minimum number of queries required by any given quantum query algorithm to compute $F(\mathbf{X})$ for any $\mathbf{X} \in \{0,1\}^N$.

The bounded-error quantum query complexity of a Boolean function F is defined as follows:

Definition 7.12. The bounded-error quantum query complexity $Q_2(F)$ of F refers to the minimum number of queries required by any given quantum query algorithm to compute $F(\mathbf{X})$ with a probability of at least $\frac{2}{3}$ for any $\mathbf{X} \in \{0, 1\}^N$.

7.2 Quantum state distinguishability

Denote $|\psi^{\mathbf{X}}\rangle$ and $|\psi^{\mathbf{Y}}\rangle$ as the quantum states generated by a quantum query algorithm $\mathcal{A}$ querying the strings $\mathbf{X}$ and $\mathbf{Y}$, respectively.

Theorem 7.1. *Given a quantum state* $|\psi^{\mathbf{Z}}\rangle$ *with* $|\psi^{\mathbf{Z}}\rangle \in \{|\psi^{\mathbf{X}}\rangle, |\psi^{\mathbf{Y}}\rangle\}$, *then for any quantum state discrimination algorithm guessing* $\mathbf{Z} = \mathbf{X}$ *or* $\mathbf{Z} = \mathbf{Y}$, *the maximum correct probability is* $1 - \epsilon = \frac{1}{2} + \frac{1}{2}\sqrt{1 - \delta^2}$, *where* ϵ *is the probability of error, and* $\delta = |\langle \psi^{\mathbf{X}} | \psi^{\mathbf{Y}} \rangle|$.

Proof. For a given quantum state discrimination algorithm described as a unitary operator U, suppose

$$U|\psi^{\mathbf{X}}\rangle = |\phi^{\mathbf{X}}\rangle = \cos\theta|0\rangle + \sin\theta|1\rangle, \tag{7.6}$$

$$U|\psi^{\mathbf{Y}}\rangle = |\phi^{\mathbf{Y}}\rangle = \sin\theta|0\rangle + \cos\theta|1\rangle, \tag{7.7}$$

where we assume $0 \le \theta \le \frac{\pi}{4}$, without loss of generality.

Measure the quantum states $|\phi^{\mathbf{X}}\rangle$ or $|\phi^{\mathbf{Y}}\rangle$ by the measurement operators $\{|0\rangle\langle 0|, |1\rangle\langle 1|\}$. Suppose that if the measurement result is 0, then the algorithm outputs $\mathbf{X}$; if the result is 1, it outputs $\mathbf{Y}$. It is clear that the success probability is $\cos^2\theta = 1 - \epsilon$, that is, $\epsilon = \sin^2\theta$.

By

$$\begin{aligned}
\delta &= |\langle \psi^{\mathbf{X}} | \psi^{\mathbf{Y}} \rangle| && (7.8)\\
&= |\langle \psi^{\mathbf{X}} | U^\dagger U | \psi^{\mathbf{Y}} \rangle| && (7.9)\\
&= |\langle \phi^{\mathbf{X}} | \phi^{\mathbf{Y}} \rangle| && (7.10)\\
&= \sin 2\theta, && (7.11)
\end{aligned}$$

we can get

$$\epsilon = \frac{1}{2} - \frac{1}{2}\sqrt{1 - \delta^2}, \tag{7.12}$$

$$\delta = 2\sqrt{\epsilon(1 - \epsilon)}. \tag{7.13}$$

In the following, we prove that the earlier quantum state discrimination algorithm is optimal, that is, there is no better quantum state discrimination algorithm that can output the correct solution with a probability higher than $\frac{1}{2} + \frac{1}{2}\sqrt{1-\delta^2}$.

In general, in quantum state discrimination algorithms we can add a number of auxiliary qubits to the input state, which are denoted as anc. Then the unitary operator is applied to the whole state with added auxiliary bits. Finally, the first bit of the state is measured.

Suppose an algorithm denoted as U' correctly recognizes $|\psi^{\mathbf{X}}\rangle$ with probability $1-\epsilon_x$ and $|\psi^{\mathbf{Y}}\rangle$ with probability $1-\epsilon_y$. Denote $\epsilon = \max(\epsilon_x, \epsilon_y)$, and then the probability that the algorithm outputs the correct solution is $1-\epsilon$. Furthermore, suppose

$$U'|\psi^{\mathbf{X}}\rangle|00\cdots 0\rangle = \sqrt{1-\epsilon_x}|0\rangle|\text{anc}(x,0)\rangle + \sqrt{\epsilon_x}|1\rangle|\text{anc}(x,1)\rangle, \tag{7.14}$$

$$U'|\psi^{\mathbf{Y}}\rangle|00\cdots 0\rangle = \sqrt{\epsilon_y}|0\rangle|\text{anc}(y,0)\rangle + \sqrt{1-\epsilon_y}|1\rangle|\text{anc}(y,1)\rangle. \tag{7.15}$$

In summary, we can obtain

$$\delta = |\langle\psi^{\mathbf{X}}|\psi^{\mathbf{Y}}\rangle| \tag{7.16}$$

$$= |\langle\psi^{\mathbf{X}}|\langle 00\cdots 0|U'^{\dagger}U'|\psi^{\mathbf{Y}}\rangle|00\cdots 0\rangle| \tag{7.17}$$

$$= |\sqrt{(1-\epsilon_x)\epsilon_y}\langle\text{anc}(x,0)|\text{anc}(y,0)\rangle + \sqrt{(1-\epsilon_y)\epsilon_x}\langle\text{anc}(x,1)|\text{anc}(y,1)\rangle| \tag{7.18}$$

$$\leq \sqrt{(1-\epsilon_x)\epsilon_y} + \sqrt{(1-\epsilon_y)\epsilon_x}. \tag{7.19}$$

To minimize ϵ satisfying the above inequality, set $\epsilon = \epsilon_x = \epsilon_y$, and we can get

$$\epsilon \geq \frac{1}{2} - \frac{1}{2}\sqrt{1-\delta^2}. \tag{7.20}$$

The theorem is proved. □

Questions

7.7. Try to encode the 3-SAT problem with a bit string.

7.3 Lower bound for the search problem

Given a Boolean function $f : \{0, 1\}^n \to \{0, 1\}$, the search problem is to find an $x \in \{0, 1\}^n$ such that $f(x) = 1$. The decision problem is to determine whether a given problem has a solution. Since the solution of decision problem can be obtained by searching the solution to the problem, the lower bound on the decision problem implies the same bound on the search problem.

The query complexity of the bounded-error quantum search algorithm with N elements is $O(\sqrt{N})$. A natural question is whether a quantum algorithm with fewer queries can be designed with the expectation of complexity advantage. In the following, we will prove the lower bound on the query complexity of the search problem, and this result shows that Grover's algorithm is optimal, that is, there are no quantum search algorithms with a query complexity less than $\Omega(\sqrt{N})$.

Definition 7.13. Suppose $\mathbf{X}_s = X_0X_1\cdots X_{N-1} \in \{0, 1\}^N$ and $X_r = 1$ if and only if $r = s$, where $s \in \{0, 1, \cdots, N-1\}$. Denote $S = \{\mathbf{X}_s \mid s = 0, 1, \cdots, N-1\}$ as the set of strings with only one 1.

Lemma 7.1. *For any given quantum query algorithm $\mathcal{A}$ with bounded error, $\mathcal{A}$ acts on zero string and before the $(j+1)$-th query the state is denoted as $|\psi_j\rangle = \sum_{r=0}^{N-1} \alpha_{r,j}|r\rangle|\phi_{r,j}\rangle$; $\mathcal{A}$ acts on $\mathbf{X}_s$ and before the $(j+1)$-th query the state is denoted as $|\psi_j^s\rangle = \sum_{r=0}^{N-1} \beta_{r,j}|r\rangle|\phi_{r,j}^s\rangle$. Suppose $|\widetilde{\psi}_{j+1}^s\rangle = U_{j+1}|\psi_j^s\rangle$, where $j \in \{0, 1, \ldots, T-1\}$. Then we have*

$$\||\widetilde{\psi}_{j+1}^s\rangle - |\psi_{j+1}^s\rangle\| \le 2|\beta_{s,j}|, \tag{7.21}$$

$$\||\psi_j\rangle - |\psi_j^s\rangle\| \le 2|\beta_{s,0}| + \cdots + 2|\beta_{s,j-1}|. \tag{7.22}$$

Proof. First, we prove inequality (7.21) as follows:

$$\||\widetilde{\psi}_{j+1}^s\rangle - |\psi_{j+1}^s\rangle\| \tag{7.23}$$

$$=\|U_{j+1}|\psi_j^s\rangle - U_{j+1}O_{\mathbf{X}_s}|\psi_j^s\rangle\| \tag{7.24}$$

$$=\|\sum_{r=0}^{N-1} \beta_{r,j}|r\rangle|\phi_{r,j}^s\rangle - O_{\mathbf{X}_s}\left(\sum_{r=0}^{N-1} \beta_{r,j}|r\rangle|\phi_{r,j}^s\rangle\right)\| \tag{7.25}$$

$$=\|\sum_{r\ne s} \beta_{r,j}|r\rangle|\phi_{r,j}^s\rangle + \beta_{s,j}|s\rangle|\phi_{s,j}^s\rangle \tag{7.26}$$

$$- \left(\sum_{r \neq s} \beta_{r,j} |r\rangle |\phi^s_{r,j}\rangle + O_{\mathbf{X}_s} \beta_{s,j} |s\rangle |\phi^s_{s,j}\rangle \right) ||$$

$$= || \beta_{s,j} |s\rangle |\phi^s_{s,j}\rangle - O_{\mathbf{X}_s} \beta_{s,j} |s\rangle |\phi^s_{s,j}\rangle || \tag{7.27}$$

$$\leq || \beta_{s,j} |s\rangle |\phi^s_{s,j}\rangle || + || O_{\mathbf{X}_s} \beta_{s,j} |s\rangle |\phi^s_{s,j}\rangle || \tag{7.28}$$

$$= || \beta_{s,j} |s\rangle |\phi^s_{s,j}\rangle || + || \beta_{s,j} |s\rangle |\phi^s_{s,j}\rangle || \tag{7.29}$$

$$= 2 |\beta_{s,j}|. \tag{7.30}$$

Next, we prove inequality (7.22) by mathematical induction. For $j = 1$, we have

$$||\,|\psi_1\rangle - |\psi^s_1\rangle|| \tag{7.31}$$

$$= || U_1 |\psi_0\rangle - |\psi^s_1\rangle || \tag{7.32}$$

$$= || U_1 U_0 |00\ldots0\rangle - |\psi^s_1\rangle || \tag{7.33}$$

$$= || U_1 |\psi^s_0\rangle - |\psi^s_1\rangle || \tag{7.34}$$

$$= ||\,|\widetilde{\psi}^s_1\rangle - |\psi^s_1\rangle || \tag{7.35}$$

$$\leq 2 |\beta_{s,0}|. \tag{7.36}$$

Assume it holds for $j = k$ with $k \geq 1$, that is, $||\,|\psi_k\rangle - |\psi^s_k\rangle|| \leq 2|\beta_{s,0}| + \cdots + 2|\beta_{s,k-1}|$, and we proceed to proving that it also holds for $j = k+1$:

$$||\,|\psi_{k+1}\rangle - |\psi^s_{k+1}\rangle|| \tag{7.37}$$

$$= || U_{k+1} |\psi_k\rangle - U_{k+1} O_{\mathbf{X}_s} |\psi^s_k\rangle || \tag{7.38}$$

$$= ||\,|\psi_k\rangle - O_{\mathbf{X}_s} |\psi^s_k\rangle || \tag{7.39}$$

$$= ||\,|\psi_k\rangle - O_{\mathbf{X}_s} |\psi^s_k\rangle + |\psi^s_k\rangle - |\psi^s_k\rangle || \tag{7.40}$$

$$= ||\,|\psi_k\rangle - |\psi^s_k\rangle + |\psi^s_k\rangle - O_{\mathbf{X}_s} |\psi^s_k\rangle || \tag{7.41}$$

$$\leq ||\,|\psi_k\rangle - |\psi^s_k\rangle|| + ||\,|\psi^s_k\rangle - O_{\mathbf{X}_s} |\psi^s_k\rangle || \tag{7.42}$$

$$\leq 2|\beta_{s,0}| + \cdots + 2|\beta_{s,k-1}| + || U_{k+1} |\psi^s_k\rangle - U_{k+1} O_{\mathbf{X}_s} |\psi^s_k\rangle || \tag{7.43}$$

$$= 2|\beta_{s,0}| + \cdots + 2|\beta_{s,k-1}| + ||\,|\widetilde{\psi}^s_{k+1}\rangle - |\psi^s_{k+1}\rangle || \tag{7.44}$$

$$\leq 2|\beta_{s,0}| + \cdots + 2|\beta_{s,k-1}| + 2|\beta_{s,k}|. \tag{7.45}$$

The proof is completed. □

Lemma 7.2. *If $|\phi_1\rangle$ and $|\phi_2\rangle$ are two quantum states with the same dimension, then*

$$||\,|\phi_1\rangle - |\phi_2\rangle|| \leq c \Rightarrow |\langle \phi_1 | \phi_2 \rangle| \geq 1 - \frac{c^2}{2}. \tag{7.46}$$

Proof. Since

$$|||\phi_1\rangle - |\phi_2\rangle|| \leq c \Rightarrow |||\phi_1\rangle - |\phi_2\rangle||^2 \leq c^2 \tag{7.47}$$

$$\Leftrightarrow (\langle\phi_1| - \langle\phi_2|)(|\phi_1\rangle - |\phi_2\rangle) \leq c^2 \tag{7.48}$$

$$\Leftrightarrow 1 - \langle\phi_1|\phi_2\rangle - \langle\phi_2|\phi_1\rangle + 1 \leq c^2 \tag{7.49}$$

$$\Leftrightarrow \frac{\langle\phi_1|\phi_2\rangle + \langle\phi_2|\phi_1\rangle}{2} \geq 1 - \frac{c^2}{2}, \tag{7.50}$$

and

$$|\langle\phi_1|\phi_2\rangle| \geq \frac{\langle\phi_1|\phi_2\rangle + \langle\phi_2|\phi_1\rangle}{2}, \tag{7.51}$$

we have

$$|\langle\phi_1|\phi_2\rangle| \geq 1 - \frac{c^2}{2}. \tag{7.52}$$

□

Lemma 7.3. *Any bounded-error quantum query algorithm requires $\Omega(\sqrt{N})$ queries to successfully distinguish between zero string and N strings $\mathbf{X}_s$ belonging to the set S, where $S = \{\mathbf{X}_s \mid s = 0, 1, \ldots, N-1\}$ is the set of strings with only one 1.*

Proof. Given any bounded-error quantum query algorithm $\mathcal{A}$ with T queries, as earlier,

$$|\psi_j\rangle = \sum_{r=0}^{N-1} \alpha_{r,j}|r\rangle|\phi_{r,j}\rangle. \tag{7.53}$$

Then

$$|\psi_T\rangle = \sum_{r=0}^{N-1} \alpha_{r,T}|r\rangle|\phi_{r,T}\rangle \tag{7.54}$$

is the final state of $\mathcal{A}$ querying all zero string. Similarly, $\mathcal{A}$ acts on $\mathbf{X}_s$ and before the $(j+1)$-th query the state is denoted as

$$|\psi_j^s\rangle = \sum_{r=0}^{N-1} \beta_{r,j}|r\rangle|\phi_{r,j}^s\rangle. \tag{7.55}$$

Then

$$|\psi_T^s\rangle = \sum_{r=0}^{N-1} \beta_{r,T}|r\rangle|\phi_{r,T}^s\rangle \tag{7.56}$$

is the final state of $\mathcal{A}$ querying all string $\mathbf{X}_s$.

The algorithm $\mathcal{A}$ needs to make $|\psi_T^s\rangle$ and $|\psi_T\rangle$ nearly orthogonal to distinguish the nonzero string $\mathbf{X}_s$ from the zero string with bounded error. By Lemma 7.1, after $\mathcal{A}$ queries $\mathbf{X}_s$ T times, it holds

$$|||\psi_T\rangle - |\psi_T^s\rangle|| \leq 2\sum_{t=0}^{T-1} |\beta_{s,t}|. \tag{7.57}$$

According to Theorem 7.1, for algorithm $\mathcal{A}$ distinguishing $\mathbf{X}_s$ from the zero string with bounded error, if the success probability is at least $\frac{2}{3}$, then the following inequality needs to be satisfied:

$$1 - \epsilon = \frac{1}{2} + \frac{1}{2}\sqrt{1 - \delta^2} \geq \frac{2}{3}, \tag{7.58}$$

where ϵ is the error of algorithm $\mathcal{A}$, and $\delta = |\langle\psi_T|\psi_T^s\rangle$. Therefore, we obtain

$$\delta = |\langle\psi_T|\psi_T^s\rangle| \leq \frac{2\sqrt{2}}{3}. \tag{7.59}$$

In addition, the following inequality follows from Lemma 7.2:

$$|\langle\psi_T|\psi_T^s\rangle| \leq 1 - \frac{c^2}{2} \Rightarrow |||\psi_T\rangle - |\psi_T^s\rangle|| \geq c. \tag{7.60}$$

To make $|\langle\psi_T|\psi_T^s\rangle| \leq \frac{2\sqrt{2}}{3}$, we set $1 - \frac{c^2}{2} \leq \frac{2\sqrt{2}}{3}$, which leads to $c^2 \geq 2 - \frac{4\sqrt{2}}{3}$. Therefore,

$$|||\psi_T\rangle - |\psi_T^s\rangle|| \geq c > \frac{1}{3}. \tag{7.61}$$

Since $|||\psi_T\rangle - |\psi_T^s\rangle|| \leq 2\sum\limits_{t=0}^{T-1} |\beta_{s,t}|$, we have

$$\sum_{t=0}^{T-1} |\beta_{s,t}| \geq \frac{1}{2}|||\psi_T\rangle - |\psi_T^s\rangle|| \geq \frac{c}{2} > \frac{1}{6}. \tag{7.62}$$

If algorithm $\mathcal{A}$ distinguishes N's strings $\mathbf{X}_s$ from the zero string with success probability at least $\frac{2}{3}$, where $s = 0, 1, \cdots, N-1$, then we have

$$\sum_{s=0}^{N-1}\sum_{t=0}^{T-1} |\beta_{s,t}| > \frac{1}{6}N. \tag{7.63}$$

Clearly, $\sum_{s=0}^{N-1} |\beta_{s,t}|^2 = 1$, due to $|\psi_t^s\rangle = \sum_{s=0}^{N-1} \beta_{s,t}|s\rangle|\phi_{s,t}^s\rangle$ being a unit vector. By the Cauchy–Schwarz inequality, we have $\sum_{s=0}^{N-1} |\beta_{s,t}| \leq \sqrt{N}$. Therefore, there is

$$\sum_{s=0}^{N-1}\sum_{t=0}^{T-1} |\beta_{s,t}| = \sum_{t=0}^{T-1}\sum_{s=0}^{N-1} |\beta_{s,t}| \leq T\sqrt{N}. \tag{7.64}$$

Finally, by combining inequality (7.63) with inequality (7.64), it concludes $T > \frac{1}{6}\sqrt{N}$, and the lemma is proved. □

Remark 7.5. The Cauchy–Schwarz inequality means that for any real numbers $a_1, a_2, \cdots, a_N$ and $b_1, b_2, \cdots, b_N$, there is $(a_1b_1 + a_2b_2 + \cdots + a_Nb_N)^2 \leq (a_1^2 + a_2^2 + \cdots + a_N^2)(b_1^2 + b_2^2 + \cdots + b_N^2)$.

Theorem 7.2. *Suppose $\mathcal{A}$ is any given quantum query algorithm. Then for each $\mathbf{X} = X_0X_1 \cdots X_{N-1} \in S \cup \{\mathbf{0}\}$, the query complexity of $\mathcal{A}$ to determine whether there exists $X_j = 1$ with bounded error is $\Omega(\sqrt{N})$, where S is the set of strings with only one 1.*

Proof. If $\mathcal{A}$ can determine whether there exists $X_j = 1$ for each $\mathbf{X} \in S \cup \{\mathbf{0}\}$, then it can also distinguish between $\mathbf{X} \in S$ or $\mathbf{X} \in \{\mathbf{0}\}$. According to Lemma 7.3, algorithm $\mathcal{A}$ requires $\Omega(\sqrt{N})$ queries to distinguish whether $\mathbf{X} \in S$ or $\mathbf{X} \in \{\mathbf{0}\}$ for each $\mathbf{X} \in S \cup \{\mathbf{0}\}$. Therefore, the query complexity of algorithm $\mathcal{A}$ to determine whether there exists $X_j = 1$ with bounded error for each $\mathbf{X} \in S \cup \{\mathbf{0}\}$ is $\Omega(\sqrt{N})$. The theorem is proved. □

By means of Theorem 7.2 mentioned previously, we can further obtain three corollaries in the following.

Corollary 7.1. *Let $T \subseteq \{0, 1\}^N$, with $S \cup \{\mathbf{0}\} \subseteq T$. Then the quantum query complexity of determining whether there exists $X_j = 1$ with bounded error for each $\mathbf{X} \in T$ is $\Omega(\sqrt{N})$, where $\mathbf{X} = X_0X_1 \cdots X_{N-1}$.*

Proof. For any given quantum query algorithm $\mathcal{A}$, if it can determine whether there exists $X_j = 1$ with bounded error for each $\mathbf{X} \in T$, then by $S \cup \{\mathbf{0}\} \subseteq T$ it follows that for each $\mathbf{X} \in S \cup \{\mathbf{0}\}$, $\mathcal{A}$ can determine whether there exists $X_j = 1$ with bounded error. By combining Theorem 7.2, the query complexity of $\mathcal{A}$ to determine whether there exists $X_j = 1$ with bounded error for each $\mathbf{X} \in T$ is $\Omega(\sqrt{N})$. The corollary is proved. □

In the light of Corollary 7.1, another corollary follows directly.

Corollary 7.2. *Let $T \subseteq \{0, 1\}^N$ satisfy $S \cup \{\mathbf{0}\} \subseteq T$. Then the quantum query complexity to find $X_j = 1$ with bounded error for each $\mathbf{X} \in T$ is $\Omega(\sqrt{N})$, where $\mathbf{X} = X_0X_1 \cdots X_{N-1}$.*

Proof. If $\mathcal{A}$ can find $X_j = 1$ with bounded error for each $\mathbf{X} \in T$, then it can determine whether there exists $X_j = 1$ with bounded error. Then the corollary follows by Corollary 7.1. □

Corollary 7.3. *The quantum query complexity of deciding whether there exists a satisfiable assignment for each 3-SAT formula Φ with n variables with bounded error is $\Omega(\sqrt{N})$, where $N = 2^n$.*

Proof. Denote $3\mathcal{SAT}$ as the set consisting of all 3-SAT formulas. From Exercise 7.8 of this section, we have

$$S \cup \{\mathbf{0}\} \subseteq \{\mathbf{X}_\Phi \mid \mathbf{X}_\Phi = X_0X_1 \cdots X_{N-1}, X_j = f_\Phi(j), \Phi \in 3\mathcal{SAT}\}.$$

Given any quantum query algorithm $\mathcal{A}$, if $\mathcal{A}$ can determine whether each 3-SAT formula has a satisfiable assignment with bounded error, then it can determine whether there exists $X_j = 1$ with bounded error for each $\mathbf{X}_\Phi \in \{\mathbf{X}_\Phi \mid \mathbf{X}_\Phi = X_0X_1 \cdots X_{N-1}, X_j = f_\Phi(j), \Phi \in 3\mathcal{SAT}\}$. Consequently, the corollary follows from Corollary 7.1. □

Exercises

7.8. Prove that

$$S \cup \{\mathbf{0}\} \subseteq \{\mathbf{X}_\Phi \mid \mathbf{X}_\Phi = X_0X_1 \cdots X_{N-1}, X_j = f_\Phi(j), \Phi \in 3\mathcal{SAT}\},$$

where $S \cup \{\mathbf{0}\}$ represents the set of N-bit strings containing at most one 1, $N = 2^n$ for some n.

7.4 Polynomial method

The polynomial method is an important method to solve the lower bound on the complexity of problems in quantum query complexity. For the details, we can refer to [1,2]. In the following, we first give the basic definition of multi-linear polynomials.

For the N-bit string $\mathbf{X} = X_0X_1 \cdots X_{N-1} \in \{0, 1\}^N$, $I \subseteq [N]$, where $[N] = \{0, 1, \cdots, N-1\}$. The monomial is defined as

$$X_I = \prod_{i \in I} X_i, \tag{7.65}$$

and the degree of a monomial is defined as the cardinality of the set I, that is, $|I|$.

The multi-linear polynomial with N variables is defined as

$$p(\mathbf{X}) = \sum_{I \subseteq [N]} c_I X_I, \tag{7.66}$$

where c_I is a complex number.

The degree of a multi-linear polynomial p is defined as the maximum of the degrees of all its monomials, that is,

$$\deg(p) = \max\{|I| \mid c_I \neq 0\}. \tag{7.67}$$

Definition 7.14. For an N-variable multi-linear polynomial $p : \mathbb{R}^N \to \mathbb{R}$, if for any $\mathbf{X} \in \{0, 1\}^N$, there is $p(\mathbf{X}) = F(\mathbf{X})$, then p represents the Boolean function F, where $F : \{0, 1\}^N \to \{0, 1\}$.

Lemma 7.4. *Any N-variable function $F : \{0, 1\}^N \to \{0, 1\}$ can be represented by a unique multi-linear polynomial $p : \mathbb{R}^N \to \mathbb{R}$.*

Proof. The existence of a polynomial representation is obvious, that is,

$$p(\mathbf{X}) = \sum_{\mathbf{Y} \in \{0,1\}^N} F(\mathbf{Y}) \prod_{k=0}^{N-1} [1 - (Y_k - X_k)^2]. \tag{7.68}$$

In the following, we prove that the uniqueness of polynomial representation. Suppose $p_1(\mathbf{X}) = p_2(\mathbf{X})$, then $p_0(\mathbf{X}) = p_1(\mathbf{X}) - p_2(\mathbf{X})$, where $\mathbf{X} \in \{0, 1\}^N$. If $p_0(\mathbf{X})$ is not a zero polynomial, without loss of generality, let $\alpha X_0 X_1 \ldots X_{k-1}$ be the monomial with the minimum degree of $p_0(\mathbf{X})$, where $\alpha \neq 0$. For a string $\mathbf{X}$, if $X_0 = X_1 = \cdots = X_{k-1} = 1$, and the rest of X_j are 0, then $p_0(\mathbf{X}) = \alpha \neq 0$, which contradicts that $p_0(\mathbf{X}) = 0$. Therefore, $p_0(\mathbf{X})$ is a zero polynomial and $p_1(\mathbf{X}) = p_2(\mathbf{X})$, where $\mathbf{X} \in \{0, 1\}^N$. The lemma is proved. □

Definition 7.15. The degree deg(F) of a Boolean function F is the degree of the multi-linear polynomial p representing F.

Example 7.6. The multi-linear polynomial representation of OR_N function with N variables is $1 - \prod_{j=0}^{N-1}(1 - X_j)$, and the degree of OR_N function is $\deg(\mathrm{OR}_N) = N$.

Definition 7.16. For an N-variable multi-linear polynomial $p : \mathbb{R}^N \to \mathbb{R}$, if $|p(\mathbf{X}) - F(\mathbf{X})| \leq \frac{1}{3}$ for all $\mathbf{X} \in \{0, 1\}^N$, then p approximates the Boolean function $F : \{0, 1\}^N \to \{0, 1\}$.

Definition 7.17. The approximation degree $\widetilde{\deg}(F)$ of the Boolean function F is the minimum degree of all multi-linear polynomials p that approximate F.

In the following, we describe the symmetrization of polynomials. Let $p : \mathbb{R}^N \to \mathbb{R}$ be a polynomial. Suppose π is a permutation. For $\mathbf{X} = X_0 \ldots X_{N-1}$, there is $\pi(\mathbf{X}) = X_{\pi(0)} \ldots X_{\pi(N-1)}$. Suppose S_N is the set of all $N!$ permutations. The symmetric polynomial p^{sym} after the symmetrization of polynomial p is defined as

$$p^{sym}(\mathbf{X}) = \frac{\sum_{\pi \in S_N} p(\pi(\mathbf{X}))}{N!}, \tag{7.69}$$

where the degree of p^{sym} is not greater than the degree of p. If $p = X_0 - X_1$, then $p^{sym} = 0$. In the following, we describe a lemma for reducing an N-variable multi-linear polynomial to a single-variable multi-linear polynomial.

Lemma 7.5. *If $p : \mathbb{R}^N \to \mathbb{R}$ is a multi-linear polynomial, then there exists a single-variable polynomial $q : \mathbb{R} \to \mathbb{R}$ of degree at most as that of p such that $p^{sym}(\mathbf{X}) = q(|\mathbf{X}|)$ for any $\mathbf{X} \in \{0, 1\}^N$, where $|\mathbf{X}|$ denotes the Hamming weight of $\mathbf{X}$.*

Proof. Suppose that the degree of p^{sym} is d, and d is not greater than the degree of p. Since p^{sym} is symmetric, it can be written as

$$p^{sym}(\mathbf{X}) = a_0 + a_1 V_1 + a_2 V_2 + \cdots + a_d V_d, \tag{7.70}$$

where $a_i \in \mathbb{R}$, and

$$V_j = \binom{|\mathbf{X}|}{j} \tag{7.71}$$

$$= \frac{|\mathbf{X}|(|\mathbf{X}|-1)(|\mathbf{X}|-2)\dots(|\mathbf{X}|-j+1)}{j!}, \tag{7.72}$$

where V_j is a polynomial about $|\mathbf{X}|$ with degree j.

Therefore, if the single-variable polynomial q is defined as

$$q(|\mathbf{X}|) = a_0 + a_1\binom{|\mathbf{X}|}{1} + a_2\binom{|\mathbf{X}|}{2} + \cdots + a_d\binom{|\mathbf{X}|}{d}, \tag{7.73}$$

then $p^{sym}(\mathbf{X}) = q(|\mathbf{X}|)$. The lemma is proved. □

Lemma 7.6. *Let $\mathcal{A}$ be a quantum query algorithm with T queries. Then there exists an N-variable complex-valued multi-linear polynomial α_i of degree at most T such that for any $\mathbf{X} \in \{0,1\}^N$, the final state of $\mathcal{A}$ is $\sum_{i\in\{0,1\}^m} \alpha_i(\mathbf{X})|i\rangle$.*

Proof. We prove by induction on the number of queries for $\mathcal{A}$. When $T = 0$, the final state of $\mathcal{A}$ is $U_0|00\cdots0\rangle$, and obviously the degree of the polynomial is 0. Suppose that the state after $\mathcal{A}$ performing k queries and acting U_k ($U_k O_\mathbf{X} U_{k-1} O_\mathbf{X} \cdots U_1 O_\mathbf{X}\ U_0|0\cdots0\rangle$) is

$$\sum_{z\in\{0,1\}^m} \alpha_z(\mathbf{X})|z\rangle,$$

where $\alpha_z(\mathbf{X})$ is a multi-linear polynomial of degree at most k. Note that

$$O_\mathbf{X}\left(\alpha_{i,0,w}(\mathbf{X})|i,0,w\rangle + \alpha_{i,1,w}(\mathbf{X})|i,1,w\rangle\right) \tag{7.74}$$

$$= \begin{cases} \alpha_{i,0,w}(\mathbf{X})|i,0,w\rangle + \alpha_{i,1,w}(\mathbf{X})|i,1,w\rangle, & \mathbf{X}_i = 0; \\ \alpha_{i,1,w}(\mathbf{X})|i,0,w\rangle + \alpha_{i,0,w}(\mathbf{X})|i,1,w\rangle, & \mathbf{X}_i = 1; \end{cases} \tag{7.75}$$

$$\begin{aligned} &= ((1-\mathbf{X}_i)\alpha_{i,0,w}(\mathbf{X}) + \mathbf{X}_i\alpha_{i,1,w}(\mathbf{X}))|i,0,w\rangle \\ &\quad + (\mathbf{X}_i\alpha_{i,0,w}(\mathbf{X}) + (1-\mathbf{X}_i)\alpha_{i,1,w}(\mathbf{X}))|i,1,w\rangle, \end{aligned} \tag{7.76}$$

and the effect of U_{k+1} does not change the degree of polynomial, so the lemma is proved. □

In the following, we present some theorems to characterize the quantum query complexity of Boolean functions.

Theorem 7.3. *Let F be a Boolean function, then $Q_E(F) \geq \frac{\deg(F)}{2}$.*

Proof. Consider the quantum query algorithm $\mathcal{A}$ that computes F exactly with query complexity $Q_E(F)$. Let $\mathcal{B}$ be the set of basic states for which the algorithm $\mathcal{A}$ outputs 1. Then the probability that algorithm $\mathcal{A}$ outputs 1 is

$$p(\mathbf{X}) = \sum_{z \in \mathcal{B}} |\alpha_z(\mathbf{X})|^2. \tag{7.77}$$

From Lemma 7.6, α_z is a polynomial of degree at most $Q_E(F)$, so $p(\mathbf{X})$ has a degree at most $2Q_E(F)$. Since the polynomial p represents the function F, the degree of p is $\deg(F)$. Thus we have $\deg(F) \le 2Q_E(F)$, that is, $Q_E(F) \ge \frac{\deg(F)}{2}$. The theorem is proved. □

Example 7.7. Since $\deg(\mathrm{OR}_N) = N$, $Q_E(\mathrm{OR}_N) \ge \frac{N}{2}$.

Example 7.8. The function PARITY is defined as: if $\mathbf{X}$ has odd numbers 1, then $\mathrm{PARITY}(\mathbf{X}) = 1$; if $\mathbf{X}$ has even numbers 1, then $\mathrm{PARITY}(\mathbf{X}) = 0$. From Exercise 7.10 in this section, we can get $\deg(\mathrm{PARITY}) = N$, so $Q_E(\mathrm{PARITY}) \ge \lceil \frac{N}{2} \rceil$.

Theorem 7.4. *If F is a Boolean function, then $Q_2(F) \ge \frac{\widetilde{\deg}(F)}{2}$.*

Proof. Consider the bounded-error quantum query algorithm $\mathcal{A}$ that approximates F with query complexity $Q_2(F)$. Let $\mathcal{C}$ be the set of basic states for which the algorithm $\mathcal{A}$ outputs 1. The probability that $\mathcal{A}$ outputs 1 is $p(\mathbf{X}) = \sum_{z \in \mathcal{C}} |\alpha_z(\mathbf{X})|^2$. By Lemma 7.6, α_z is a polynomial with degrees of at most $Q_2(F)$, and hence the degree of $p(\mathbf{X})$ is at most $2Q_2(F)$. If $F(\mathbf{X}) = 1$, then $p(\mathbf{X}) \ge \frac{2}{3}$; if $F(\mathbf{X}) = 0$, then $p(\mathbf{X}) \le \frac{1}{3}$, that is, for any $\mathbf{X} \in \{0, 1\}^N$, there is $|p(\mathbf{X}) - F(\mathbf{X})| \le \frac{1}{3}$, so p approximates F. Since p approximates F, the approximation degree $\widetilde{\deg}(F)$ of F is not greater than the degree of p, that is, $\widetilde{\deg}(F) \le 2Q_2(F)$, which is $Q_2(F) \ge \frac{\widetilde{\deg}(F)}{2}$. The theorem is proved. □

In the following, we introduce some examples to illustrate the utility of the previous theorem.

Example 7.9. By Exercise 7.11 of this section, we can get $\widetilde{\deg}(\mathrm{OR}) \in \Theta(\sqrt{N})$, so $Q_2(\mathrm{OR}) \in \Omega(\sqrt{N})$. Since the query complexity of the quantum search algorithm for estimating the OR function with bounded error is $O(\sqrt{N})$, the lower bound $\Omega(\sqrt{N})$ is tight.

Example 7.10. From Exercise 7.12 in this section, we can get $\widetilde{\deg}(\mathrm{PARITY}) = N$, so $Q_2(\mathrm{PARITY}) \ge \lceil \frac{N}{2} \rceil$.

Example 7.11. Consider the function MAJORITY, which is defined as $\mathrm{MAJORITY}(\mathbf{X}) = 1$ if $\mathbf{X}$ contains more than $\frac{N}{2}$ ones, and $\mathrm{MAJORITY}(\mathbf{X}) = 0$ if $\mathbf{X}$ contains no more than $\frac{N}{2}$ ones, where $\mathbf{X} \in \{0, 1\}^N$. From Exercise 7.14 in this section, we can obtain $\widetilde{\deg}(\mathrm{MAJORITY}) \in \Theta(N)$, so $Q_2(\mathrm{MAJORITY}) \in \Omega(N)$.

Example 7.12. Consider the function THRESHOLD_M, which is defined as: if the number of $\mathbf{X}$ containing 1 is at least M, then $\text{THRESHOLD}_M(\mathbf{X}) = 1$, otherwise $\text{THRESHOLD}_M(\mathbf{X}) = 0$, where $\mathbf{X} \in \{0,1\}^N$. By Exercise 7.15 in this section, we can get

$$\widetilde{\deg}(\text{THRESHOLD}_M) \in \Theta(\sqrt{M(N-M+1)}). \tag{7.78}$$

Therefore, $Q_2(\text{THRESHOLD}_M) \in \Omega(\sqrt{M(N-M+1)})$.

Sensitivity is an important metric to describe the query complexity of Boolean functions. In the following, we describe the definitions of sensitivity and block sensitivity, as well as the related theorems [1].

Definition 7.18. For a string $\mathbf{X} \in \{0,1\}^N$, let $\mathbf{X}^I$ denote the string obtained by flipping the variable corresponding to the index set I. Generally, $\mathbf{X}^{\{i\}}$ is abbreviated to $\mathbf{X}^i$, where $I \subseteq \{0, 1, \ldots, N-1\}$. For example, for $\mathbf{X} = 10101$, we have $\mathbf{X}^{\{0,1,2\}} = 01001$, $\mathbf{X}^4 = 10100$.

The sensitivity $s_{\mathbf{X}}(F)$ of a Boolean function F on $\mathbf{X} = X_0 \ldots X_{N-1} \in \{0,1\}^N$ is defined as

$$s_{\mathbf{X}}(F) = |\{X_i | F(\mathbf{X}) \neq F(\mathbf{X}^i), 0 \leq i \leq N-1\}|. \tag{7.79}$$

The sensitivity of a Boolean function F is defined as $s(F) = \max_{\mathbf{X}\in\{0,1\}^N} s_{\mathbf{X}}(F)$.

If $F(\mathbf{X}) \neq F(\mathbf{X}^B)$, then F is sensitive to the block B on $\mathbf{X}$. If a Boolean function F is sensitive to the disjoint sets $B_1, \ldots, B_b$ on $\mathbf{X}$, then the maximum value of b is the block sensitivity of F on $\mathbf{X}$, denoted as $bs_{\mathbf{X}}(F)$. The block sensitivity of a Boolean function F is defined as $bs(F) = \max_{\mathbf{X}\in\{0,1\}^N} bs_{\mathbf{X}}(F)$.

If F is a constant function, then $s(F) = bs(F) = 0$. In fact, the sensitivity of a Boolean function F is a special case that limits the size of each sensitive block B_i to 1 in the block sensitivity of F.

Theorem 7.5. [2] *Let $p : \mathbb{R} \to \mathbb{R}$ be a polynomial. If it satisfies $b_1 \leq p(i) \leq b_2$ for any integer $0 \leq i \leq N$, and there exists a real number $0 \leq x \leq N$ satisfying $|p'(x)| \geq c$, then $\deg(p) \geq \sqrt{\frac{cN}{c+b_2-b_1}}$.*

Theorem 7.6. [2] *If F is a Boolean function, then $Q_2(F) \geq \sqrt{\frac{bs(F)}{16}}$ and $Q_E(F) \geq \sqrt{\frac{bs(F)}{8}}$.*

Proof. In the following, we prove that $Q_2(F) \geq \sqrt{\frac{bs(F)}{16}}$. Consider a quantum query algorithm $\mathcal{A}$ of query complexity $Q_2(F)$ that computes the function F with bounded error and error probability not greater than $\frac{1}{3}$.

Denote that the acceptance probability of the function F computed by algorithm $\mathcal{A}$ with bounded error is a polynomial p of degree no greater than $2Q_2(F)$, and p approximates F. Since p represents the probability, $p(\mathbf{X}) \in [0, 1]$ for any $\mathbf{X} \in \{0, 1\}^N$. Set $b = bs(F)$, and let $B_0, \ldots, B_{b-1}$ be the set of block sensitivity. Suppose $\mathbf{X}$ is the input to F. Without loss of generality, we can set $F(\mathbf{X}) = 0$.

Denote $\mathbf{Y} = (Y_0, \ldots, Y_{b-1}) \in \mathbb{R}^b$. Define $\mathbf{Z} = (Z_0, \ldots, Z_{N-1}) \in \mathbb{R}^N$, which satisfies

$$Z_j = \begin{cases} Y_i, & \text{if } X_j = 0 \text{ and } j \in B_i, \\ 1 - Y_i, & \text{if } X_j = 1 \text{ and } j \in B_i, \\ X_j, & \text{if } j \notin B_i. \end{cases} \tag{7.80}$$

In summary, if $\mathbf{Y} = \vec{0}$, then $\mathbf{Z} = \mathbf{X}$; if $i \neq j$, $\mathbf{Y}_i = 1$ and $\mathbf{Y}_j = 0$, then $\mathbf{Z} = \mathbf{X}^{B_i}$. $q(\mathbf{Y}) = p(\mathbf{Z})$ is a polynomial of degree no greater than $2Q_2(F)$ with b variables, which satisfies the following conditions:

1. Since p represents probability, $q(\mathbf{Y}) \in [0, 1]$ for any $\mathbf{Y} \in \{0, 1\}^b$;
2. Since $|q(\vec{0}) - 0| = |p(\mathbf{X}) - F(\mathbf{X})| \leq \frac{1}{3}$, $0 \leq q(\vec{0}) \leq \frac{1}{3}$.
3. If $\mathbf{Y}_i = 1$ and $\mathbf{Y}_j = 0$ for $i \neq j$, then $|q(\mathbf{Y}) - 1| = |p(\mathbf{X}^{B_i}) - F(\mathbf{X}^{B_i})| \leq \frac{1}{3}$.

Thus, if $|\mathbf{Y}| = 1$, that is, $\mathbf{Y}$ contains a 1, then $\frac{2}{3} \leq q(\mathbf{Y}) \leq 1$.

Suppose r is a symmetrized polynomial of a single variable of q over $\{0, 1\}^b$, it follows that the degree of r is not greater than $2Q_2(F)$. For any $0 \leq i \leq b$, there is $0 \leq r(i) \leq 1$. Since $r(0) = q(\vec{0}) \leq \frac{1}{3}$ and $r(1) = q(\mathbf{Y}) \geq \frac{2}{3}$, there exists an $x \in [0, 1]$ such that $r'(x) \geq \frac{1}{3}$, where $|\mathbf{Y}| = 1$. By Theorem 7.5, we have $\deg(r) \geq \sqrt{\frac{b}{4}}$. Since $\deg(r) \leq 2Q_2(F)$, we have

$$Q_2(F) \geq \sqrt{\frac{b}{16}} = \sqrt{\frac{bs(F)}{16}}. \tag{7.81}$$

Similarly, it can be shown that $Q_E(F) \geq \sqrt{\frac{bs(F)}{8}}$. The theorem is proved. □

Example 7.13. Since $bs_0(\mathrm{OR}) = N$, the block sensitivity of function OR is N. By Theorem 7.6, we have $Q_2(\mathrm{OR}) \geq \frac{\sqrt{N}}{4}$.

Lemma 7.7. [1] *If F is a Boolean function, then $D(F) \leq bs(F)^3$.*

Theorem 7.7. *If F is a Boolean function, then $D(F) \leq 2^{12} Q_2(F)^6$.*

Proof. From Lemma 7.7 it follows that

$$D(F) \leq bs(F)^3. \tag{7.82}$$

By means of Theorem 7.6, we have

$$bs(F) \leq 16 Q_2(F)^2. \tag{7.83}$$

By Eq. (7.82) and Eq. (7.83), we get

$$D(F) \leq 2^{12} Q_2(F)^6, \tag{7.84}$$

and the proof is completed. □

A Boolean function F is symmetric if $F(\mathbf{X})$ depends only on the Hamming weight $|\mathbf{X}|$ of $\mathbf{X}$, that is, the number of ones in $\mathbf{X}$. The symmetric Boolean function F can be described by a vector $(F_0, F_1, \ldots, F_N) \in \{0,1\}^{N+1}$, where F_k is the value of $F(\mathbf{X})$ for $|\mathbf{X}| = k$.

Denote

$$\Gamma(F) = \min\{|2k - N + 1| : F_k \neq F_{k+1}, 0 \leq k \leq N-1\}, \tag{7.85}$$

$\Gamma(F)$ is a variable with respect to a symmetric function F and $0 \leq \Gamma(F) \leq N-1$.

Lemma 7.8. [1] *If F is a nonconstant symmetric Boolean function, then* $D(F) = (1 - o(1))N$, $Q_2(F) = \Theta(\sqrt{N(N - \Gamma(F))})$.

Theorem 7.8. *If F is a nonconstant symmetric Boolean function, then* $D(F) \in O((Q_2(F))^2)$.

Proof. Due to Lemma 7.8, we have

$$D(F) = (1 - o(1))N \tag{7.86}$$

$$= O(N), \tag{7.87}$$

$$Q_2(F) = \Theta(\sqrt{N(N - \Gamma(F))}) \tag{7.88}$$

$$= \Omega(\sqrt{N(N - (N-1))}) \tag{7.89}$$

$$= \Omega(\sqrt{N}). \tag{7.90}$$

As a result, we get

$$D(F) \in O((Q_2(F))^2), \tag{7.91}$$

and the theorem is proved. □

The polynomial method can be extended to partial functions defined on true subsets of $\{0,1\}^N$ [3–5]. It can also be proved that the lower bound of search problem is $\Omega(\sqrt{N})$ by the polynomial method.

Exercises

7.9. Prove that $Q_E(\mathrm{OR}) = N$.

7.10. Represent PARITY function by using a real polynomial of degree N.

7.11. Prove that $\widetilde{\deg}(\mathrm{OR}) \in \Theta(\sqrt{N})$.

7.12. Prove that $\widetilde{\deg}(\mathrm{PARITY}) = N$.

7.13. Prove that $Q_E(\mathrm{PARITY}) = Q_2(\mathrm{PARITY}) = \lceil \frac{N}{2} \rceil$, and design the corresponding quantum query algorithm to compute the PARITY function.

7.14. Prove that $\widetilde{\deg}(\mathrm{MAJORITY}) \in \Theta(N)$.

7.15. Prove that $\widetilde{\deg}(\mathrm{THRESHOLD}_M) \in \Theta(\sqrt{M(N-M+1)})$.

7.16. Prove that the block sensitivity of $\mathrm{THRESHOLD_M}$ is $N - M + 1$.

7.5 Adversary method

Adversary method [6] is another important method to solve the lower bound on the quantum query complexity of problems in quantum computational complexity.

Consider quantum query algorithm $\mathcal{A}$ with t queries to compute Boolean function $F:\{0,1\}^N \to \{0,1\}$ with bounded error. Suppose $|\psi_j^{\mathbf{X}}\rangle$ and $|\psi_j^{\mathbf{Y}}\rangle$ are the states of $\mathcal{A}$ querying $\mathbf{X}$ and $\mathbf{Y}$ for j times, respectively. Suppose $|\psi_t^{\mathbf{X}}\rangle$ and $|\psi_t^{\mathbf{Y}}\rangle$ are the final states of $\mathcal{A}$ querying $\mathbf{X}$ and $\mathbf{Y}$ for t times, respectively. If $\mathcal{A}$ can distinguish $|\psi_t^{\mathbf{X}}\rangle$ from $|\psi_t^{\mathbf{Y}}\rangle$ with probability at least $1-\epsilon$, where ϵ is the error, then from Theorem 7.1 it follows that

$$|\langle\psi_t^{\mathbf{X}}|\psi_t^{\mathbf{Y}}\rangle| \le 2\sqrt{\epsilon(1-\epsilon)}. \tag{7.92}$$

Suppose $\mathcal{X} = \{\mathbf{X} \mid F(\mathbf{X}) = 0\}$, $\mathcal{Y} = \{\mathbf{Y} \mid F(\mathbf{Y}) = 1\}$, and $R \subseteq \mathcal{X} \times \mathcal{Y}$. Since for any $\mathbf{X}$ and $\mathbf{Y}$, $|\psi_0^{\mathbf{X}}\rangle = |\psi_0^{\mathbf{Y}}\rangle$, it holds

$$\sum_{|\psi_0^{\mathbf{X}}\rangle, |\psi_0^{\mathbf{Y}}\rangle : (\mathbf{X},\mathbf{Y}) \in R} |\langle\psi_0^{\mathbf{X}}|\psi_0^{\mathbf{Y}}\rangle| = |R|. \tag{7.93}$$

If $\mathcal{A}$ can distinguish $|\psi_t^{\mathbf{X}}\rangle$ from $|\psi_t^{\mathbf{Y}}\rangle$ with probability at least $1-\epsilon$, then

$$\sum_{(\mathbf{X},\mathbf{Y})\in R} |\langle \psi_t^{\mathbf{X}} | \psi_t^{\mathbf{Y}} \rangle| \leq 2\sqrt{\epsilon(1-\epsilon)}|R|. \tag{7.94}$$

If $\epsilon < \frac{1}{2}$, then

$$2\sqrt{\epsilon(1-\epsilon)}|R| < |R|. \tag{7.95}$$

Denote $W^j = \sum_{(\mathbf{X},\mathbf{Y})\in R} \frac{1}{\sqrt{|\mathcal{X}||\mathcal{Y}|}} |\langle \psi_j^{\mathbf{X}} | \psi_j^{\mathbf{Y}} \rangle|$. Then

$$W^0 - W^t \geq |R| \frac{(1-2\sqrt{\epsilon(1-\epsilon)})}{\sqrt{|\mathcal{X}||\mathcal{Y}|}} \tag{7.96}$$

$$\in \Omega\left(\frac{|R|}{\sqrt{|\mathcal{X}||\mathcal{Y}|}}\right). \tag{7.97}$$

If there exists a $\Delta > 0$ such that $W^{j-1} - W^j \leq \Delta$, then

$$W^0 - W^t \leq t\Delta, \tag{7.98}$$

that is,

$$t \geq \frac{W^0 - W^t}{\Delta}. \tag{7.99}$$

The lower bound on the number of queries t for algorithm $\mathcal{A}$ can be obtained from Eq. (7.99).

Lemma 7.9. *For any $a, b \in \mathbb{R}$ with $r > 0$, there is*

$$2ab \leq \frac{1}{r}a^2 + rb^2. \tag{7.100}$$

Proof. From $(\frac{a}{\sqrt{r}} - \sqrt{r}b)^2 \geq 0$, we can get

$$2ab \leq \frac{1}{r}a^2 + rb^2. \tag{7.101}$$

The lemma is proved. □

Lemma 7.10. *For any $R \subseteq \mathcal{X} \times \mathcal{Y}$, there is $W^{j-1} - W^j \leq 2\sqrt{ll'}$, where $1 \leq j \leq t$, and the integers l and l' satisfy the following conditions:*

1. *For each* $\mathbf{X} \in \mathcal{X}$ *and* $i \in \{0, 1, \ldots, N-1\}$, *there exist at most* l *distinct* $\mathbf{Y} \in \mathcal{Y}$ *such that* $(\mathbf{X}, \mathbf{Y}) \in R$ *and* $X_i \neq Y_i$;

2. *For each* $\mathbf{Y} \in \mathcal{Y}$ *and* $i \in \{0, 1, \ldots, N-1\}$, *there exist at most* l' *distinct* $\mathbf{X} \in \mathcal{X}$ *such that* $(\mathbf{X}, \mathbf{Y}) \in R$ *and* $X_i \neq Y_i$.

Proof. According to the definition of W^j, we can obtain

$$W^{j-1} - W^j = \frac{1}{\sqrt{|\mathcal{X}||\mathcal{Y}|}} \sum_{(\mathbf{X},\mathbf{Y})\in R} \left(|\langle \psi_{j-1}^{\mathbf{X}} | \psi_{j-1}^{\mathbf{Y}} \rangle| - |\langle \psi_j^{\mathbf{X}} | \psi_j^{\mathbf{Y}} \rangle|\right) \tag{7.102}$$

$$\leq \frac{1}{\sqrt{|\mathcal{X}||\mathcal{Y}|}} \sum_{(\mathbf{X},\mathbf{Y})\in R} |\langle \psi_{j-1}^{\mathbf{X}} | \psi_{j-1}^{\mathbf{Y}} \rangle - \langle \psi_j^{\mathbf{X}} | \psi_j^{\mathbf{Y}} \rangle|. \tag{7.103}$$

Denote

$$|\psi_{j-1}^{\mathbf{X}}\rangle = \sum_{i=0}^{N-1} \alpha_{i,j-1}^{\mathbf{X}} |i\rangle |\phi_{i,j-1}^{\mathbf{X}}\rangle, \tag{7.104}$$

$$|\psi_{j-1}^{\mathbf{Y}}\rangle = \sum_{i=0}^{N-1} \alpha_{i,j-1}^{\mathbf{Y}} |i\rangle |\phi_{i,j-1}^{\mathbf{Y}}\rangle. \tag{7.105}$$

Recall the definition of query operator:

$$\hat{O}_{\mathbf{X}} |i\rangle |\phi_{i,j-1}^{\mathbf{X}}\rangle = (-1)^{X_i} |i\rangle |\phi_{i,j-1}^{\mathbf{X}}\rangle, \tag{7.106}$$

$$\hat{O}_{\mathbf{Y}} |i\rangle |\phi_{i,j-1}^{\mathbf{Y}}\rangle = (-1)^{Y_i} |i\rangle |\phi_{i,j-1}^{\mathbf{Y}}\rangle. \tag{7.107}$$

We have

$$|\psi_j^{\mathbf{X}}\rangle = U_j \hat{O}_{\mathbf{X}} |\psi_{j-1}^{\mathbf{X}}\rangle \tag{7.108}$$

$$= U_j \hat{O}_{\mathbf{X}} \left(\sum_{i:X_i\neq 1} \alpha_{i,j-1}^{\mathbf{X}} |i\rangle |\phi_{i,j-1}^{\mathbf{X}}\rangle + \sum_{i:X_i=1} \alpha_{i,j-1}^{\mathbf{X}} |i\rangle |\phi_{i,j-1}^{\mathbf{X}}\rangle \right) \tag{7.109}$$

$$= U_j \left(\sum_{i:X_i\neq 1} \alpha_{i,j-1}^{\mathbf{X}} |i\rangle |\phi_{i,j-1}^{\mathbf{X}}\rangle - \sum_{i:X_i=1} \alpha_{i,j-1}^{\mathbf{X}} |i\rangle |\phi_{i,j-1}^{\mathbf{X}}\rangle \right) \tag{7.110}$$

$$= U_j \left(|\psi_{j-1}^{\mathbf{X}}\rangle - 2 \sum_{i:X_i=1} \alpha_{i,j-1}^{\mathbf{X}} |i\rangle |\phi_{i,j-1}^{\mathbf{X}}\rangle \right). \tag{7.111}$$

Similarly, it can be obtained that

$$|\psi_j^{\mathbf{Y}}\rangle = U_j \hat{O}_{\mathbf{Y}} |\psi_{j-1}^{\mathbf{Y}}\rangle \tag{7.112}$$

$$= U_j\left(|\psi_{j-1}^{\mathbf{Y}}\rangle - 2\sum_{i:Y_i=1}\alpha_{i,j-1}^{\mathbf{Y}}|i\rangle|\phi_{i,j-1}^{\mathbf{Y}}\rangle\right). \tag{7.113}$$

Therefore, we have

$$\langle\psi_j^{\mathbf{X}}|\psi_j^{\mathbf{Y}}\rangle = \left(\langle\psi_{j-1}^{\mathbf{X}}| - 2\sum_{i:X_i=1}\alpha_{i,j-1}^{\mathbf{X}*}\langle i|\langle\phi_{i,j-1}^{\mathbf{X}}|\right)U_j^\dagger$$

$$U_j\left(|\psi_{j-1}^{\mathbf{Y}}\rangle - 2\sum_{i:Y_i=1}\alpha_{i,j-1}^{\mathbf{Y}}|i\rangle|\phi_{i,j-1}^{\mathbf{Y}}\rangle\right) \tag{7.114}$$

$$\begin{aligned} &= \langle\psi_{j-1}^{\mathbf{X}}|\psi_{j-1}^{\mathbf{Y}}\rangle - 2\sum_{i:X_i=1}\alpha_{i,j-1}^{\mathbf{X}*}\alpha_{i,j-1}^{\mathbf{Y}}\langle\phi_{i,j-1}^{\mathbf{X}}|\phi_{i,j-1}^{\mathbf{Y}}\rangle \\ &\quad - 2\sum_{i:Y_i=1}\alpha_{i,j-1}^{\mathbf{X}*}\alpha_{i,j-1}^{\mathbf{Y}}\langle\phi_{i,j-1}^{\mathbf{X}}|\phi_{i,j-1}^{\mathbf{Y}}\rangle \\ &\quad + 4\sum_{i:X_i=Y_i=1}\alpha_{i,j-1}^{\mathbf{X}*}\alpha_{i,j-1}^{\mathbf{Y}}\langle\phi_{i,j-1}^{\mathbf{X}}|\phi_{i,j-1}^{\mathbf{Y}}\rangle \end{aligned} \tag{7.115}$$

$$= \langle\psi_{j-1}^{\mathbf{X}}|\psi_{j-1}^{\mathbf{Y}}\rangle - 2\sum_{i:X_i\neq Y_i}\alpha_{i,j-1}^{\mathbf{X}*}\alpha_{i,j-1}^{\mathbf{Y}}\langle\phi_{i,j-1}^{\mathbf{X}}|\phi_{i,j-1}^{\mathbf{Y}}\rangle, \tag{7.116}$$

that is,

$$\langle\psi_{j-1}^{\mathbf{X}}|\psi_{j-1}^{\mathbf{Y}}\rangle - \langle\psi_j^{\mathbf{X}}|\psi_j^{\mathbf{Y}}\rangle = 2\sum_{i:X_i\neq Y_i}\alpha_{i,j-1}^{\mathbf{X}*}\alpha_{i,j-1}^{\mathbf{Y}}\langle\phi_{i,j-1}^{\mathbf{X}}|\phi_{i,j-1}^{\mathbf{Y}}\rangle. \tag{7.117}$$

As a result, we can get

$$W^{j-1} - W^j \tag{7.118}$$

$$\leq \frac{1}{\sqrt{|\mathcal{X}||\mathcal{Y}|}}\sum_{(\mathbf{X},\mathbf{Y})\in R}|2\sum_{i:X_i\neq Y_i}\alpha_{i,j-1}^{\mathbf{X}*}\alpha_{i,j-1}^{\mathbf{Y}}\langle\phi_{i,j-1}^{\mathbf{X}}|\phi_{i,j-1}^{\mathbf{Y}}\rangle| \tag{7.119}$$

$$\leq \frac{1}{\sqrt{|\mathcal{X}||\mathcal{Y}|}}\sum_{(\mathbf{X},\mathbf{Y})\in R}2\sum_{i:X_i\neq Y_i}|\alpha_{i,j-1}^{\mathbf{X}*}\alpha_{i,j-1}^{\mathbf{Y}}\langle\phi_{i,j-1}^{\mathbf{X}}|\phi_{i,j-1}^{\mathbf{Y}}\rangle| \tag{7.120}$$

$$\leq \sum_{(\mathbf{X},\mathbf{Y})\in R}\sum_{i:X_i\neq Y_i}2\frac{|\alpha_{i,j-1}^{\mathbf{X}}|}{\sqrt{|\mathcal{X}|}}\frac{|\alpha_{i,j-1}^{\mathbf{Y}}|}{\sqrt{|\mathcal{Y}|}}. \tag{7.121}$$

In Lemma 7.9, denote $a = \frac{|\alpha_{i,j-1}^{\mathbf{X}}|}{\sqrt{|\mathcal{X}|}}$, $b = \frac{|\alpha_{i,j-1}^{\mathbf{Y}}|}{\sqrt{|\mathcal{Y}|}}$, $r = \sqrt{\frac{l}{l'}}$. Then we have

$$
\begin{aligned}
& W^{j-1} - W^{j} && (7.122)\\
& \leq \sum_{(\mathbf{X},\mathbf{Y})\in R}\sum_{i:X_i\neq Y_i}\left(\sqrt{\frac{l'}{l}}\frac{|\alpha_{i,j-1}^{\mathbf{X}}|^2}{|\mathcal{X}|}+\sqrt{\frac{l}{l'}}\frac{|\alpha_{i,j-1}^{\mathbf{Y}}|^2}{|\mathcal{Y}|}\right) && (7.123)\\
& = \sum_{(\mathbf{X},\mathbf{Y})\in R}\sum_{i:X_i\neq Y_i}\sqrt{\frac{l'}{l}}\frac{|\alpha_{i,j-1}^{\mathbf{X}}|^2}{|\mathcal{X}|}+\sum_{(\mathbf{X},\mathbf{Y})\in R}\sum_{i:X_i\neq Y_i}\sqrt{\frac{l'}{l}}\frac{|\alpha_{i,j-1}^{\mathbf{Y}}|^2}{|\mathcal{Y}|} && (7.124)\\
& = \sum_{i}\sum_{\mathbf{X}\in\mathcal{X}}\sum_{\mathbf{Y}\in\mathcal{Y}:(\mathbf{X},\mathbf{Y})\in R,X_i\neq Y_i}\sqrt{\frac{l'}{l}}\frac{|\alpha_{i,j-1}^{\mathbf{X}}|^2}{|\mathcal{X}|}\\
& \quad + \sum_{i}\sum_{\mathbf{Y}\in\mathcal{Y}}\sum_{\mathbf{X}\in\mathcal{X}:(\mathbf{X},\mathbf{Y})\in R,X_i\neq Y_i}\sqrt{\frac{l}{l'}}\frac{|\alpha_{i,j-1}^{\mathbf{Y}}|^2}{|\mathcal{Y}|} && (7.125)\\
& \leq \sum_{i}\sum_{\mathbf{X}\in\mathcal{X}} l\sqrt{\frac{l'}{l}}\frac{|\alpha_{i,j-1}^{\mathbf{X}}|^2}{|\mathcal{X}|}+\sum_{i}\sum_{\mathbf{Y}\in\mathcal{Y}} l'\sqrt{\frac{l}{l'}}\frac{|\alpha_{i,j-1}^{\mathbf{Y}}|^2}{|\mathcal{Y}|} && (7.126)\\
& = \frac{\sqrt{ll'}}{|\mathcal{X}|}\sum_{\mathbf{X}\in\mathcal{X}}\sum_{i}|\alpha_{i,j-1}^{\mathbf{X}}|^2+\frac{\sqrt{ll'}}{|\mathcal{Y}|}\sum_{\mathbf{Y}\in\mathcal{Y}}\sum_{i}|\alpha_{i,j-1}^{\mathbf{Y}}|^2 && (7.127)\\
& = \frac{\sqrt{ll'}}{|\mathcal{X}|}\sum_{\mathbf{X}\in\mathcal{X}}1+\frac{\sqrt{ll'}}{|\mathcal{Y}|}\sum_{\mathbf{Y}\in\mathcal{Y}}1 && (7.128)\\
& = 2\sqrt{ll'}, && (7.129)
\end{aligned}
$$

and thus the lemma is proved. □

Lemma 7.11. *For any $R \subseteq \mathcal{X}\times\mathcal{Y}$, if the integers l and l' satisfy the conditions of Lemma 7.10, then the number of queries t for any quantum algorithm $\mathcal{A}$ that distinguishes $|\psi_t^{\mathbf{X}}\rangle$ from $|\psi_t^{\mathbf{Y}}\rangle$ with probability at least $1-\epsilon$ ($\epsilon < \frac{1}{2}$) satisfies*

$$
t \geq |R|\frac{(1-2\sqrt{\epsilon(1-\epsilon)})}{\sqrt{|\mathcal{X}||\mathcal{Y}|}2\sqrt{ll'}} \in \Omega\left(\frac{|R|}{\sqrt{|\mathcal{X}||\mathcal{Y}|}\sqrt{ll'}}\right). \tag{7.130}
$$

Proof. Denote $\Delta = 2\sqrt{ll'}$. Combining Eq. (7.99) with Eq. (7.96) and Lemma 7.10, we have

$$
\begin{aligned}
t & \geq \frac{W^0 - W^t}{\Delta} && (7.131)\\
& \geq |R|\frac{(1-2\sqrt{\epsilon(1-\epsilon)})}{\sqrt{|\mathcal{X}||\mathcal{Y}|}\Delta} && (7.132)\\
& = |R|\frac{(1-2\sqrt{\epsilon(1-\epsilon)})}{\sqrt{|\mathcal{X}||\mathcal{Y}|}2\sqrt{ll'}} && (7.133)
\end{aligned}
$$

$$\in \Omega\left(\frac{|R|}{\sqrt{|\mathcal{X}||\mathcal{Y}|}\sqrt{ll'}}\right). \tag{7.134}$$

The lemma is proved. □

Lemma 7.12. *For any $R \subseteq \mathcal{X} \times \mathcal{Y}$, there is $|R| \geq \sqrt{|\mathcal{X}||\mathcal{Y}|mm'}$, where the integers m and m' satisfy the following conditions:*

1. *For each $\mathbf{X} \in \mathcal{X}$, there exist at least m distinct $\mathbf{Y} \in \mathcal{Y}$ such that $(\mathbf{X}, \mathbf{Y}) \in R$;*
2. *For each $\mathbf{Y} \in \mathcal{Y}$, there exist at least m' distinct $\mathbf{X} \in \mathcal{X}$ such that $(\mathbf{X}, \mathbf{Y}) \in R$.*

Proof. Since for each $\mathbf{X} \in \mathcal{X}$, there exist at least m distinct $\mathbf{Y} \in \mathcal{Y}$ such that $(\mathbf{X}, \mathbf{Y}) \in R$, we have $|R| \geq m|\mathcal{X}|$. Similarly, $|R| \geq m'|\mathcal{Y}|$ can be obtained. $|R|$ is not less than the average of $m|\mathcal{X}|$ and $m'|\mathcal{Y}|$, that is,

$$|R| \geq \frac{m|\mathcal{X}| + m'|\mathcal{Y}|}{2} \tag{7.135}$$

$$\geq \sqrt{|\mathcal{X}||\mathcal{Y}|mm'}. \tag{7.136}$$

The lemma is proved. □

Theorem 7.9. *For any $R \subseteq \mathcal{X} \times \mathcal{Y}$, if the integers l and l' satisfy the conditions of Lemma 7.10, and the integers m and m' satisfy the conditions of Lemma 7.12, then the query complexity of any quantum algorithm $\mathcal{A}$ that distinguishes $|\psi_t^{\mathbf{X}}\rangle$ and $|\psi_t^{\mathbf{Y}}\rangle$ with probability at least $1 - \epsilon$ ($\epsilon < \frac{1}{2}$) is*

$$Q_2(F) \in \Omega\left(\sqrt{\frac{mm'}{ll'}}\right). \tag{7.137}$$

Proof. If the integers l and l' satisfy the conditions of Lemma 7.10, then from Lemma 7.11 it follows that

$$t \geq |R|\frac{(1 - 2\sqrt{\epsilon(1-\epsilon)})}{\sqrt{|\mathcal{X}||\mathcal{Y}|}2\sqrt{ll'}}. \tag{7.138}$$

If the integers m and m' satisfy the conditions of Lemma 7.12, then from Lemma 7.12 it follows that

$$t \geq |R|\frac{(1 - 2\sqrt{\epsilon(1-\epsilon)})}{\sqrt{|\mathcal{X}||\mathcal{Y}|}2\sqrt{ll'}} \tag{7.139}$$

$$\geq \sqrt{|\mathcal{X}||\mathcal{Y}|mm'}\frac{(1 - 2\sqrt{\epsilon(1-\epsilon)})}{\sqrt{|\mathcal{X}||\mathcal{Y}|}2\sqrt{ll'}} \tag{7.140}$$

$$= \frac{1 - 2\sqrt{\epsilon(1-\epsilon)}}{2}\sqrt{\frac{mm'}{ll'}} \tag{7.141}$$

$$\in \Omega\left(\sqrt{\frac{mm'}{ll'}}\right), \tag{7.142}$$

that is,

$$Q_2(F) \in \Omega\left(\sqrt{\frac{mm'}{ll'}}\right). \tag{7.143}$$

The theorem is proved. □

Example 7.14. To solve the lower bound on the query complexity of the search problem, we assume that $\mathcal{X}$ is a set containing only zero string of N bits, i.e., $\mathcal{X} = \{0^N\}$, and $\mathcal{Y}$ is a set consisting of strings of N bits with exactly one 1 as well as $R = \mathcal{X} \times \mathcal{Y}$. For search problem, by Lemma 7.10 and Lemma 7.12, $m = N$, $m' = l = l' = 1$. According to Theorem 7.9, the lower bound on the query complexity of search problem is $\Omega(\sqrt{N})$.

Example 7.15. Suppose N is a perfect square, $m = \sqrt{N}$, and $\mathbf{X} = X_0X_1 \ldots X_{N-1}$. Let the Boolean function $F : \{0, 1\}^N \to \{0, 1\}$ compute the AND-OR tree problem defined as follows:

$$\begin{aligned} F(\mathbf{X}) = (X_0 \vee X_1 \vee \cdots \vee X_{m-1}) \wedge (X_m \vee X_{m+1} \vee \cdots \vee X_{2m-1}) \\ \wedge (X_{2m} \vee X_{2m+1} \vee \cdots \vee X_{3m-1}) \wedge \cdots \\ \wedge (X_{(m-1)m} \vee X_{(m-1)m+1} \vee \cdots \vee X_{m^2-1}). \end{aligned} \tag{7.144}$$

Fig. 7.2 shows a schematic of $F : \{0, 1\}^N \to \{0, 1\}$ computing the AND-OR tree problem.

Fig. 7.3 shows a schematic of $F : \{0, 1\}^N \to \{0, 1\}$ computing the AND-OR tree problem, where the input to F is $\mathbf{X}$ and $F(\mathbf{X}) = 0$.

Fig. 7.4 shows a schematic of $F : \{0, 1\}^N \to \{0, 1\}$ computing the AND-OR tree problem, where the input to F is $\mathbf{Y}$ and $F(\mathbf{Y}) = 1$.

Theorem 7.10. *Let $F : \{0, 1\}^N \to \{0, 1\}$ be a Boolean function computing the* AND-OR *tree. Then we have $Q_2(F) \in \Omega(\sqrt{N})$.*

Proof. In Fig. 7.3, let $\mathcal{X}$ be the set of bit strings where the input to exactly one OR function is zero string, and each input to each other OR functions has exactly one 1. In Fig. 7.4, let $\mathcal{Y}$ be the set of bit strings where the input to each OR function has exactly one 1. Define the relation $R \subseteq \mathcal{X} \times \mathcal{Y}$, where $(\mathbf{X}, \mathbf{Y}) \in R$ if and only if $\mathbf{X} = X_0X_1 \ldots X_{N-1}$ and $\mathbf{Y} = Y_0Y_1 \ldots Y_{N-1}$ have only one different bit.

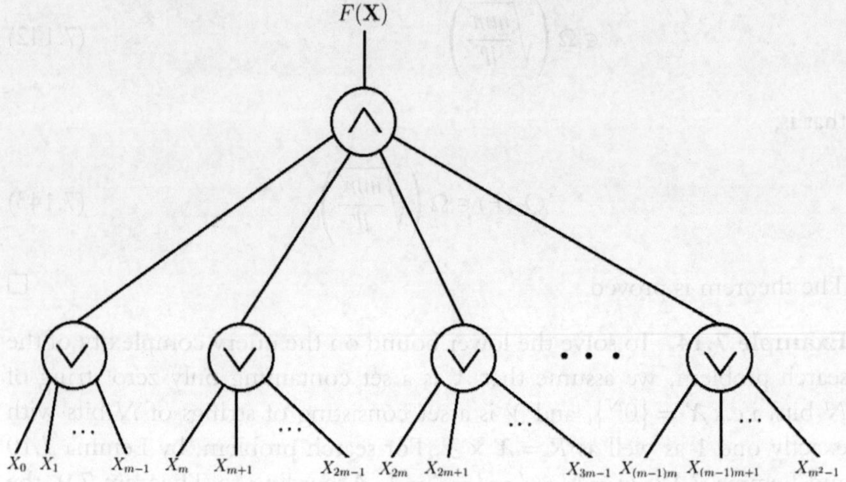

Figure 7.2 $F : \{0, 1\}^N \rightarrow \{0, 1\}$ computes the AND-OR tree problem.

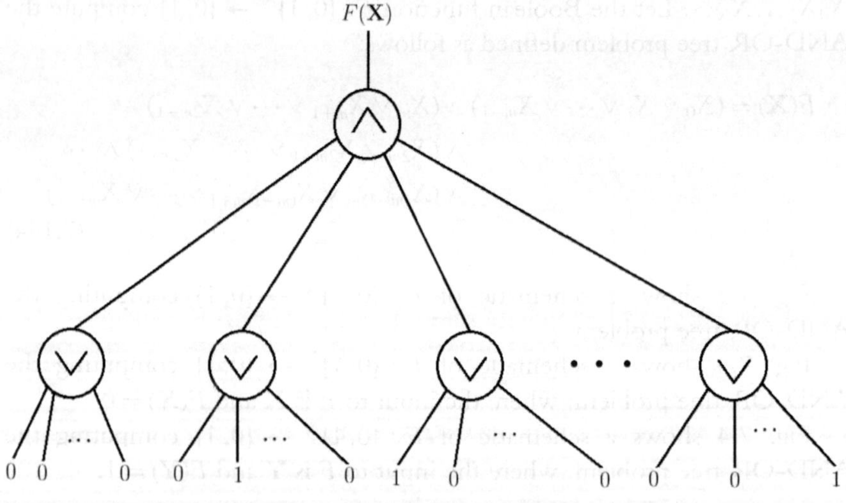

Figure 7.3 $F : \{0, 1\}^N \rightarrow \{0, 1\}$ computes the AND-OR tree problem, where the input to F is $\mathbf{X}$ and $F(\mathbf{X}) = 0$.

- For each $\mathbf{X} \in \mathcal{X}$, there exists exactly one OR function whose $\sqrt{N}$ inputs are all zeros. Flipping any one of these $\sqrt{N}$ zeros to 1 gives a bit string $\mathbf{Y} \in \mathcal{Y}$. Therefore, for each $\mathbf{X} \in \mathcal{X}$, there exist $\sqrt{N}$ strings $\mathbf{Y} \in \mathcal{Y}$ such that $(\mathbf{X}, \mathbf{Y}) \in R$. Consequently, $m = \sqrt{N}$.

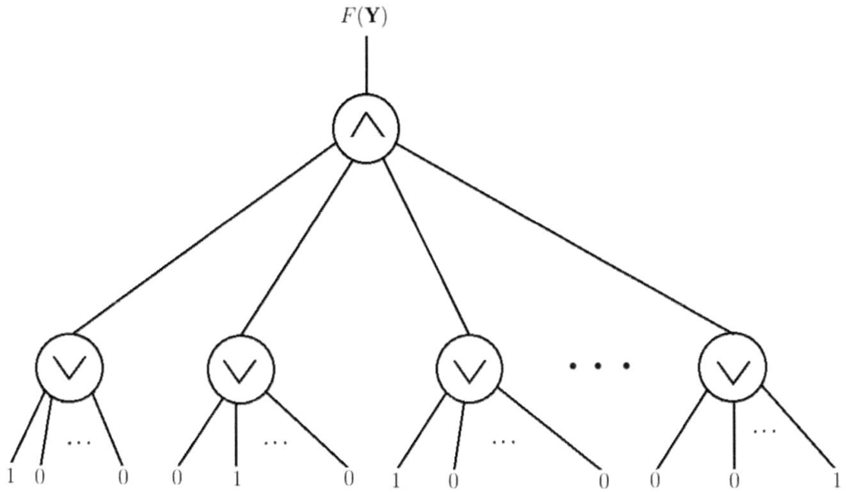

Figure 7.4 $F : \{0, 1\}^N \rightarrow \{0, 1\}$ computes the AND-OR tree problem, where the input to F is $\mathbf{Y}$ and $F(\mathbf{Y}) = 1$.

- For each $\mathbf{Y} \in \mathcal{Y}$, there exists exactly one 1 in the input for each of the $\sqrt{N}$ OR functions. Flipping any one of these 1s to 0 gives a bit string $\mathbf{X} \in \mathcal{X}$. Therefore, for each $\mathbf{Y} \in \mathcal{Y}$, there exist $\sqrt{N}$ strings $\mathbf{X} \in \mathcal{X}$ such that $(\mathbf{X}, \mathbf{Y}) \in R$. As a result, $m' = \sqrt{N}$.
- For each $\mathbf{X} \in \mathcal{X}$ and each $i \in \{0, 1, \ldots, N-1\}$, there exists at most one $\mathbf{Y} \in \mathcal{Y}$ such that $(\mathbf{X}, \mathbf{Y}) \in R$ and $X_i \neq Y_i$. Thus, $l = 1$.
- For each $\mathbf{Y} \in \mathcal{Y}$ and each $i \in \{0, 1, \ldots, N-1\}$, there exists at most one $\mathbf{X} \in \mathcal{X}$ such that $(\mathbf{X}, \mathbf{Y}) \in R$ and $X_i \neq Y_i$. Thus, $l' = 1$.

Finally, according to Theorem 7.9, we can obtain

$$Q_2(F) \in \Omega\left(\sqrt{\frac{mm'}{ll'}}\right) = \Omega\left(\sqrt{\frac{\sqrt{N} \cdot \sqrt{N}}{1 \cdot 1}}\right) = \Omega(\sqrt{N}), \tag{7.145}$$

and the theorem is proved. □

There is a quantum query algorithm with query complexity of $O(\sqrt{N})$ to compute the AND-OR tree problem with bounded error. The classical query complexity for computing the AND-OR tree problem with bounded error is $\Theta(N)$.

In addition, there are the weighted adversary method, the spectral method, and the Kolmogorov method for computing the lower bound on the quantum query complexity of a given problem [7]. In a way, these methods are equivalent, and the lower bounds on the quantum query complexity obtained by them for some problems are equal, but the details are omitted here. We can refer to [7] for further learning of these profound insights.

Exercises

7.17. Show that the query complexity of computing the function MAJORITY with bounded error by the adversary method is $\Omega(N)$. Hint: Suppose X is a string with $\frac{N}{2}$ ones. Let Y be a string with $\frac{N}{2}+1$ ones.

7.18. Prove that the quantum query complexity of the function PARITY computed by the adversary method is $\Omega(N)$.

7.19. Design a quantum query algorithm with query complexity $O(\sqrt{N} \times \log N)$ to compute the AND-OR problem with bounded error.

7.20. Prove that $Q_2(F) \in \Omega(\sqrt{bs(F)})$ can be obtained by applying the adversary method. Hint: Let $\mathcal{X}$ be a string that obtains $bs(F)$.

7.6 Summary

Quantum computational complexity is an important part of computational complexity theory [8,9], which describes the difficulty of solving problems in the framework of quantum computing.

In this chapter, we first introduced the basic definitions of computational complexity classes, including classical computational complexity classes and quantum computational complexity classes. Then the definitions of the quantum query model, classical query complexity, and quantum query complexity were given. The quantum query model is an important class of theoretical models in quantum computing, and it implies basic ideas and presents a general formalization of many quantum query algorithms.

Then, to prove a lower bound on the query complexity of search problem, we provided a lower bound on the success probability of distinguishing quantum states. Finally, we introduced in detail two important methods for deriving the lower bounds on quantum query complexity, namely the polynomial method and the adversary method.

References

[1] H. Buhrman, R. de Wolf, Complexity measures and decision tree complexity: a survey, Theoretical Computer Science 288 (1) (2002) 21–43.

[2] R. Beals, H. Buhrman, R. Cleve, et al., Quantum lower bounds by polynomials, in: Proceedings of the 39th Annual Symposium on Foundations of Computer Science (Cat. No. 98CB36280), 1998, pp. 352–361.

[3] D.W. Qiu, S.G. Zheng, Characterizations of symmetrically partial Boolean functions with exact quantum query complexity, arXiv:1603.06505, 2016.

[4] D.W. Qiu, S.G. Zheng, Generalized Deutsch–Jozsa problem and the optimal quantum algorithm, Physical Review A 97 (6) (2018) 062331.

[5] D.W. Qiu, S.G. Zheng, Revisiting Deutsch–Jozsa algorithm, Information and Computation 275 (2020) 104605.

[6] A. Ambainis, Quantum lower bounds by quantum arguments, Journal of Computer and System Sciences 64 (4) (2002) 750–767.

[7] R. Špalek, M. Szegedy, All quantum adversary methods are equivalent, Theory of Computing 2 (1) (2006) 1–18.

[8] H. Buhrman, Quantum computing and communication complexity, Bulletin of the EATCS 70 (2000) 131–141.

[9] R. de Wolf, Quantum communication and complexity, Theoretical Computer Science 287 (1) (2002) 337–353.

CHAPTER 8

Quantum error correction⊛

The realization of quantum computers and quantum communication in practice requires quantum error correction to address errors caused by noise. In information theory, error correction is generally achieved by adding redundant information. Even if some information is damaged due to noise interference, sufficient redundant information can be utilized to restore the information through error correction. Coding theory, which is closely related to information theory, is a mathematical theory that studies the rules of signal encoding during the process of information transmission. Its main goal is to construct codes with good properties, allowing the encoded source messages to be corrected at the receiving end after transmission through a channel. Classical error correction is the foundation of quantum error correction and new methods are required to achieve quantum error correction.

8.1 Classical bit-flip error correction

In classical information theory, bit information may experience a flip when transmitted through a noisy channel. In the following paragraphs, we introduce a number of basic concepts and methods of classical bit-flip error correction.

Let Alice send 1 bit to Bob through a noisy channel, where the probability of the bit flip is p (with $0 \le p < \frac{1}{2}$). That is, if Alice sends a bit b to Bob, Bob receives $\neg b$ with probability p and receives b with probability $1-p$, as shown in Fig. 8.1.

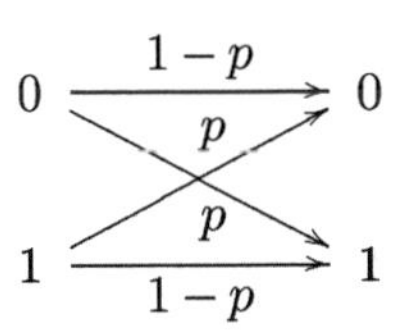

Figure 8.1 Classical bit-flip.

⊛ This book has a companion website hosting complementary materials. Visit this URL to access it: https://www.elsevier.com/books-and-journals/book-companion/9780443277047.

Theoretical Foundations of Quantum Computing
https://doi.org/10.1016/B978-0-44-327704-7.00013-X

If Alice wants to send an important bit of information to Bob through a noisy channel, and the bit may flip during transmission, while Bob hopes to receive the bit correctly, then classical 3-bit repetition coding can be used for error correction. In the following, we provide the definition and related theorems of classical 3-bit repetition code error correction.

Definition 8.1. The classical 3-bit repetition code is defined as encoding one bit of information by repeating it 3 times, and the bit that appears most frequently is selected as the decoded bit.

Theorem 8.1. *If Alice wants to send 1 bit to Bob through a noisy channel, with the probability of bit flip being p (where $0 \le p < \frac{1}{2}$), there exists an error correction method of classical 3-bit repetition code that allows the original bit to be recovered with a probability* $1 - (3p^2 - 2p^3)$.

Proof. First, if the bit Alice wants to send is 0, she encodes it as 000; if the bit Alice wants to send is 1, she encodes it as 111. Then Alice sends the encoded 3 bits to Bob.

The probability of at most 1-bit flip during the transmission of these 3 bits over a noisy channel is given by

$$\begin{aligned} & \mathrm{P}[0 \text{ bit flip}] + \mathrm{P}[1 \text{ bit flip}] \\ & = (1-p)^3 + 3(1-p)^2 p \qquad (8.1) \\ & = 1 - (3p^2 - 2p^3). \qquad (8.2) \end{aligned}$$

In the case of at most 1 bit being flipped, if Bob receives the 3 bits as abc, he will take the bit that appears most frequently among abc as the decoded bit. This bit is the original bit that Alice sent. □

Exercises

8.1. Alice wants to send 1 bit to Bob through a noisy channel, with a bit flip probability 0.07. By using the classical 3-bit repetition code for error correction, write out the probability of recovering the original bit.

8.2. Alice wants to send 1 bit to Bob through a noisy channel, with a bit flip probability p (where $0 \le p < \frac{1}{2}$). If two bits are flipped, can the classical 3-bit repetition code successfully correct errors?

8.2 Quantum bit-flip error correction

If Alice sends $|\psi\rangle$ to Bob through a noisy channel, according to the no-cloning theorem, Alice cannot encode $|\psi\rangle$ as $|\psi\rangle|\psi\rangle|\psi\rangle$. Furthermore, Bob cannot directly measure the received quantum state, as doing so would collapse the state and make it impossible to restore.

In summary, it is clear that quantum error correction and classical error correction are fundamentally different, and classical error correction methods cannot be directly applied to address quantum error issues. Therefore new approaches are required. Now, let us first consider the occurrence of a qubit flip error. We provide the definition of qubit flip and the relevant theorems as follows.

Definition 8.2. Let $|\psi\rangle = \alpha|0\rangle + \beta|1\rangle$. If $|\psi\rangle$ changes to $|\neg\psi\rangle = \alpha|1\rangle + \beta|0\rangle$, then $|\psi\rangle$ undergoes a bit flip. Clearly, $|\neg\psi\rangle = \sigma_x|\psi\rangle$, where $\sigma_x = \begin{bmatrix} 0 & 1 \\ 1 & 0 \end{bmatrix}$.

Definition 8.3. Let $|\psi\rangle = \alpha|0\rangle + \beta|1\rangle$ be the qubit to be transmitted. If there exists a protocol in which the sender Alice encodes $|\psi\rangle$ as $\alpha|0\rangle^{\otimes k} + \beta|1\rangle^{\otimes k}$, and during transmission, at most k_1 (with $k_1 \leq k$) qubits undergo a bit flip, then the receiver Bob can decode the received quantum state to obtain $|\psi\rangle$. This protocol is referred to as a (k_1, k) bit-flip protocol, where k and k_1 are positive integers.

Theorem 8.2. *If Alice sends the qubit $|\psi\rangle = \alpha|0\rangle + \beta|1\rangle$ to Bob through a noisy channel, then there exists a $(1, 3)$ bit-flip protocol that Alice transmits to Bob.*

Proof. First, Alice encodes $\alpha|0\rangle + \beta|1\rangle$ into

$$\alpha|000\rangle + \beta|111\rangle$$

using the circuit shown in Fig. 8.2. Then she sends $\alpha|000\rangle + \beta|111\rangle$ to Bob through a noisy channel, during which one of the qubits of the state may undergo a bit flip.

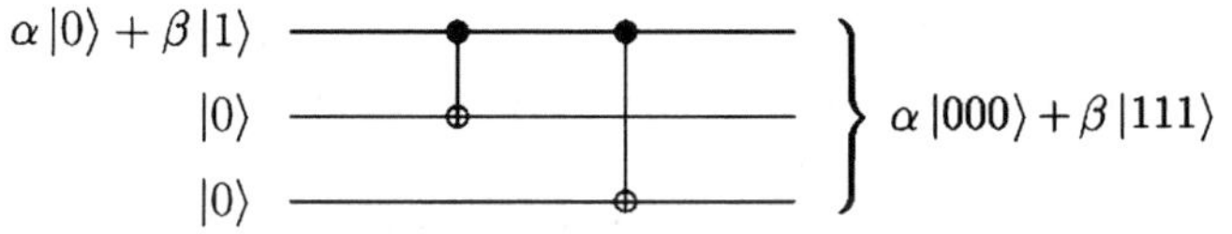

Figure 8.2 Quantum bit flip encoding circuit.

If the quantum state received by Bob is $\alpha|abc\rangle+\beta|\neg a\neg b\neg c\rangle$, he decodes it using the circuit shown in Fig. 8.3. This circuit introduces two auxiliary qubits that serve as redundancy checks. The redundancy checks are data encodings that can detect or automatically correct errors, also known as error detection and correction codes.

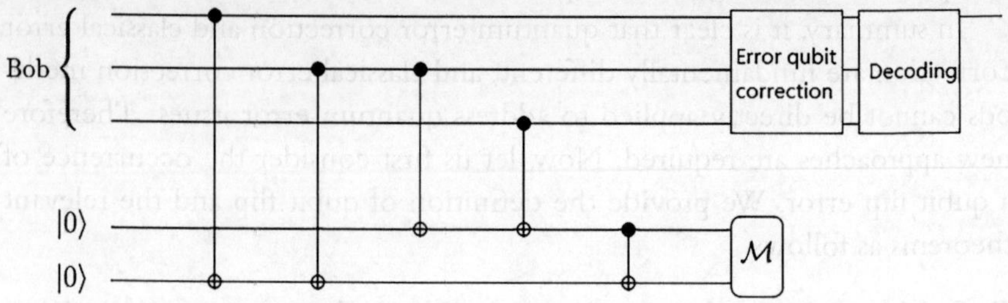

Figure 8.3 Quantum bit flip decoding circuit.

The evolution process of the quantum state $\alpha|abc\rangle+\beta|\neg a\neg b\neg c\rangle$ through the circuit in Fig. 8.3 is as follows:

$$(\alpha|abc\rangle+\beta|\neg a\neg b\neg c\rangle)|00\rangle$$
$$=\alpha|abc\rangle|00\rangle+\beta|\neg a\neg b\neg c\rangle|00\rangle \tag{8.3}$$
$$\to \alpha|abc\rangle|b\oplus c\rangle|a\oplus c\rangle+\beta|\neg a\neg b\neg c\rangle|\neg b\oplus\neg c\rangle|\neg a\oplus\neg c\rangle \tag{8.4}$$
$$=\alpha|abc\rangle|b\oplus c\rangle|a\oplus c\rangle+\beta|\neg a\neg b\neg c\rangle|b\oplus c\rangle|a\oplus c\rangle \tag{8.5}$$
$$=(\alpha|abc\rangle+\beta|\neg a\neg b\neg c\rangle)|b\oplus c\rangle|a\oplus c\rangle. \tag{8.6}$$

Expression (8.4) is obtained from the five CNOT gates in the circuit shown in Fig. 8.3. Then Bob measures the fourth and fifth qubits of the quantum state $(\alpha|abc\rangle+\beta|\neg a\neg b\neg c\rangle)|b\oplus c\rangle|a\oplus c\rangle$, specifically $|b\oplus c\rangle$ and $|a\oplus c\rangle$, to obtain the check code in binary representation.

If $a=b=c$, then $b\oplus c=0$ and $a\oplus c=0$. This indicates that the quantum state $\alpha|abc\rangle+\beta|\neg a\neg b\neg c\rangle$ has not experienced any bit flip.

If $\neg a=b=c$, then $b\oplus c=0$ and $a\oplus c=1$. This indicates that the first qubit of the quantum state $\alpha|abc\rangle+\beta|\neg a\neg b\neg c\rangle$ undergoes a flip.

If $a=\neg b=c$, then $b\oplus c=1$ and $a\oplus c=0$. This indicates that the second qubit of the quantum state $\alpha|abc\rangle+\beta|\neg a\neg b\neg c\rangle$ undergoes a flip.

If $a=b=\neg c$, then $b\oplus c=1$ and $a\oplus c=1$. This indicates that the third qubit of the quantum state $\alpha|abc\rangle+\beta|\neg a\neg b\neg c\rangle$ undergoes a flip.

Next, Bob corrects the flipped qubit by applying σ_x operation based on the check code. The quantum state evolves as follows:

$$\alpha|abc\rangle+\beta|\neg a\neg b\neg c\rangle\to\alpha|000\rangle+\beta|111\rangle. \tag{8.7}$$

Finally, Bob decodes as follows:

$$\alpha|000\rangle + \beta|111\rangle \rightarrow (\alpha|0\rangle + \beta|1\rangle)|00\rangle, \tag{8.8}$$

and Bob takes the first qubit, which is the quantum state $|\psi\rangle$ sent by Alice. The proof is completed. □

Exercises

8.3. In the proof of Theorem 8.2, if the second qubit of the quantum state $\alpha|000\rangle + \beta|111\rangle$ encoded by Alice undergoes a bit flip, write out the evolution of the quantum state during the decoding phase for Bob.

8.4. In the proof of Theorem 8.2, if the third qubit of the quantum state $\alpha|000\rangle + \beta|111\rangle$ encoded by Alice undergoes a bit flip, write out the evolution of the quantum state during the decoding phase for Bob.

8.3 Quantum phase-flip error correction

Now we consider the occurrence of quantum phase-flip errors. In the following, we provide the definition of quantum phase flips and related theorems.

Definition 8.4. Suppose $|\psi\rangle = \alpha|0\rangle + \beta|1\rangle$. If $|\psi\rangle$ changes to $|\phi\rangle = \alpha|0\rangle - \beta|1\rangle$, then $|\psi\rangle$ undergoes a phase flip. Clearly, $|\phi\rangle = \sigma_z|\psi\rangle$, where $\sigma_z = \begin{bmatrix} 1 & 0 \\ 0 & -1 \end{bmatrix}$.

Definition 8.5. Let $|\psi\rangle = \alpha|0\rangle + \beta|1\rangle$ be the qubit to be transmitted. If there exists a protocol where the sender Alice encodes $|\psi\rangle$ as $\alpha|+\rangle^{\otimes k} + \beta|-\rangle^{\otimes k}$, and during transmission at most k_2 ($k_2 \leq k$) qubits undergo phase flips, and the receiver Bob decodes the received quantum state to obtain $|\psi\rangle$, then this protocol is called a (k_2, k) phase-flip protocol, where k and k_2 are positive integers.

Theorem 8.3. *If Alice sends $|\psi\rangle = \alpha|0\rangle + \beta|1\rangle$ to Bob through a noisy channel, then there exists a $(1, 3)$ phase-flip protocol that Alice transmits the qubit to Bob.*

Proof. First, Alice uses the circuit in Fig. 8.4 to encode the quantum state $|\psi\rangle = \alpha|0\rangle + \beta|1\rangle$ as

$$\alpha|+\rangle|+\rangle|+\rangle + \beta|-\rangle|-\rangle|-\rangle, \tag{8.9}$$

and then sends the encoded quantum state $\alpha|+\rangle|+\rangle|+\rangle+\beta|-\rangle|-\rangle|-\rangle$ to Bob through a noisy channel. During the transmission, one of the qubits in this quantum state may undergo a phase flip.

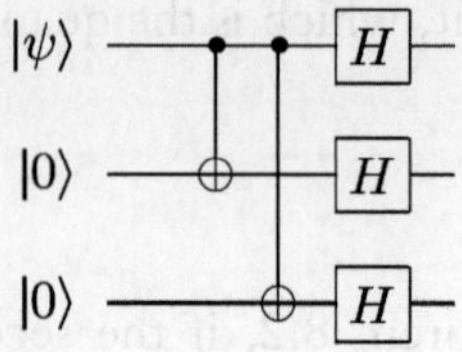

Figure 8.4 Quantum phase-flip encoding circuit.

During the transmission of the quantum state $\alpha|+\rangle|+\rangle|+\rangle+\beta|-\rangle|-\rangle|-\rangle$ through the channel, if a qubit undergoes a phase flip, it is equivalent to the operator σ_z acting on that qubit. The action of the operator σ_z on the basis $\{|+\rangle, |-\rangle\}$ is as follows:

$$\sigma_z|+\rangle = |-\rangle, \quad \sigma_z|-\rangle = |+\rangle. \tag{8.10}$$

If Bob receives the quantum state sent by Alice through the noisy channel, he can decode it using the circuit in Fig. 8.5.

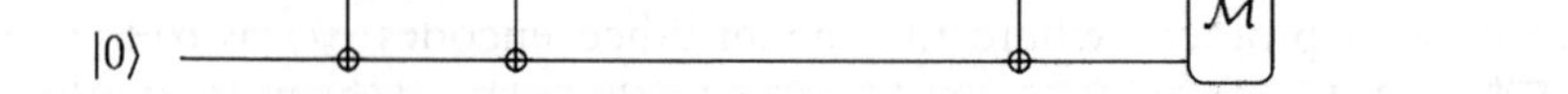

Figure 8.5 Quantum phase-flip decoding circuit.

First, Bob applies the Hadamard transform to each qubit of the received quantum state, transforming the received state $|+\rangle$ to $|0\rangle$ and the received state $|-\rangle$ to $|1\rangle$. At this point, let $\alpha|abc\rangle+\beta|\neg a\neg b\neg c\rangle$. Then, similar to the quantum bit-flip error correction process, he uses the check code to detect errors. If the check code is 00, it indicates that no qubit has undergone a phase flip; if the result is 01, it indicates that the first qubit has undergone a phase flip; if the result is 10, it indicates that the second qubit has undergone a phase flip; if the result is 11, it indicates that the third qubit has undergone a phase flip. Finally, to decode, if a qubit has undergone a phase flip, he applies the operator σ_z to that qubit to restore the original quantum state $|\psi\rangle$ that Alice intended to send. This completes the proof. □

Exercises

8.5. In the proof of Theorem 8.3, if the first qubit of the quantum state $\alpha|+\rangle|+\rangle|+\rangle + \beta|-\rangle|-\rangle|-\rangle$ encoded by Alice undergoes a phase flip, write out the evolution process of the quantum state during the decoding stage by Bob.

8.6. In the proof of Theorem 8.3, if the second qubit of the quantum state $\alpha|+\rangle|+\rangle|+\rangle + \beta|-\rangle|-\rangle|-\rangle$ encoded by Alice undergoes a phase flip, write out the evolution process of the quantum state during the decoding stage by Bob.

8.4 Shor code

A natural question is whether there is a method to simultaneously correct both quantum bit-flip errors and quantum phase-flip errors. The answer is yes, and this can be achieved by cascading quantum phase-flip error correction with quantum bit-flip error correction. A related theorem is presented in the following, and its proof involves the construction of a class of quantum codes known as Shor codes [1].

Definition 8.6. Let $|\psi\rangle = \alpha|0\rangle + \beta|1\rangle$ be the qubit to be transmitted. If there exists a protocol in which the sender Alice encodes $|\psi\rangle$ as

$$\alpha\frac{(|0\rangle^{\otimes k} + |1\rangle^{\otimes k})^{\otimes m}}{(\sqrt{2})^m} + \beta\frac{(|0\rangle^{\otimes k} - |1\rangle^{\otimes k})^{\otimes m}}{(\sqrt{2})^m},$$

where m is the number of blocks and k is the number of qubits per block, and during transmission, each block undergoes at most k_1 bit-flip errors, and at most one block among the m blocks undergoes k_2 phase-flip errors, then the receiver Bob can decode the received quantum state to obtain $|\psi\rangle$. This protocol is called a $(k_1, k_2, m[k])$ bit-phase flip protocol, where k, m, k_1 $(k_1 \leq k)$, and k_2 $(k_2 \leq k)$ are positive integers.

Theorem 8.4. *If Alice sends the qubit* $|\psi\rangle = \alpha|0\rangle + \beta|1\rangle$ *to Bob through a noisy channel, there exists a* $(1, 1, 3[3])$ *bit-phase flip protocol that Alice transmits* $|\psi\rangle$ *to Bob.*

Proof. First, Alice uses a quantum phase-flip error correction code to encode $|0\rangle$ and $|1\rangle$ as follows:

$$|0\rangle \to |+++\rangle, \tag{8.11}$$

$$|1\rangle \to |---\rangle. \tag{8.12}$$

Then Alice uses a quantum bit-flip error correction code to encode $|+\rangle$ and $|-\rangle$ as follows:

$$|+\rangle = \frac{|0\rangle + |1\rangle}{\sqrt{2}} \to \frac{|000\rangle + |111\rangle}{\sqrt{2}}, \tag{8.13}$$

$$|-\rangle = \frac{|0\rangle - |1\rangle}{\sqrt{2}} \to \frac{|000\rangle - |111\rangle}{\sqrt{2}}. \tag{8.14}$$

Thus Alice encodes the quantum state $\alpha|0\rangle + \beta|1\rangle$ as

$$\begin{aligned} &\alpha\frac{(|000\rangle + |111\rangle)(|000\rangle + |111\rangle)(|000\rangle + |111\rangle)}{2\sqrt{2}} \\ &+\beta\frac{(|000\rangle - |111\rangle)(|000\rangle - |111\rangle)(|000\rangle - |111\rangle)}{2\sqrt{2}}, \end{aligned} \tag{8.15}$$

which is generally referred to as the Shor code.

Alice can complete the encoding of the Shor code using the circuit shown in Fig. 8.6. This encoding circuit cascades the quantum phase-flip error correction code with the quantum bit-flip error correction code, which is one of the methods to construct new quantum error correction codes.

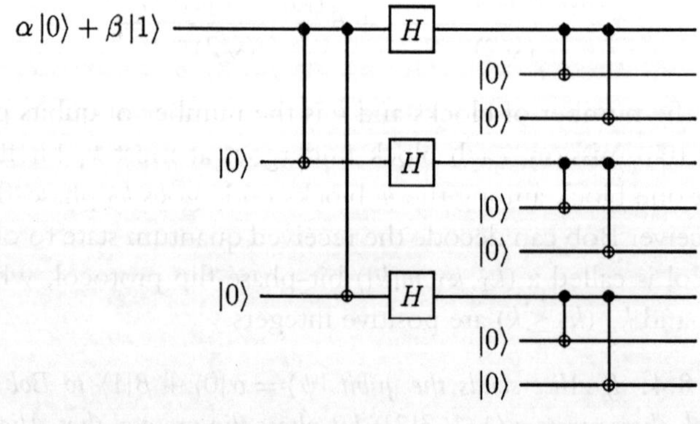

Figure 8.6 Encoding circuit of Shor code.

After completing the encoding, Alice sends the Shor code to Bob through a noisy channel. During transmission, one of the qubits in the Shor code may undergo a bit flip, another may undergo a phase flip, or a certain qubit in the Shor code may simultaneously undergo both a bit flip and a phase flip. After receiving the potentially erroneous quantum state, Bob decodes it using the circuit shown in Fig. 8.7 to retrieve the original quantum state $|\psi\rangle$ that Alice sent.

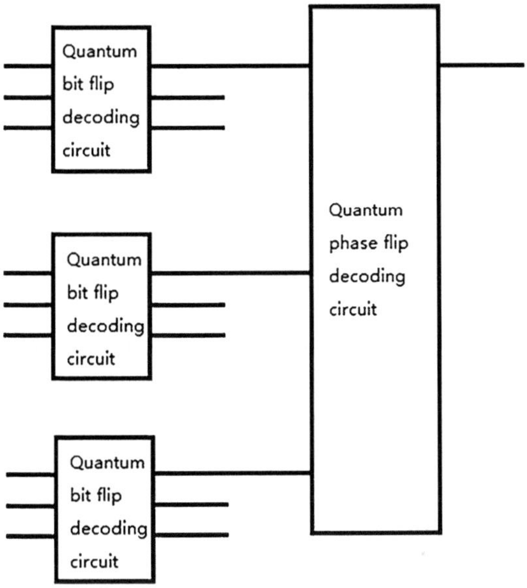

Figure 8.7 Decoding circuit of Shor code.

In the Shor code decoding circuit shown in Fig. 8.7, the specific details of the quantum bit flip decoding circuit are illustrated in Fig. 8.3, and the specific details of the quantum phase-flip decoding circuit are illustrated in Fig. 8.5.

During the decoding phase, Bob will divide the received 9 qubits into 3 groups, each containing 3 qubits. Specifically, the 1st, 2nd, and 3rd qubits form the 1st group, the 4th, 5th, and 6th qubits form the 2nd group, and the 7th, 8th, and 9th qubits form the 3rd group.

First, Bob applies the quantum bit-flip decoding circuit to each group to perform quantum bit-flip error correction. Then, since a phase flip on any one qubit within a group has an equivalent effect on that group, it is sufficient to perform quantum phase-flip error correction on any single qubit from any of the three groups. In the Shor code decoding circuit shown in Fig. 8.7, the first qubit from each group is selected, specifically the 1st, 4th, and 7th qubits of the Shor code, as the input. Finally, after applying the quantum phase flip decoding circuit, Bob can recover the original quantum state $|\psi\rangle$ that Alice sent. □

Remark 8.1. The Shor code can also simultaneously correct bit-flip errors on any single qubit within each group, as well as phase-flip errors on any number of qubits within any single group.

Example 8.1. Assume the 7th qubit of the Shor code undergoes both a phase flip and a bit flip. Then the Shor code becomes

$$\begin{aligned} &\alpha\frac{(|000\rangle+|111\rangle)(|000\rangle+|111\rangle)(|100\rangle-|011\rangle)}{2\sqrt{2}} \\ &+\beta\frac{(|000\rangle-|111\rangle)(|000\rangle-|111\rangle)(|100\rangle+|011\rangle)}{2\sqrt{2}}. \end{aligned} \tag{8.16}$$

First, perform bit-flip error correction on each group to obtain three 2-bit check code, which are 00, 00, and 01, respectively. This indicates that there is no bit flip in the 1st group, no bit flip in the 2nd group, and a bit flip on the 1st qubit of the 3rd group.

Next, perform bit-flip error correction on the 1st qubit of the 3rd group, resulting in the quantum state:

$$\begin{aligned} &\alpha\frac{(|000\rangle+|111\rangle)(|000\rangle+|111\rangle)(|000\rangle-|111\rangle)}{2\sqrt{2}} \\ &+\beta\frac{(|000\rangle-|111\rangle)(|000\rangle-|111\rangle)(|000\rangle+|111\rangle)}{2\sqrt{2}}. \end{aligned} \tag{8.17}$$

Then perform phase-flip error correction to obtain a check code 11, indicating a phase-flip error in the 3rd group.

After performing phase-flip error correction on the 3rd group, the quantum state becomes

$$\begin{aligned} &\alpha\frac{(|000\rangle+|111\rangle)(|000\rangle+|111\rangle)(|000\rangle+|111\rangle)}{2\sqrt{2}} \\ &+\beta\frac{(|000\rangle-|111\rangle)(|000\rangle-|111\rangle)(|000\rangle-|111\rangle)}{2\sqrt{2}}, \end{aligned} \tag{8.18}$$

which is the Shor code.

Exercises

8.7. In the proof of Theorem 8.4, if the 1st and 5th qubits of the Shor code undergo bit flips simultaneously, and the 9th qubit undergoes a phase flip, write down the check code and the quantum state evolution process during error correction.

8.8. In the proof of Theorem 8.4, if the 3rd and 7th qubits of the Shor code undergo bit flips simultaneously, and the 5th qubit undergoes a phase flip, write down the check code and the quantum state evolution process during error correction.

8.5 Linear code

In coding theory, linear codes form the foundation for the study of various types of codes. The encoding and decoding schemes of linear codes are very simple. In the following, we first provide a general definition of codes, followed by an introduction to concepts related to linear codes.

Definition 8.7. Let Σ be a finite set, referred to as the alphabet. A finite sequence composed of elements from Σ is called a word, and the set of all words over Σ is denoted by Σ^*. Given a subset $C \subseteq \Sigma^*$, if

$$c_1 c_2 \cdots c_m = c'_1 c'_2 \cdots c'_n \tag{8.19}$$

holds for any $c_1, c_2, \cdots, c_m, c'_1, c'_2, \cdots, c'_n \in C$, it necessarily follows that $c_i = c'_i$ $(1 \leq i \leq n)$ and $m = n$, then C is called a code over the alphabet Σ.

Let C be a code over Σ. If $|\Sigma| = q$, then C is called a q-ary code. Words in the code are called codewords. The number of elements in a codeword is referred to as the codeword length. If all codewords in the code have the same length, it is called a fixed-length code; otherwise, it is called a variable-length code.

Example 8.2. Let the alphabet $\Sigma = \{0, 1\}$, and $C = \{0, 10, 110, 111\}$. It is easy to see that C is a binary variable-length code over Σ. Its codewords are $0, 10, 110, 111$, with lengths of $1, 2, 3, 3$, respectively.

Example 8.3. Let the alphabet $\Sigma = \{0, 1\}$, and $C = \{0, 11, 011\}$. According to the definition of a code, C is not a code.

Definition 8.8. Let F be a non-empty set, and the members of F are called elements. Suppose that two operations, addition and multiplication, are defined in F. For any two elements a and b in F, the result of the addition operation is denoted by $a+b$, and the result of the multiplication operation is denoted by $a \cdot b$. The set F is closed under the operations of addition and multiplication, meaning that for any $a, b \in F$, we have $a+b \in F$ and $a \cdot b \in F$. If the following operational rules are satisfied:

(1) For any $a, b \in F$,

$$a+b=b+a \quad \text{(commutative law of addition);} \tag{8.20}$$

(2) For any $a, b, c \in F$,

$$(a+b)+c=a+(b+c) \quad \text{(associative law of addition);} \tag{8.21}$$

(3) There exists an element in F, denoted by 0, with the property

$$a+0=a, \forall a \in F; \tag{8.22}$$

(4) For any $a \in F$, there exists an element $-a$ in F with the property

$$a+(-a)=0; \tag{8.23}$$

(5) For any $a, b \in F$,

$$a \cdot b=b \cdot a \quad \text{(commutative law of multiplication);} \tag{8.24}$$

(6) For any $a, b, c \in F$,

$$(a \cdot b) \cdot c=a \cdot (b \cdot c) \quad \text{(associative law of multiplication);} \tag{8.25}$$

(7) There exists a non-zero element in F, denoted by 1, with the property

$$a \cdot 1=a, \forall a \in F; \tag{8.26}$$

(8) For any $a \in F$, where $a \neq 0$, there exists an element a^{-1} in F with the property

$$a \cdot a^{-1}=1; \tag{8.27}$$

(9) For any $a, b, c \in F$,

$$a \cdot (b+c)=a \cdot b+a \cdot c \quad \text{(distributive law);} \tag{8.28}$$

then F is called a field with respect to the defined operations of addition and multiplication.

Definition 8.9. If the number of elements in the field F is finite, then F is called a finite field.

Example 8.4. If p is a prime number, then the set $\{0, 1, 2, \cdots, p-1\}$ forms a finite field under addition modulo p and multiplication modulo p, denoted as GF(p).

In the following text, let the alphabet Σ be GF(p), where GF(p) denotes the finite field with p elements. Let $V(n, p)$ represent the n-dimensional vector space over GF(p). Any $a \in V(n, p)$ has the following form: $a = (a_1, a_2, \cdots, a_n)^T$, where $a_i \in \mathrm{GF}(p)$, $i = 1, 2, \cdots, n$.

The definition of Hamming distance is provided in the following.

Definition 8.10. Let $x, y \in V(n, p)$. The Hamming distance between x and y, denoted as $d_H(x, y)$, is defined as the number of positions at which they differ. If $x = x_1x_2 \cdots x_n$ and $y = y_1y_2 \cdots y_n$, then

$$d_H(x, y) = |\{i \mid x_i \neq y_i, 1 \leq i \leq n\}|. \tag{8.29}$$

Example 8.5. Let $x, y \in V(7, 2)$, with $x = 1010101$ and $y = 0001111$. It is easy to obtain $d_H(x, y) = 4$. In $V(7, 3)$, $d_H(0120120, 0011222) = 5$.

Theorem 8.5. *For any $x, y, z \in V(n, p)$, the Hamming distance satisfies the following properties:*

(1) *Non-negativity: $d_H(x, y) \geq 0$, and $d_H(x, y) = 0$ if and only if $x = y$;*

(2) *Symmetry: $d_H(x, y) = d_H(y, x)$;*

(3) *Triangle inequality: $d_H(x, y) \leq d_H(x, z) + d_H(y, z)$.*

From Theorem 8.5, it is known that $V(n, p)$ is a metric space, which is also referred to as Hamming space.

Now, we consider the decoding problem and provide the definition of nearest-neighbor decoding.

Definition 8.11. Let $C \subseteq V(n, p)$ be a code. After transmitting $x \in C$ through the channel, the received vector at the receiving end is y. The vector y is decoded to the codeword $z' \in C$ that has the smallest Hamming distance to y, that is, $z' \in \{z \mid \min_{z \in C} d_H(z, y)\}$, which is referred to as nearest-neighbor decoding.

Example 8.6. Let $C = \{000, 111\} \subseteq V(3, 2)$, and let $x = 000$ be a codeword in C. Assume that after the codeword x is transmitted through the channel, the received vector at the receiving end is $y = 001$. According to nearest-neighbor decoding, the vector y is decoded to the codeword 000 in C.

The minimum distance of a code is an important parameter that characterizes the error-correcting performance of the code. The minimum distance of a code is defined as follows.

Definition 8.12. Let $C \subseteq V(n,p)$ be a code. Its minimum distance is defined as the minimum Hamming distance between any two different codewords in C, denoted as $d(C)$, that is,

$$d(C) = \min_{x,y \in C, x \neq y} d_H(x,y). \tag{8.30}$$

Example 8.7. Let the code $C = \{000, 001, 010\} \subseteq V(3,2)$. It is easy to obtain that the minimum distance of C is 1.

Definition 8.13. Let $C \subseteq V(n,p)$ be a code. After transmitting $x \in C$ through the noisy channel, the receiver obtains $y \in V(n,p)$, if $d_H(x,y) = t$, it is said that x has incurred t errors. If the vector y can be decoded as x, then C is said to be able to completely correct t errors in x.

A theorem regarding the relationship between the minimum distance of a code and its error-correcting capability is presented here.

Theorem 8.6. *Let $C \subseteq V(n,p)$ be a code. The necessary and sufficient condition for C to correct at most t errors is $d(C) = 2t+1$ or $d(C) = 2t+2$.*

Proof. First, we prove the sufficiency. Let $d(C) = 2t+1$ or $2t+2$. When the codeword x is sent through a noisy channel, it becomes the vector y, and if $d_H(x,y) \leq t$, then for any $x' \in C$ with $x' \neq x$, according to the triangle inequality property of the Hamming distance, we have

$$d_H(x,y) + d_H(y,x') \geq d_H(x,x') \tag{8.31}$$
$$\geq d(C) \tag{8.32}$$
$$\geq 2t+1. \tag{8.33}$$

Therefore we have

$$d_H(y,x') \geq 2t+1 - d_H(x,y) \tag{8.34}$$
$$\geq t+1 \tag{8.35}$$
$$> d_H(x,y). \tag{8.36}$$

According to nearest-neighbor decoding, the vector y will most likely be decoded as the codeword x.

Now we prove that the code C cannot correct $t+1$ errors. Since $d(C) = 2t+1$ or $2t+2$, there exist $x = x_1x_2\cdots x_n \in C$ and $x' = x'_1x'_2\cdots x'_n \in C$ such that $d_H(x, x') = d(C) = 2t+1$ or $2t+2$.

If $d_H(x, x') = d(C) = 2t+1$, without loss of generality, let

$$x_i \neq x'_i, i = 1, \cdots, 2t+1; \tag{8.37}$$

$$x_j = x'_j, j = 2t+2, \cdots, n. \tag{8.38}$$

Consider $y = y_1y_2\cdots y_n$, and

$$y_i = \begin{cases} x_i, & \text{if } 1 \le i \le t, \\ x'_i, & \text{if } t+1 \le i \le 2t+1, \\ x_i = x'_i, & \text{if } 2t+2 \le i \le n. \end{cases} \tag{8.39}$$

Clearly, we have

$$d_H(y, x) = t+1 \text{ and } d_H(y, x') = t. \tag{8.40}$$

From Eq. (8.40), we obtain

$$d_H(y, x') < d_H(y, x). \tag{8.41}$$

According to nearest-neighbor decoding, the vector y is highly likely to be decoded as the codeword x', rather than being correctly decoded as the codeword x. In other words, the code C cannot correct $t+1$ errors. If $d_H(x, x') = d(C) = 2t+2$, without loss of generality, let

$$x_i \neq x'_i, i = 1, \cdots, 2t+2; \tag{8.42}$$

$$x_j = x'_j, j = 2t+3, \cdots, n. \tag{8.43}$$

Let $y = y_1y_2\cdots y_n$, and

$$y_i = \begin{cases} x_i\ , & 1 \le i \le t+1, \\ x'_i\ , & t+2 \le i \le 2t+2, \\ x_i = x'_i\ , & 2t+3 \le i \le n. \end{cases} \tag{8.44}$$

Clearly, we have

$$d_H(y, x) = t+1 \text{ and } d_H(y, x') = t+1. \tag{8.45}$$

From Eq. (8.45), we have

$$d_H(y, x') = d_H(y, x). \tag{8.46}$$

According to the nearest-neighbor decoding, the vector y could be decoded as the codeword x' or as the codeword x. This implies that the code C cannot fully correct $t+1$ errors. In summary, the code C can correct at most t errors. Now, we prove the necessity. If the code C can correct at most t errors, then it must hold that

$$2t+1 \leq d(C) \leq 2t+2. \tag{8.47}$$

Otherwise, if $d(C) \geq 2t+3 = 2(t+1)+1$, then by sufficiency, the code C could correct $t+1$ errors, which contradicts the fact that the code C can correct at most t errors. On the other hand, if $d(C) \leq 2t$, then by sufficiency, the number of errors the code C can correct is at most $t-1$, which also contradicts the fact that the code C can correct at most t errors. Therefore $d(C) = 2t+1$ or $d(C) = 2t+2$, which completes the proof of the theorem. □

Next, we discuss an important class of codes—linear codes. First, we present a proposition.

Proposition 8.1. *If C is a subspace of $V(n, p)$, then C is a p-ary linear code.*

Definition 8.14. If $C \subseteq V(n, p)$ is a p-ary linear code of dimension k, then C is called a p-ary $[n, k]$ linear code. If the minimum distance of the p-ary $[n, k]$ linear code is d, then it is called a p-ary $[n, k, d]$ linear code.

Example 8.8. $C = \{0000000, 0001111, 0110011, 1010101, 0111100, 1011010, 1100110, 1101001\}$ is a binary $[7, 3, 4]$ linear code.

Since a p-ary $[n, k]$ linear code C is a k-dimensional subspace of $V(n, p)$, it is sufficient to provide a set of basis vectors of C to completely generate the linear code C. The definition of the generator matrix is given as follows.

Definition 8.15. Let C be a p-ary $[n, k]$ linear code. The elements of a basis of C are arranged as row vectors to form a $k \times n$ matrix G, which is called the generator matrix of the linear code C.

Example 8.9. A binary $[3, 1]$ linear code

$$C = \{000, 111\}$$

has the generator matrix $G = \begin{bmatrix} 1 & 1 & 1 \end{bmatrix}$.

Example 8.10. A binary [7, 4, 3] linear code

$$\begin{aligned} C = \{&0000000, 0001111, 0110011, 1010101, \\ &0111100, 1011010, 1100110, 1101001, \\ &1111111, 1110000, 1001100, 0101010, \\ &1000011, 0100101, 0011001, 0010110\} \end{aligned} \tag{8.48}$$

has a generator matrix given by

$$G = \begin{bmatrix} 1 & 0 & 0 & 0 & 0 & 1 & 1 \\ 0 & 1 & 0 & 0 & 1 & 0 & 1 \\ 0 & 0 & 1 & 0 & 1 & 1 & 0 \\ 0 & 0 & 0 & 1 & 1 & 1 & 1 \end{bmatrix}. \tag{8.49}$$

The definition of the coset of a linear code is provided as follows.

Definition 8.16. Let C be a p-ary $[n, k]$ linear code. For any $a \in V(n, p)$, define

$$a + C = \{a + x \mid x \in C\}, \tag{8.50}$$

then $a + C$ is called a coset of C.

Example 8.11. For a binary [2, 1] linear code $C = \{00, 11\}$ over $V(2, 2)$, there are two cosets, namely $\{00, 11\}$ and $\{01, 10\}$.

The vector inner product operation on the vector space $V(n, p)$ is defined as follows.

Let $x = x_1x_2 \cdots x_n$ and $y = y_1y_2 \cdots y_n \in V(n, p)$. The inner product of x and y is defined as

$$x \cdot y = x_1y_1 + x_2y_2 + \cdots + x_ny_n, \tag{8.51}$$

where the operations on the right-hand side are performed modulo p. For any $x, y \in V(n, p)$, if the inner product $x \cdot y = 0$, then x and y are said to be orthogonal.

In the following paragraphs, we introduce dual codes.

Proposition 8.2. *Let C be a p-ary $[n, k]$ linear code. Define*

$$C^{\perp} = \{x \in V(n, p) \mid \forall y \in C,\ x \cdot y = 0\}, \tag{8.52}$$

then $C^{\perp}$ is a subspace of $V(n, p)$, and it is called the dual code of C.

Proof. It is easy to prove that $C^{\perp}$ is a subspace of $V(n,p)$ due to the closure properties of addition and scalar multiplication. □

Example 8.12. Given a binary $[7,4,3]$ linear code

$$\begin{aligned} C = \{&0000000, 0001111, 0110011, 1010101, \\ &0111100, 1011010, 1100110, 1101001, \\ &1111111, 1110000, 1001100, 0101010, \\ &1000011, 0100101, 0011001, 0010110\}, \end{aligned} \tag{8.53}$$

it can be verified that

$$\begin{aligned} C^{\perp} = \{&0000000, 0001111, 0110011, 1010101, \\ &0111100, 1011010, 1100110, 1101001\}. \end{aligned} \tag{8.54}$$

In fact, $C^{\perp}$ is a binary $[7,3,4]$ linear code.

The definition of the parity-check matrix is provided as follows.

Definition 8.17. If C is a p-ary $[n,k]$ linear code, then the generator matrix of $C^{\perp}$ is called the parity-check matrix of C.

Since the basis of the dual code $C^{\perp}$ is not unique, the parity-check matrix of C is also not unique.

Proposition 8.3. *Let C be a p-ary $[n,k]$ linear code. The following conclusions hold:*

(1) *The parity-check matrix of C is an $(n-k)\times n$ matrix.*
(2) *If H is a parity-check matrix of C, then we have*

$$C = \{x \in V(n,q) \mid xH^T = \mathbf{0}\}. \tag{8.55}$$

The proof of this proposition is left as an exercise.

Example 8.13. Let $C = \{0000000, 0001111, 0110011, 1010101, 0111100, 1011010, 1100110, 1101001\}$ be a binary $[7,3,4]$ linear code. One possible parity-check matrix for this code is

$$H = \begin{bmatrix} 1 & 0 & 0 & 0 & 0 & 1 & 1 \\ 0 & 1 & 0 & 0 & 1 & 0 & 1 \\ 0 & 0 & 1 & 0 & 1 & 1 & 0 \\ 0 & 0 & 0 & 1 & 1 & 1 & 1 \end{bmatrix}. \tag{8.56}$$

Proposition 8.4. *Let C be a binary [n, k] linear code. Then we have*

$$\sum_{y\in C}(-1)^{x\cdot y} = \begin{cases} |C|, & x \in C^{\perp}; \\ 0, & x \notin C^{\perp}. \end{cases} \tag{8.57}$$

Proof. When $x \in C^{\perp}$, for any $y \in C$, we have $(-1)^{x\cdot y} = 1$. Thus $\sum_{y\in C}(-1)^{x\cdot y} = |C|$. When $x \notin C^{\perp}$, there exists $s \in C$ such that $x \cdot s = 1$. Let $f(y) = y + s$, for $y \in C$. Then f is a bijection from C to C. Therefore

$$\sum_{y\in C}(-1)^{x\cdot y} + \sum_{y\in C}(-1)^{x\cdot y} = \sum_{y\in C}(-1)^{x\cdot y} + \sum_{y\in C}(-1)^{x\cdot(y+s)} \tag{8.58}$$

$$= [1 + (-1)^{x\cdot s}]\sum_{y\in C}(-1)^{x\cdot y} \tag{8.59}$$

$$= 0. \tag{8.60}$$

□

Hamming codes are a special type of linear code. The definition of binary Hamming codes is provided as follows.

Definition 8.18. Let r be a positive integer, and let H be an $r \times (2^r - 1)$ matrix whose column vectors are formed by all distinct non-zero vectors from $V(r, 2)$. The linear code with H as its parity-check matrix is called a binary Hamming code, denoted as $\text{Ham}(r, 2)$.

Remark 8.2. $\text{Ham}(r, 2)$ refers to any one of the equivalent codes within a certain class. In the context of equivalence, $\text{Ham}(r, 2)$ is unique. Here, equivalence means that the codes C and C' have the same parameters and both are p-ary $[n, k, d]$ linear codes.

Clearly, the code length of $\text{Ham}(r, 2)$ is $n = 2^r - 1$, and the dimension is $k = n - r = 2^r - 1 - r$. Therefore $\text{Ham}(r, 2)$ is a binary $[2^r - 1, 2^r - 1 - r]$ linear code.

Example 8.14. For $r = 3$, one of the parity-check matrices for $\text{Ham}(3, 2)$ is

$$H = \begin{bmatrix} 0 & 0 & 0 & 1 & 1 & 1 & 1 \\ 0 & 1 & 1 & 0 & 0 & 1 & 1 \\ 1 & 0 & 1 & 0 & 1 & 0 & 1 \end{bmatrix}. \tag{8.61}$$

It can be verified that the minimum distance of $\text{Ham}(3, 2)$ is 3, so $\text{Ham}(3, 2)$ is a binary $[7, 4, 3]$ linear code.

Exercises

8.9. Prove that the three properties regarding Hamming distance in Theorem 8.5 hold.

8.10. Let $C=\{1100, 1010, 1001, 0110, 0101, 0011\}$ be a binary code. Find the minimum distance of code C.

8.11. Prove that the two conclusions of Proposition 8.3 hold.

8.12. Let C be a q-ary $[n, k]$ linear code with its generator matrix G and parity-check matrix H. Prove that $GH^T=0$.

8.13. Let C be a q-ary $[3, 1]$ linear code with its generator matrix $G=\begin{bmatrix}1 & 1 & 1\end{bmatrix}$. Write down the parity-check matrix of C.

8.6 CSS code

Between 1995 and 1997, Calderbank, Shor [2], Steane [3], and other researchers independently constructed a class of quantum codes based on classical linear codes. These codes are commonly referred to as CSS codes. In the following, we provide the definition and related theorems of CSS codes.

Definition 8.19. A complex subspace of $\mathbb{C}^{2^n}$ with a dimension greater than or equal to 1 is called a quantum code.

Definition 8.20. Let C_1 and C_2 be binary linear codes of type $[n, k_1]$ and $[n, k_2]$, respectively, with $C_2 \subseteq C_1$. For any given $x \in C_1$, denote

$$|x+C_2\rangle = \frac{1}{\sqrt{|C_2|}} \sum_{y \in C_2} |x+y\rangle, \tag{8.62}$$

and denote

$$\mathrm{CSS}(C_1, C_2) = \{|x+C_2\rangle | x \in C_1\}, \tag{8.63}$$

which is called the quantum code $\mathrm{CSS}(C_1, C_2)$.

For any $x, x' \in C_1$, let $|x'+C_2\rangle = \frac{1}{\sqrt{|C_2|}} \sum_{y' \in C_2} |x'+y'\rangle$. The inner product in $\mathrm{CSS}(C_1, C_2)$ is defined as

$$\langle x'+C_2|x+C_2\rangle = \frac{1}{|C_2|} \sum_{y', y \in C_2} \langle x'+y'|x+y\rangle.$$

Proposition 8.5. $\mathrm{CSS}(C_1, C_2)$ *is a* $[n, 2^{k_1-k_2}]$ *linear code.*

Proof. It is easy to prove that $\mathrm{CSS}(C_1, C_2)$ satisfies closure under addition and scalar multiplication. □

The cosets of C_2 in C_1 are $\{|x + C_2\rangle \mid x \in C_1\}$. Furthermore, it can be proven that the CSS code can correct t quantum bit-flip and phase-flip errors.

Theorem 8.7. *Let C_1 and C_2 be binary linear codes of $[n, k_1]$ and $[n, k_2]$, respectively. The parity-check matrices of C_1 and $C_2^{\perp}$ are respectively H_1 and H_2. If $C_2 \subseteq C_1$, and both C_1 and $C_2^{\perp}$ can correct t bit-flip errors, then the* $\mathrm{CSS}(C_1, C_2)$ *code can correct up to t quantum bit-flip errors and t phase-flip errors.*

Proof. The $\mathrm{CSS(C_1, C_2)}$ code is composed of quantum states given by

$$\frac{1}{\sqrt{|C_2|}}\sum_{y\in C_2}|x+y\rangle. \tag{8.64}$$

It is easy to prove that if $x, x' \in C_1$, and $x - x' \in C_2$, then $|x + C_2\rangle = |x' + C_2\rangle$. If $x, x' \in C_1$, and $x - x' \notin C_2$, then $|x + C_2\rangle$ and $|x' + C_2\rangle$ are orthogonal. To prove $\langle x + C_2|x' + C_2\rangle = 0$, we only need to show that $A \cap B = \varnothing$, where $A = \{x + y \mid y \in C_2\}$ and $B = \{x' + y \mid y \in C_2\}$. Thus $|x + C_2\rangle$ and $|x' + C_2\rangle$ do not share any common basis states. If $|x + C_2\rangle$ and $|x' + C_2\rangle$ are not orthogonal, then $A \cap B \neq \varnothing$. This means there exist $y, y' \in C_2$ such that $x + y = x' + y'$, leading to $x - x' = y' - y \in C_2$. This contradicts the assumption, so $|x + C_2\rangle$ and $|x' + C_2\rangle$ are orthogonal.

The following proof can use the error-correcting properties of the linear code C_1 and the linear code $C_2^{\perp}$ to detect and correct quantum errors.

First, use an n-bit vector e_b to describe quantum bit-flip errors across n qubits, and an n-bit vector e_p to describe quantum phase-flip errors across n qubits, where a component value of 1 indicates that the corresponding qubit has flipped, and 0 indicates no flip. Since both C_1 and $C_2^{\perp}$ can correct up to t bit-flip and t phase-flip errors, we have $|e_b| \leq t$ and $|e_p| \leq t$.

If the state $|x+C_2\rangle$ undergoes bit-flip and phase-flip errors, it transforms into

$$\frac{1}{\sqrt{|C_2|}}\sum_{y\in C_2}(-1)^{(x+y)\cdot e_p}|x+y+e_b\rangle. \tag{8.65}$$

To detect bit-flip errors, we introduce auxiliary qubits $|0\rangle$ to store the check bits of C_1.

By applying the check matrix H_1 of C_1, the quantum state $|x+y+e_b\rangle|0\rangle$ is transformed into the quantum state $|x+y+e_b\rangle|H_1(x+y+e_b)\rangle$.

Since $x+y \in C_1$, we have $|x+y+e_b\rangle|H_1(x+y+e_b)\rangle = |x+y+e_b\rangle|H_1 e_b\rangle$. Therefore after the application of the check matrix H_1, we obtain the following state:

$$\frac{1}{\sqrt{|C_2|}} \sum_{y \in C_2} (-1)^{(x+y)\cdot e_p} |x+y+e_b\rangle|H_1 e_b\rangle. \tag{8.66}$$

By measuring the auxiliary qubits and obtaining the result $H_1 e_b$, a bit-flip error is detected. Discarding the auxiliary qubits, we obtain the following state:

$$\frac{1}{\sqrt{|C_2|}} \sum_{y \in C_2} (-1)^{(x+y)\cdot e_p} |x+y+e_b\rangle. \tag{8.67}$$

Since C_1 can correct t bit-flip errors, e_b can be uniquely determined from the syndrome $H_1 e_b$. The specific process is as follows: there exists an $m \in V(n,2)$ such that $H_1 e_b = H_1 m$, which implies $H_1(m - e_b) = 0$. Let $m - e_b = h$, then $h \in C_1$. Further, h is transformed into m by the bit-flip error e_b. Since $|e_b| \leq t$, and C_1 can correct up to t bit-flip errors, m is corrected to h, from which e_b is obtained, completing the error detection process.

Then apply a NOT gate to the bit positions indicated by e_b. After correcting the bit-flip errors, the following state is obtained:

$$\frac{1}{\sqrt{|C_2|}} \sum_{y \in C_2} (-1)^{(x+y)\cdot e_p} |x+y\rangle. \tag{8.68}$$

Next, to detect phase-flip errors, we apply the Hadamard transform to each qubit, resulting in the following state:

$$\frac{1}{\sqrt{|C_2| 2^n}} \sum_{z \in \{0,1\}^n} \sum_{y \in C_2} (-1)^{(x+y)\cdot(e_p+z)} |z\rangle. \tag{8.69}$$

Let $z' \equiv z + e_p$. The state in Eq. (8.69) can be expressed as follows:

$$\frac{1}{\sqrt{|C_2| 2^n}} \sum_{z' \in \{0,1\}^n} \sum_{y \in C_2} (-1)^{(x+y)\cdot z'} |z' + e_p\rangle. \tag{8.70}$$

Since

$$\sum_{y\in C_2}(-1)^{y\cdot z'}=\begin{cases}|C_2|, & z'\in C_2^{\perp},\\ 0, & z'\notin C_2^{\perp}.\end{cases} \tag{8.71}$$

The state in Eq. (8.70) can be expressed as follows:

$$\sqrt{\frac{|C_2|}{2^n}}\sum_{z'\in C_2^{\perp}}(-1)^{x\cdot z'}|z'+e_p\rangle. \tag{8.72}$$

From Eq. (8.72), it can be seen that after the Hadamard transform, a phase-flip error can be converted into a bit-flip error.

By applying the parity-check matrix H_2 of $C_2^{\perp}$, we obtain the syndrome H_2e_p. Based on the syndrome H_2e_p, the error e_p can be uniquely determined. The specific process is as follows: there exists an $a\in V(n,2)$ such that $H_2e_p=H_2a$, which implies $H_2(a-e_p)=0$. Let $a-e_p=h'$. Then $h'\in C_2^{\perp}$. Furthermore, h' becomes a after the bit-flip error e_p. Since $|e_p|\le t$ and $C_2^{\perp}$ can correct t bit-flip errors, we can obtain h' by correcting a, and thus determine e_p, completing the error detection.

Correcting the error bits indicated by e_p, we obtain the following state:

$$\sqrt{\frac{|C_2|}{2^n}}\sum_{z'\in C_2^{\perp}}(-1)^{x\cdot z'}|z'\rangle. \tag{8.73}$$

Finally, apply the Hadamard transform to each qubit to complete the error correction.

Equivalently, this is the result of applying the Hadamard transform to the quantum state represented by Eq. (8.72) when $e_p=0$. Since the Hadamard transform is its own inverse, the transformation yields the quantum state in Eq. (8.68) when $e_p=0$, namely

$$\frac{1}{\sqrt{|C_2|}}\sum_{y\in C_2}|x+y\rangle. \tag{8.74}$$

This results in the quantum state in Eq. (8.64) through error correction. The proof of the theorem is completed. □

Example 8.15. Let C_1 be a binary $[7,4,3]$ linear code,

$$\begin{aligned}C_1 = \{&0000000, 0001111, 0110011, 1010101,\\ &0111100, 1011010, 1100110, 1101001,\\ &1111111, 1110000, 1001100, 0101010,\\ &1000011, 0100101, 0011001, 0010110\}.\end{aligned} \tag{8.75}$$

It can correct at most 1 bit-flip error, and let C_2 be the dual code of C_1. Then the CSS(C_1, C_2) is a [7, 2] quantum error correction code, which can correct 1 bit-flip error and phase-flip error. This CSS(C_1, C_2) quantum code is referred to as the Steane code, and its encoding is as follows:

$$\begin{aligned}|0000000 + C_2\rangle = \frac{1}{\sqrt{8}}(&|0000000\rangle + |0001111\rangle + |0110011\rangle + |1010101\rangle\\ &+ |0111100\rangle + |1011010\rangle + |1100110\rangle + |1101001\rangle),\end{aligned} \tag{8.76}$$

$$\begin{aligned}|1111111 + C_2\rangle = \frac{1}{\sqrt{8}}(&|1111111\rangle + |1110000\rangle + |1001100\rangle + |0101010\rangle\\ &+ |1000011\rangle + |0100101\rangle + |0011001\rangle + |0010110\rangle).\end{aligned} \tag{8.77}$$

Exercises

8.14. Let C_1 be the binary [7, 4, 3] linear code from Example 8.15, and let C_2 be the dual code of C_1. Prove:

(1) If $x, x' \in C_1$ and $x - x' \in C_2$, then $|x + C_2\rangle = |x' + C_2\rangle$;

(2) If $x, x' \in C_1$ and $x - x' \notin C_2$, then $|x + C_2\rangle$ and $|x' + C_2\rangle$ are orthogonal.

8.15. Let C_1 be the binary [7, 4, 3] linear code from Example 8.15, and let C_2 be the dual code of C_1. Write out all the cosets of C_2 in C_1.

8.16. Let C_1 be the binary [7, 4, 3] linear code from Example 8.15, and let C_2 be the dual code of C_1. For the CSS(C_1, C_2)[7, 2] quantum code, if the first qubit undergoes a bit-flip and the seventh qubit undergoes a phase-flip, write out the evolution process of the quantum state during the error correction stage according to Theorem 8.7.

8.7 * Stabilizer code

From 1996 to 1997, Gottesman, Calderbank, and others [4–6] discovered the group structure of quantum error-correcting codes, introduced the concept of stabilizers, and developed a systematic theory for the construction of quantum error-correcting codes. Next, the fundamental theory of stabilizer codes is introduced.

First, we provide an example related to the concept of stabilizers.

Example 8.16. For the quantum state

$$|\psi\rangle = \frac{|00\rangle + |11\rangle}{\sqrt{2}}, \tag{8.78}$$

it can be verified that it satisfies

$$(X \otimes X)|\psi\rangle = |\psi\rangle, \tag{8.79}$$

$$(Z \otimes Z)|\psi\rangle = |\psi\rangle. \tag{8.80}$$

The state $|\psi\rangle$ is said to be stabilized by the operators $X \otimes X$ and $Z \otimes Z$.

A concept closely related to stabilizers is the Pauli operator group. Under matrix multiplication, the matrices formed by multiplying Pauli matrices by ± 1 and $\pm i$ constitute a group, known as the single-qubit Pauli operator group, denoted as

$$G_1 \equiv \{\pm I, \pm iI, \pm X, \pm iX, \pm Y, \pm iY, \pm Z, \pm iZ\}. \tag{8.81}$$

Furthermore, under matrix multiplication, the n-qubit Pauli operator group is denoted as

$$G_n \equiv \{P_1 \otimes P_2 \otimes \cdots \otimes P_n \mid P_j \in G_1, j = 1, 2, \cdots, n\}. \tag{8.82}$$

The definition of a stabilizer is provided as follows.

Definition 8.21. Assume $S \subseteq G_n$ is a subgroup, and V_S is the vector space composed of n-qubit quantum states. If for any $|\psi\rangle \in V_S$ and any $T \in S$, it holds that $|\psi\rangle = T|\psi\rangle$, then V_S is said to be stabilized by S, and S is referred to as the stabilizer of V_S.

The definition of a generating set for a group is provided as follows.

Definition 8.22. Suppose G is a group with multiplication denoted by $\cdot$, and $g_1, \cdots, g_l$ are elements in G. If for any $g \in G$, there exist $g_1, \cdots, g_l$ such that $g = g_1 \cdot g_2 \cdot \ldots \cdot g_l$, then $g_1, \cdots, g_l$ are called a generating set for the group G, denoted as $G = \langle g_1, \cdots, g_l \rangle$.

Example 8.17. Let $S = \{I \otimes I \otimes I, Z_1 \otimes Z_2 \otimes I, I \otimes Z_2 \otimes Z_3, Z_1 \otimes I \otimes Z_3\}$ be a set that forms a group under matrix multiplication. Since $Z_1 \otimes I \otimes Z_3 = (Z_1 \otimes Z_2 \otimes I)(I \otimes Z_2 \otimes Z_3)$ and $I = (Z_1 \otimes Z_2 \otimes I)^2$, it follows that $S = \langle Z_1 \otimes Z_2 \otimes I, I \otimes Z_2 \otimes Z_3 \rangle$.

As follows, the definition of an independent generating set is provided.

Definition 8.23. Let G be a group with the group operation denoted by $\cdot$. If a generating set of G is $g_1, \ldots, g_l$, and removing any element g_i from $g_1, \ldots, g_l$ results in the condition that

$$\langle g_1, \cdots, g_{i-1}, g_{i+1}, \cdots, g_l \rangle \neq \langle g_1, \cdots, g_l \rangle, \tag{8.83}$$

then $g_1, \ldots, g_l$ is called an independent generating set.

The definition of elements commuting in a group is given as follows.

Definition 8.24. Let G be a group with the group operation denoted by $\cdot$. If for any $g_i, g_j \in G$, it holds that $g_i \cdot g_j = g_j \cdot g_i$, then the elements g_i and g_j are said to commute with each other.

In the following paragraphs, the definition of a stabilizer code is provided.

Proposition 8.6. *Let $S \subseteq G_n$ be a subgroup. If $-I \notin S$, S has $n-k$ independent generators that commute, that is, $S = \langle g_1, \ldots, g_{n-k} \rangle$ with $-I \notin S$, then V_S is a 2^k-dimensional vector space.*

Definition 8.25. Let $S \subseteq G_n$ be a subgroup such that $-I \notin S$ and S has $n-k$ independent generators that commute, that is, $S = \langle g_1, \ldots, g_{n-k} \rangle$. The vector space V_S that is stabilized by S is referred to as a $[n, 2^k]$ stabilizer code, denoted as $C(S)$.

Example 8.18. For the Steane code with 7 qubits, a generating set for its stabilizer is constructed as follows (Fig. 8.8):

Name	Operator
g_1	IIIXXXX
g_2	IXXIIXX
g_3	XIXIXIX
g_4	$IIIZZZZ$
g_5	$IZZIIZZ$
g_6	$ZIZIZIZ$

Figure 8.8 Generators of the stabilizer of the Steane code.

Example 8.19. For the Shor code with 9 qubits, a generating set for its stabilizer is constructed as follows (Fig. 8.9):

Name	Operator
g_1	$Z Z I I I I I I I$
g_2	$I Z Z I I I I I I$
g_3	$I I I Z Z I I I I$
g_4	$I I I I Z Z I I I$
g_5	$I I I I I I Z Z I$
g_6	$I I I I I I I Z Z$
g_7	$X X X X X X I I I$
g_8	$I I I X X X X X X$

Figure 8.9 Generators of the stabilizer of the Shor code.

8.8 * Binary quantum MDS code

A quantum code is a subspace of the Hilbert space $\mathbb{C}^{2^n}$. In a quantum code, there are three fundamental parameters: the codeword length n, the dimension of the code 2^k, and the minimum distance d. In binary quantum codes, the parameters must satisfy the Singleton bound. The Singleton bound is an upper bound on the dimension 2^k of the code given n and d. A quantum maximum distance separable code, referred to as a quantum Maximum Distance Separable (MDS) code, is an important class of quantum error-correcting codes that are easy to construct, encode, and decode while also possessing strong error correction capabilities and practicality, along with a good algebraic structure. This section mainly introduces binary quantum MDS codes [7].

In quantum codes, quantum errors are typically described using unitary operators, which act on the complex vector space $\mathbb{C}^{2^n}$.

Any change to a single qubit can be represented as the action of a linear combination of Pauli operators. A quantum error on an n-qubit can be expressed in the following form:

$$\epsilon = i^{\lambda}\omega_1 \otimes \omega_2 \otimes \cdots \otimes \omega_n,$$

where $\lambda \in \{0, 1, 2, 3\}$ and $\omega_j \in \{I, \sigma_x, \sigma_y, \sigma_z\}$ for $j = 1, \cdots, n$.

All quantum errors can be constructed from the following group of operators:

$$E_n = \{i^\lambda \omega_1 \otimes \omega_2 \otimes \cdots \otimes \omega_n \mid \lambda \in \{0, 1, 2, 3\}, \omega_j \in \{I, \sigma_x, \sigma_y, \sigma_z\}\}.$$

Let $e = i^\lambda \omega_1 \otimes \omega_2 \otimes \cdots \otimes \omega_n$, $e' = i^{\lambda'} \omega'_1 \otimes \omega'_2 \otimes \cdots \otimes \omega'_n$. The operation $\cdot$ of the group E_n is defined as

$$e \cdot e' = i^{\lambda+\lambda'} \omega_1\omega'_1 \otimes \omega_2\omega'_2 \otimes \cdots \otimes \omega_i\omega'_i \cdots \otimes \omega_n\omega'_n,$$

where ω_i acts on the i-th qubit of the quantum state, with $i = 1, \ldots, n$.

Definition 8.26. Let $e \in E_n$. The quantum weight of e is defined as

$$\omega(e) = |\{j \mid 1 \le j \le n, \ \omega_j \ne I\}|.$$

Assume $\{|0\rangle, |1\rangle, \cdots, |k\rangle, \cdots, |2^n - 1\rangle\}$ is an orthonormal basis on $\mathbb{C}^{2^n}$, and $\{|0\rangle, |1\rangle, \cdots, |2^k - 1\rangle\}$ is an orthonormal basis for the quantum code Q.

Definition 8.27. Let Q be a binary quantum code. For any vector $|\mu\rangle \in Q$, we have $|\mu\rangle = |a_1\rangle \otimes |a_2\rangle \otimes \cdots \otimes |a_n\rangle$, where $a_i \in \{0, 1\}$ for $i = 1, 2, \cdots, n$. The vector $|\mu\rangle$ is called a codeword of Q, and n is referred to as the length of the code Q.

Definition 8.28. Let Q be a quantum code of length n. For any two orthogonal codewords $|\nu\rangle$ and $|\mu\rangle$ in Q (i.e., $\langle \nu|\mu\rangle = 0$), if for any $e_1, e_2 \in E_n(l) = \{e \in E_n \mid \omega(e) \le l\}$, $0 \le l \le n$, it holds that $\langle \nu|e_1e_2|\mu\rangle = 0$, then Q can correct at most l qubit errors.

Proposition 8.7. *Let Q be a quantum code of length n. If Q can correct at most l qubit errors, then for any $e \in E_n(2l)$, any two orthogonal codewords $|\nu\rangle$ and $|\mu\rangle$ in Q satisfy $\langle \nu|e|\mu\rangle = 0$.*

Theorem 8.8. *A quantum code Q can correct at most l qubit errors if and only if for every $e \in E_n(2l)$, it holds that $PeP = \lambda_e P$, where λ_e is a complex number that depends only on e, and P is the projection operator from $\mathbb{C}^{2^n}$ onto Q.*

Proof. "$\Leftarrow$" For $|c\rangle, |c'\rangle \in Q$ with $\langle c|c'\rangle = 0$, for every $e \in E_n(l)$, we have

$$\begin{aligned}\langle c|e|c'\rangle &= \langle cP|e|Pc'\rangle \\ &= \langle c|PeP|c'\rangle \\ &= \langle c|\lambda_e P|c'\rangle\end{aligned}$$

$$= \lambda_e \langle c|c' \rangle = 0.$$

"$\Rightarrow$" If $|c\rangle$ and $|c'\rangle$ are orthonormal bases in Q, then $|c + c'\rangle$ and $|c - c'\rangle$ are also orthonormal bases in Q. Since Q can correct at most l qubit errors, for any $e \in E_n(2l)$, we have $\langle c + c'|e|c - c'\rangle = \langle c|e|c\rangle - \langle c'|e|c'\rangle = 0$, which implies that $\langle c|e|c\rangle = \langle c'|e|c'\rangle$. Let Q have an orthonormal basis $\{|c_1\rangle, |c_2\rangle, \cdots, |c_{2^k}\rangle\}$. Then

$$\begin{aligned} PeP &= (\sum_{i=1}^{2^k} |c_i\rangle\langle c_i|)e(\sum_{j=1}^{2^k} |c_j\rangle\langle c_j|) \\ &= \sum_{i,j=1}^{2^k} |c_i\rangle\langle c_i|e|c_j\rangle\langle c_j| \\ &= \lambda_e P, \end{aligned}$$

where $\lambda_e = \langle c_i|e|c_i\rangle$ and $P = \sum_{i=1}^{2^k} |c_i\rangle\langle c_i|$. □

Definition 8.29. Let Q be a quantum code of length n. The largest positive integer d (with $d \le n$) that satisfies the following property is called the minimum distance of Q: for any $|\nu\rangle, |\mu\rangle \in Q$ such that $\langle \nu|\mu\rangle = 0$, and for any $e \in E_n$ with $\omega(e) \le d - 1$, it holds that $\langle \nu|e|\mu\rangle = 0$.

A quantum code Q is typically represented as $[[n, 2^k, d]]$, where n is the code length, 2^k is the dimension of the code, and d is the minimum distance. Similar to the classical case, the three parameters n, k, and d of a quantum code are interconnected, which will be discussed in detail as follows.

Definition 8.30. Suppose $(G, \cdot)$ is a group where $\cdot$ is the group operation, and $N \subseteq G$. If every element a in G commutes with every element in N, that is, $a \cdot N = N \cdot a$, then N is called the center of the group.

For example, the center of the group E_n is $C(E_n) = \{\pm I, \pm iI\}$, where $\pm I = \pm I_1 \otimes I_2 \otimes \cdots \otimes I_n$ and $\pm iI = \pm iI_1 \otimes I_2 \otimes \cdots \otimes I_n \in E_n$. We denote $\overline{E_n} = E_n / C(E_n) = \{e \cdot C(E_n) \mid \forall e \in E_n\}$.

Definition 8.31. Let Q be a quantum code of type $[[n, 2^k, d]]$, and let $l = \left[\frac{d-1}{2}\right]$. If the linear subspace of $\mathbb{C}^{2^n}$ given by $\{\overline{e}Q \mid \overline{e} \in \overline{E_n}, \omega(\overline{e}) \le l\}$ is mutually orthogonal, where $\overline{e}Q$ denotes the operator $\overline{e}$ acting on each codeword in Q via multiplication $\cdot$, then Q is called a pure quantum code.

Theorem 8.9. (Quantum Hamming bound) *If Q is a pure quantum code of type* $[[n, 2^k, d]]$, *then*

$$2^n \geq 2^k \sum_{i=0}^{l} 3^i \binom{n}{i}. \tag{8.84}$$

Proof. First, the dimension of $\bar{e}Q$ is equal to the dimension of Q, which is 2^k. This is because the unitary operator $\bar{e}$ acts on an orthogonal basis of Q, namely $\{|c_1\rangle, |c_2\rangle, \ldots, |c_{2^k}\rangle\}$, and the set $\{\bar{e}|c_1\rangle, \bar{e}|c_2\rangle, \ldots, \bar{e}|c_{2^k}\rangle\}$ remains an orthogonal basis. In an n-qubit system, there are $\binom{n}{i}$ ways to choose i bits, so there are a total of $3^i\binom{n}{i}$ quantum weights with weight i. Furthermore, from the definition of pure quantum codes, it can be seen that the $\sum_{i=0}^{l} 3^i\binom{n}{i}$ vector subspaces $\bar{e}Q$ are mutually orthogonal, so the dimension of the entire space 2^n is greater than or equal to the sum of the dimensions of these subspaces, that is,

$$2^n \geq 2^k \sum_{i=0}^{l} 3^i \binom{n}{i}. \tag{8.85}$$

□

Definition 8.32. Assume Q is a $[[n, 2^k]]$ quantum code, and P is the projection operator from $\mathbb{C}^{2^n}$ onto Q. Let

$$P = \sum_{i=0}^{2^k-1} |i\rangle\langle i|,$$

$$S_n = \{e = \sigma_0 \otimes \cdots \otimes \sigma_{n-1} \mid \sigma_j \in \{I, \sigma_x, \sigma_y, \sigma_z\}, j = 0, 1, \cdots, n-1\}.$$

Define

$$B_i = \frac{1}{2^{2k}} \sum_{\substack{e \in S_n \\ \omega(e)=i}} \mathrm{Tr}^2(eP),$$

$$B_i^{\perp} = \frac{1}{2^k} \sum_{\substack{e \in S_n \\ \omega(e)=i}} \mathrm{Tr}(ePeP),$$

for $0 \leq i \leq n$. The polynomials

$$B(x, y) = \sum_{i=0}^{n} B_i x^{n-i} y^i,$$

$$B^{\perp}(x,y)=\sum_{i=0}^{n}B_i^{\perp}x^{n-i}y^i\in\mathbb{R}[x,y]$$

are called the weight polynomial of the quantum code Q, where $\mathbb{R}[x,y]$ denotes the set of bivariate polynomials with real coefficients.

Theorem 8.10. *If Q is a $[[n,2^k,d]]$ quantum code, the following conclusions hold:*
(1) $B_0=B_0^{\perp}=1$, $B_i^{\perp}\geq B_i\geq 0$ for $0\leq i\leq n$;
(2) If $t\leq n-1$ and $B_i^{\perp}=B_i$ for $0\leq i\leq t$, while $B_{t+1}^{\perp}>B_{t+1}$, then the minimum distance d of the code Q is $t+1$.

Proof. (1) Since P is a projection operator, P acts as the identity operator on Q, and $\mathrm{Tr}(P)=\mathrm{Tr}(P^2)=2^k$. Therefore $B_0=\frac{1}{2^{2k}}\mathrm{Tr}^2(P)=1$ and $B_0^{\perp}=\frac{1}{2^k}\mathrm{Tr}(P^2)=1$. By Definition 8.32, $B_i\geq 0$. For linear operators A and B, by Cauchy–Schwarz inequality, we have

$\mathrm{Tr}^2\left(A^{\dagger}B\right)\leq\mathrm{Tr}\left(A^{\dagger}A\right)\cdot\mathrm{Tr}\left(B^{\dagger}B\right)$ (equality holds if and only if $A=\alpha B$, $\alpha\in\mathbb{C}$), and since $\mathrm{Tr}(AB)=\mathrm{Tr}(BA)$, for $e\in S_n$, we have

$$\begin{aligned}\mathrm{Tr}^2(eP)&=\mathrm{Tr}^2(ePPP)\\&=\mathrm{Tr}^2(PePP)\\&\leq\mathrm{Tr}(PePPeP)\,\mathrm{Tr}\left(P^2\right)\\&=2^k\cdot\mathrm{Tr}(ePeP).\end{aligned}$$

Thus we have $B_i^{\perp}\geq B_i$, and $\mathrm{Tr}^2(eP)=2^k\cdot\mathrm{Tr}(ePeP)$ if and only if $PeP=\lambda_eP$.

(2) From the definitions of B_i and $B_i^{\perp}$, it is known that for $0\leq i\leq n$,

$$\begin{aligned}B_j^{\perp}=B_j\ (0\leq j\leq i)&\Leftrightarrow\mathrm{Tr}^2(eP)=2^k\cdot\mathrm{Tr}(ePeP)\ (\forall e\in S_n,w(e)\leq i)\\&\Leftrightarrow PeP=\lambda_eP\ \ (\forall e\in E_n(i)),\end{aligned}\tag{8.86}$$

where $E_n(i)=\{e\in E_n\mid\omega(e)\leq i\}$. According to Theorem 8.8, the right side of Eq. (8.86) is equivalent to: if $c,c'\in Q$ and $\langle c|c'\rangle=0$, then for every $e\in E_n(i)$, $\langle c|e|c'\rangle=0$. Therefore from the definition of the minimum distance d, we have $d=t+1$. The proof of the theorem is completed. □

Definition 8.33. Given any positive integer n, we define

$$P_i(x)=\sum_{j=0}^{i}(-1)^j3^{i-j}\binom{x}{j}\binom{n-x}{i-j}\quad(0\leq i\leq n)$$

as the Krawtchouk polynomial, where x is a real number and $\binom{x}{j}=\frac{x!}{j!(x-j)!}$.

$P_i(x)$ is a polynomial of degree i in x, that is, $\deg(P_i(x)) = i$. For example,

$$P_0(x) = 1,$$
$$P_1(x) = 3n - 4x,$$
$$P_2(x) = \frac{1}{2}\left(16x^2 + 8(1-3n)x + 9n(n-1)\right).$$

There is the following lemma regarding $P_i(x)$.

Lemma 8.1. *$P_i(x)$ has the following properties:*

(1) (Symmetry) $3^i\binom{n}{i}P_j(i) = 3^j\binom{n}{j}P_i(j)$, *where* $0 \le i, j \le n$.

(2) (Orthogonality)

$$\sum_{i=0}^{n} P_r(i)P_i(s) = 4^n \delta_{rs},$$

$$\sum_{i=0}^{n} 3^i \binom{n}{i} P_r(i)P_s(i) = 4^n \cdot 3^r \binom{n}{r} \delta_{rs}.$$

(3) *Every real coefficient polynomial* $f(x) \in \mathbb{R}[x]$ *can be expressed as*

$$f(x) = \sum_{i=0}^{d} f_i P_i(x),$$

where $f_i \in \mathbb{R}$, $d = \deg(f(x))$, *and the coefficients* f_i *are given by*

$$f_i = 4^{-n} \sum_{j=0}^{n} f(j)P_j(i).$$

(4) *Let the weight polynomial of a quantum code* $[[n, 2^k]]$ *be* $B(x, y) = \sum_{t=0}^{n} B_t x^{n-t} y^t$ *and* $B^{\perp}(x, y) = \sum_{t=0}^{n} B_t^{\perp} x^{n-t} y^t$. *Then*

$$B_i = \frac{1}{2^{n+k}} \sum_{j=0}^{n} P_i(j) B_j^{\perp}.$$

Proof. (1) For all $z \in \mathbb{R}$, from the definition of $P_i(x)$, we have

$$\sum_{i=0}^{n} P_i(j)z^i = \sum_{i=0}^{n}\sum_{\mu=0}^{i} (-1)^{\mu} 3^{i-\mu} \binom{n-j}{i-\mu}\binom{j}{\mu} z^i$$

$$= \sum_{\mu=0}^{n} (-1)^{\mu} \binom{j}{\mu} \sum_{i=\mu}^{n} 3^{i-\mu} \binom{n-j}{i-\mu} z^i$$

$$= \sum_{\mu=0}^{n} (-1)^{\mu} \binom{j}{\mu} z^{\mu} \sum_{i=0}^{n-j} 3^i \binom{n-j}{i} z^i$$

$$= (1-z)^j (1+3z)^{n-j}.$$

Therefore for all $\omega \in \mathbb{R}$,

$$\begin{aligned} \sum_{i,j=0}^{n} 3^j \binom{n}{j} P_i(j) z^i \omega^j &= \sum_{j=0}^{n} \binom{n}{j} (3\omega)^j \left(\frac{1-z}{1+3z}\right)^j (1+3z)^n \\ &= (1+3z)^n \left(1 + 3\omega \cdot \frac{1-z}{1+3z}\right)^n \\ &= (1+3z+3\omega-3z\omega)^n. \end{aligned} \tag{8.87}$$

The expression in (8.87) is symmetric in z and ω, and thus the left side is also symmetric, leading to

$$\sum_{i,j=0}^{n} 3^j \binom{n}{j} P_i(j) z^i \omega^j = \sum_{i,j=0}^{n} 3^i \binom{n}{i} P_j(i) z^i \omega^j.$$

So, we conclude that $3^j \binom{n}{j} P_i(j) = 3^i \binom{n}{i} P_j(i)$.

(2) From the proof in (1), we have

$$\begin{aligned} &\sum_{r,s=0}^{n} \sum_{i=0}^{n} 3^i \binom{n}{i} P_r(i) P_s(i) z^r \omega^s \\ &= \sum_{i=0}^{n} 3^i \binom{n}{i} (1-z)^i (1+3z)^{n-i} (1-\omega)^i (1+3\omega)^{n-i} \\ &= [(1+3z)(1+3\omega) + 3(1-z)(1-\omega)]^n \\ &= (4+12z\omega)^n = 4^n (1+3z\omega)^n. \end{aligned}$$

By comparing the coefficients on both sides of the last equality, we obtain $\sum_{i=0}^{n} 3^i \binom{n}{i} P_r(i) P_s(i) = 4^n 3^r \binom{n}{r} \delta_{rs}$. The other orthogonality can be easily derived from the symmetry of $P_i(x)$ in (1).

(3) Because $\deg(P_i(x)) = i$, we can expand $f(x)$ as $\sum_{i=0}^{d} f_i P_i(x)$. Then, using the orthogonality, we have

$$\begin{aligned}\sum_{j=0}^{n} f(j)P_j(i) &= \sum_{j=0}^{n} P_j(i) \sum_{k=0}^{n} f_k P_k(j) \\ &= \sum_{k=0}^{n} f_k \sum_{j=0}^{n} P_j(i)P_k(j) \\ &= 4^n f_i.\end{aligned}$$

(4) From the MacWilliams identity $B(x, y) = \frac{1}{K} B^{\perp}\left(\frac{x+3y}{2}, \frac{x-y}{2}\right)$, we have

$$\begin{aligned}\sum_{t=0}^{n} B_t x^{n-t} y^t &= \frac{1}{2^k} \sum_{i=0}^{n} B_i^{\perp} \left(\frac{x+3y}{2}\right)^{n-i} \left(\frac{x-y}{2}\right)^{i} \\ &= \frac{1}{2^{n+k}} \sum_{i=0}^{n} B_i^{\perp} \sum_{\lambda,\mu \geq 0} \binom{n-i}{\lambda}\binom{i}{\mu} x^{n-i-\lambda}(3y)^{\lambda} x^{i-\mu}(-y)^{\mu}.\end{aligned}$$

Thus

$$\begin{aligned}B_t &= \frac{1}{2^{n+k}} \sum_{i=0}^{n} B_i^{\perp} \sum_{\substack{\lambda,\mu > 0 \\ \lambda+\mu=t}} \binom{n-i}{\lambda}\binom{i}{\mu} 3^{\lambda}(-1)^{\mu} \\ &= \frac{1}{2^{n+k}} \sum_{i=0}^{n} B_i^{\perp} P_t(i).\end{aligned}$$

The lemma is proved. □

Now, we use Krawtchouk polynomials to estimate the bounds of quantum codes, which is also a commonly used method in classical coding.

Lemma 8.2. *Let $f(x)$ be a polynomial with real coefficients and its expansion in terms of $P_i(x)$ is given by*

$$f(x) = \sum_{i=0}^{n} f_i P_i(x) \quad (f_i \in \mathbb{R}).$$

If the following conditions hold:
(1) $f_i \geq 0$ for $0 \leq i \leq n$;

(2) $f(j) > 0$ for $0 \le j \le d-1$ and $f(j) \le 0$ for $d \le j \le n$, then for a quantum code Q of type $[[n, 2^k, d]]$, we have

$$2^k \le 2^{-n} \max_{0 \le j \le d-1} \frac{f(j)}{f_j}.$$

Proof. From Lemma 8.1 and the conditions of this lemma, we have

$$\begin{aligned} 2^{n+k} \sum_{i=0}^{d-1} f_i B_i &\le 2^{n+k} \sum_{i=0}^{n} f_i B_i = \sum_{i=0}^{n} f_i \sum_{j=0}^{n} B_j^{\perp} P_i(j) \\ &= \sum_{j=0}^{n} B_j^{\perp} \sum_{i=0}^{n} f_i P_i(j) = \sum_{j=0}^{n} B_j^{\perp} f(j) \\ &\le \sum_{j=0}^{d-1} B_j^{\perp} f(j) \\ &= \sum_{j=0}^{d-1} B_j f(j) \quad \text{(according to Theorem 8.10).} \end{aligned}$$

Thus

$$2^{n+k} \le \frac{\sum_{j=0}^{d-1} B_j f(j)}{\sum_{j=0}^{d-1} B_j f_j} \le \max_{0 \le j \le d-1} \frac{f(j)}{f_j}.$$

The lemma is proved. □

Theorem 8.11. (Quantum singleton bound) *For any quantum code $[[n, 2^k, d]]$, if $d \le \frac{n}{2} + 1$, then $k \le n - 2d + 2$.*

Proof. Consider the following polynomial with real coefficients:

$$f(x) = 4^{n-d+1} \prod_{j=d}^{n} \left(1 - \frac{x}{j}\right) = 4^{n-d+1} \frac{\binom{n-x}{n-d+1}}{\binom{n}{n-d+1}}.$$

The function value $f(j)$ satisfies condition (2) of Lemma 8.2. Next, we calculate the coefficients f_i in $f(x) = \sum_{i \ge 0} f_i P_i(x)$. To do this, we consider

$$\begin{aligned} \sum_{\lambda=0}^{n} 3^{\lambda} \binom{n}{\lambda} f(\lambda) z^{\lambda} &= \frac{4^{n-d+1}}{\binom{n}{n-d+1}} \sum_{\lambda=0}^{n} 3^{\lambda} \binom{n}{\lambda} \binom{n-\lambda}{n-d+1} z^{\lambda} \\ &= 4^{n-d+1} \sum_{\lambda=0}^{n} \binom{d-1}{\lambda} (3z)^{\lambda} = 4^{n-d+1} (1+3z)^{d-1}. \end{aligned}$$

Moreover,

$$\begin{aligned}\sum_{\lambda=0}^{n} 3^{\lambda}\binom{n}{\lambda} f(\lambda) z^{\lambda} &= \sum_{\lambda=0}^{n} 3^{\lambda}\binom{n}{\lambda} z^{\lambda} \sum_{i=0}^{n} f_i P_i(\lambda) \\ &= \sum_{i,\lambda=0}^{n} 3^{i}\binom{n}{i} z^{\lambda} f_i P_{\lambda}(i) \\ &= \sum_{i=0}^{n} 3^{i}\binom{n}{i} f_i \sum_{\lambda=0}^{n} P_{\lambda}(i) z^{\lambda} \\ &= \sum_{i=0}^{n} 3^{i}\binom{n}{i} f_i (1+3z)^n \left(\frac{1-z}{1+3z}\right)^i.\end{aligned}$$

Thus we have

$$\sum_{i=0}^{n} 3^{i}\binom{n}{i} f_i \left(\frac{1-z}{1+3z}\right)^i = \frac{4^{n-d+1}}{(1+3z)^{n-d+1}}. \tag{8.88}$$

Let $\omega = \frac{1-z}{1+3z}$. Then $z = \frac{1-\omega}{1+3\omega}$. Substituting into Eq. (8.88) yields

$$\begin{aligned}\sum_{i=0}^{n} 3^{i}\binom{n}{i} f_i \omega^i &= \frac{4^{n-d+1}}{\left(\frac{4}{1+3\omega}\right)^{n-d+1}} = (1+3\omega)^{n-d+1} \\ &= \sum_{i=0}^{n-d+1} \binom{n-d+1}{i} 3^i \omega^i.\end{aligned}$$

This indicates that

$$f_i = \frac{\binom{n-d+1}{i}}{\binom{n}{i}} = \frac{\binom{n-i}{d-1}}{\binom{n}{d-1}} \quad (0 \le i \le n),$$

and satisfies condition (1) of Lemma 8.2. Therefore using Lemma 8.2, we have

$$\begin{aligned}2^k &\le 2^{-n} \max_{0\le j\le d-1} \frac{f(j)}{f_j} \\ &= 2^{-n} \max_{0\le j\le d-1} \left\{ 4^{n-d+1} \frac{\binom{n-j}{n-d+1}\binom{n}{d-1}}{\binom{n}{n-d+1}\binom{n-j}{d-1}} \right\} \\ &= 2^{n-2d+2} \max_{0\le j\le d-1} \frac{\binom{n-j}{n-d+1}}{\binom{n-j}{d-1}}.\end{aligned}$$

Let

$$g(j) = \frac{\binom{n-j}{n-d+1}}{\binom{n-j}{d-1}} \quad (0 \le j \le d-1).$$

Then, when $d \le \frac{n}{2} + 1$,

$$\frac{g(j)}{g(j+1)} = \frac{n-j-d+1}{d-1-j} \ge 1.$$

Thus we have $2^k \le 2^{n-2d+2} g(0) = 2^{n-2d+2}$, concluding the proof of the theorem. □

Definition 8.34. Let C be a quantum code $[[n, 2^k, d]]$. If $k = n - 2d + 2$ (which satisfies the quantum Singleton bound), then C is called a quantum MDS code.

8.9 Summary

In quantum communication, various types of noise and the coherence of quantum states can easily lead to errors in quantum information. To overcome the errors caused by this, quantum information science introduces the channel coding system from classical information theory, which constructs self-replication of information states and adds redundancy to enable the system to automatically correct erroneous information, ensuring the accuracy of the information. Quantum error correction coding is an essential method to combat quantum decoherence effects and is a key technology for ensuring the effective operation of quantum computing and quantum communication.

This chapter starts with classical bit error correction, first introducing the classical 3-bit repetition code, and then focusing on the basic theory of quantum bit error correction. It designs encoding and decoding circuits and introduces parity-check codes to handle errors caused by qubit flips and phase flips. The definitions of Shor code, nearest-neighbor decoding, linear codes, CSS codes, and stabilizer codes are provided, along with theorems related to them.

References

[1] P.W. Shor, Scheme for reducing decoherence in quantum computer memory, Physical Review A 52 (1995) R2493–R2496.

[2] A.R. Calderbank, P.W. Shor, Good quantum error-correcting codes exist, Physical Review A 54 (1996) 1098–1105.
[3] A. Steane, Multiple-particle interference and quantum error correction, Proceedings of the Royal Society of London. Series A, Mathematical, Physical and Engineering Sciences 452 (1954) (1996) 2551–2577.
[4] D. Gottesman, Stabilizer Codes and Quantum Error Correction, California Institute of Technology, 1997.
[5] D. Gottesman, Class of quantum error-correcting codes saturating the quantum Hamming bound, Physical Review A 54 (1996) 1862–1868.
[6] A.R. Calderbank, E.M. Rains, P.W. Shor, et al., Quantum error correction and orthogonal geometry, Physical Review Letters 78 (3) (1997) 405–408.
[7] K.Q.C.H. Feng, Quantum Error Correction Code, Science Press, 2010.

Index

0–9

1QFA, 73
  with classical states, 57, 71
  with control languages, 57, 73
1QFA together with classical states (1QFAC), 71
1QFAC, 71, 72
2-letter 1QFA, 76
2QCFA, 5, 84
2QFA, 78
2RFA, 79
3-bit repetition code, 240
3-CNF formula, 209
3-colorable problem, 209
3-SAT problem, 209, 210
$\frac{\pi}{8}$ gate, 106

A

Abelian
  groups, 171
  stabilizer, 171
    problem, 171
Accepting states, 65
Adjoint operators, 26
Admissible quantum operation, 39
Adversary method, 227, 236
Algorithm
  designing quantum, 143, 203
  Deutsch, 119, 127
  Deutsch–Jozsa, 119, 130
  fastest classical, 160
  Fourier transform, 146
  Gram–Schmidt, 31
  Grover's, 4, 176
    search, 119
  HHL, 6, 119, 190–192
  hidden subgroup, 169, 175
  probabilistic, 119
  quantum, 2–4, 119, 171, 201, 203
    amplitude amplification, 179
    amplitude estimation, 183
    approximate optimization, 119, 201
    hidden subgroup, 171
    phase estimation, 119
    search, 6
    state discrimination, 212, 213
  query quantum, 2, 3, 123, 125, 214, 222, 235
  Shor's, 4, 119
    discrete logarithm, 165, 166, 168
    factorization, 159
  Simon, 3, 119, 133
  VQE, 196
Alice's encoded quantum state, 48
AND gate, 15
AND-OR tree problem, 233
Automata theory, 57

B

B92 protocol, 49
BB84 protocol, 45
Bell state, 12, 18, 36
Binary
  Hamming code, 257
  linear codes, 258, 259
  quantum codes, 265, 266
Biomedical industry, 6
Bit-flip
  error, 239
  protocol, 241
Bit-phase flip
  protocol, 245
Bloch
  sphere, 106
  vector, 36
Block sensitivity, 224, 227
Boolean function, 3, 124, 183, 222–224
  nonconstant symmetric, 226
  symmetric, 226
  symmetric partial, 125, 132

C

Cauchy sequence, 14
Cauchy–Schwarz inequality, 24, 218
CCNOT gate, 17
Circuit
  decoding, 247, 275
  diagram, 16, 137
  encoding, 246, 275
Circuit satisfiability (CSAT) problem, 209
Classical
  3-bit repetition code, 275
  automata theory, 63
  error correction, 241
  query complexity, 236
  states, 84
Classical pushdown automata (PDA), 94
CNOT gate, 18, 22, 54, 108
Code
  correction, 242
  CSS, 258, 275
  dual, 255
  error detection, 242
  fixed-length, 249
  Hamming, 257
  linear, 249, 255, 275
  over the alphabet, 249
  pure quantum, 267
  q-ary, 249
  quantum, 245, 258, 265–267
    error correction, 246
  Shor, 245, 246, 248, 275
  stabilizer, 262, 275
  Steane, 262, 264
  variable-length, 249
Codewords, 249
Complete inner product space, 14
Complete set of Boolean operations, 15
Completely positive operator, 39
Complexity classes, 105
  BPP, 105
  BQP, 105
  EQP, 105
  P, 105
  PSPACE, 105
Computational
  basis states, 11
  model, 2
  process, 2, 60, 67, 71, 75
Conjugate
  linearity, 14
  symmetry, 14
  transpose, 13, 22
Context-free grammar (CFG), 97, 98
Context-free languages (CFL), 94, 97
Controlled NOT gate, 16
Correction codes, 242
Coset, 255
CSS code, 258, 275
Cut-point languages, 63

D

D-J algorithm, 3
D-J problem, 8
Decidable, 63
Decoding circuits, 247, 275
Density
  matrix, 33, 35
  operator, 33
Designing quantum algorithm, 143, 203
Deterministic finite automata (DFA), 57, 59
Deterministic polynomial-time, 208
Deterministic Turing machines, 64, 102, 104, 209
Deutsch algorithm, 119, 127
Deutsch problem, 127, 129, 130, 170
Deutsch–Jozsa algorithm, 119, 130
Deutsch–Jozsa problem, 130, 131
DFA, 58, 64
Diagonal representation, 25
Dirac notation, 23
Discrete logarithm, 170
  problem, 166, 169, 170
Double quantum bits, 12
Dual code, 255

E

E91 protocol, 51
Eigenvalues, 25
Eigenvectors, 25
Encoding circuit, 246, 275
End-mark, 74
Ensemble of pure states, 33
Entangled state, 18

EPR pair, 12
Error correction, 239
  method, 240
  quantum, 48, 239, 241, 262
Error detection codes, 242
Error probability, 131
Euclidean norm, 69
Evolution process, 43, 79, 242, 245, 262
  quantum state, 249
EXSPACE, 64, 69

F

Fastest classical algorithm, 160
Final configuration, 103
Final state, 58
Financial services, 7
Finite Abelian hidden subgroup problem, 175
Finite automata
  deterministic, 59
  non-deterministic, 98
  one-way multi-head, 75
  one-way quantum, 57
  probabilistic, 59
  quantum, 4, 57, 59, 116
  reversible, 62
  two-way deterministic, 79
  two-way quantum, 5, 78, 116
    with quantum and classical states, 5, 83
Finite field, 251
Finite input alphabet, 74
Finite-dimensional Hilbert space, 45, 96
Fixed-length code, 249
Fourier transform algorithm, 146
Function
  Boolean, 3, 124, 183, 222–224
  MAJORITY, 223
  PARITY, 223
  $\mathrm{THRESHOLD}_M$, 224

G

Gate
  $\frac{\pi}{8}$, 106
  AND, 15
  CCNOT, 17
  CNOT, 18, 22, 54, 108
  description, 15
  Hadamard, 19, 22, 36, 54, 106, 115
  logic, 14
  model, 199
  NAND, 15
  NOT, 15
    controlled, 16
  OR, 15
  phase, 106
  quantum, 18, 22, 53, 106
  single-qubit, 108
  Toffoli, 17
  universal, 16
  X, 22
  XOR, 15
  Y, 22
Gaussian elimination, 138
General graph automorphism problem, 171
Generating set, 263
Generator matrix, 254
Gram–Schmidt algorithm, 31
Graph isomorphism problem, 209
Grover's algorithm, 4, 176
Grover's operator, 183
Grover's search algorithm, 119

H

Hadamard gate, 19, 22, 36, 54, 106, 115
Hadamard transform, 32
Hamming
  code, 257
    binary, 257
  distance, 251
  space, 251
Hermitian
  adjoint operator, 26
  operators, 26
HHL algorithm, 6, 119, 190–192
Hidden linear function problem, 170
Hidden subgroup
  algorithm, 169, 175
  problem, 169, 171
  quantum
    algorithm, 171
Hilbert space, 14, 24, 31, 74, 103, 109
  finite-dimensional, 45, 96
  infinite-dimensional, 45, 96
Holevo bound, 48

I

Infinite-dimensional Hilbert space, 45, 96
Information encryption, 7
Initial configuration, 103
Initial state, 58
Inner product, 14, 42
  space, 14
    complete, 14
Integer factorization problem, 209
Inverse quantum Fourier transform, 147, 175

K

k-letter 1QFA, 75, 76
Kraus operator, 39
Krawtchouk polynomials, 272

L

Language class
  BPP, 208
  BQP, 208
  NP, 208
  P, 208
  PSPACE, 209
Linear
  code, 249, 255, 275
    binary, 258, 259
    p-ary $[n, k]$, 254–256, 258
  independence, 23
  operator, 23, 25, 26
Logic gates, 14
  circuit representation, 16

M

Maximum Distance Separable (MDS) code, 265
Measure-many 1QFA, 57, 65
Measure-once 1QFA, 57
Method
  adversary, 227, 236
  error correction, 240
  polynomial, 220, 227, 236
Minimum distance, 267
Minimum Hamming distance, 252
Mixed states, 33
MM-1QFA, 65, 67, 68
MO-1QFA, 57, 59, 67
MO-QPDA, 97
Model
  computational, 2
  gate, 199
  probabilistic, 122
  quantum
    adiabatic computation, 199
    computation, 116, 121, 122
    query, 119, 123, 201, 210, 211
Multi-letter 1QFA, 57, 75, 77
Multi-linear polynomial, 220

N

NAND gate, 15, 17
Nearest-neighbor decoding, 251–253, 275
NFA, 64
No-cloning theorem, 19, 22
Noisy Intermediate-Scale Quantum (NISQ), 201
Non-Abelian groups, 171
Non-deterministic finite automata (NFA), 98
Non-halting state, 65
Non-negativity, 251
Non-reversible languages, 77
Nonconstant symmetric Boolean function, 226
Nondeterministic Turing machines, 209
Nonorthogonal quantum states, 49
Normal operator, 26
NOT gate, 15
  controlled, 16
NP problems, 209
NPC problems, 209

O

One-way multi-head finite automata, 75
One-Way Quantum Finite Automata (1QFA), 57
Operator
  adjoint, 26
  completely positive, 39
  decomposition theorem, 27
  density, 33
  Grover's, 183
  Hermitian, 26
    adjoint, 26

Kraus, 39
linear, 23, 25, 26
normal, 26
phase, 202
positive semi-definite, 26, 28
projection, 26, 27
query, 210, 229
unitary, 26, 28
OR gate, 15
Order-finding problem, 169
Orthonormal basis, 25, 26, 28, 266

P

p-ary [*n*, *k*] linear code, 254–256, 258
Parity-check matrix, 256
Partial trace, 36
Pauli matrices, 24, 106
PFA, 58, 64
Phase flips, 275
Phase gate, 106
Phase operator, 202
Phase-flip protocol, 243
Polar decomposition, 27
Polynomial
degree, 124
Krawtchouk, 272
method, 220, 227, 236
multi-linear, 220
weight, 269
Positive definiteness, 14
Positive semi-definite operator, 26, 28
PRIME, 207
Privacy amplification, 46
Probabilistic
algorithms, 119
model, 122
Turing machines, 105
Probabilistic finite automata (PFA), 57, 59
Probability distribution, 58
Problem
3-colorable, 209
3-SAT, 209, 210
Abelian stabilizer, 171
AND-OR tree, 233
CSAT, 209
D-J, 8
Deutsch, 127, 129, 130, 170
Deutsch–Jozsa, 130, 131
discrete logarithm, 166, 169, 170
finite Abelian hidden subgroup, 175
general graph automorphism, 171
graph isomorphism, 209
hidden linear function, 170
hidden subgroup, 169, 171
integer factorization, 209
NP, 209
NPC, 209
order-finding, 169
quantum static, 199
search, 214
self-shift-equivalent polynomial, 170
Simon, 3, 133, 135, 142
subset sum, 209
traveling salesman, 209
Projection operator, 26, 27
Protocol
B92, 49, 55
BB84, 45, 55
bit-flip, 241
bit-phase flip, 245
E91, 51, 55
phase-flip, 243
quantum
communication, 51, 55
key distribution, 51, 55
teleportation, 55
Pure quantum code, 267

Q

q-ary code, 249
QAOA, 119, 201–203
QCFG, 100, 101
QKD protocols, 55
qQPDA, 96
q quantum pushdown automaton (qQPDA), 95
QTM, 103
Quantum
algorithm, 2–4, 119, 171, 201, 203
amplitude estimation, 183
automata, 57
basis states, 74, 75, 92
bit, 11, 148
bit-flip error, 241

channel, 46, 47
chemistry, 196
circuit, 22, 57, 110, 116, 144, 147, 191
code, 245, 258, 265–267
  binary, 265, 266
coherence, 127
communication, 45, 239, 275
  complexity, 5
  protocols, 51, 55
  technology, 55
complexity, 5
computation, 24, 116
  models, 116, 121, 122
computational complexity, 5
computers, 239
computing, 1, 5, 6, 203
encryption technology, 7
error correction, 48, 239, 241, 262
  codes, 246
  coding, 275
Fourier transform, 143, 144
gates, 18, 22, 53, 106
grammars, 5, 97, 116
Hall effect, 2
Hamming bound, 268
hardware development, 7
information science, 275
key distribution protocol, 51, 55
logic, 116
MDS, 265
  code, 265, 275
measurement, 32, 35
mechanics, 1, 7, 47
  assumptions, 32
parallelism, 127
phase
  estimation, 4, 119, 147, 148, 152, 162, 166
  flip decoding circuit, 247
  flips, 243
phase-flip error, 243
query
  algorithm, 2, 3, 123, 125, 214, 222, 235
  complexity, 142, 211, 212, 236
  model, 119, 123, 201, 210, 211, 236
regular grammar, 98, 99
search algorithm, 6
singleton bound, 273, 275
state, 1, 60, 84, 88, 162, 242, 263
  discrimination algorithm, 212, 213
  distinguishability, 212
  evolution process, 249
static problem, 199
superdense coding protocol, 52
superposition state, 99
teleportation, 45, 53, 54
  protocols, 45, 54, 55
transition function, 103
Quantum adiabatic
  computation model, 199
  theorem, 199
Quantum amplitude
  amplification algorithm, 179
  amplification technique, 119
  estimation algorithm, 183
Quantum approximate optimization algorithm (QAOA), 119, 201
Quantum context-free grammars (QCFG), 100
Quantum context-free languages (QCFL), 101
Quantum Finite Automata (QFA), 4, 57, 59, 116
Quantum key distribution (QKD), 45
Quantum pushdown automaton (QPDA), 94, 96, 116
Quantum Turing machine (QTM), 57, 102, 108
Qubits, 11
  errors, 266
  flip, 241, 275
    error, 241
  state, 49
Query
  complexity, 4, 124, 211, 214
  operators, 210, 229

R

Raw key, 49, 50
Regular
  grammar, 97, 98
  languages, 98
Rejecting states, 65

Representation of sum of operators, 39
Reversible
  languages, 62
  logic gates, 16
  Turing machines, 2, 104
Reversible finite automaton (RFA), 62, 63

S

Schmidt decomposition theorem, 28, 42
Search problem, 214
Self-shift-equivalent polynomial problem, 170
Shor code, 245, 246, 248, 275
  decoding circuit, 247, 248
Shor's algorithm, 4, 119
Shor's discrete logarithm algorithm, 165, 166, 168
Shor's factorization algorithm, 159
Shor's integer factorization, 6
Simon algorithm, 3, 119, 133
Simon problem, 133, 135, 142
Simple quantum circuits, 20
Simultaneous diagonalization, 27
Single-qubit
  gates, 108
  Pauli operator group, 263
  X-Y decomposition, 115
Singular value decomposition, 28
Spectral decomposition, 27
Stabilizer code, 262, 275
State
  accepting, 65
  classical, 84
  entangled, 18
  final, 58
  initial, 58
  non-halting, 65
  quantum, 1, 60, 84, 88, 162, 242, 263
  qubits, 49
  rejecting, 65
  space, 33
Steane code, 262, 264
Subset sum problem, 209
Superoperator, 39
Symmetric Boolean function, 226
Symmetric partial Boolean function, 125, 132
Symmetry, 251

T

Tape alphabet, 74
Tensor product operation, 20
Theorem
  no-cloning, 19, 22
  operator decomposition, 27
  quantum adiabatic, 199
  Schmidt decomposition, 28, 42
Toffoli gate, 17
Transition probability vector, 58
Traveling salesman problem (TSP), 209
Triangle inequality, 251
Turing machine, 102, 104, 105, 110
  deterministic, 64, 102, 104, 209
  nondeterministic, 209
  probabilistic, 105
  quantum, 57, 102, 108
  reversible, 2, 104
  universal, 104
    deterministic, 104
    quantum, 104
Two-qubit
  entangled state, 12
  system, 12
Two-way deterministic finite automata (2DFA), 79
Two-way quantum finite automata (2QFA), 5, 78, 116
Two-way quantum finite automata with quantum and classical states (2QCFA), 5, 83
Two-way reversible finite automaton (2RFA), 79

U

UMO, 63
Unbounded error, 63
Unitary Coupled Cluster (UCC) theory, 200
Unitary operator, 26, 28
Universal
  gate, 16
  Turing machine, 104
    deterministic, 104
    quantum, 104

V
Variable-length code, 249
Variational quantum eigensolver (VQE), 119
algorithm, 196
Vector space, 13

W
Weather forecasting, 7
Weight polynomial, 269

X
X gate, 22
XOR gate, 15

Y
Y gate, 22